TExES Pedagogy and Professional Responsibilities EC-12 Bonus Edition

Bonus Edition: PPR EC-12 THEA eneralist 4-8

Teacher Certification Exam

By: Sharon Wynne, M.S.

XAMonline, INC.
Boston

Copyright © 2011 XAMonline, Inc.
All rights reserved. No part of the material protected by this copyright notice may be reproduced or utilized in any form or by any means, electronic or mechanical, including photocopying, recording or by any information storage and retrievable system, without written permission from the copyright holder.

To obtain permission(s) to use the material from this work for any purpose including workshops or seminars, please submit a written request to

XAMonline, Inc.
25 First Street, Suite 106
Cambridge, MA 02141
Toll Free 1-800-301-4647
Email: info@xamonline.com
Web: www.xamonline.com
Fax: 1-617-583-5552

Library of Congress Cataloging-in-Publication Data
Wynne, Sharon A.
TExES Pedagogy and Professional Responsibilities EC-12 Bonus Edition: PPR EC-12, THEA, Generalist 4-8 / Sharon A. Wynne.
ISBN: 978-1-60787-315-0, 1st edition
1. TExES Pedagogy and Professional Responsibilities EC-12   2. Study Guides.
3. TExES   4. Teachers' Certification & Licensure. 5. Careers

Disclaimer:
The opinions expressed in this publication are the sole works of XAMonline and were created independently from the National Education Association (NES), Educational Testing Service (ETS), or any State Department of Education, National Evaluation Systems or other testing affiliates. Between the time of publication and printing, state specific standards as well as testing formats and website information may change that are not included in part or in whole within this product. XAMonline develops sample test questions, and they reflect similar content as on real tests; however, they are not former tests. XAMonline assembles content that aligns with state standards but makes no claims nor guarantees teacher candidates a passing score. Numerical scores are determined by testing companies such as NES or ETS and then are compared with individual state standards. A passing score varies from state to state.

Printed in the United States of America   œ-1
TExES Pedagogy and Professional Responsibilities EC-12 Bonus Edition: PPR EC-12, THEA, Generalist 4-8
ISBN: 978-1-60787-315-0

TEACHER CERTIFICATION STUDY GUIDE

TABLE OF CONTENTS

DOMAIN I — DESIGNING INSTRUCTION AND ASSESSMENT TO PROMOTE STUDENT LEARNING..1

COMPETENCY 001 — THE TEACHER UNDERSTANDS HUMAN DEVELOPMENTAL PROCESSES AND APPLIES THIS KNOWLEDGE TO PLAN INSTRUCTION AND ONGOING ASSESSMENT THAT MOTIVATE STUDENTS AND ARE RESPONSIVE TO THEIR DEVELOPMENTAL CHARACTERISTICS AND NEEDS..1

Skill 1.1   Knows the typical stages of cognitive, social, physical, and emotional development of students in early childhood through grade 12..1

Skill 1.2   Recognizes the wide range of individual developmental differences that characterizes students in early childhood through grade 12 and the implications of this developmental variation for instructional planning..3

Skill 1.3   Analyzes ways in which developmental characteristics of students in early childhood through grade 12 impact learning and performance and applies knowledge of students' developmental characteristics and needs to plan effective learning experiences and assessments..5

Skill 1.4   Demonstrates an understanding of physical changes that occur in early childhood through adolescence, factors that affect students' physical growth and health (e.g., nutrition, sleep, prenatal exposure to drugs, abuse) and ways in which physical development impacts development in other domains (i.e., cognitive, social, emotional)..6

Skill 1.5   Recognizes factors affecting the social and emotional development of students in early childhood through adolescence (e.g., lack of affection and attention, parental divorce, homelessness) and knows that students' social and emotional development impacts their development in other domains (i.e., cognitive, physical)..7

Skill 1.6   Uses knowledge of cognitive changes in students in early childhood through adolescence (e.g., from an emphasis on concrete thinking to the emergence and refinement of abstract thinking and reasoning, increased ability to engage in reflective thinking, increased focus on the world beyond the school setting) to plan developmentally appropriate instruction and assessment that promote learning and development..9

Skill 1.7   Understands that development in any one domain (i.e., cognitive, social, physical, emotional) impacts development in other domains..10

Skill 1.8   Recognizes signs of developmental delays or impairments in students in early childhood through grade 4..11

TEACHER CERTIFICATION STUDY GUIDE

Skill 1.9	Knows the stages of play development (i.e., from solitary to cooperative) and the important role of play in young children's learning and development...	12
Skill 1.10	Uses knowledge of the developmental characteristics and needs of students in early childhood through grade 4 to plan meaningful, integrated, and active learning and play experiences that promote the development of the whole child..	13
Skill 1.11	Recognizes that positive and productive learning environments involve creating a culture of high academic expectations, equity throughout the learning community and developmental responsiveness..	13
Skill 1.12	Recognizes the importance of helping students in early childhood through grade 12 learn and apply life skills (e.g., decision-making skills, organizational skills, goal-setting skills, self-direction, workplace skills)..	16
Skill 1.13	Knows the rationale for appropriate middle-level education and how middle-level schools are structured to address the characteristics and needs of young adolescents...	18
Skill 1.14	Recognizes typical challenges for students during later childhood, adolescence and young adulthood (e.g., self-image, physical appearance, eating disorders, feelings of rebelliousness, identity formation, educational and career decisions) and effective ways to help students address these challenges..	19
Skill 1.15	Understands ways in which student involvement in risky behaviors (e.g., drug and alcohol use, gang involvement) impacts development and learning...	20
Skill 1.16	Demonstrates knowledge of the importance of peers, peer acceptance and conformity to peer group norms and expectations for adolescents and understands the significance of peer-related issues for teaching and learning..	22
COMPETENCY 002	**THE TEACHER UNDERSTANDS STUDENT DIVERSITY AND KNOWS HOW TO PLAN LEARNING EXPERIENCES AND DESIGN ASSESSMENTS THAT ARE RESPONSIVE TO DIFFERENCES AMONG STUDENTS AND THAT PROMOTE ALL STUDENTS' LEARNING...**	**23**
Skill 2.1	Demonstrates knowledge of students with diverse personal and social characteristics (e.g., those related to ethnicity, gender, language background, exceptionality) and the significance of student diversity for teaching, learning, and assessment......................	23
Skill 2.2	Accepts and respects students with diverse backgrounds and needs...	24
Skill 2.3	Knows how to use diversity in the classroom and the community to enrich all students' learning experiences..	26

TEACHER CERTIFICATION STUDY GUIDE

Skill 2.4	Knows strategies for enhancing one's own understanding of students' diverse backgrounds and needs..	27
Skill 2.5	Knows how to plan and adapt lessons to address students' varied backgrounds, skills, interests and learning needs, including the needs of English language learners and students with disabilities...	28
Skill 2.6	Understands cultural and socioeconomic differences (including differential access to technology) and knows how to plan instruction that is responsive to cultural and socioeconomic differences among students...	31
Skill 2.7	Understands the instructional significance of varied student learning needs and preferences...	33
COMPETENCY 003	**THE TEACHER UNDERSTANDS PROCEDURES FOR DESIGNING EFFECTIVE AND COHERENT INSTRUCTION AND ASSESSMENT BASED ON APPROPRIATE LEARNING GOALS AND OBJECTIVES**..	**34**
Skill 3.1	Understands the significance of the Texas Essential Knowledge and Skills (TEKS) and of prerequisite knowledge and skills in determining instructional goals and objectives...	34
Skill 3.2	Uses appropriate criteria to evaluate the appropriateness of learning goals and objectives (e.g., clarity; relevance; significance; age-appropriateness; ability to be assessed; responsiveness to students' current skills and knowledge, background, needs, and interests; alignment with campus and district goals...	35
Skill 3.3	Uses assessment to analyze students' strengths and needs, evaluate teacher effectiveness, and guide instructional planning for individuals and groups..	37
Skill 3.4	Understands the connection between various components of the Texas statewide assessment program, the TEKS and instruction, and analyzes data from state and other assessments using common statistical measures to help identify students' strengths and needs...	40
Skill 3.5	Demonstrates knowledge of various types of materials and resources (including technological resources and resources outside the school) that may be used to enhance student learning and engagement and evaluates the appropriateness of specific materials and resources for use in particular situations, to address specific purposes and to meet varied student needs..	42
Skill 3.6	Plans lessons and structures units so that activities progress in a logical sequence and support stated instructional goals..	44

TEACHER CERTIFICATION STUDY GUIDE

Skill 3.7　Plans learning experiences that provide students with developmentally appropriate opportunities to explore content from integrated and varied perspectives (e.g., by presenting thematic units that incorporate different disciplines, providing intradisciplinary and interdisciplinary instruction, designing instruction that enables students to work cooperatively, providing multicultural learning experiences, prompting students to consider ideas from multiple viewpoints, encouraging students' application of knowledge and skills to the world beyond the school).. 46

Skill 3.8　Allocates time appropriately within lessons and units, including providing adequate opportunities for students to engage in reflection, self-assessment, and closure.. 48

COMPETENCY 004　THE TEACHER UNDERSTANDS LEARNING PROCESSES AND FACTORS THAT IMPACT STUDENT LEARNING AND DEMONSTRATES THIS KNOWLEDGE BY PLANNING EFFECTIVE, ENGAGING INSTRUCTION AND APPROPRIATE ASSESSMENTS.. 52

Skill 4.1　Understands the role of learning theory in the instructional process and uses instructional strategies and appropriate technologies to facilitate student learning (e.g., connecting new information and ideas to prior knowledge, making learning meaningful and relevant to students).. 52

Skill 4.2　Understands that young children think concretely and rely primarily on motor and sensory input and direct experience for development of skills and knowledge and uses this understanding to plan effective, developmentally appropriate learning experiences and assessments.. 55

Skill 4.3　Understands that the middle-level years are a transitional stage in which students may exhibit characteristics of both older and younger children, and that these are critical years for developing important skills and attitudes (e.g., working and getting along with others, appreciating diversity, making a commitment to continued schooling)... 56

Skill 4.4　Recognizes how characteristics of students at different developmental levels (e.g., limited attention span and need for physical activity and movement for younger children; importance of peers, search for identity, questioning of values and exploration of long-term career and life goals for older students) impact teaching and learning.. 57

Skill 4.5　Applies knowledge of the implications for learning and instruction of the range of thinking abilities found among students in any one grade level and students' increasing ability over time to engage in abstract thinking and reasoning... 58

TEACHER CERTIFICATION STUDY GUIDE

Skill 4.6   Stimulates reflection, critical thinking and inquiry among students (e.g., supports the concept of play as a valid vehicle for young children's learning; provides opportunities for young children to manipulate materials and to test ideas and hypotheses; engages students in structured, hands-on problem-solving activities that are challenging; encourages exploration and risk-taking; creates a learning community that promotes positive contributions, effective communication and the respectful exchange of ideas).. 60

Skill 4.7   Enhances learning for students by providing age-appropriate instruction that encourages the use and refinement of higher-order thinking skills (e.g., prompting students to explore ideas from diverse perspectives; structuring active learning experiences involving cooperative learning, problem solving, open-ended questioning and inquiry; promoting students' development of research skills)... 62

Skill 4.8   Teaches, models, and monitors organizational and time-management skills at an age-appropriate level (e.g., establishing regular places for classroom toys and materials for young children, keeping related materials together, using organizational tools, using effective strategies for locating information and organizing information systematically)... 63

Skill 4.9   Teaches, models and monitors age-appropriate study skills (e.g., using graphic organizers, outlining, note-taking, summarizing, test-taking) and structures research projects appropriately (e.g., teaches students the steps in research, establishes checkpoints during research projects, helps students use time-management tools)... 64

Skill 4.10   Analyzes ways in which teacher behaviors (e.g., teacher expectations, student grouping practices, teacher-student interactions) impact student learning and plans instruction and assessment that minimizes the effects of negative factors and enhance all students' learning... 68

Skill 4.11   Analyzes ways in which factors in the home and community (e.g., parent expectations, availability of community resources, community problems) impact student learning and plans instruction and assessment with awareness of social and cultural factors to enhance all students' learning... 69

Skill 4.12   Understands the importance of self-directed learning and plans instruction and assessment that promote students' motivation and their sense of ownership of and responsibility for their own learning.. 70

Skill 4.13   Analyzes ways in which various teacher roles (e.g., facilitator, lecturer) and student roles (e.g., active learner, observer, group participant) impact student learning... 72

Skill 4.14   Incorporates students' different approaches to learning (e.g., auditory, visual, tactile, kinesthetic) into instructional practices... 73

TEACHER CERTIFICATION STUDY GUIDE

DOMAIN II   CREATING A POSITIVE, PRODUCTIVE CLASSROOM ENVIRONMENT..74

COMPETENCY 005   THE TEACHER KNOWS HOW TO ESTABLISH A CLASSROOM CLIMATE THAT FOSTERS LEARNING, EQUITY AND EXCELLENCE AND USES THIS KNOWLEDGE TO CREATE A PHYSICAL AND EMOTIONAL ENVIRONMENT THAT IS SAFE AND PRODUCTIVE..74

Skill 5.1   Uses knowledge of the unique characteristics and needs of students at different developmental levels to establish a positive, productive classroom environment (e.g., encourages cooperation and sharing among younger students; provides middle-level students with opportunities to collaborate with peers; encourages older students' respect for the community and the people in it).. 74

Skill 5.2   Establishes a classroom climate that emphasizes collaboration and supportive interactions, respect for diversity and individual differences and active engagement in learning by all students.. 76

Skill 5.3   Analyzes ways in which teacher-student interactions and interactions among students impact classroom climate and student learning and development.. 77

Skill 5.4   Presents instruction in ways that communicate the teacher's enthusiasm for learning.. 77

Skill 5.5   Uses a variety of means to convey high expectations for all students... 78

Skill 5.6   Knows characteristics of physical spaces that are safe and productive for learning, recognizes the benefits and limitations of various arrangements of furniture in the classroom and applies strategies for organizing the physical environment to ensure physical accessibility and facilitate learning in various instructional contexts.. 78

Skill 5.7   Creates a safe, nurturing, and inclusive classroom environment that addresses students' emotional needs and respects students' rights and dignity.. 80

COMPETENCY 006   THE TEACHER UNDERSTANDS STRATEGIES FOR CREATING AN ORGANIZED AND PRODUCTIVE LEARNING ENVIRONMENT AND FOR MANAGING STUDENT BEHAVIOR...81

Skill 6.1   Analyzes the effects of classroom routines and procedures on student learning, and knows how to establish and implement age-appropriate routines and procedures to promote an organized and productive learning environment... 81

Skill 6.2	Demonstrates an understanding of how young children function in groups and designs group activities that reflect a realistic understanding of the extent of young children's ability to collaborate with others..	83
Skill 6.3	Organizes and manages group activities that promote students' ability to work together cooperatively and productively, assume responsible roles and develop collaborative skills and individual accountability..	84
Skill 6.4	Recognizes the importance of creating a schedule for young children that balances restful and active movement activities and that provides large blocks of time for play, projects, and learning centers..	85
Skill 6.5	Schedules activities and manages time in ways that maximize student learning, including using effective procedures to manage transitions; to manage materials, supplies, and technology; and to coordinate the performance of noninstructional duties (e.g., taking attendance) with instructional activities..	88
Skill 6.6	Uses technological tools to perform administrative tasks such as taking attendance, maintaining grade books and facilitating communication..	88
Skill 6.7	Works with volunteers and paraprofessionals to enhance and enrich instruction and applies procedures for monitoring the performance of volunteers and paraprofessionals in the classroom..	89
Skill 6.8	Applies theories and techniques related to managing and monitoring student behavior..	91
Skill 6.9	Demonstrates awareness of appropriate behavior standards and expectations for students at various developmental levels..	94
Skill 6.10	Applies effective procedures for managing student behavior and for promoting appropriate behavior and ethical work habits (e.g., academic integrity) in the classroom (e.g., communicating high and realistic behavior expectations, involving students in developing rules and procedures, establishing clear consequences for inappropriate behavior, enforcing behavior standards consistently, encouraging students to monitor their own behavior to use conflict resolution skills, responding appropriately to various types of behavior)..	96
DOMAIN III	**IMPLEMENTING EFFECTIVE, RESPONSIVE INSTRUCTION AND ASSESSMENT**..	99
COMPETENCY 007	**THE TEACHER UNDERSTANDS AND APPLIES PRINCIPLES AND STRATEGIES FOR COMMUNICATING EFFECTIVELY IN VARIED TEACHING AND LEARNING CONTEXTS**..	99
Skill 7.1	Demonstrates clear, accurate communication in the teaching and learning process and uses language that is appropriate to students' ages, interests, and backgrounds..	99

Skill 7.2	Engages in skilled questioning and leads effective student discussions, including using questioning and discussion to engage all students in exploring content; extends students' knowledge; and fosters active student inquiry, higher-order thinking, problem solving and productive, supportive interactions, including appropriate wait time...	100
Skill 7.3	Communicates directions, explanations and procedures effectively and uses strategies for adjusting communication to enhance student understanding (e.g., by providing examples, simplifying complex ideas, using appropriate communication tools)...............	103
Skill 7.4	Practices effective communication techniques and interpersonal skills (including both verbal and nonverbal skills and electronic communication) for meeting specified goals in various contexts...	104
COMPETENCY 008	**THE TEACHER PROVIDES APPROPRIATE INSTRUCTION THAT ACTIVELY ENGAGES STUDENTS IN THE LEARNING PROCESS..**	**105**
Skill 8.1	Employs various instructional techniques (e.g., discussion, inquiry, problem solving) and varies teacher and student roles in the instructional process and provides instruction that promotes intellectual involvement and active student engagement and learning...	105
Skill 8.2	Applies various strategies to promote student engagement and learning (e.g., by structuring lessons effectively, using flexible instructional groupings, pacing lessons flexibly in response to student needs, including wait time)...	107
Skill 8.3	Presents content to students in ways that are relevant and meaningful and that link with students' prior knowledge and experience	109
Skill 8.4	Applies criteria for evaluating the appropriateness of instructional activities, materials, resources and technologies for students with varied characteristics and needs...	110
Skill 8.5	Engages in continuous monitoring of instructional effectiveness..	112
Skill 8.6	Applies knowledge of different types of motivation (i.e., internal, external) and factors affecting student motivation...	112
Skill 8.7	Employs effective motivational strategies and encourages students' self-motivation...	114
COMPETENCY 009	**THE TEACHER INCORPORATES THE EFFECTIVE USE OF TECHNOLOGY TO PLAN, ORGANIZE, DELIVER, AND EVALUATE INSTRUCTION FOR ALL STUDENTS...**	**116**

TEACHER CERTIFICATION STUDY GUIDE

Skill 9.1	Demonstrates knowledge of basic terms and concepts of current technology (e.g., hardware, software applications and functions, input/output devices, networks)...	116
Skill 9.2	Understands issues related to the appropriate use of technology in society and follows guidelines for the legal and ethical use of technology and digital information (e.g., privacy guidelines, copyright laws, acceptable use policies)...	118
Skill 9.3	Applies procedures for acquiring, analyzing and evaluating electronic information (e.g., locating information on networks, accessing and manipulating information from secondary storage and remote devices, using online help and other documentation, evaluating electronic information for accuracy and validity)..	119
Skill 9.4	Knows how to use task-appropriate tools and procedures to synthesize knowledge, create and modify solutions and evaluate results to support the work of individuals and groups in problem-solving situations and project-based learning activities (e.g., planning, creating and editing word processing documents, spreadsheet documents and databases; using graphic tools; participating in electronic communities as learner, initiator and contributor; sharing information through online communication)..	121
Skill 9.5	Knows how to use productivity tools to communicate information in various formats (e.g., slide show, multimedia presentation, newsletter) and applies procedures for publishing information in various ways (e.g., printed copy, monitor display, Internet document, video)...	122
Skill 9.6	Knows how to incorporate the effective use of current technology; use technology applications in problem-solving and decision-making situations; implement activities that emphasize collaboration and teamwork; and use developmentally appropriate instructional practices, activities and materials to integrate the Technology Applications TEKS into the curriculum..	123
Skill 9.7	Knows how to evaluate students' technologically produced products and projects using established criteria related to design, content delivery, audience and relevance to assignment...	125
Skill 9.8	Identifies and addresses equity issues related to the use of technology...	126
COMPETENCY 010	**THE TEACHER MONITORS STUDENT PERFORMANCE AND ACHIEVEMENT; PROVIDES STUDENTS WITH TIMELY, HIGH-QUALITY FEEDBACK; AND RESPONDS FLEXIBLY TO PROMOTE LEARNING FOR ALL STUDENTS.**...	**127**
Skill 10.1	Demonstrates knowledge of the characteristics, uses, advantages and limitations of various assessment methods and strategies, including technological methods and methods that reflect real-world applications...	127

Skill 10.2	Creates assessments that are congruent with instructional goals and objectives and communicates assessment criteria and standards to students based on high expectations for learning..	132
Skill 10.3	Uses appropriate language and formats to provide students with timely, effective feedback that is accurate, constructive, substantive and specific...	133
Skill 10.4	Knows how to promote students' ability to use feedback and self-assessment to guide and enhance their own learning...	135
Skill 10.5	Responds flexibly to various situations (e.g., lack of student engagement in an activity, the occurrence of an unanticipated learning opportunity) and adjusts instructional approaches based on ongoing assessment of student performance........................	135
DOMAIN IV	**FULFILLING PROFESSIONAL ROLES AND RESPONSIBILITIES**..	**137**
COMPETENCY 011	**THE TEACHER UNDERSTANDS THE IMPORTANCE OF FAMILY INVOLVEMENT IN CHILDREN'S EDUCATION AND KNOWS HOW TO INTERACT AND COMMUNICATE EFFECTIVELY WITH FAMILIES**...	**137**
Skill 11.1	Applies knowledge of appropriate ways (including electronic communication) to work and communicate effectively with families in various situations...	137
Skill 11.2	Engages families, parents, guardians and other legal caregivers in various aspects of the educational program..	137
Skill 11.3	Interacts appropriately with all families, including those that have diverse characteristics, backgrounds and needs..	138
Skill 11.4	Communicates effectively with families on a regular basis (e.g., to share information about students' progress) and responds to their concerns..	139
Skill 11.5	Conducts effective conferences with parents, guardians and other legal caregivers..	140
Skill 11.6	Effectively uses family support resources (e.g., community, interagency) to enhance family involvement in student learning..	141
COMPETENCY 012	**THE TEACHER ENHANCES PROFESSIONAL KNOWLEDGE AND SKILLS BY EFFECTIVELY INTERACTING WITH OTHER MEMBERS OF THE EDUCATIONAL COMMUNITY AND PARTICIPATING IN VARIOUS TYPES OF PROFESSIONAL ACTIVITIES**...	**144**

TEACHER CERTIFICATION STUDY GUIDE

Skill 12.1	Interacts appropriately with other professionals in the school community (e.g., vertical teaming, horizontal teaming, team teaching, mentoring)..	144
Skill 12.2	Maintains supportive, cooperative relationships with professional colleagues and collaborates to support students' learning and to achieve campus and district goals..	145
Skill 12.3	Knows the roles and responsibilities of specialists and other professionals at the building and district levels (e.g., department chairperson, principal, board of trustees, curriculum coordinator, technology coordinator, special education professional)................................	145
Skill 12.4	Understands the value of participating in school activities and contributes to school and district (e.g., by participating in decision making and problem solving, sharing ideas and expertise, serving on committees, volunteering to participate in events and projects)	147
Skill 12.5	Uses resources and support systems effectively (e.g., mentors, service centers, state initiatives, universities) to address professional development needs..	148
Skill 12.6	Recognizes characteristics, goals and procedures associated with teacher appraisal and uses appraisal results to improve teaching skills...	149
Skill 12.7	Works productively with supervisors, mentors and other colleagues to address issues and to enhance professional knowledge and skills...	149
Skill 12.8	Understands and uses professional development resources (e.g., mentors and other support systems, conferences, online resources, workshops, journals, professional associations, coursework) to enhance knowledge, pedagogical skills and technological expertise...	149
Skill 12.9	Engages in reflection and self-assessment to identify strengths, challenges and potential problems; improve teaching performance; and achieve professional goals..	150
COMPETENCY 013	**THE TEACHER UNDERSTANDS AND ADHERES TO LEGAL AND ETHICAL REQUIREMENTS FOR EDUCATORS AND IS KNOWLEDGEABLE OF THE STRUCTURE OF EDUCATION IN TEXAS...**	**151**
Skill 13.1	Knows legal requirements for educators (e.g., those related to special education, students' and families' rights, student discipline, equity, child abuse) and adheres to legal guidelines in education-related situations...	151
Skill 13.2	Knows and adheres to legal and ethical requirements regarding the use of educational resources and technologies (e.g., copyright, Fair Use, data security, privacy, acceptable use policies)...	154

TEACHER CERTIFICATION STUDY GUIDE

Skill 13.3	Applies knowledge of ethical guidelines for educators in Texas (e.g., those related to confidentiality, interactions with students and others in the school community), including policies and procedures described in the *Code of Ethics and Standard Practices for Texas Educators*... 157
Skill 13.4	Follows procedures and requirements for maintaining accurate student records... 158
Skill 13.5	Understands the importance of and adheres to required procedures for administering state- and district-mandated assessments... 160
Skill 13.6	Uses knowledge of the structure of the state education system, including relationships among campus, local and state components, to seek information and assistance.. 161
Skill 13.7	Advocates for students and for the profession in various situations.. 161

TEXES PEDAGOGY AND PROFESSIONAL RESPONSIBILITIES EC-12

Sample Test 164

Answer Key 182

Rationales for Sample Questions.. 184

BONUS: THEA TEXAS HIGHER EDUCATION ASSESSMENT

Reading Sample Test.. 225

Reading Answer Key 233

Reading Rationales for Sample Questions 235

Mathematics Sample Test 248

Mathematics Answer Key... 260

Mathematics Rationales for Sample Questions... 262

Writing/Elements of Composition Sample Test.. 289

Writing/Elements of Composition Answer Key.. 299

Writing/Elements of Composition Rationales for Sample Questions 301

BONUS: TEXES GENERALIST 4-8

Language Arts Sample Test... 320

TEACHER CERTIFICATION STUDY GUIDE

Language Arts Answer Key 327

Language Arts Rationales for Sample Questions 329

Mathematics Sample Test 342

Mathematics Answer Key 348

Mathematics Rationales for Sample Questions 350

Social Science Sample Test 366

Social Science Answer Key 371

Social Science Rationales for Sample Questions 373

Science Sample Test 386

Science Answer Key 393

Science Rationales for Sample Questions 395

Science Essays 413

TEACHER CERTIFICATION STUDY GUIDE

Section 1 About XAMonline

XAMonline – A Specialty Teacher Certification Company
Created in 1996, XAMonline was the first company to publish study guides for state-specific teacher certification examinations. Founder Sharon Wynne found it frustrating that materials were not available for teacher certification preparation and decided to create the first single, state-specific guide. XAMonline has grown into a company of over 1800 contributors and writers and offers over 300 titles for the entire PRAXIS series and every state examination. No matter what state you plan on teaching in, XAMonline has a unique teacher certification study guide just for you.

XAMonline – Value and Innovation
We are committed to providing value and innovation. Our print-on-demand technology allows us to be the first in the market to reflect changes in test standards and user feedback as they occur. Our guides are written by experienced teachers who are experts in their fields. And, our content reflects the highest standards of quality. Comprehensive practice tests with varied levels of rigor means that your study experience will closely match the actual in-test experience.

To date, XAMonline has helped nearly 600,000 teachers pass their certification or licensing exams. Our commitment to preparation exceeds simply providing the proper material for study - it extends to helping teachers **gain mastery** of the subject matter, giving them the **tools** to become the most effective classroom leaders possible, and ushering today's students toward a **successful future**.

Section 2 About this Study Guide

Purpose of this Guide
Is there a little voice inside of you saying, "Am I ready?" Our goal is to replace that little voice and remove all doubt with a new voice that says, "I AM READY. **Bring it on**!" by offering the highest quality of teacher certification study guides.

Organization of Content
You will see that while every test may start with overlapping general topics, each are very unique in the skills they wish to test. Only XAMonline presents custom content that analyzes deeper than a title, a subarea, or an objective. Only XAMonline presents content and sample test assessments along with **focus statements**, the deepest-level rationale and interpretation of the skills that are unique to the exam.

Title and field number of test
→Each exam has its own name and number. XAMonline's guides are written to give you the content you need to know for the specific exam you are taking. You can be confident when you buy our guide that it contains the information you need to study for the specific test you are taking.

Subareas
→These are the major content categories found on the exam. XAMonline's guides are written to cover all of the subareas found in the test frameworks developed for the exam.

Objectives
→These are standards that are unique to the exam and represent the main subcategories of the subareas/content categories. XAMonline's guides are written to address every specific objective required to pass the exam.

TEACHER CERTIFICATION STUDY GUIDE

Focus statements
→These are examples and interpretations of the objectives. You find them in parenthesis directly following the objective. They provide detailed examples of the range, type, and level of content that appear on the test questions. **Only XAMonline's guides drill down to this level.**

How do We Compare with Our Competitors?
XAMonline – drills down to the focus statement level
CliffsNotes and REA – organized at the objective level
Kaplan – provides only links to content
MoMedia – content not specific to the test

Each subarea is divided into manageable sections that cover the specific skill areas. Explanations are easy-to-understand and thorough. You'll find that every test answer contains a rejoinder so if you need a refresher or further review after taking the test, you'll know exactly to which section you must return.

How to Use this Book
Our informal polls show that most people begin studying up to 8 weeks prior to the test date, so start early. Then ask yourself some questions: How much do you really know? Are you coming to the test straight from your teacher-education program or are you having to review subjects you haven't considered in 10 years? Either way, take a **diagnostic or assessment test** first. Also, spend time on sample tests so that you become accustomed to the way the actual test will appear.

This guide comes with an online diagnostic test of 30 questions found online at www.XAMonline.com. It is a little boot camp to get you up for the task and reveal things about your compendium of knowledge in general. Although this guide is structured to follow the order of the test, you are not required to study in that order. By finding a time-management and study plan that fits your life you will be more effective. The results of your diagnostic or self-assessment test can be a guide for how to manage your time and point you towards an area that needs more attention.

Week	Activity
8 weeks prior to test	Take a diagnostic test found at www.XAMonline.com
7 weeks prior to test	Build your Personalized Study Plan for each chapter. Determine which sections you feel strong in and can skip and which you feel weak in and need to focus on.
6-3 weeks prior to test	For each of these 4 weeks, choose a content area to study. You don't have to go in the order of the book. It may be that you start with the content that needs the most review. Alternately, you may want to ease yourself into plan by starting with the most familiar material.
2 weeks prior to test	Take the sample test, score it, and create a review plan for the final week before the test.
1 week prior to test	Following your plan (which will likely be aligned with the areas that need the most review) go back and study the sections that align with the questions you may have gotten wrong. Then go back and study the sections related to the questions you answered correctly. If need be, create flashcards and drill yourself on any area that you makes you anxious.

PPR EC-12 BONUS EDITION

TEACHER CERTIFICATION STUDY GUIDE

Section 3 About the TExES Pedagogy and Professional Responsibilities EC-12 Exam

What is the TExES Pedagogy and Professional Responsibilities EC-12 exam?
The TExES Pedagogy and Professional Responsibilities EC-12 exam is designed to ensure that certified teachers possess the necessary skills and knowledge to teach the state-approved curriculum in Texas public schools (the Texas Essential Knowledge and Skills (TEKS) curriculum).

Often **your own state's requirements** determine whether or not you should take any particular test. The most reliable source of information regarding this is your state's Department of Education. This resource should have a complete list of testing centers and dates. Test dates vary by subject area and not all test dates necessarily include your particular test, so be sure to check carefully.

If you are in a teacher-education program, check with the Education Department or the Certification Officer for specific information for testing and testing timelines. The Certification Office should have most of the information you need.

If you choose an alternative route to certification you can either rely on our website at www.XAMonline.com or on the resources provided by an alternative certification program. Many states now have specific agencies devoted to alternative certification and there are some national organizations as well, for example:
National Association for Alternative Certification
http://www.alt-teachercert.org/index.asp

Interpreting Test Results
Contrary to what you may have heard, the results of the TX PPR EC-12 test are not based on time. More accurately, you will be scored on the raw number of points you earn in relation to the raw number of points available. Each question is worth one raw point. It is likely to your benefit to complete as many questions in the time allotted, but it will not necessarily work to your advantage if you hurry through the test.

Follow the guidelines provided by Educational Testing Service for interpreting your score. The web site offers a sample test score sheet and clearly explains how/whether the scores are scaled and what to expect if you have an essay portion on your test. Scores are available in your online ETS TExES account by 5 pm of the scoring report date listed in the registration bulletin.

What's on the Test?
The TExES Pedagogy and Professional Responsibilities EC-12 exam consists of 90 multiple-choice questions. The breakdown of the questions is as follows:

Category	Question	Approximate Percentage of the test
I. Designing Instruction and Assessment to Promote Student Learning	Multiple	31%

TEACHER CERTIFICATION STUDY GUIDE

II. Domain II: Creating a Positive, Productive Classroom Environment	Multiple	15%
III. Implementing Effective, Responsive Instruction and Assessment	Multiple	31%
IV. Health-Related Skills and Resources	Multiple	23%

Question Types

You're probably thinking, enough already, I want to study! Indulge us a little longer while we explain that there is actually more than one type of multiple-choice question. You can thank us later after you realize how well prepared you are for your exam.

1. **Complete the Statement.** The name says it all. In this question type you'll be asked to choose the correct completion of a given statement. For example: The Dolch Basic Sight Words consist of a relatively short list of words that children should be able to:
   A. Sound out
   B. Know the meaning of
   C. Recognize on sight
   D. Use in a sentence

   The correct answer is C. In order to check your answer, test out the statement by adding the choices to the end of it.

2. **Which of the Following.** One way to test your answer choice for this type of question is to replace the phrase "which of the following" with your selection. Use this example: Which of the following words is one of the twelve most frequently used in children's reading texts:
   A. There
   B. This
   C. The
   D. An

   Don't look! Test your answer. ____ is one of the twelve most frequently used in children's reading texts. Did you guess C? Then you guessed correctly.

TEACHER CERTIFICATION STUDY GUIDE

3. **Roman Numeral Choices.** This question type is used when there is more than one possible correct answer. For example: Which of the following two arguments accurately supports the use of cooperative learning as an effective method of instruction?
   I. Cooperative learning groups facilitate healthy competition between individuals in the group.
   II. Cooperative learning groups allow academic achievers to carry or cover for academic underachievers.
   III. Cooperative learning groups make each student in the group accountable for the success of the group.
   IV. Cooperative learning groups make it possible for students to reward other group members for achieving.
   - A. I and II
   - B. II and III
   - C. I and III
   - D. III and IV

   Notice that the question states there are **two** possible answers. It's best to read all the possibilities first before looking at the answer choices. In this case, the correct answer is D.

4. **Negative Questions.** This type of question contains words such as "not," "least," and "except." Each correct answer will be the statement that does **not** fit the situation described in the question. Such as: Multicultural education is **not**
   - A. An idea or concept
   - B. A "tack-on" to the school curriculum
   - C. An educational reform movement
   - D. A process

   Think to yourself that the statement could be anything but the correct answer. This question form is more open to interpretation than other types, so read carefully and don't forget that you're answering a negative statement.

5. **Questions That Include Graphs, Tables, or Reading Passages.** As ever, read the question carefully. It likely asks for a very specific answer and not broad interpretation of the visual. Here is a simple (though not statistically accurate) example of a graph question: In the following graph in how many years did more men take the NYSTCE exam than women?

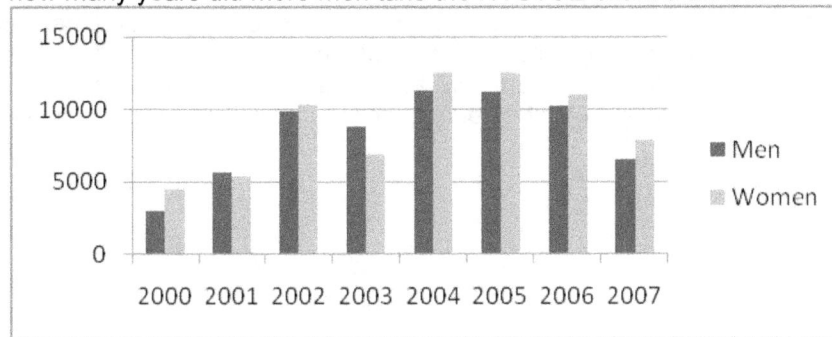

   A. None
   B. One
   C. Two
   D. Three

It may help you to simply circle the two years that answer the question. Make sure you've read the question thoroughly and once you've made your determination, double check your work. The correct answer is C.

TEACHER CERTIFICATION STUDY GUIDE

Section 4 Helpful Hints

Study Tips

1. **You are what you eat.** Certain foods aid the learning process by releasing natural memory enhancers called CCKs (cholecystokinin) composed of tryptophan, choline, and phenylalanine. All of these chemicals enhance the neurotransmitters associated with memory and certain foods release memory enhancing chemicals. A light meal or snacks from the following foods fall into this category:
   - Milk
   - Nuts and seeds
   - Rice
   - Oats
   - Eggs
   - Turkey
   - Fish

   The better the connections, the more you comprehend!

2. **See the forest for the trees.** In other words, get the concept before you look at the details. One way to do this is to take notes as you read, paraphrasing or summarizing in your own words. Putting the concept in terms that are comfortable and familiar may increase retention.

3. **Question authority.** Ask why, why, why. Pull apart written material paragraph by paragraph and don't forget the captions under the illustrations. For example, if a heading reads *Stream Erosion* put it in the form of a question (why do streams erode? Or what is stream erosion?) then find the answer within the material. If you train your mind to think in this manner you will learn more and prepare yourself for answering test questions.

4. **Play mind games**. Using your brain for reading or puzzles keeps it flexible. Even with a limited amount of time your brain can take in data (much like a computer) and store it for later use. In ten minutes you can: read two paragraphs (at least), quiz yourself with flash cards, or review notes. Even if you don't fully understand something on the first pass, your mind stores it for recall, which is why frequent reading or review increases chances of retention and comprehension.

5. **The pen is mightier than the sword.** Learn to take great notes. A by-product of our modern culture is that we have grown accustomed to getting our information in short doses. We've subconsciously trained ourselves to assimilate information into neat little packages. Messy notes fragment the flow of information. Your notes can be much clearer with proper formatting. ***The Cornell Method*** is one such format. This method was popularized in *How to Study in College*, Ninth Edition, by Walter Pauk. You can benefit from the method without purchasing an additional book by simply looking the method up online.

TEACHER CERTIFICATION STUDY GUIDE

Below is a sample of how *The Cornell Method* can be adapted for use with this guide.

Cue Column (2 ½")	Note Taking Column (6")
	1. **Record:** During your reading, use the note-taking column to record important points.
	2. **Questions:** As soon as you finish a section, formulate questions based on the notes in the right-hand column. Writing questions helps to clarify meanings, reveal relationships, establish community, and strengthen memory. Also, the writing of questions sets the state for exam study later.
	3. **Recite:** Cover the note-taking column with a sheet of paper. Then, looking at the questions or cue-words in the question and cue column only, say aloud, in your own words, the answers to the questions, facts, or ideas indicated by the cue words.
	4. **Reflect:** Reflect on the material by asking yourself questions.
	5. **Review:** Spend at least ten minutes every week reviewing all your previous notes. Doing so helps you retain ideas and topics for the exam.
Summary (2")	
After reading, use this space to summarize the notes from each page.	

*Adapted from *How to Study in College,* Ninth Edition, by Walter Pauk, ©2008 Wadsworth

6. **Place yourself in exile and set the mood.** Set aside a particular place and time to study that best suits your personal needs and biorhythms. If you're a night person, burn the midnight oil. If you're a morning person set yourself up with some coffee and get to it. Make your study time and place as free from distraction as possible and surround yourself with what you need, be it silence or music. Studies have shown that music can aid in concentration, absorption, and retrieval of information. Not all music, though. Classical music is said to work best.

7. **Get pointed in the right direction.** Use arrows to point to important passages or pieces of information. It's easier to read than a page full of yellow highlights. Highlighting can be used sparingly, but add an arrow to the margin to call attention to it.

8. **Check your budget.** You should at least review all the content material before your test, but allocate the most amount of time to the areas that need the most refreshing. It sounds obvious, but it's easy to forget. You can use the study rubric above to balance your study budget.

TEACHER CERTIFICATION STUDY GUIDE

Testing Tips

1. **Get smart, play dumb.** Sometimes a question is just a question. No one is out to trick you, so don't assume that the test writer is looking for something other than what was asked. Stick to the question as written and don't overanalyze.

2. **Do a double take.** Read test questions and answer choices at least twice because it's easy to miss something, to transpose a word or some letters. If you have no idea what the correct answer is, skip it and come back later if there's time. If you're still clueless, it's okay to guess. Remember, you're scored on the number of questions you answer correctly and you're not penalized for wrong answers. The worst case scenario is that you miss a point from a good guess.

3. **Turn it on its ear.** The syntax of a question can often provide a clue, so make things interesting and turn the question into a statement to see if it changes the meaning or relates better (or worse) to the answer choices.

4. **Get out your magnifying glass.** Look for hidden clues in the questions because it's difficult to write a multiple-choice question without giving away part of the answer in the options presented. In most questions you can readily eliminate one or two potential answers, increasing your chances of answering correctly to 50/50, which will help out if you've skipped a question and gone back to it (see tip #2).

5. **Call it intuition.** Often your first instinct is correct. If you've been studying the content you've likely absorbed something and have subconsciously retained the knowledge. On questions you're not sure about trust your instincts because a first impression is usually correct.

6. **Graffiti.** Sometimes it's a good idea to mark your answers directly on the test booklet and go back to fill in the optical scan sheet later. You don't get extra points for perfectly blackened ovals. If you choose to manage your test this way, be sure not to mismark your answers when you transcribe to the scan sheet.

7. **Become a clock-watcher.** You have a set amount of time to answer the questions. Don't get bogged down laboring over a question you're not sure about when there are ten others you could answer more readily. If you choose to follow the advice of tip #6, be sure you leave time near the end to go back and fill in the scan sheet.

TEACHER CERTIFICATION STUDY GUIDE

Do the Drill

No matter how prepared you feel it's sometimes a good idea to apply Murphy's Law. So the following tips might seem silly, mundane, or obvious, but we're including them anyway.

1. **Remember, you are what you eat, so bring a snack.** Choose from the list of energizing foods that appear earlier in the introduction.

2. **You're not too sexy for your test.** Wear comfortable clothes. You'll be distracted if your belt is too tight, or if you're too cold or too hot.

3. **Lie to yourself.** Even if you think you're a prompt person, pretend you're not and leave plenty of time to get to the testing center. Map it out ahead of time and do a dry run if you have to. There's no need to add road rage to your list of anxieties.

4. **Bring sharp, number 2 pencils.** It may seem impossible to forget this need from your school days, but you might. And make sure the erasers are intact, too.

5. **No ticket, no test.** Bring your admission ticket as well as **two** forms of identification, including one with a picture and signature. You will not be admitted to the test without these things.

6. **You can't take it with you.** Leave any study aids, dictionaries, notebooks, computers and the like at home. Certain tests **do** allow a scientific or four-function calculator, so check ahead of time if your test does.

7. **Prepare for the desert.** Any time spent on a bathroom break **cannot** be made up later, so use your judgment on the amount you eat or drink.

8. **Quiet, Please!** Keeping your own time is a good idea, but not with a timepiece that has a loud ticker. If you use a watch, take it off and place it nearby but not so that it distracts you. And **silence your cell phone.**

To the best of our ability, we have compiled the content you need to know in this book and in the accompanying online resources. The rest is up to you. You can use the study and testing tips or you can follow your own methods. Either way, you can be confident that there aren't any missing pieces of information and there shouldn't be any surprises in the content on the test.

If you have questions about test fees, registration, electronic testing, or other content verification issues please visit www.texes.ets.org.

Good luck!
Sharon Wynne
Founder, XAMonline

TEACHER CERTIFICATION STUDY GUIDE

DOMAIN I DESIGNING INSTRUCTION AND ASSESSMENT TO PROMOTE STUDENT LEARNING

COMPETENCY 001 THE TEACHER UNDERSTANDS HUMAN DEVELOPMENTAL PROCESSES AND APPLIES THIS KNOWLEDGE TO PLAN INSTRUCTION AND ONGOING ASSESSMENT THAT MOTIVATE STUDENTS AND ARE RESPONSIVE TO THEIR DEVELOPMENTAL CHARACTERISTICS AND NEEDS

Skill 1.1 Knows the typical stages of cognitive, social, physical, and emotional development of students in early childhood through grade 12

Teachers should have a broad knowledge and thorough understanding of the development that typically occurs during students' current period of life. More importantly, the teacher should understand how children learn best during each period of development. The most important premise of child development is that all domains of development (physical, social, and academic) are integrated. Development in each dimension is influenced by the other dimensions. Moreover, today's educator must also have knowledge of exceptionalities and how these exceptionalities affect all domains of a child's development.

PHYSICAL DEVELOPMENT
It is important for the teacher to be aware of the physical stages of development and how changes to the child's physical attributes (which include internal developments, increased muscle capacity, improved coordination, and other attributes as well as obvious growth) affect the child's ability to learn. Factors determined by the physical stage of development include: ability to sit and attend, the need for activity, the relationship between physical coordination and self-esteem, and the degree to which physical involvement in an activity (as opposed to being able to understand an abstract concept) affects learning and the child's sense of achievement.

Early Childhood
Children ages 3.5–5 are typically referred to as preschoolers, and this age comprises the area of early childhood education. In their physicality, this age group begins to resemble miniature adults, rather than the physique of a baby. Arms and legs stretch to catch up with their torso and head, baby fat decreases, and their bodies become sleeker and ready for more complex activities. Within this age range, typical gross motor skills acquired include climbing stairs; catching, kicking, and throwing a ball; peddling; standing on one leg; jumping; and skipping. Fine motor skills include drawing a circle, triangle, square, basic people, and large letters; zippering and buttoning; use of scissors; and twisting doorknobs and lids.

Once students enter kindergarten, they are referred to as grade schoolers. Here, students refine the skills that they learned over the past few years, including running faster, more complex climbing, improved ball skills, and early exploration of organized sports. Fine motor development also progresses as students' drawings, lettering, and painting improves.

Early Adolescence

Early adolescence is characterized by dramatic physical changes, moving the individual from childhood toward physical maturity. Early, prepubescent changes are noted with the appearance of secondary sexual characteristics. Girls experience a concurrent rapid growth in height that occurs between the ages of about 9.5 and 14.5 years, peaking somewhere around 12 years of age. Boys experience a concurrent rapid growth in height that occurs between the ages of about 10.5 to 11 and 16 to 18, peaking around age 14.

The sudden and rapid physical changes that young adolescents experience typically cause this period of development to be one of self-consciousness, sensitivity, and concern over one's own body changes and excruciating comparisons between oneself and peers. Because physical changes may not occur in a smooth, regular schedule, adolescents may go through stages of awkwardness, both in terms of appearance and physical mobility and coordination.

For more information on physical development, **SEE** Skills 1.3 and 1.4

COGNITIVE (ACADEMIC) DEVELOPMENT

Jean Piaget, a European scientist who studied cognitive development in the 20th century, developed many theories about the way humans learn. Most famously, he developed a theory about the stages of the development of human minds. The first stage is the **sensory-motor stage** that lasts until a child is in the toddler years. In this stage, children begin to understand their senses.

The next stage, called the **pre-operational stage**, is where children begin to understand symbols. For example, as they learn language, they begin to realize that words are symbols of thoughts, actions, items, and other elements in the world. This stage lasts into early elementary school.

The third stage is referred to as the **concrete operations stage**. This lasts until late elementary school. In this stage, children go one step beyond learning what a symbol is. They learn how to manipulate symbols, objects, and other elements. A common example of this stage is the ability to understand the displacement of water. In this stage, children can reason that a wide and short cup of water poured into a tall and thin cup of water can actually have the same amount of water.

The next stage is called the **formal operations stage**. It usually starts in adolescence or early teen years, and it continues on into adulthood. This stage allows for the development of abstract thinking, logic, critical thinking, hypothesis, systematic organization of knowledge, and other highly sophisticated thinking skills.

For more information on cognitive development, **SEE** Skills 1.6 and 4.1.

SOCIAL DEVELOPMENT

Children progress through a variety of social stages, beginning with an awareness of peers but a lack of concern for their presence. Young children engage in "parallel" activities playing alongside their peers without directly interacting with one another. During the primary years, children develop an intense interest in peers. They establish productive and positive social and working relationships with one another. This stage of social growth continues to increase in importance throughout the child's school years, including intermediate, middle school, and high school years. It is necessary for the teacher to recognize the importance of developing positive peer group relationships and to provide opportunities and support for cooperative small group projects that not only develop cognitive ability but promote peer interaction.

The Role of Peers

The ability to work and relate effectively with peers contributes greatly to the child's sense of competence. In order to develop this sense of competence, students need to successfully acquire the information base and social skill sets that promote cooperative effort in achieving academic and social objectives.

Middle-level students develop a deep social and emotional association with their peers. While young people are often self-conscious and perceive deficits in their intelligence, physical makeup, and personalities when compared to their peers, they also want to be accepted by their peers. Usually, they establish productive, positive social and working relationships with one another. Often, they are inclined to consider the perceptions and reactions of peers and value their opinions, above all else.

Some students not only perceive themselves as outsiders, but are, in fact, treated as such by their peers. While many schools provide training in social skills for students who experience peer rejection, the success of these programs is often limited by the lack of social context in the exercises. A recent study in the *Journal of Primary Prevention* evaluated and documented the effectiveness of classroom-level rather than individual-oriented approaches. Team-led groups consisting of "accepted" and "rejected" students in 24 middle-school classrooms met weekly to participate in non-academic, cooperative activities and cooperative academic work. The study found that, after the experiment, there was a significant increase in the number of students who reported that "almost all" or "all" of their peers respected them and their opinions.

Acceptance by, and interaction with, one's peers is an overwhelming priority in the life of most middle-level students. And pursuit of this social necessity is not restricted to school-time; it permeates their entire lives. But it is within the classroom setting where the positive and negative aspects of peer relations can be monitored, evaluated, and focused through planning and instruction into constructive, enabling relationships.

For more information on social development, **SEE** Skill 1.5.

Skill 1.2   **Recognizes the wide range of individual developmental differences that characterizes students in early childhood through grade 12 and the implications of this developmental variation for instructional planning**

Those who study childhood development recognize that young students grow and mature in common, recognizable patterns, but at different rates that cannot be effectively accelerated.

This can result in variance in the academic performance of different children in the same classroom. With the establishment of inclusion as a standard in the classroom, it is necessary for all teachers to understand that variation in development among the student population is another aspect of diversity within the classroom. This has implications for the ways in which instruction is planned and delivered and the ways in which students learn and are evaluated.

Knowledge of age-appropriate expectations is fundamental to the teacher's positive relationship with students and effective instructional strategies. Equally important is the knowledge of what is individually appropriate for the specific children in a classroom. Developmentally oriented teachers approach classroom groups and individual students with a respect for their emerging capabilities. Developmentalists recognize that kids grow in common patterns but at different rates that usually cannot be accelerated by adult pressure or input. Developmentally oriented teachers know that variance in the school performance of different children often results from differences in their general growth.

CHILD-CENTERED TEACHING
The effective teacher selects learning activities based on specific learning objectives. Ideally, teachers should not plan activities that fail to augment the specific objectives of the lesson. Additionally, selected learning objectives should be consistent with state and district educational goals that focus on national educational goals (Goals 2000) and the specific strengths and weaknesses of individual students assigned to the teacher's class.

The effective teacher takes care to select appropriate activities and classroom situations in which learning is optimized. The classroom teacher should manipulate instructional activities and classroom conditions in a manner that enhances group and individual learning opportunities. For example, the classroom teacher can organize group learning activities in which students are placed in a situation in which cooperation, sharing ideas, and discussion occurs. Cooperative learning activities can assist students in learning to collaborate and share personal and cultural ideas and values in a classroom learning environment.

If an educational program is child-centered, then it will surely address the abilities and needs of the students because it will take its cues from students' interests, concerns, and questions. Making an educational program child-centered involves building on the natural curiosity children bring to school, and asking children what they want to learn.

Teachers help students to identify their own questions, puzzles, and goals, and then structure for them widening circles of experience and investigation of those topics. Teachers manage to infuse all the skills, knowledge, and concepts that society mandates into a child-driven curriculum. This does not mean passive teachers who respond only to students' explicit cues. Teachers also draw on their understanding of children's developmentally characteristic needs and enthusiasms to design experiences that lead children into areas they might not choose but that they do enjoy and that engage them. Teachers also bring their own interests and enthusiasms into the classroom to share and to act as a motivational means of guiding children.

TEACHER CERTIFICATION STUDY GUIDE

INSTRUCTIONAL PLANNING

Implementing such a child-centered curriculum is the result of very careful and deliberate planning. Well thought-out planning includes specifying behavioral objectives, specifying students' entry behavior (knowledge and skills), selecting and sequencing learning activities so as to move students from entry behavior to objective, and evaluating the outcomes of instruction in order to improve planning.

Planning for instructional activities entails identification or selection of the activities the teacher and students will engage in during a period of instruction. Planning is a multifaceted activity which includes the following considerations:

- The determination of the order in which activities will be completed
- The specification of the component parts of an activity, including their order
- The materials to be used for each part
- The particular roles of the teacher and students
- Decisions about the amount of time to be spent on a given activity
- The number of activities to be completed during a period of instruction
- Judgment of the appropriateness of an activity for a particular situation
- Specifications of the organization of the class for the activity

Attention to learner needs during planning is foremost and includes identification of that which the students already know or need to know; the matching of learner needs with instructional elements such as content, materials, activities, and goals; and the determination of whether or not students have performed at an acceptable level following instruction.

Skill 1.3   **Analyzes ways in which developmental characteristics of students in early childhood through grade 12 impact learning and performance and applies knowledge of students' developmental characteristics and needs to plan effective learning experiences and assessments**

For a general outline of physical development, **SEE** Skill 1.1.

Teachers should have a broad knowledge and understanding of the phases of development which typically occur in each stage of life, and the teacher must be aware of how receptive children are to specific methods of instruction and learning during each period of development. It is important for the teacher to be aware of the physical stages of development and how changes to the child's physical attributes affect the child's ability to learn.

IDENTIFYING DELAYS IN COGNITIVE DEVELOPMENT

Early childhood and grade school is a critical time for learning as rapid cognitive and language development occur. Typical children begin to significantly develop language around age 2, and many other foundational aspects of learning occur at this time. Development certainly has many basic milestones in the early childhood years, and knowledge of what development is within a typical range versus what constitutes a delay is crucial for early childhood and elementary teachers. The earlier parents and teachers identify a delay, the more likely the child will make successful progress, many times eliminating the need for later special education services. Early intervention programs for delays such as speech, hearing, motor skills, social skills, and more are often available for parents and teachers. **SEE** also "Prenatal Concerns" in Skill 1.4 and the general content of Skill 1.8.

MEETING THE NEEDS OF GROWING STUDENTS

The impact of physical changes on individual students is to make them more self-aware, more self-conscious, and more self-absorbed. Constant comparison with peers developing at different rates will cause many individuals to feel inadequate or inferior, at least at times. While remaining sensitive to the genuine, emotional response of early adolescents to changes they cannot control and do not fully comprehend, the teacher will find it necessary to be more proactive in bringing students out of themselves and becoming interactive participants in the classroom learning experience.

In selecting learning activities for older children, teachers should focus on more complex ideas as older students are capable of understanding more complex instructional activities. Moreover, effective teachers maintain a clear understanding of the developmental appropriateness of activities selected and select and present these activities in a manner consistent with the level of readiness of his/her students.

For information on how to plan effective learning experiences and assessments based on individual development, **SEE** Skill 1.2.

Skill 1.4   **Demonstrates an understanding of physical changes that occur in early childhood through adolescence, factors that affect students' physical growth and health (e.g., nutrition, sleep, prenatal exposure to drugs, abuse) and ways in which physical development impacts development in other domains (i.e., cognitive, social, emotional)**

For more information on physical development, **SEE** Skills 1.1 and 1.3.

PRENATAL CONCERNS

Issues of physical health might include the prenatal exposure to drugs, alcohol, or nicotine. In all cases, moderate to severe brain damage is possible; however, more subtle impairment can also occur (trouble with breathing, attention deficit disorder, etc.). For example, prenatal exposure to marijuana is harmful to the infant and has later developmental repercussions. It damages forming brain cells in an unborn fetus and harms existing brain cells in a student. Because drugs, alcohol, and nicotine can impair brain development, children exposed to such things in the womb may need significant extra classroom support. Some of these children will also need to be referred to the Special Education teacher in order to be tested for learning disabilities.

EARLY CHILDHOOD AND ELEMENTARY CHANGES

As stated in the previous skill, the early childhood and elementary years are both a time of rapid physical growth. Teachers must consider these tremendous changes and how they can affect learning in the classroom.

TEACHER CERTIFICATION STUDY GUIDE

Nutrition and Sleep
At any age, but especially with younger students, day-to-day issues such as lack of sufficient sleep or nutrition can harm children. While a child who has had sleep disruptions or insufficient nutrition can bounce back easily when these are attended to, it is often the case that children living in environments where sleep and proper nutrition are not available will continue to struggle through childhood. Symptoms of a lack of nutrition and sleep most notably include a lack of concentration, particularly in the classroom. Furthermore, children who lack sufficient sleep or nutrition may become agitated more easily than other children.

Through federal and local funds, many schools are able to provide free or reduced-price breakfasts and lunches for children; however, some children may not get a decent dinner, and during weekends and holidays, they may struggle even more.

ADOLESCENT CHANGES
Like younger students, students at the middle and early high school level are continually undergoing physical and emotional changes and development. No matter how well educators might try to prepare them for this, they have no point of reference within their own life experiences for such changes. Everything that is occurring to them is new and unfamiliar and often makes them uncomfortable about themselves and in the company of others. Often these physical, hormonal, and emotional changes will occur in spurts, moving some ahead of their peers and leaving some behind. In most cases, the individual feels different and often is treated as different by his or her peers. The student may feel socially awkward, and this may be reflected in schoolwork and especially in classroom participation. The teacher must be sensitive to the issues of a developing child and aware of the impact this may have on student learning, classroom decorum, and the cohesion among classmates which the teacher is trying to foster.

Abuse
At any age and in any community, abuse can occur. Abuse can take the form of emotional and/or physical abuse, and it can severely increase the risk of lower academic achievement. Maltreated children experience such emotional trauma that it can lead to less focus and motivation in school (therefore, less academic learning), increased social problems, and lower emotional stability. Once lower achievement is realized by these students, they often continue along this path of failure and are more likely to display behavior problems and engage in risky behaviors as they age. Teachers must be able to recognize possible signs of abuse and know the proper approach in their school district for reporting possible cases of child abuse.

Skill 1.5   **Recognizes factors affecting the social and emotional development of students in early childhood through adolescence (e.g., lack of affection and attention, parental divorce, homelessness) and knows that students' social and emotional development impacts their development in other domains (i.e., cognitive, physical)**

LACK OF AFFECTION AND ATTENTION
When children are emotionally neglected or have recently endured family upsets, their level of attention toward school will be greatly reduced. They may also show signs of jealousy towards

other children or they may feel a sense of anger toward other children, the teacher, or their parents. Aggression is a very common behavior of emotionally neglected children.

When a child has had little verbal interaction, the symptoms can be similar to the symptoms of abuse or neglect. The child might have a "deer in the headlights" look and maintain a very socially awkward set of behaviors. In general, such a child will have a drastically reduced ability to express him or herself in words and often uses aggression as a tool to get his or her thoughts across.

Although cognitive ability is not lost due to such circumstances (abuse, neglect, emotional upset, lack of verbal interaction), the child will most likely not be able to provide as much intellectual energy as the child not experiencing these issues. Note though that the classroom can be seen as a "safe" place by a child, so it is imperative that teachers be attentive to the needs and emotions of their students.

SENSE OF SELF
Helping students to develop healthy self-images and self-worth are integral to the learning and development experiences. For students who are experiencing negative self-image and peer isolation, learning is not necessarily the top priority. When a student is attending school from a homeless shelter, is living through a parental divorce, or feeling a need to conform to fit into a certain student group, the student is being compromised and may be unable to effectively navigate the educational process or engage in the required academic expectations towards graduation or promotion to the next grade level or subject core level.

Most schools offer health classes that address teen issues around sexuality, self-image, peer pressure, nutrition, wellness, gang activity, drug engagement, and a variety of other relevant teen experiences. Some schools have contracted with outside agencies to develop collaborative partnerships to bring in after-school tutorial classes; often, these are gender and cultural specific groupings where students can deal authentically with integration of cultural and ethnic experiences and lifestyles. Drug intervention programs and speakers on gang issues have created dynamic opportunities for school communities to bring the "undiscussable" issues to the forefront. Both students and teachers must be taught about the world of teenagers and understand the social, psychological, and learning implications of teenage development.

WHEN TO BE CONCERNED
Lying, stealing, and fighting are atypical behaviors that most children may exhibit occasionally, but if a child lies, steals, or fights regularly or blatantly then these behaviors may be indicative of emotional distress. Emotional disturbances in childhood are not uncommon and take a variety of forms. Usually these problems show up in the form of uncharacteristic behaviors. Most of the time, children respond favorably to brief treatment programs of psychotherapy. At other times, disturbances may need more intensive therapy and are harder to resolve. All stressful behaviors need to be addressed, and any type of chronic antisocial behavior needs to be examined as a possible symptom of deep-seated emotional upset.

Skill 1.6   **Uses knowledge of cognitive changes in students in early childhood through adolescence (e.g., from an emphasis on concrete thinking to the emergence and refinement of abstract thinking and reasoning, increased ability to engage in reflective thinking, increased focus on the world beyond the school setting) to plan developmentally appropriate instruction and assessment that promote learning and development**

For a basic outline of cognitive development, **SEE** Skill 1.1

ADDRESSING THE STAGES OF COGNITIVE DEVELOPMENT
In early childhood and early elementary school years, children are in the learning stage known as pre-operational. In this stage (ages 2–7), students learn to represent objects by images, objects, signs, and words. Students this age remain quite ego-centric and have a hard time understanding that other people have a point of view or perspective.

Later in elementary school (around age 8), students begin to transition into the next stage of learning, known as the concrete operational stage. In this stage, intelligence is demonstrated through logical and systematic manipulation of symbols related to concrete objects. Operational thinking develops (mental actions that are reversible), egocentric thought gradually diminishes, and students begin to think concretely and logically about concepts and ideas.

At this stage of development, the student is becoming able to accept, and process, comprehend, and retain more challenging concepts, materials, instruction, and skills. Learning from instruction through multiple perspectives is more effective as the student's mind is less focused on the self and the environment that supports the self. The increasing ability to use reason and think abstractly during this stage of development makes the mind more receptive to varied input and able to process this input without suffering intellectual "overload." But, of course, not all young minds are cognitively receptive to the same degree at the same age or grade level. Providing all students with the same knowledge base and the same skills can be challenging in a cognitively diverse classroom.

The requirement for students within a diverse classroom to acquire the same academic skills (at the same levels) can sometimes be achieved with programmed learning instructional materials. While not widely available for every subject, at every level, a great deal of useful material is in publication. Professional teachers familiar with the format have often created their own modules for student use to be incorporated within their lesson planning.

Around the beginning of middle school (age 11 through to high school), concrete operation thinkers begin to move toward the formal operational stage (generally, identified with full adolescence and adulthood), where intelligence is demonstrated through the logical use of symbols related to abstract concepts. Students can really begin to consider abstract concepts, representations, and various perspectives, probabilities, and ideologies. Students at this age are capable of creating hypotheses, testing them, anticipating outcomes, and engaging in higher levels of problem solving.

Skill 1.7   **Understands that development in any one domain (i.e., cognitive, social, physical, emotional) impacts development in other domains**

UNDERSTANDING DOMAINS OF DEVELOPMENT

Child development does not occur in a vacuum. Each element of development impacts other elements of development. A significant premise in the study of child development holds that all domains of development (physical, social, and academic) are integrated. Development in each dimension is influenced by the others. For example, as cognitive development progresses, social development often follows.

When it is said that development takes place within domains, it is simply meant that different aspects of a human are undergoing change. For example, physical changes take place (e.g., body growth, sexuality); cognitive changes take place (e.g., better ability to reason); linguistic changes take place (e.g., a child's vocabulary develops further); social changes take place (e.g., figuring out identity); emotional changes take place (e.g., changes in ability to be concerned about other people); and moral changes take place (e.g., testing limits).

Developmental Advancement

Developmental advances within the domains occur neither simultaneously nor parallel to one another, necessarily. People often comment that adolescents develop slower in the physical domain than they do in the social or cognitive domain (e.g., they may think like teenagers, but they still look like children), however, the truth is that even in such cases, physical development is under progress—just not as evident on the surface. And as children develop physically, they develop the dexterity to demonstrate cognitive development, such as writing something on a piece of paper (in this case, this is cognitive development that only can be demonstrated by physical development). Or, as they develop emotionally, they learn to be more sensitive to others and therefore enhance social development.

What does this mean for teachers? The concept of latent development is particularly important. While teachers may not see some aspects of development present in their students, other areas of development may give clues as to a child's current or near-future capabilities. For example, as students' linguistic development increases, observable ability may not be present (i.e., a student may know a word but cannot quite use it yet). As the student develops emotionally and socially, the ability to use more advanced words and sentence structures develops because the student will have a greater need to express him or herself.

An important thing to remember about adolescent development within each of these domains is that they are not exclusive. For example, physical and emotional development are tied intricately, particularly when one feels awkward about his or her body, when emotional feelings are tied to sexuality, or when one feels that he or she does not look old enough (as rates of growth are obviously not similar). Moral and cognitive development often goes hand in hand when an adolescent gives reasons for behavior or searches for role models.

In general, by understanding that developmental domains are not exclusive, teachers can identify current needs of students better and they can plan for future instructional activities meant to assist students as they develop into adults.

Skill 1.8   Recognizes signs of developmental delays or impairments in students in early childhood through grade 4

Children develop at rapidly different rates and therefore there is always a range in what is considered "typical" development. It is very important for teachers to be familiar with the range of typical development so that concerns regarding delays and/or impairments can be identified and addressed early.

DEVELOPMENTAL DELAYS
The term "developmental delay" refers to a significant lag in a student's cognitive, physical, social, behavioral, or emotional development. Cognitive delays can include delays in both verbal and non-verbal domains (e.g., verbal communication, mathematical reasoning, logical reasoning, visual processing, auditoring processing, memorization, etc.). Physical delays refer to delays in gross and/or fine motor skills (e.g., the inability to stand up straight, walk normally, play simple sport-like activities, hold a pencil). In very young children (i.e, infants and toddlers), physical delays include limitations in milestones such as sitting up, crawling, or walking. Social delays refer to a lag in a child's ability to relate to others. Behavioral delays can include a slower progression into and then out of the more egocentric toddler stage or may include atypical behaviors (e.g., handflapping). Emotional delays revolve around a student's understanding and ability to convey feelings.

Some developmental delays may exist in isolation, such as a specific language impairment, while others are more global in nature (e.g., mental retardation). Likewise, delays might relate to specific disabilities that can stay with a child the rest of his or her life (everything from problems with eyesight to autism) or learning disabilities (everything from attention deficit disorder to dyslexia). They might also be things that fade as a child gets older or can be addressed with remediation and/or therapy (such as problems with motor skills).

Dealing with Delays
Generally, teachers and parents should know the range of attributes that develop over time in children. There is usually no cause for alarm, as many children do develop skills later in childhood (and certain domains may be developed later than others). When concern regarding the need for intervention does arise, it may be because the teacher observes a child struggling with certain tasks as compared to peers. This may be noted via observation of student behaviors, student frustration, work samples, or by student report. The fear or presence of bullying can also be a harsh reality for the student who is struggling with a developmental delay. The teacher must be aware of peer interactions in order to ensure that all children are fully protected.

When in doubt, the teacher should privately discuss any concern regarding a student with a special education teacher or school psychologist first. That professional may be able to assist the teacher in determining whether it would be important to evaluate the child, or whether it would be important to contact the parent to ask questions, seek clarification, or point out a potential delay. Very often though, parents will be aware of the delay and the child will be able to receive special accomodations in the classroom. Teachers should be forewarned about this by the special education personnel prior to the beginning of the schoolyear.

Skill 1.9   Knows the stages of play development (i.e., from solitary to cooperative) and the important role of play in young children's learning and development

THE IMPORTANCE OF PLAY

Too often, recess and play is considered peripheral or unimportant to a child's development. It is sometimes regarded as a way for kids to just get physical energy out or a "tradition" of childhood. The truth is, though, that play is very important to human development. First, in this country, even though most people are very industrious, they also believe strongly that all individuals deserve time to relax and enjoy the "fruits of our labors." But even more importantly, for the full development of children (who will soon be active citizens of our democracy, parents, spouses, friends, colleagues, and neighbors), play is an activity that helps teach basic values such as sharing and cooperation. It also teaches that taking care of oneself (as opposed to constantly working) is good for human beings and creates a more enjoyable society.

The stages of play development move from solitary (particularly in infancy stages) to cooperative (in early childhood), but even in early childhood children should be able to play on their own and entertain themselves from time to time. Children who do not know what to do with themselves when they are bored should be encouraged to think about particular activities that might be of interest. It is also extremely important that children play with peers. While the emerging stages of cooperative play may be awkward (as children will at first not want to share toys, for example), with some guidance and experience children will learn how to be good peers and friends.

Contributions to Development

Playing with objects helps children to develop motor skills. The objects that children play with should be varied and age appropriate. For example, playing with a doll can actually help to develop hand-eye coordination. Sports, for both boys and girls, can be equally valuable. Parents and teachers need to remember that sports at young ages should only be for the purpose of development of interests and motor skills—not competition. Many children will learn that they do not enjoy sports, and parents and teachers should be respectful of these decisions.

In general, play is an appropriate way for children to learn many things about themselves, their world, and their interests. Children should be encouraged to participate in different types of play and they should be watched over as they encounter new types of play.

TEACHER CERTIFICATION STUDY GUIDE

Skill 1.10 **Uses knowledge of the developmental characteristics and needs of students in early childhood through grade 4 to plan meaningful, integrated, and active learning and play experiences that promote the development of the whole child**

SELECTING ACTIVITIES

The effective teacher is aware of students' individual learning styles and human growth and development theory and applies these principles in the selection and implementation of appropriate instructional activities.

Learning activities selected for younger students (below age eight) should focus on short time frames in highly simplified form. The nature of the activity and the content in which the activity is presented affects the approach that the students will take in processing the information. Younger children tend to process information at a slower rate than older children (age eight and older).

For more information on adjusting instruction to individual learning needs, **SEE** Skill 1.2.

For more information on play experiences, **SEE** Skill 1.9.

Skill 1.11 **Recognizes that positive and productive learning environments involve creating a culture of high academic expectations, equity throughout the learning community and developmental responsiveness**

HIGH EXPECTATIONS

In a document prepared for the Southern Regional Education Board, titled *Strategies for Creating a Classroom Culture of High Expectations*, Myra Cloer Reynolds summarized the process necessary to meet the stated objective when she wrote, "Motivation and classroom management skills are essential to creating and sustaining an environment of high expectations and improvement in today's schools."

In some school systems, there are very high expectations placed on certain students and little expectation placed on others. Often, the result is predictable: you get exactly what you expect to get and you seldom get more out of a situation or person than you are willing to put in. A teacher is expected to provide the same standards of excellence in education for all students. This standard cannot be upheld or met unless the teacher has (and conveys) high expectations for all students.

Considerable research has been done, over several decades, regarding student performance. Time and again, a direct correlation has been demonstrated between the teacher's expectations for a particular student and that student's academic performance. This may be unintended and subtle, but the effects are manifest and measurable. For example, a teacher may not provide the fullest effort on behalf of the student when there are low expectations of success. And the student may "buy into" this evaluation of his or her potential, possibly becoming further scholastically burdened by low self-esteem. Other students, with more self-confidence in their own abilities, might still go along with this "free ride," willing to do only what is expected of them and unwittingly allowing this disservice to hamper their academic progress.

Conveying High Expectations
There are a variety of ways in which a teacher can convey high expectations to students. Much has to do with the attitude of the teacher and positive interactions with the students—clearly stating expectations and reinforcing this at every opportunity.

- Notify the class of your high expectations for their academic success. Let them know that they will be able to acquire all the skills in which you will be instructing them, and you take personal responsibility and pride in their success.
- Speak to the class about the opportunity to support your goals for their success. Let them know that you appreciate having a student approach you with questions, problems, or doubts about her or his performance, understanding of class work, or ability to succeed. That sort of help enables you to help them and helps you succeed as a teacher.
- Never lower standards or "dilute" instruction for certain students. It is the teacher's responsibility to ascertain the means to bring the student's academic performance up to standards.
- Use all forms of teacher communication with students to reinforce your high expectations for them—as a class, and especially as individuals. What we internalize as individuals, we utilize in group settings.

An example of an opportunity to communicate expectations would be when writing comments on exams and papers being returned to individual students. Positive reinforcement should be provided regarding the progress that the student is making regarding the high expectations for his or her academic achievement. If the work itself is below expectations—perhaps even substandard—provide positive, constructive comments about what should be done to meet the expectations. Express confidence in the student's ability to do so. A negative comment, like a negative attitude, is unacceptable on the part of the teacher. The teacher may deem it necessary to speak one-on-one with the student regarding his or her performance. Remember, however, that no student ever feels motivated when reading the words "see me" on an exam or assignment.

DEVELOPMENTAL RESPONSIVENESS
Within the school system, administrators, faculty as a whole, and the individual classroom teacher strive to develop an environment which provides for personalized support of each student's intellectual, physical, emotional, social, and ethical development. Members of the faculty and staff are assigned to provide mentoring, advice, and advocacy in response to the varying needs of students during their educational experience. Along with in-house professionals who are prepared to meet the developmental requirements of a diverse student population, many school systems provide programs and individuals who reach out to parents and families and the community on behalf of the students.

Curriculum is developed which is socially significant and relevant to the personal interests of students. Classroom teachers plan, prepare, and deliver instructional modules that are directed toward specific issues of childhood development (physical, intellectual, emotional, etc.) and incorporate student participation in all related discussions and activities. Wherever possible, interdisciplinary instructional modules (devised, developed, and presented by teachers from different disciplines—each providing his/her own skill sets to achieve comprehensive understanding of the subjects/issues) should be employed to provide the most efficient use of faculty resources and the most effective means of introducing the students to all aspects and skills related to a subject.

EQUITY

- **Equal Access** requires that there be no impediment (physical, cultural, intellectual, social, and economic, etc.) or bias which restricts some students from access which is available to others.
- **Equal Treatment** ensures that no student is valued above or below the others. Physical, intellectual, cultural, economic, or other criteria may not be applied in determining how a student is treated. Equally high academic expectations are afforded all students, with the assurance that this objective is achievable and will be supported by the teacher and the educational system.
- **Equal Opportunity to Learn** requires that every student have equal access to all resources, physical and intellectual, as well as equal instruction and support from the classroom teacher and staff.
- **Equal Outcomes** requires that instruction and evaluation are structured to ensure all students acquire the skills being taught.

While equal treatment and equal access for all individuals is mandated under various state and federal statutes, not every issue has necessarily been considered and addressed. There can be difficulties with interpretation of these statutes. There may also be inconsistencies between the letter of the law and the intent of the law. Significant differences in the implementation and conduct of policy and procedure within institutions can also hamper the effectiveness of the laws and the intent with which these statutes were created.

Achieving Equity
Equity may not be fully achieved if practices are instituted or changed, superficially, only to comply with statutory regulations rather than internalized and embraced by the entire learning community as an opportunity to improve the educational system.

In an educational environment, from the classroom throughout the entire school system, there should be no such impediments to achieving equity. The primary responsibility of the educator is to ensure that all aspects of the educational process, and all information necessary to master specified skills, are readily accessible to all students. There should be no conflict between laws mandating equity and educational philosophy. Policies, practices, and procedures instituted to comply with (or surpass the requirements of) these laws support our educational objectives. By creating, internalizing, and practicing the values of an academic culture with high expectations for all students and inclusion of all students in every aspect of the educational process, educators provide for equity in education and fulfill their primary responsibility.

Skill 1.12 **Recognizes the importance of helping students in early childhood through grade 12 learn and apply life skills (e.g., decision-making skills, organizational skills, goal-setting skills, self-direction, workplace skills)**

BEYOND ACADEMICS

Public education should be concerned with more than academic standards. School is a place where children can learn skills of good citizenship, time management, goal setting, and decision-making. But teachers must be deliberate about teaching these skills. Like most good teaching, students will have much more success learning these things if they get the opportunity to practice them. That is why a classroom should be like a little "community" where children get opportunities to help with chores and maintain responsibility for certain things. Some of the ways teachers can do this include setting up stations and centers throughout the classroom. With a classroom that contains various centers, student desks consist of only one physical component of the classroom. Teachers can set up student mailboxes to store certain materials. They can also arrange manipulatives and other classroom objects in various places that students are required to maintain and keep clean.

Time Management and Organization

A technique that many teachers use is rotating various chores each week. One student might be responsible for ensuring that materials get distributed to students. Another student might supervise clean-up time. Another student might assist with preparation of manipulatives. Not only does this type of activity improve time management and organizational skills in students, it creates a type of classroom community that is motivating to students. In a way, it causes students to feel safer and more included in their classroom environment.

In addition to physical classroom arrangement and student responsibility, teachers should focus on teaching children skills for time management and goal setting. Teachers can use a variety of materials and expectations to do this. For example, many teachers have students write down class-time agendas each morning and then set personal goals for the school-day. Then, they might have their students reflect on whether or not they met these goals and whether or not they successfully completed all agenda items.

Long Term Goals and Responsibility

Longer-term goals can be discussed, as well. Teachers might work with students on an individual basis to set personal academic goals for students. Students should be encouraged to come up with their own goals but with the assistance of teachers. Teachers can help students focus on goals that might be related to current performance and/or interests. Then, students should get opportunities quite often to reflect on their goals, consider their work toward those goals, and alter goals as they go along.

Finally, learning centers, although usually used for the purpose of teaching content-area skills, can be great tools for teaching responsibility and independence. Teachers can use this time to work independently with students. While they do so, students in small groups travel from one center to another, completing various learning activities. For example, one center might ask students to read a story together and answer a few questions. Another center might have computers and require students to complete various computer-based learning activities. Doing this promotes independent and group learning skills and gives students opportunities to set and monitor short-term goals.

In addressing the needs of middle-level students to acquire decision making, organizational, and goal-setting skills, the teacher is establishing a foundation which will contribute to each student's success in education and beyond. As young people mature and are put in a position of making more choices, independent of adult advice or supervision, their abilities at decision-making and goal setting become vital. They will be faced with making choices ranging from prioritizing time and effort in their studies and aspects of their social lives, to decisions regarding "at-risk" behaviors (e.g., smoking, drug and alcohol use, sexual activity).

Things to Keep in Mind
Cognitive, psychological, social, cultural, and even socioeconomic factors can all influence how young people approach decision-making, goal-setting, and being organized. Impediments to overcome include:
- Inability to see a variety of options—may view any necessary choice as an either-or decision only
- Accepting personal disorganization and indecision—feeling they have no real control over their lives, lacking experience, knowledge, and basic skills in these areas
- Harboring misconceptions about their own abilities to recognize risks, or misperceptions about behaviors generally considered as "at-risk"
- Depending on their own limited experiences when determining the possible consequences of their actions, rather than considering the probabilistic evidence
- Inclined to consider the reactions of peers, and value their opinions, before all else
- Unable to estimate the probability of negative consequences regarding any given decision
- Often will succumb to emotion over logic, negating the decision-making process

Structured lessons to teach the appropriate skills will address the following:
- Identifying (precisely and concisely) the issue
- Defining the objective—the decision(s) to be made and the goal(s) or objective(s) to attain
- Listing relevant options/choices
- Evaluating each possible option/choice—considering all likely outcomes
- Identifying negative consequences of any particular option/choice
- Identifying which options/choices have few or no negative consequences
- Reducing the number of options/choices based on the previous identification of consequences
- Evaluating the remaining options/choices against the stated objectives
- Making a decision and acting upon it

Materials for Teaching Beyond Academics

For classroom use, there are numerous resources (instructional videos, printed materials, instructional games) that provide for controlled interaction among the students and between teacher and student and address issues of concern to students. They are usually age and/or grade specific, activity-driven, and employ multimedia. Examples of pertinent topics, with stated educational goals, available for instructional use would include, "How to Handle Your Emotions," "Respecting Others," "The Three R's of Growing Up," "Preventing Conflicts and Violence," "Speaking of Sex," "You and Your Values," "Getting Along with Parents," "Friendship," "Enhancing Self-Esteem," "Dealing with Pressures," and "Setting & Achieving Goals."

It is often possible to include part or all of such instructional materials in a broader lesson plan which incorporates adopting life-skills with learning subject matter. The technology and varieties of media available to the teacher today enable the teacher to provide a multifaceted, instructional experience in the classroom. It is the teacher's responsibility to the students to remain aware of these and exercise her or his professional judgment as to what is beneficial and when it should be introduced into the classroom environment.

For more on organizational skills, **SEE** Skills 4.8, 4.9, 5.6, and 6.1.

Skill 1.13   **Knows the rationale for appropriate middle-level education and how middle-level schools are structured to address the characteristics and needs of young adolescents**

MIDDLE-LEVEL EDUCATION

Middle-level education and the school systems that provide it were conceived and developed specifically as a unique middle tier of education that would bridge the gap between elementary and secondary education and focus on meeting the academic and personal needs of the students in this category.

Proponents and advocates for a middle school system claimed that the existing junior high school system had failed to realize its philosophy because it simply imitated the senior high school's subject orientation, departmentalized teaching, reliance on lecture methods, sophisticated social activities, and competitive interscholastic sports. Arguing that younger children and early adolescents need more acceptance and less competition, these advocates offered alternative practices. In her publication "Practitioner's Monograph, No. 9," professional educator Sara Lake enumerated these alternative practices as:

- A more intimate, personal environment created by team organization and teacher advisor programs
- Interdisciplinary instruction
- Varied learning strategies to accommodate adolescent curiosity and restlessness
- Exploratory and elective programs to help expand students' horizons
- Appropriately designed co-curricular programs where grade organization is not as important as program quality

TEACHER CERTIFICATION STUDY GUIDE

Skill 1.14   **Recognizes typical challenges for students during later childhood, adolescence and young adulthood (e.g., self-image, physical appearance, eating disorders, feelings of rebelliousness, identity formation, educational and career decisions) and effective ways to help students address these challenges**

POSITIVE SELF-CONCEPT

A positive self-concept for a child or adolescent is a very important element in terms of the students' ability to learn and to be an integral member of society. If students think poorly of themselves or have sustained feelings of inferiority, they probably will not be able to optimize their potential for learning. It is therefore part of the teacher's task to ensure that each student develops a positive self-concept.

A positive self-concept does not imply feelings of superiority, perfection, or competence/efficacy. Instead, a positive self-concept involves self-acceptance as a person and having a proper respect for oneself.

Students generally do not realize their own abilities and frequently lack self-confidence. Teachers can instill positive self-concept in children and thereby enhance their innate abilities by providing certain types of feedback. Such feedback includes attributing students' successes to their efforts and specifying what the student did that produced the success. Qualitative comments influence attitudes more than quantitative feedback such as grades.

Factors Affecting Positive Self-Concept

Many factors can affect how students perceive themselves including academics, appearance, peer acceptance, gender roles, sexuality, racial identity, and more. Around the onset of adolescence, factors such as physical appearance and a strong drive for autonomy become prominent in a student's mind. How an adolescent characterizes their body image is strongly influenced by family, culture, media, peers, and their own individual feelings.

Girls, especially, are subject to physical appearance pressures. Research shows that women's mass media magazines had more than 10 times more marketing advertisements promoting weight loss than men's magazines. When pressured with negative perceptions of their self-image and physical appearance, some young girls become prone to dangerous behaviors concerning their eating (such as bulimia, anorexia, dieting pills, etc.), their actions (rebellion, drugs, smoking, etc.) or other risky behaviors.

SEE also Skill 4.3.

ENHANCING SELF-CONCEPT

Process Approach

Teachers may take a number of approaches to enhancement of self-concept among students. One such scheme is the process approach, which proposes a three-phase model for teaching. This model includes a sensing function, a transforming function, and an acting function. These three factors can be simplified into the words by which the model is usually given: **reach**, **touch**, and **teach**.

The sensing, or perceptual, function incorporates information or stimuli in an intuitive manner. The transforming function conceptualizes, abstracts, evaluates, and provides meaning and value to perceived information. The acting function chooses actions from several different alternatives to be set forth overtly. The process model may be applied to almost any curricular field.

Invitational Education
According to the invitational education approach, teachers and their behaviors may be inviting, or they may be disinviting. Inviting behaviors enhance self-concept among students, while disinviting behaviors diminish self-concept. Inviting teacher behaviors reflect an attitude of "doing with" rather than "doing to." Students are "invited" or "disinvited" depending on the teacher behaviors.

Invitational teachers exhibit the following skills (Biehler and Snowman, 394):

- Reaching each student (e.g., learning names, having one-to-one contact)
- Listening with care (e.g., picking up subtle cues)
- Being real with students (e.g., providing only realistic praise, "coming on straight")
- Being real with oneself (e.g., honestly appraising your own feelings and disappointments)
- Inviting good discipline (e.g., showing students you have respect in personal ways)
- Handling rejection (e.g., not taking lack of student response in personal ways)
- Inviting oneself (e.g., thinking positively about oneself)

Disinviting behaviors include those that demean students, as well as those that may be chauvinistic, sexist, condescending, thoughtless, or insensitive to student feelings. Inviting behaviors are the opposite of these, and characterize teachers who act with consistency and sensitivity.

SEE also "Sense of Self" in Skill 1.5.

Skill 1.15 **Understands ways in which student involvement in risky behaviors (e.g., drug and alcohol use, gang involvement) impacts development and learning**

RISKY BEHAVIORS AND EMOTIONAL DISTRESS
Risky behaviors, including (but not limited to) cigarette/drug/alcohol abuse, gangs, and sexual activity, are most likely to emerge during the middle or high school years. However, this does not mean that elementary school children are exempt from exploring or being exposed to such behaviors. According to the Institute of Youth Development (www.youthdevelopment.org), many children experience their first encounters with drugs, cigarettes, and sexual activity by age 12

(and sometimes even younger). It is possible that children as young as sixth grade (or perhaps even younger) may be exploring risky behaviors.

Effects of Risky Behaviors
Researchers have shown that when students engage in risky behaviors, it often negatively impacts their learning and development. Academically, students tend to start struggling and failing earlier, which further results in a lack of commitment to school. Socially, students demonstrate anti-social behaviors, begin to have trouble with friends, and start to display behavioral issues. These negative outcomes then impact their physical, emotional, and further cognitive development.

In middle-level students, decision-making skills are often deficient. This, coupled with erroneous messages from the media, the community and even the family, can make at-risk behavior appear attractive, acceptable, and desirable. As young people mature and are put in a position of making more choices, independent of adult advice or supervision, they will be faced with making choices regarding involvement in "at-risk" behaviors.

Reasons for Risky Behaviors
While young people are often self-conscious and perceive deficits in themselves when compared to their peers, they also want to be accepted by their peers. Some adolescents (and even pre-adolescents) will deliberately adopt certain behaviors as a statement to their peers that they are "special." In practice, this can range from acting-out, or mild, antisocial behavior, to the adoption of at-risk behaviors that can impede physical, emotional, and intellectual development, restrict appropriate social development, impair judgment and functionality, and possibly impair health or even become life-threatening.

Although peer acceptance or making a statement before one's peers may be the motivation, involvement in at-risk behaviors will quite often put the young individual's future at risk. Choosing behaviors that society deems as unacceptable places the individual outside of the "norm". As that individual's peers continue to mature and develop socially and intellectually, he or she may be perceived as an outsider—and he or she may come to share and accept this perception. Unfortunately, this negative reinforcement may result in continued or increased involvement in at-risk behaviors and the consequences are many. Academically, the consequences of this are reflected in the high drop-out rate for students who became involved in at-risk behaviors during early adolescence.

Signs of Emotional Distress
All students demonstrate some behaviors that may indicate emotional distress from time to time since all children experience stressful periods within their lives. However, the emotionally healthy students can maintain control of their own behavior even during stressful times. Teachers need to be mindful that the difference between typical stressful behavior and severe emotional distress is determined by the frequency, duration, and intensity of stressful behavior.

Lying, stealing, and fighting are atypical behaviors that most children may exhibit occasionally, but if a child lies, steals, or fights regularly or blatantly then these behaviors may be indicative of emotional distress. Lying is especially common among young children who feel the need to avoid punishment or seek a means to make themselves feel more important. As children become older, past the ages of six or seven, lying is often a signal that the child is feeling insecure. These feelings of insecurity may escalate to the point of being habitual or obvious and then may indicate that the child is seeking attention because of emotional distress. Fighting, especially among siblings, is a common occurrence. However, if a child fights, is unduly aggressive, or is belligerent towards others on a consistent basis, teachers and parents need to consider the possibility of emotional problems.

Helping Students
How can a teacher know when a child needs help with his/her behavior? The child will indicate by what they do that they need and want help. Breaking rules established by parents, teachers, and other authorities or destroying property can signify that a student is losing control, especially when these behaviors occur frequently. Other signs that a child needs help may include frequent bouts of crying, a quarrelsome attitude, and constant complaints about school, friends, or life in general. Anytime a child's disposition, attitude, or habits change significantly, teachers and parents need to seriously consider the existence of emotional difficulties.

As stated in Skill 1.5, emotional disturbances in childhood are not uncommon and take a variety of forms. Usually these problems show up in the form of uncharacteristic behaviors. Most of the time, children respond favorably to brief treatment programs of psychotherapy. At other times, disturbances may need more intensive therapy and are harder to resolve. All stressful behaviors need to be addressed, and any type of chronic antisocial behavior needs to be examined as a possible symptom of deep-seated emotional upset.

Behaviors indicating a tendency toward the use of drugs and/or alcohol usually are behaviors that suggest low self-esteem. Such behaviors might be academic failure, social maladaptation, antisocial behavior, truancy, disrespect, chronic rule breaking, aggression and anger, and depression. The student tending toward the use of drugs and/or alcohol will exhibit losses in social and academic functional levels that were previously attained. He may begin to experiment with substances. The adage, "Pot makes a smart kid average and an average kid dumb," is right on the mark. In some families, substance abuse is a known habit of the parents. Thus modeled, the children may assume this to be acceptable behavior, making it very difficult to convince them that drugs and alcohol are not good for them.

Skill 1.16   **Demonstrates knowledge of the importance of peers, peer acceptance and conformity to peer group norms and expectations for adolescents and understands the significance of peer-related issues for teaching and learning**

SEE "The Role of Peers" in Skill 1.1.

COMPETENCY 002 THE TEACHER UNDERSTANDS STUDENT DIVERSITY AND KNOWS HOW TO PLAN LEARNING EXPERIENCES AND DESIGN ASSESSMENTS THAT ARE RESPONSIVE TO DIFFERENCES AMONG STUDENTS AND THAT PROMOTE ALL STUDENTS' LEARNING

Skill 2.1 Demonstrates knowledge of students with diverse personal and social characteristics (e.g., those related to ethnicity, gender, language background, exceptionality) and the significance of student diversity for teaching, learning, and assessment

CLASSROOM DIVERSITY

Diversity in the classroom includes race, ethnicity, gender, and varying socioeconomic situations but also includes students who are physically or intellectually challenged or who have exceptionalities. All students must be included in the learning process and all students can contribute and add value to the learning process. Acceptance of diversity and any specific requirements necessary to aid individuals to accomplish on a par with classmates, must be incorporated in lesson planning, teacher presentation, and classroom activities.

Oftentimes, students absorb the culture and social environment around them without deciphering contextual meaning of the experiences. When provided with a diversity of cultural contexts, students are able to adapt and incorporate multiple meanings from cultural cues vastly different from their own socioeconomic backgrounds. Socio-cultural factors provide a definitive impact on a students' psychological, emotional, affective, and physiological development, along with a students' academic learning and future opportunities.

Teaching Diversity

The primary responsibility of the classroom teacher is to ensure that all aspects of the educational process, and all information necessary to master specified skills, are readily accessible by all students in the classroom. In the classroom, the teacher must actively promote inclusion and devise presentations which address commonalities among heterogeneous groups. In the development of lesson plans and presentation formats, this should be evident in the concept and in the language used (e.g., incorporating ideas and phrases that suggest "we" rather than "they" whenever possible).

The prescribed teaching material in a given subject area will usually provide an adequate format appropriate to the grade level and the diversity of a general student population. By assuring that any additional content or instructional aides used in classroom are thematically the same as the prescribed material, the teacher can usually assure these will also be appropriate. The teacher is the final arbiter regarding content, format, and presentation in the classroom, so the teacher must exercise judgment when reviewing all classroom materials, lesson plans, presentations, and activities against set criteria. For example:

- **Offensive**: Anything that might be considered derogatory regarding any individual or group; any comment or material which is insensitive to any nationality, religion, culture, race, family structure, etc.; Regardless the composition of a particular classroom, negativism about any group harbors an acceptance of such negativism and contributes to a "them" versus "us" attitude

- **Exclusive**: Anything which ignores or nullifies the needs, rights, or value of an individual or any group; anything which stratifies society, placing some group or groups above others in significance
- **Inappropriate**: Below or beyond the suitable comprehension level; imprecise, inadequate for mastery of specific skills within the subject matter; fails to provide for accurately measurable skill acquisition

SEE also Skill 2.3.

For information on assessments in a diverse classroom, **SEE** Skill 2.5.

Skill 2.2 **Accepts and respects students with diverse backgrounds and needs**

RESPECTING CLASSROOM DIVERSITY
Effective teaching begins with teachers who can demonstrate sensitivity for diversity in teaching and in relationships within school communities. The teacher must take the time to know each student as an individual and demonstrate a sincere interest in each student. For example, it is important to know the correct spelling and pronunciation of each student's name and any preference in how the student would like to be addressed.

Teachers should plan time for interaction in the classroom when the teacher and the class can become familiar with each student's interests and experiences. This will help the teacher and the students avoid making assumptions based on any individual's background or appearance.

Promoting an Accepting Environment
Encourage all students to respond to each other's questions and statements in the classroom. Be prepared to respond, appropriately, should any issue or question regarding diversity arise during classroom discussions or activities. If necessary to promote or control discussion in the classroom, the teacher should provide the students with specific guidelines (which are easy to understand and to follow) defining the intended objectives and any restrictions. Inclusion means involving everyone in classroom discussions. The teacher should allow the students to volunteer and then call on the more reluctant students to provide additional information or opinions. All opinions (which are not derogatory in case or by nature) are valid and should be reinforced as such by the teacher's approval.

Teachers should also continuously make cultural connections that are relevant and empowering for all students and communicate academic and behavioral expectations. Cultural sensitivity is communicated beyond the classroom with parents and community members to establish and maintain relationships.

Rules in the classroom that respect all students regardless of background can make inroads on the thinking of children who may come from bigoted families. For example, projects with relation to people they don't know, such as the victims of a hurricane, will give them an experience of caring for someone who is suffering. Trips to nursing homes and taking cards or gifts can have a great impact on children of all ages.

PERSONALIZED LEARNING COMMUNITIES
In personalized learning communities, relationships and connections between students, staff, parents, and community members promote lifelong learning for all students. School communities that promote an inclusion of diversity in the classroom, community, curriculum, and connections enable students to maximize their academic capabilities and educational opportunities. Setting school climates that are inclusive of the multicultural demographic student population create positive and proactive mission and vision themes that align student and staff expectations.

The following factors enable students and staff to emphasize and integrate diversity in student learning:

- Inclusion of multicultural themes in curriculum and assessments
- Creation of a learning environment that promotes multicultural research, learning, collaboration, and social construction of knowledge and application
- Providing learning tasks that emphasize student cognitive, critical thinking, and problem-solving skills
- Learning tasks that personalize the cultural aspects of diversity and celebrate diversity in the subject matter and student projects
- Promotion of intercultural, positive, social, peer interrelationships and connections

Teachers communicate diversity in instructional practices and experiential learning activities that create curiosity in students who want to understand the interrelationship of cultural experiences. Students become self-directed in discovering the global world in and outside the classroom. Teachers understand that when diversity becomes an integral part of the classroom environment, students become global thinkers and doers.

In the intercultural communication model, students are able to learn how different cultures engage in both verbal and nonverbal modes of communicating meaning. Students who become multilingual in understanding the stereotypes that have defined other cultures are able to create new bonding experiences that will typify a more integrated global culture. Students who understand how to effectively communicate with diverse cultural groups are able to maximize their own learning experiences by being able to transmit both verbally and non-verbally cues and expectations in project collaborations and in performance-based activities.

The learning curve for teachers in intercultural understanding is exponential in that they are able to engage all learners in the academic process and learning engagement. Teaching students how to incorporate learning techniques from a cultural aspect enriches the cognitive expansion experience since students are able to expand their cultural knowledge bases.

Skill 2.3   **Knows how to use diversity in the classroom and the community to enrich all students' learning experiences**

METHODS FOR TEACHING DIVERSITY

Teachers must establish a classroom climate that is culturally respectful and engaging for students. In a culturally sensitive classroom, teachers maintain equity and fairness in student interactions and curriculum implementation. Teachers are responsible for including cultural and diverse resources in their curriculum and instructional practices. Exposing students to culturally sensitive room decorations and posters that show positive and inclusive messages is one way to demonstrate inclusion of multiple cultures.

Artifacts that could reflect teacher/student sensitivity to diversity might consist of the following:

- Student portfolios reflecting multicultural/multiethnic perspectives
- Journals and reflections about field trips/guest speakers from diverse cultural backgrounds
- Printed materials and wall displays from multicultural perspectives
- Parent/guardian letters in a variety of languages reflecting cultural diversity
- Projects that include cultural history and diverse inclusions
- Disaggregated student data reflecting cultural groups
- Classroom climate of professionalism that fosters diversity and cultural inclusion

Teachers must create personalized learning communities where every student is a valued member and contributor of the classroom experiences. In classrooms where socio-cultural attributes of the student population are incorporated into the fabric of the learning process, dynamic interrelationships are created that enhance the learning experience and the personalization of learning. When students are provided with numerous academic and social opportunities to share cultural incorporations into the learning, everyone in the classroom benefits from bonding through shared experiences and having an expanded viewpoint of a world experience and culture that vastly differs from their own.

Benefits of Teaching Diversity

Researchers continue to show that personalized learning environments increase the learning effect for students; decrease drop-out rates among marginalized students; and reduce unproductive student behavior that can result from constant cultural misunderstandings or miscues between students. Promoting diversity of learning and cultural competency in the classroom for students and teachers creates a world of multicultural opportunities and learning.

When students are able to step outside their comfort zones and share the world of a homeless student or empathize with an English Language Learner (ELL) student who has just immigrated to the United States and is learning English for the first time and is still trying to keep up with the academic learning in an unfamiliar language; then students grow exponentially in social understanding and cultural connectedness.

ELL Students and Diversity

Because ELL students are often grouped in classes that take a different approach to teaching English than those for native speakers, it is easy to assume that they all present with the same needs and characteristics. Nothing could be further from the truth, even in what they need when it comes to learning English. It is important that their backgrounds and personalities be observed just as with native speakers. Anyone who is in an environment where his language is not the standard one feels embarrassed and inferior. The student who is in that situation expects to fail. Encouragement is even more important for these students. They need many opportunities to succeed.

Personalized learning communities provide supportive learning environments that address the academic and emotional needs of students. As socio-cultural knowledge is conveyed continuously in the interrelated experiences shared cooperatively and collaboratively in student groupings and individualized learning, the current and future benefits will continue to present the case and importance of understanding the "whole" child, inclusive of the social and the cultural context.

Skill 2.4   Knows strategies for enhancing one's own understanding of students' diverse backgrounds and needs

STRATEGIES FOR ASSESSING DIVERSITY NEEDS IN THE CLASSROOM

Diversity is a factor in virtually every classroom today. It is important for teachers to be aware that diversity applies to many areas of a student's life including race, socioeconomic status, ethnicity, religion, and individual abilities. Together, all of these variations provide for a unique set of students with each class and as teachers become aware of the increasing complexity of student makeup, as well as increase their knowledge of and experiences with various cultures, the teacher becomes more able to work with intercultural relationships.

Teachers must know how to inform themselves of their class's diverse needs. To do so, teachers must work to build a multicultural classroom. In doing so, they will learn about the backgrounds, interests, and needs of their students. First, be open and communicate with students in and out of class. Not only does this promote a positive learning environment, it shows the teacher is genuine and interested in really knowing the students. Another idea is to attend seminars regarding various backgrounds to be educated on various ethnicities, races, and religions. For example, Mexican-American students are more accustomed to physical gestures such as hugging or touching an arm when talking. This might make an unaware teacher uncomfortable until she realizes it is a cultural norm.

Taking a genuine approach with students not only applies to their learning but to their well-being as well. The teacher-student relationship requires trust and care and so showing genuine care develops this trust between teachers and their students. This will play a role not only in academics but also in behavior and a teacher's responsiveness to student needs (academic, physical, emotional, and more). If a teacher has developed a trusting relationship with a child, the reasons for the child's behavior may come out. It might be that the child needs to tell someone what is going on and is seeking a confidant and a trusted teacher can intervene.

TEACHER CERTIFICATION STUDY GUIDE

Understanding Cultural Learning Patterns
Another strategy to learn more about students is to understand cultural learning patterns. For example, some cultures encourage high degrees of questioning, debating, and criticizing as part of the learning process, while others revere strict listening and no speaking while learning. These various learning patterns may not be evident to some teachers and knowledge of this will help a teacher better understand students. Utilizing literature, music, customs, and art from various backgrounds demonstrates an appreciation for various cultures.

Also, teachers should be sure not to over-generalize with these patterns. Just because a student looks to be of Asian descent does not mean s/he adheres to that cultural learning pattern. That student may have grown up his/her whole life in America and his/her learning pattern would likely adhere to that of an American student instead.

Language is another factor. Teachers who attempt to learn even a word or two of a student's foreign language is conveying a respect for individual cultures and therefore increasing the student's perception that the teacher genuinely cares.

SEE also Skill 2.3.

Skill 2.5   **Knows how to plan and adapt lessons to address students' varied backgrounds, skills, interests and learning needs, including the needs of English language learners and students with disabilities**

ADDRESSING LEARNING DIFFERENCES
No two students are alike. It follows, then, that no students *learn* alike. To apply a one-dimensional instructional approach and a strict tunnel vision perspective of testing is to impose learning limits on students. All students have the right to an education, but there cannot be a singular path to that education. A teacher must acknowledge the variety of learning styles and abilities among students within a class (and, indeed, the varieties from class to class) and apply multiple instructional and assessment processes to ensure that every child has appropriate opportunities to master the subject matter, demonstrate such mastery, and improve and enhance learning skills with each lesson.

Teachers are learning the value of giving assignments that meet the individual abilities and needs of students. After instruction, discussion, questioning, and practice have been provided, rather than assigning one task to all students, teachers are asking students to generate tasks that will show their knowledge of the information presented. Students are given choices and thereby have the opportunity to demonstrate more effectively the skills, concepts, or topics that they as individuals have learned. It has been established that student choice increases student originality, intrinsic motivation, and higher mental processes.

Students' attitudes and perceptions about learning are the most powerful factors influencing academic focus and success. When instructional objectives center on students' interests and are relevant to their lives, effective learning occurs. Learners must believe that the tasks they are asked to perform have some value and that they have the ability and resources to perform them. If a student thinks a task is unimportant, he/she will not put much effort into it.

If a student thinks s/he lacks the ability or resources to successfully complete a task, even attempting the task becomes too great a risk. Not only must the teacher understand the students' abilities and interests, the teacher must also help students develop positive attitudes and perceptions about tasks and learning.

Teachers must avoid teaching tasks that fit their own interests and goals and instead design activities that address the students' concerns. In order to do this, it is necessary to find out about students and to have a sense of their interests and goals. Teachers can do this by conducting student surveys and simply by questioning and listening to students. Once this information is obtained the teacher can link students' interests with classroom tasks.

DIFFERENTIATED INSTRUCTION

The effective teacher will seek to connect all students to the subject matter through multiple techniques, with the goal that each student, through their own abilities, will relate to one or more techniques and excel in the learning process. Differentiated instruction encompasses several areas:

- **Content**: What is the teacher going to teach? Or, better put, what does the teacher want the students to learn? Differentiating content means that students will have access to content that piques their interest about a topic, with a complexity that provides an appropriate challenge to their intellectual development.
- **Process**: A classroom management technique where instructional organization and delivery is maximized for the diverse student group. These techniques should include dynamic, flexible grouping activities, where instruction and learning occurs both as whole-class, teacher-led activities, as well as peer learning and teaching (while teacher observes and coaches) within small groups or pairs.
- **Product**: The expectations and requirements placed on students to demonstrate their knowledge or understanding. The type of product expected from each student should reflect each student's own capabilities.

COOPERATIVE LEARNING

Cooperative learning situations, as practiced in today's classrooms, grew out of searches conducted by several groups in the early 1970's. Cooperative learning situations can range from very formal applications such as STAD (Student Teams-Achievement Divisions) and CIRC (Cooperative Integrated Reading and Composition) to less formal groupings known variously as "group investigation," "learning together," and "discovery groups." Cooperative learning as a general term is now firmly recognized and established as a teaching and learning technique in American schools.

Since cooperative learning techniques are so widely diffused in the schools, it is necessary to orient students in the skills by which cooperative learning groups can operate smoothly, and thereby enhance learning. Students who cannot interact constructively with other students will not be able to take advantage of the learning opportunities provided by the cooperative learning situations and will furthermore deprive their fellow students of the opportunity for cooperative learning.

These skills form the hierarchy of cooperation in which students first learn to work together as a group, so they may then proceed to levels at which they may engage in simulated conflict situations. This cooperative setting allows different points of view to be constructively entertained. For more information on cooperative learning, **SEE** Skills 5.2, 6.2, 6.3 and 9.6.

Most classrooms contain a mixture of the following:

- Differences among learners, classroom settings, and academic outcomes
- Biological, sociological, ethnicity, socioeconomic status, psychological needs, learning modalities, and styles among learners
- Differences in classroom settings that promote learning opportunities such as collaborative, participatory, and individualized learning groupings
- Expected learning outcomes that are theoretical, affective, and cognitive for students

SELF CONFIDENCE IN STUDENTS

SEE Skill 1.14

DIFFERENCES IN ABILITIES

Common learning disabilities include attention disorders such as ADD/ADHD (where concentration can be very tough), auditory processing disorders (where listening comprehension is very difficult), visual processing disorders (where reading can be tough and visual memory may be impaired), dyslexia (where reading can be confusing), and many others. Physical disabilities include Down's syndrome, where mental retardation may be a factor; cerebral palsy, where physical movement is impaired; and many others. Developmental disabilities might include the lack of ability to use fine motor skills. When giftedness is observed, teachers should also concern themselves with ensuring that such children get the attention they need and deserve so that they can continue to learn and grow.

ENGLISH LANGUAGE LEARNERS

Below are some of the more common approaches used in today's K-12 classrooms for children still acquiring English. Cognitive approaches to language learning focus on concepts. While words and grammar are important, when teachers use the cognitive approach, they focus on using language for conceptual purposes—rather than learning words and grammar for the sake of simply learning new words and grammatical structures. This approach focuses heavily on students' learning styles, and it cannot necessarily be pinned down as having specific techniques. Rather, it is more of a philosophy of instruction.

Another very common motivational approach is **Total Physical Response**. This is a kinesthetic approach that combines language learning and physical movement. In essence, students learn new vocabulary and grammar by responding with physical motion to verbal commands. Some people say it is particularly effective because the physical actions create good brain connections with the words.

In general, the best methods do not treat students as if they have a language deficit. Rather, the best methods build upon what students already know, and they help to instill the target language as a communicative process rather than a list of vocabulary words that have to be memorized.

EMERGENT CURRICULUM
Emergent curriculum describes the projects and themes that classrooms embark on that have been inspired by the children's interests. The teacher uses all the tools of assessment available to know as much as possible about the students and then continually assesses them over the period of the unit or semester. As the teacher gets to know the students, s/he listens to what their interests are and creates a curriculum in response to what s/he learns from observations.

Webbing
Webbing is a recent concept related to the idea of emergent curriculum. The two main uses are planning and recording curriculum. Planning webs are used to generate ideas for activities and projects for the children from an observed interest, such as rocks.

Teachers work together to come up with ideas and activities for the children and to record them in a "web" format. Activities can be grouped by different areas of the room or by developmental domains. For example, clusters either fall under areas such as dramatic play or science or around domains such as language, cognitive, and physical development. Either configuration works, but being consistent in each web is important. This format will work as a unit, weekly, or monthly program plan. Any new activities that emerge throughout the unit can also be added to the web. The record will serve in the future to plan activities that emerge from the children's play and ideas.

Skill 2.6   **Understands cultural and socioeconomic differences (including differential access to technology) and knows how to plan instruction that is responsive to cultural and socioeconomic differences among students**

CULTURAL AND SOCIOECONOMIC ISSUES
A positive environment, where open, discussion-oriented, non-threatening communication among all students can occur, is a critical factor in creating an effective learning culture. The teacher must take the lead and model appropriate actions and speech and intervene quickly when a student makes a misstep and offends (often inadvertently) another.

Communication issues that the teacher in a diverse classroom should be aware of include:

- Be sensitive to terminology and language patterns that may exclude or demean students. Regularly switch between the use of "he" and "she" in speech and writing. Know and use the current terms that ethnic and cultural groups use to identify themselves (e.g., "Latinos" [favored] vs. "Hispanics").

- Be aware of body language that is intimidating or offensive to some cultures, such as direct eye contact, and adjust accordingly.
- Monitor your own reactions to students to ensure equal responses to males and females, as well as differently-performing students.
- Don't "protect" students from criticism because of their ethnicity or gender. Likewise, acknowledge and praise all meritorious work without singling out any one student. Both actions can make all students hyper-aware of ethnic and gender differences and cause anxiety or resentment throughout the class.
- Emphasize the importance of discussing and considering different viewpoints and opinions. Demonstrate and express value for all opinions and comments, and lead students to do the same.

Possible Cultural and Language Issues

Most class rosters will consist of students from a variety of cultures. Teachers should get to know their students (of all cultures) so that they may incorporate elements of their cultures into classroom activities and planning. Also, getting to know about a student's background/cultural traditions helps to build a rapport with each student, as well as further educate the teacher about the world in which he or she teaches. **SEE** Skill 3.5 for more information about a culturally diverse classroom.

For students still learning English, teachers must make every attempt to communicate with that student daily. Whether it is with another student who speaks the same language, word cards, computer programs, drawings, or other methods, teachers must find ways to encourage each student's participation. The teacher must also be sure the appropriate language services begin for the student in a timely manner.

Possible Socioeconomic Issues

Teachers must also consider students from various socioeconomic backgrounds. Teachers should watch these students carefully for signs of malnutrition, fatigue, and possible learning disorders. In many cases, however, these students are just as likely as anyone else to work well in a classroom. Unfortunately, sometimes students from lower SES backgrounds may need help deriving a homework system or perhaps need more attention on study or test-taking skills. Difficulties sometimes occur with these students when it comes to completing homework consistently. For example, access to technology and media may vary greatly within the student population. In planning classroom work, homework assignments and other projects, the teacher must take this into account.

DEALING WITH THESE ISSUES

First, be knowledgeable about the resources available to the students within the school, the library system, and the community. Be sure that any issues which might restrict a student's access (physical impediments, language difficulties, expenses, etc.) are addressed. Secondly, never plan for work or assignments where every student would not have equal access to information and technology. As in all aspects of education, each student must have an equal opportunity to succeed. Teachers should encourage these students as much as possible and offer positive reinforcements when they meet or exceed classroom expectations.

Skill 2.7   **Understands the instructional significance of varied student learning needs and preferences**

VARIED STUDENT NEEDS
The classrooms of today are characterized by students with broadly diverse cultures, economic backgrounds, learning problems; highly advanced learners; ESL students; migrant students; highly motivated students; and also under- achievers. Nearly half of all children will live in single-parent homes at some time during their school years.

Teachers have a critical responsibility to respond to these challenging and academically diverse populations in their classrooms. Successful teachers should learn to develop teaching and classroom routines that address the student learner variations in readiness, interest, and learning styles.

STRATEGIES FOR DEALING WITH VARIED STUDENTS
One strategy in which teachers can model in their classrooms is differentiation learning. Differentiation learning is an approach to teaching in which teachers "proactively modify curricula, teaching methods, resources, learning activities, and student products" to address the diverse needs of individual students in order to take full advantage of learning opportunities for every student in the classroom (Bearne, 1996; Tomlinson, 1999).

For more information on differentiated learning, **SEE** Skill 2.5.

TEACHER CERTIFICATION STUDY GUIDE

COMPETENCY 003   **THE TEACHER UNDERSTANDS PROCEDURES FOR DESIGNING EFFECTIVE AND COHERENT INSTRUCTION AND ASSESSMENT BASED ON APPROPRIATE LEARNING GOALS AND OBJECTIVES**

Skill 3.1   **Understands the significance of the Texas Essential Knowledge and Skills (TEKS) and of prerequisite knowledge and skills in determining instructional goals and objectives**

TEXAS ESSENTIAL KNOWLEDGE AND SKILLS
The Texas Essential Knowledge and Skills have been formulated as the standards by which students will be officially evaluated. These skills and areas of knowledge are the areas that the state believes all students should know and be able to perform by the time they exit each respective grade level. While all states have similar standards, each state considers different skills and areas of knowledge necessary and requires teachers to fully and successfully teach these to students.

Although teachers have access to and should use the TEKS in planning instruction, these standards do not automatically translate into classroom activities and learning. In other words, teachers have a lot of work to do to ensure that students learn those standards. The standards inform teachers about what students need to know and be able to do. Once teachers have this information, it is their responsibility to determine how students will best learn the standards.

PREREQUISITE SKILLS
Teachers must appropriately arrange material throughout the school year so that they teach prerequisite skills more advanced ones. For example, while teaching social studies, teachers may want to teach in a chronological fashion (and therefore would have to map out the chronology and how long they want to spend teaching each component throughout the year so that they cover the entire course of history required in the standards), or a math teacher might want to build on skills, such as teaching addition before multiplication.

In addition to considering the hierarchy of prerequisite skills when completing yearlong planning, as teachers plan from day to day, they need to be aware of their learning goals for their students, as well as their daily objectives within their lessons. Broadly, goals and objectives can be distinguished by suggesting that goals are long-term and often more abstract, immeasurable and vague. Objectives are short-term, specific, measurable, and must be clear.

Here are some examples; there might be a goal that students learn how to write a book report, but the objectives might include teaching children how to summarize a book, how to set up a report, or how to identify the source of a story. There might be the goal that students will learn phonemic awareness (the ability to identify and manipulate the sounds in words), but there might be a lesson by which our objective is to have students distinguish between the "t" sound and the "d" sound in a word. **SEE** also Skill 3.2.

Skill 3.2 **Uses appropriate criteria to evaluate the appropriateness of learning goals and objectives (e.g., clarity; relevance; significance; age-appropriateness; ability to be assessed; responsiveness to students' current skills and knowledge, background, needs, and interests; alignment with campus and district goals)**

GOALS AND OBJECTIVES

Teacher must be very knowledgeable about the writing of behavioral objectives that fall within the guidelines of the state and local expectations, and objectives must be measurable so that when the unit or semester is complete, teachers can know for sure whether accomplishments have been made. One might think that an objective would work well for a lesson and a goal might be better for a unit; that would definitely be correct. Each lesson should have at least one objective. That is, by the time the students finish the lesson, they should be able to demonstrate learning of SOMETHING that the teacher has decided to teach that day.

One of the major differences between a goal and an objective is that a goal is long-term and an objective is specific and observable. Once long-range goals have been identified and established, it is important to ensure that all goals and objectives are in conjunction with student ability and needs. Some objectives may be too basic for a higher level student, while others cannot be met with a student's current level of knowledge.

Evaluating Student Needs

There are many forms of evaluating student needs to ensure that all goals set are challenging yet achievable. Teachers should check a student's cumulative file, located in guidance, for reading level and prior subject area achievement. This provides a basis for goal setting but shouldn't be the only method used. Depending on the subject area, basic skills test, reading level evaluations, writing samples, and/or interest surveys can all be useful in determining if all goals are appropriate. Informal observation should always be used as well. Finally, it is important to take into consideration the student's level of motivation when addressing student needs.

When given objectives by the school or county, teachers may wish to adapt them so that they can meet the needs of their student population. For example, if a high level advanced class is given the objective, "*State five causes of World War II,*" a teacher may wish to adapt the objective to a higher level. "*State five causes of World War II and explain how they contributed to the start of the war.*" Subsequently, objectives can be modified for a lower level as well. "*From a list of causes, pick three that specifically caused World War II.*"

Setting Effective Goals and Objectives

First, goals and objectives must be clear. Clarity implies that the goal and objective must be clear for not only the teacher, but also the student and anyone else who might step into class on a particular day. If the objective is not clear in everyone's mind, it is probably not going to be clearly taught.

Here is a quick example: the teacher has a *goal* of teaching about nouns and verbs and an *objective* focusing on nouns, verbs, other parts of speech, and the uses of each one in a sentence. Given this goal and objective, most people would likely be confused as to what the teacher is really working on with students. In contrast, an objective such as this is much clearer: "Students will learn to contrast nouns and verbs in already-written sentences." Now there is an objective with clarity. The reader knows that the students should be able to get a sentence (age-appropriate length and complexity, by the way) and possibly circle the words that are nouns and underline the sentences that are verbs.

The goal and objective must also be significant and truly have purpose for both the standards and the life-long learning needs of students. Just because learning the parts of speech might be part of the state standards (such as the noun/verb example above), teachers might want to think twice about spending weeks upon weeks focusing on teaching this material. The significance is present, of course (all educated individuals SHOULD know the difference between the two parts of speech), but there are many other areas that students should focus on, as well.

Teachers must ensure that all goals and objectives are age-appropriate. This implies that the lessons teachers teach (and therefore the material the students are assessed on) should be appropriate to the developmental levels of the children in their classrooms. Typically, standards are defined very appropriately for each grade level. However, when a teacher takes a standard and translates it into a learning goal and an objective for a particular lesson, the teacher should remember that students will not learn the standard well if it is taught in a way that is completely too complex for their grade level and age. For information on developmental stages, **SEE** Skill 1.1

Assessing Goals and Objectives
Teachers should judge all objectives on their ability to be assessed. This is, in many ways, the most important concept in evaluating the appropriateness of learning goals and objectives. Everything else can in many ways be judged on the assessment of how well students have learned the new information or skills. For example, say there is an objective that suggests that students will learn about the solar system. How is this assessed? There is so much to know about the solar system. Perhaps, the teacher will teach everything s/he knows about the solar system, but then s/he is teaching more about what s/he knows than about what students need to know. And when s/he assesses, s/he will assess them on what he taught, not what they should have learned. Therefore, an objective such as "Students will identify all the planets in the solar system" is much better because it can simply be assessed.

Here is another example to consider. If a teacher has the goal of teaching first graders advanced calculus, when the teacher thinks about assessing the students, s/he might realize that no matter how well a lesson was taught, the students did not have any context or background knowledge to make this an age-appropriate skill to learn about. In many ways, judging an objective on its ability to be assessed can highlight strengths and/or weaknesses in the other appropriateness criteria.

Addressing Standards

When an objective is responsive to students' current skills and knowledge, background, needs, and interests, this means there are multiple routes to learning a standard. Standards may seem very specific but when thought about closely, they can be approached from a variety of angles. While teachers may be more willing to teach the standards based on what they know about them or what they find to be interesting in them, teachers should remember that it would be more productive if they thought about their students' prior knowledge and personal interests. The learning will be more engaging and effective this way. For further information regarding planning and adapting lessons to address students' varied backgrounds, skills, interests and learning needs, **SEE** Skill 2.5.

Finally, when objectives are aligned with campus and district goals, one can see that objectives can be tailored for various purposes but that they still can meet the learning needs of the standards. When a school has a mission, for example, of ensuring that students become aware of their communities and their environments (many charter and magnet schools have focus areas like this), the objectives can focus on these elements.

Outcomes of Successful Goals and Objectives

If the teacher stays right on the cutting edge of children's experience, they will become more and more curious about what is out there in the world that they do not know about. A lesson on a particular country or even a tribe in the world that the children may not even know exists that will use various kinds of media to reveal to them what life is like there for children their own age is a good way to introduce the world out there. In such a presentation, positive aspects of the lives of those "other" children should be included. Perhaps a correspondence with a village could be developed. It is good for children, some of whom may not live very high on the social scale in this country, to know what the rest of the world is like, and in so doing, develop a curiosity to know more.

In general, teachers should realize that the higher the quality of the objective (if it is adhered to in the lesson), the higher the quality of instruction, and therefore, the higher the quality of learning.

For information on utilizing relevant information, **SEE** Skill 8.3.

SEE also "Develop Success-Oriented Activities" in Skill 4.12.

Skill 3.3   **Uses assessment to analyze students' strengths and needs, evaluate teacher effectiveness, and guide instructional planning for individuals and groups**

EVALUATING STUDENT NEEDS

There are many ways to evaluate a child's knowledge and assess his/her learning needs. In recent years, the emphasis has shifted from "mastery testing" of isolated skills to authentic assessments of what children know. Authentic assessments allow the teacher to know more precisely what each individual student knows, can do, and needs to do. Authentic assessments can work for both the student and the teacher in becoming more responsible for learning. For definitions and examples of formal assessment (both objective and subjective), as well as informal assessment, **SEE** Skill 10.1.

To determine the abilities of incoming students, it may be helpful to consult their prior academic records. Letter grades assigned at previous levels of instruction as well as scores on standardized tests may be taken into account. In addition, the teacher may choose to administer pre-tests at the beginning of the school year, and perhaps also at the initial stage of each new unit of instruction. The textbooks available for classroom use may provide suitable pre-tests, tests of student progress, and post-tests.

In addition to administering tests, the teacher may assess the readiness of students for a particular level of instruction by having them demonstrate their ability to perform some relevant task. In a class that emphasizes written composition, for example, students may be asked to submit writing samples.

Teachers should also gauge student readiness by simply asking them about their previous knowledge of the subject or task at hand. While their comments may not be completely reliable indicators of what they know or understand, such discussions have the advantage of providing an idea of the students' interest in what is being taught. Instruction has a greater impact when the material being introduced is of student interest and relevant to the students' lives.

Tailoring Individual Evaluations
After initial evaluations have been conducted and appropriate instruction follows, teachers will need to fine tune individual evaluations in order to provide optimum learning experiences. Some of the same types of evaluations can be used on an ongoing basis to determine individual learning needs as were used to determine initial general learning needs. It is somewhat more difficult to choose an appropriate evaluation instrument for elementary-aged students than for older students.

Therefore, teachers must be mindful of developmentally appropriate instruments. At the same time, teachers must be cognizant of the information that they wish to attain from a specific evaluation instrument. Ultimately, these two factors—students' developmental stage and the information to be derived—will determine which type of evaluation will be most appropriate and valuable. There are few commercially designed assessment tools that will prove to be as effective as the tool that is constructed by the teacher.

Using Portfolios
The ability to create a personal and professional charting of student's academic and emotional growth found within the performance-based assessment of individualized portfolios becomes a toolkit for both students and teachers. Teachers can use semester portfolios to gauge student academic progress and personal growth of students who are constantly changing their self-images and worldviews on a daily basis. When a student is studying to master a math concept and is able to create a visual of the lessons learned that transcend beyond the initial concept to

create a bridge connecting a higher level of thinking and application of knowledge, then the teacher can share a moment of enjoyable math comprehension with the student.

Teachers who are innovative and creative in instructional practices are able to model and foster creative thinking in their students. Encouraging students to maintain journals and portfolios of their valued work from projects and assignments will allow students to make conscious choices on including a diversity of their creative endeavors in a filing format that can be treasured throughout the educational journey.

EVALUATING TEACHER EFFECTIVENESS

It is important for teachers to involve themselves in constant periods of reflection and self-reflection to ensure they are meeting the needs of the students. There are several avenues a teacher might take in order to assess his or her own teaching strengths and weaknesses. Early indicators that a self-evaluation might be necessary include having several students that do not understand a concept. In such a case, a teacher might want to go over his or her lesson plans to make sure the topic is being covered thoroughly and in a clear fashion. Brainstorming other ways to tackle the content might also help. Speaking to other teachers, asking how they teach a certain skill, might give new insight to one's own teaching tactics.

The very nature of the teaching profession—the yearly cycle of doing the same thing over and over again—creates the tendency to fossilize, to quit growing, and to become complacent. The teachers who are truly successful are those who have built into their own approach to their jobs and to their lives safeguards against that. They see themselves as constant learners, and believe that learning never ends. They are careful never to teach their classes the same as they did the last time. They build in a tendency to reflect on what is happening to their students under their care or what happened this year as compared to last year. What worked the best? What did not work so well? What can be changed to improve success rates? What about continuing education? Should they go for another degree or should they enroll in more classes?

Teachers will encounter situations daily where students have difficulty with a fact, task, concept, or idea or when the student does not get it, does not acquire the skill, or cannot internalize the information. As the teacher, what can be done? Repeat the instruction, verbatim, until it sinks in? Chastise or cajole the student into acknowledging an understanding? Since the teacher is genuinely concerned about the student's acquisition of skills and academic success, they will immediately realize that the dilemma is theirs, not the student's, and they will seek different ways to communicate an understanding of the information so that the student will completely comprehend and acquire a meaningful skill. After all, if the student does not succeed, it is the teacher who has failed.

Determining a Better Approach

In determining a better approach for providing an understanding to the student, teachers should consider many options and define the more probable ones to be used for instruction. The process for identifying viable options would include a teacher asking the following questions of themselves and answering them:

- What different words or phrasing might be used to say the same thing?
- How would I explain an opposite condition or fact, and would a negative example provide an understanding through contrast?
- If I imagined that the problem/fact/skill which I want to teach was an object which I could move around in any direction, would I be able to identify the "object's" component parts? Could I revise my explanation to provide a better understanding by starting from a different component part, reordering the component parts or redefining the component parts?
- Is there something preexisting in the student's acquired knowledge/skills which I can use to redirect or reinforce my explanation by making reference or demonstrating a link?
- Is there something specific to the student's culture or life experience which could inform my explanation/instruction?

In a student-centered learning environment, the goal is to provide the best education and opportunity for academic success for all students. Integrating the developmental patterns of physical, social, and academic norms for students will provide individual learners with student learning plans that are individualized and specific to their skill levels and needs. Teachers who effectively develop and maximize a student's potential will use pre- and post-assessments to gain comprehensive data on the existing skill level of the student in order to plan and adapt curriculum to address and grow student skills. Maintaining communication with the student and parents will provide a community approach to learning where all stakeholders are included to maximize student-learning growth.

Any good teacher will understand that he or she needs to self-evaluate and adjust his or her lessons periodically. Signing up for professional courses or workshops can also help a teacher assess his or her abilities by opening one's eyes to new ways of teaching.

Skill 3.4 Understands the connection between various components of the Texas statewide assessment program, the TEKS and instruction, and analyzes data from state and other assessments using common statistical measures to help identify students' strengths and needs

UNDERSTANDING TEXAS STATE ASSESSMENTS AND TEKS

The statewide, Texas assessment program and the TEKS have been specifically designed so that students are assessed on what is in the TEKS. In other words, the test items in the state-wide assessment focus exclusively on what the TEKS says students should know and be able to do.

Therefore, the teaching, learning, and assessing process is as follows:

1. Teachers know what is in the standards
2. Teachers develop a plan for the school year to ensure that all the standards are covered
3. Teachers develop objectives for specific lessons within the school year
4. Teachers provide various assessments throughout the year to ensure that students are progressing adequately

5. Teachers use the data from those assessments to make modifications to instruction (or to repeat certain topics)
6. Students are assessed on the state-wide assessment program
7. Schools and teachers can analyze the data from the state-wide assessment program to determine how to plan for instruction in the next year

Notice that all elements funnel back to instruction. All assessments, in fact, are designed in part to give teachers information about how they need to enhance or modify their instruction.

UTILIZING YEARLY DATA

Now, each year, teachers can use assessment data from the statewide tests to determine how well their students have done each year. But many people make the analogy that analyzing year-end test data provides as much information as the score of a basketball or baseball game gives people about the specific things that were done well and poorly throughout the game. When teachers just focus on the data from year-end tests, they see what areas students mastered and what areas they did not master.

However, to really see how instruction can be modified, teachers need to focus on providing multiple opportunities for assessment throughout the year to get as much information within the year on what could be improved. A simple and short assessment at the end of a lesson tells a teacher, for example, if students mastered the material from the lesson. Or, a reading inventory kept throughout the year tells how much a student has progressed in reading skill, rather than just giving us a "score" at the end of the year which will not show the ups and downs throughout the year.

When it is said that common statistical methods should be used to identify students' strengths and weaknesses, it is meant that different statistical methods should not be used to compare outcomes. Here is a good example: a teacher gives a student a 10 question quiz. A student gets 8 questions correct, and the teacher identifies performance as 80% correct. Yet, when the test scores from the state come back, and the teacher sees that the student is in the 60th percentile, what this means is that 60% of students taking the test scored LOWER than the student, not that the student only answered 60% correct. The point here is that it is important to know what scores mean and not to compare one type of score to another type, as the numbers may not relate.

SEE also Skills 10.1 and 10.2.

Skill 3.5   **Demonstrates knowledge of various types of materials and resources (including technological resources and resources outside the school) that may be used to enhance student learning and engagement and evaluates the appropriateness of specific materials and resources for use in particular situations, to address specific purposes and to meet varied student needs**

CHOOSING CLASSROOM MATERIALS

In considering suitable learning materials for the classroom, the teacher must have a thorough understanding of the state-mandated curriculum. According to state requirements, certain objectives must be met in each subject taught at every designated level of instruction. Keeping in mind the state requirements concerning the objectives and materials, the teacher must determine the abilities of the incoming students assigned to his/her class or supervision. It is essential to be aware of their entry behavior—that is, their current level of achievement in the relevant areas.

Teachers should have a toolkit of instructional strategies, materials, and technologies to encourage and teach students how to problem-solve and think critically about subject content. With each curriculum chosen by a district for school implementation there is an expectation that students must master benchmarks and standards of learning skills.

Textbooks

Most teachers choose to use textbooks, which are suitable to the age and developmental level of specific student populations. Textbooks reflect the values and assumptions of the society that produces them, while they also represent the knowledge and skills considered to be essential in becoming an educated adult. Finally, textbooks are useful to the school bureaucracy and the community, for they make public and accessible the private world of the classroom. Teachers should ensure that the textbooks used are current, thorough, representative of multiple perspectives, and free of cultural stereotypes.

Other Materials

Aside from textbooks, there is a wide variety of materials available to today's teachers. Computers are now commonplace in schools. Hand-held calculators support problems solving as they eliminate the need for students to be automatic with math facts in order to learn math concepts. Videocassettes (VCR's) and DVDs are common and permit the use of home-produced or commercially produced tapes. Textbook publishers often provide films, recordings, and software to accompany the text, as well as maps, graphics, and colorful posters to help students visualize what is being taught. Teachers can usually scan the educational publishers' brochures that arrive at their principal's or department head's office on a frequent basis.

Libraries and Media Centers

In addition, yesterday's libraries are today's media centers. Teachers can usually have opaque projectors delivered to the classroom to project print or pictorial images (including student work) onto a screen for classroom viewing. Some teachers have chosen to replace chalkboards or whiteboards with projectors that reproduce the print or images present on the plastic sheets known as transparencies, which the teacher can write on during a presentation or have machine-printed in advance. In either case, the transparency can easily be stored for later use.

Technology
Newer technologies such as wireless projectors make student access to teacher information even easier as they allow teachers to write and/or type onto a computer and that information is automatically projected onto the classroom screen (or even wall). Another higher-tech option that is replacing transparencies, projectors, and chalkboards is digital whiteboards, such as SMART boards. These digital screens allow teachers to project images from their computer, write on the boards, and use their hands or other implements to edit, erase, and move items on the screen. Such technology provides for a truly multi-sensory experience for students who are able to physically work with the information they are learning at the board.

This is an age where technology continues to expand at an ever increasing pace. Most students have a cursory understanding of different technologies and some are quite advanced, maybe even more so than their teachers. In order to engage students, it is important that teachers learn how to utilize now everyday tools such as the internet, blogs, wikis, podcasts, and other new digital technologies.

In an art or photography class, or any class in which it is helpful to display visual materials, slides can easily be projected onto a wall or a screen. Cameras are inexpensive enough to enable students to photograph and display their own work, as well as keep a record of their achievements in teacher files or student portfolios. Teaching students how to do this type of work digitally is also of value. Many high school courses, in particular, now allow students to access digital media and editing. Additionally, students can create their own blog to track achievements or portfolios.

Assistive Technology
In order to enhance student learning for all students, it is also crucial to have an understanding of assistive technology. Assistive technology "offers a bridge between a student's needs and his or her abilities. It connects a student's abilities with an educational opportunity that would otherwise be blocked by a disability." (Hecker, L., & Engstrom, E.U., 2005.) Familiarity with general categories of assistive technology, such as screen readers, speech-to-text software, word prediction tools, book on tape/CD, personal computers, or digital assistants for typing and even calculators, gives a teacher the means to ask questions and access resources for students that will enable a student to succeed.

Studies have shown that students learn best when what is taught in lecture and textbook reading is presented more than once in various formats. In some instances, students themselves may be asked to reinforce what they have learned by completing some original production—for example, by drawing pictures to explain some scientific process, by writing a monologue or dialogue to express what some historical figure might have said on some occasion, by devising a board game to challenge the players' mathematical skills, or by acting out (and perhaps filming) episodes from a classroom reading selection. Students usually enjoy having their work displayed or presented to an audience of peers. Thus, their productions may supplement and personalize the learning experiences that the teacher has planned for them. For more information on technology, **SEE** Competency 009, specifically Skills 9.4, 9.5, and 9.6.

Workshops and Conferences
Another way to stay current in the field is by attending workshops or conferences. Teachers will be enthusiastically welcomed on those occasions when educational publishers are asked to display their latest productions and revised editions of materials.

Cognitive Styles
Finally, in choosing materials, teachers should keep in mind that not only do students learn at different rates, but they bring a variety of cognitive styles to the learning process. **SEE** Skill 4.1 for information on these learning styles.

Skill 3.6 Plans lessons and structures units so that activities progress in a logical sequence and support stated instructional goals

LESSON PLANNING
Lesson plans are important in guiding instruction in the classroom. Incorporating the nuts and bolts of a teaching unit, the lesson plan outlines the steps of teacher implementation and assessment of teacher instructional capacity and student learning capacity. Teachers are able to objectify and quantify learning goals and targets in terms of incorporating effective performance-based assessments and projected criteria for identifying when a student has learned the material presented.

Critical Elements
The elements critical to the learning process include lesson content, quality materials, varied activities, specific goals, and consideration of learner needs. All components of a lesson plan including the unit description, learning targets, learning experiences, explanation of learning rationale and assessments must be present to provide both quantifiable and qualitative data to ascertain whether student learning has taken place and whether effective teaching has occurred for the students. A typical format would include the following items below:

1. Content of lesson plan: The plan contains guidelines for what is being taught and how the students will be able to access the information. Subsequent evaluations and assessments will determine whether students have learned or correctly processed the subject content being taught.
2. Materials: The plan provides a list of evaluated materials that will be used to implement the lesson content.
3. Unit Description: The plan provides description of the learning and classroom environment.
    a. Classroom Characteristics: The plan describes the physical arrangements of the classroom, along with the student grouping patterns for the lesson being taught. Classroom rules and consequences should be clearly posted and visible.

      b. Student Characteristics: The plan provides the demographics of the classroom that includes student number, gender, cultural and ethnic backgrounds, along with Independent Education students with IEPs (Individualized Education Plans).
4. Learning Goals/Targets/Objectives: The plan defines the expectations of each lesson. Are the learning goals appropriate to the state learning standards and District academic goals? Are the objectives appropriate for the grade level and subject content area and inclusive of a multicultural perspective and global viewpoint?
5. Learning Experiences for students: The plan describes how student learning will be supported using the learning goals
    a. What prior knowledge or experiences will the students bring to the lesson? How will you check and verify that student knowledge?
    b. How will all students in the classroom be engaged? How will students who have been identified as marginalized in the classroom be engaged in the lesson unit?
    c. How will the lesson plan be modified for students with IEPs and how will Independent Education students be evaluated for learning and processing of the modified lesson targets?
    d. How will the multicultural aspect be incorporated into the lesson plan?
    e. What interdisciplinary linkages and connections will be used to incorporate across other subject areas?
    f. What types of assessments/evaluations will be used to test student understanding and processing of the lesson plan?
    g. How will students be cooperatively grouped to engage in the lesson?
    h. What Internet linkages are provided in the lesson plan?
6. Rationales for Learning Experiences: The plan provides data on how the lesson plan addresses student learning goals and objectives. Address whether the lesson provides accommodations for students with IEPs and provides support for marginalized students in the classroom.
7. Assessments: The plan describes pre- and post-assessments that evaluate student learning as it correlates to the learning goals and objectives. Do the assessments include a cultural integration that addresses the cultural needs and inclusion of students?

All components of a lesson plan (including the unit description, learning targets, learning experiences, explanation of learning rationale and assessments) must be present to provide both quantifiable and qualitative data to ascertain whether student learning has taken place and whether effective teaching has occurred for the students. National and state learning standards must be taken into account because not only will the teacher and his students be measured by the students' scores at the end of the year, the school will also. So, not only must the teacher be knowledgeable about state and local standards, she must structure her own classes in ways that will meet those frameworks.

LARGE-SCALE CURRICULUM PLANNING
On the large scale, the teacher must think about the scope of her ambitious plans for the day, the week, the unit, the semester, and the year. The teacher must decide on the subject matter for the unit, semester, and year, making certain that it is appropriate to the age of the students,

relevant to their real lives, and in their realm of anticipated interest. Some things the teacher should consider include introducing politically controversial issues or avoiding them? Each teacher must make these decisions deliberatively on the basis of feedback from her students, at the same time keeping sight of the learning objectives.

Careful planning of the curriculum will ensure student success. The curriculum should be structured and in a progressive manner that demonstrates concepts, themes, and skills and the relationships between these modalities. The teacher should encourage students to identify and integrate these instructional concepts and relate that content to their lives and their surroundings. Also, teachers should be knowledgeable about state and local standards and structure their classes in ways that will meet the state-mandated frameworks.

SEE also Skill 8.2.

Skill 3.7 **Plans learning experiences that provide students with developmentally appropriate opportunities to explore content from integrated and varied perspectives (e.g., by presenting thematic units that incorporate different disciplines, providing intradisciplinary and interdisciplinary instruction, designing instruction that enables students to work cooperatively, providing multicultural learning experiences, prompting students to consider ideas from multiple viewpoints, encouraging students' application of knowledge and skills to the world beyond the school)**

When the teacher actively and frequently models viewing from multiple perspectives as an approach to learning in the classroom, the students not only benefit through improved academic skill development, they also begin to adopt this approach for learning and contemplating as a personal skill. This ability to consider a situation, issue, problem, or event from multiple viewpoints is a skill that will serve the individual well throughout his or her academic career and beyond.

THEMATIC UNITS
Interdisciplinary and thematic instruction, by definition and design, provide for teaching from perspective. Examples of effective, readily available instructional units are displayed below.

- **Discovering Your World** by Anita Yeoman
  This integrated unit introduces students to various countries as they plan a trip around the world. The unit is very flexible and can be adapted for any middle-level grade and time period. It consists of detailed suggestions for planning a "journey" according to the needs of each class. Worksheets for planning an itinerary, making passports and calculating distances are included, together with peer and self evaluation sheets and tracking sheets. Students will utilize research skills as they learn about language, history, geography and culture of the countries they "visit" on their world trip.

- **Let's Create an Island** by Philip Richards
  In this unit, students will create an island, following a set of suggestions, deciding on

such things as its location, topography, climate, population, employment, form of government, leisure activities, education etc. It enables students to learn important <u>geographic</u>, <u>scientific</u> and <u>civic</u> concepts in a manner that is enjoyable and imaginative. For each activity a concept is taught as a <u>class activity</u>, followed by <u>independent exercises</u> to reinforce what has been taught. The students then this use this knowledge when creating their own island. Includes tracking sheets, suggestions for teaching the unit, a rubric for evaluation and an answer key. Grades 6–9.

- **Cool Character** by Charlotte Wilcox, Sharon, Toothman, Linda Hatfield
  The objective of this unit, intended for grade 6, is to teach character education through the integration of different subject areas, primarily <u>Health</u>, <u>English/Language Arts</u>, <u>Science</u>, and <u>Social Studies</u>. This unit meets the following National Standards:
- **Language Arts:**
  - Gathers and uses information for research purposes
  - Demonstrates competence in the general skills and strategies of the writing process
  - Demonstrates competence in speaking and listening as tools for learning
- **Social Studies:**
  - Understands the importance of Americans sharing and supporting certain values, beliefs, and principles of American constitutional democracy
  - Understands economic, social, and cultural developments in the contemporary United States
- **Health:**
  - Knows how to maintain mental and emotional health
  - Understands the fundamental concepts of growth and development

COOPERATIVE LEARNING

SEE Skills 5.2, 6.2, and 6.3.

Multicultural Learning and Perspectives
When planning instruction for a diverse group (or teaching about diversity, for that matter) incorporate teaching through the use of perspective. There is always more than one way to "see" or approach a problem, an example, a process, fact or event, or any learning situation. Varying approaches for instruction helps to maintain the students' interest in the material and enables the teacher to address the diverse needs of individuals to comprehend the material. Meeting the requirement to enable students within a diverse classroom to acquire the same academic skills (at the same levels) can be aided considerably by incorporating teaching through the use of perspective into the unit plan.

Curriculum objectives and instructional strategies may be inappropriate and unsuccessful when presented in a single format which relies on the student's understanding and acceptance of the values and common attributes of a specific culture which is not his or her own. Planning, devising, and presenting material from a multicultural perspective can enable the teacher in a culturally diverse classroom to ensure that all the students achieve the stated, academic objective.

Even when the student population is largely culturally homogeneous, teaching with cultural perspective is always an asset to student comprehension and learning. History, as a subject, would be just one obvious example. The study of history includes the interactions of people from different cultures or subcultures. The point of view of, and impact on, each culture must be presented during instruction to ensure a comprehensive understanding of issues and events by the students. And in order to understand these points of view and impacts, it will be necessary to study the backgrounds of the cultures involved.

Teaching from multiple perspectives opens the door to a world of ideas teachers can use to make education an interesting, fun, and effective learning experience where every student can be included in the process and be successful in attaining the objectives. The possibilities may only be limited by the teacher's imagination. Should that limit actually be reached, the teacher has only to look to his or her colleagues to expand the horizon of teaching possibilities.

For more information on incorporating culture to enhance classroom learning, **SEE** Skills 2.1, 2.3, and 2.5.

APPLYING KNOWLEDGE TO THE WORLD
Students need to learn how to apply the practical application of knowledge to life. Many students are unaware of the correlation between knowledge and application. Once students have acquired new knowledge, they are typically asked to apply it through assignments, group projects, and examinations. Teachers can effectively content to students' life experiences, including, when appropriate, the building on prior learning in the content area or other related subject matter. Research shows that when students can engage in collaboration, their learning potential increases substantially. This is due in part to the group learning process, which provides them with the opportunity to co-construct new knowledge that has been gained and shared by other members of their group. They are made aware of the fact that the application of knowledge to the world is not done in isolation but is the combined efforts of many.

Here is a philosophy of teaching from perspective: it is less important which path we take than that we all arrive at the same destination.

Skill 3.8   Allocates time appropriately within lessons and units, including providing adequate opportunities for students to engage in reflection, self-assessment, and closure

MANAGING INSTRUCTIONAL TIME
Time is a resource which must be provided for in planning, like any other resource. Poor allocation and management of time will result in poor instruction and the inability of students to properly comprehend and internalize the skills to be mastered.

When allocating classroom time, the teacher must assume there will be nonproductive events within and between learning activities. During daily lesson planning, the teacher should identify these events and account for the time necessary to complete each one. Failure to include this in the planning process may result in classroom instruction or activities being rushed or not completed, and lessons or assignments not fully understood by the students.

Conversely, if the teacher simply allocates an estimated amount of "down time" without identifying the probable events and quantifying the time, he or she may find that instructional activities are completed much sooner than expected. Some teachers will try to cover for this by "stretching" or repeating instruction, having a "spontaneous" question and answer session, using the time for "quiet study," or simply allowing the students to socialize until the end of the period. These are unproductive uses of time and may in fact prove to be counterproductive. Unplanned time is usually wasted time.

These nonproductive events are usually organizational and administrative tasks, such as:

- Taking and recording attendance
- Processing announcements
- Gathering or issuing homework assignments
- Distributing instructional materials
- Assembling members for group activities
- Responding to students questions regarding a new or revised process

Proper time management and allocation contribute to efficient classroom management and a positive learning environment. When things seem to go in fits and starts or there are frequent lulls in activity, students may respond as if the instruction or learning activity were dull and become bored, disinterested and uninvolved. If students feel uninvolved in a lesson, the teacher is probably wasting time teaching that lesson.

Strategies for Planning Time
In order to assess the time required for particular lessons and units, specific information about the content, materials, and activities involved must be known, at a detail level, in order to allocate time appropriately. Within the specifications for most instructional materials provided by educational publishers, there are guidelines on using the material and recommendations for the allocation of time, by unit. Obviously, it is the teacher, not the textbook/media publisher, who determines what goes into a lesson plan and what is presented in the classroom—and how and when it will be presented.

Going beyond the guidelines, recommendations, and time approximations provided with such material, the teacher should decide what will and will not be used in the classroom. For each unit that will be used, the teacher should consider the component parts and ask the question, "What response do I want from the students at this point? Contemplation? Questions? Discussion or other activity? Writing or testing?" Based on his or her answers, the teacher should be able to approximate the effort involved and plan adequate time, accordingly. The same process would be used when the teacher designs and develops her or his own units or adopts them from another source.

REFLECTION

All of this is not to say that only activities conducted or directed by the teacher—with active teacher participation—have value. The needs of the students for personal review and reflection, self-assessment, to internalize ideas, information or skills, or to achieve a sense of completion should be recognized as valid, identified in the particular, and allocated appropriate time.

Purposes for allocating such time to students would include:

- After difficult or complex tasks or skills have been introduced
- After difficult or complex tasks or skills have been utilized
- After technically difficult or complex instructional materials have been introduced
- After technically difficult or complex instructional materials have been utilized
- After independent research has been conducted by students
- After student reports or presentations to the class
- After returning graded examinations, assignments, or other evaluations to students
- After planned classroom activities and discussions
- After presentation or instruction on life skills, social skills, at-risk behaviors, etc.

The process of reflection needs to be planned for both during and after learning situations. Reflective thinking refers to the process of analyzing and making judgments about what has happened. It encourages students to continuously evaluate incoming information and be flexible, if appropriate, in their approach to a task. It also allows students to store information and transfer the learning experience to novel, future tasks.

Reflective thinking helps to hone higher-order thinking skills by relating new information to prior knowledge, thinking in the abstract, and using meta-cognitive skills to think about one's own thinking and learning. When allocating time for reflective thinking, the following tasks can be considered:

- Teacher modeling of metacognitive and self-explanation strategies
- Reviews of the learning task (e.g., KWL chart: What is Known, What we Want to Know, and What we have already Learned)
- Use of, and time for, reflective journaling for students to write their hypotheses/positions, reasons behind those ideas, and questions/weaknesses in their ideas
- Teacher posed questions that seek reasoning and evidence, specifically *why*, *how*, and *what*
- Collaborative activities that allow for learning about other points of view

SELF-ASSESSMENT

Self-assessment must also have time allocated to it in the course of designing a lesson or unit. Self-assessment is the process of students judging the quality of their work, based on given criteria, with the goal of improving performance in the future. The process of self-assessment itself is also helping to teach students to think critically, so that they do not need someone else to tell them how well they are doing. There is a solid body of evidence that supports the use of self-assessment for improving student performance, particularly in writing. And, equally as convincing, students often like to do it and are more motivated to persist on difficult tasks! Research also revealed that student attitudes toward evaluations were more positive when they were involved in the assessment.

The process of self-assessment is a learning experience. The process must first begin by involving students in defining the criteria on which they will be assessed. Teachers must then instruct students on how to apply that criterion to their own work. Teacher modeling, with examples, is crucial at this step. Students must then be given feedback on their self-evaluations so that they can learn how to most effectively use the process. Finally, students must be guided on how to use those self-evaluations to develop personal goals.

One popular method of self-assessment is using rubrics. Developing rubrics with students gives them the opportunity to participate in defining important criteria and also provides students with a tool to use during the learning task. Students can then systematically proceed through the assessment procedure, discuss specific areas of strength and/or weakness, and transition to goal setting in a more systematic and structured manner.

CLOSING A UNIT

Closure within a lesson or unit plan can often be overlooked; however it is a crucial time for students and teachers. Closure is the period of time when a lesson is wrapped up and the students are assisted in storing the new information into a meaningful context that can be applied in the future.

For students, closure often provides a brief overview, a reinforcement of key ideas, an affirmation of the material learned, or a time to clear up confusions or inconsistencies. For teachers, this is a time where learning can be solidified through reinforcement of key concepts and placed in the larger context of a unit or idea. It can also provide insight into which students have a clear understanding of the task and which ones need more clarification.

Sample Closure Activities
Some sample closure activities include:

- A KWL chart, with a focus on the "L" section (What has been Learned).
- 3-2-1: 3 Things learned, 2 Questions, 1 Thing liked/Strategy I used
- Circle, Square, Triangle (for higher-level students): Things/ideas that are still circling in my mind (still thinking about), things/ideas that square with what I know/believe (confirmation of known information), three points I've learned
- 3 Whats: *What* Did I learn? So *what*? (Why is it important?) *What* now? (How does this relate to what we have learned/will learn?)

TEACHER CERTIFICATION STUDY GUIDE

COMPETENCY 004 **THE TEACHER UNDERSTANDS LEARNING PROCESSES AND FACTORS THAT IMPACT STUDENT LEARNING AND DEMONSTRATES THIS KNOWLEDGE BY PLANNING EFFECTIVE, ENGAGING INSTRUCTION AND APPROPRIATE ASSESSMENTS**

Skill 4.1 **Understands the role of learning theory in the instructional process and uses instructional strategies and appropriate technologies to facilitate student learning (e.g., connecting new information and ideas to prior knowledge, making learning meaningful and relevant to students)**

BEHAVIORAL AND COGNITIVE LEARNING

First, teachers should realize that historically, there are two broad sides regarding the construction of meaning, the application of strategies, etc. One is behavioral learning. Behavioral learning theory suggests that people learn socially or through some sort of stimulation or repetition. The other broad theory is cognitive. Cognitive learning theories suggest that learning takes place in the mind, and that the mind processes ideas through brain mapping and connections with other material and experiences. In other words, with behaviorism, learning is somewhat external. We see something, for example, and then we copy it. With cognitive theories, learning is internal. For example, we see something, analyze it in our minds, and make sense of it for ourselves. Then, if we choose to copy it, we do, but we do so having internalized the process.

There are several cognitive educational learning theories that can be applied to classroom practices. One classic learning theory is Piaget's stages of development, which consists of four learning stages: sensory motor stage (from birth to age 2); pre-operation stages (ages 2 to 7 or early elementary); concrete operational (ages 7 to 11 or upper elementary); and formal operational (ages 11- high school). Piaget believed children passed through this series of stages to develop from the most basic forms of concrete thinking to sophisticated levels of abstract thinking.

The metacognition learning theory deals with "the study of how to help the learner gain understanding about how knowledge is constructed and about the conscious tools for constructing that knowledge" (Joyce and Weil 1996). The cognitive approach to learning involves the teacher's understanding that teaching the student to process his/her own learning and mastery of skill provides the greatest learning and retention opportunities in the classroom. Students are taught to develop concepts and teach themselves skills in problem solving and critical thinking. The student becomes an active participant in the learning process, and the teacher facilitates that conceptual and cognitive learning process.

BRAIN-BASED LEARNING

Some of the most prominent learning theories in education today include brain-based learning. Supported by recent brain research, brain-based learning suggests that knowledge about the way the brain retains information enables educators to design the most effective learning environments. As a result, researchers have developed 12 principles that relate knowledge about the brain to teaching practices.

These 12 principles are:

1. The brain is a complex adaptive system
2. The brain is social
3. The search for meaning is innate
4. We use patterns to learn more effectively
5. Emotions are crucial to developing patterns
6. Each brain perceives and creates parts and whole simultaneously
7. Learning involves focused and peripheral attention
8. Learning involves conscious and unconscious processes
9. We have at least two ways of organizing memory
10. Learning is developmental
11. Complex learning is enhanced by challenged (and inhibited by threat)
12. Every brain is unique

(Caine & Caine, 1994, Mind/Brain Learning Principles)

Educators can use these principles to help design methods and environments in their classrooms to maximize student learning.

MULTIPLE INTELLIGENCE THEORY

The Multiple Intelligent Theory, developed by Howard Gardner, suggests that students learn in (at least) seven different ways. These include visually/spatially, musically, verbally, logically/mathematically, interpersonally, intrapersonally, and bodily/kinesthetically. **SEE** also Skills 4.5 and 4.14.

CONSTRUCTIVISM

The most current learning theory of constructivist learning allows students to construct learning opportunities. For constructivist teachers, the belief is that students create their own reality of knowledge and how to process and observe the world around them. Students are constantly constructing new ideas, which serve as frameworks for learning and teaching.

Researchers have shown that the constructivist model is comprised of the four components:

1. Learner creates knowledge
2. Learner constructs and makes meaningful new knowledge to existing knowledge
3. Learner shapes and constructs knowledge by life experiences and social interactions
4. In constructivist learning communities, the student, teacher and classmates establish knowledge cooperatively on a daily basis

Constructivist learning for students is dynamic and ongoing. For constructivist teachers, the classroom becomes a place where students are encouraged to interact with the instructional process by asking questions and posing new ideas to old theories. The use of cooperative learning that encourages students to work in supportive learning environments using their own ideas to stimulate questions and propose outcomes is a major aspect of a constructivist classroom.

BEHAVIORISM

Social and behavioral theories look at the social interactions of students in the classroom that instruct or impact learning opportunities in the classroom. The psychological approaches behind both theories are subject to individual variables that are learned and applied either proactively or negatively in the classroom. The stimulus of the classroom can promote learning or evoke behavior that is counterproductive for both students and teachers. Students are social beings that normally gravitate to action in the classroom, so teachers must be cognizant in planning classroom environments that provide both focus and engagement in maximizing learning opportunities.

Designing classrooms that provide optimal academic and behavioral support for a diversity of students in the classroom can be daunting for teachers. The ultimate goal for both students and teachers is creating a safe learning environment where students can construct knowledge in an engaging and positive classroom climate of learning.

APPLYING LEARNING THEORY IN THE CLASSROOM

No one of these theories will work for every classroom, and a good approach is to incorporate a range of learning styles in a classroom. Still, under the guidance of any theory, good educators will differentiate their instructional practices to meet the needs of their students' abilities and interests using various instructional practices. Today, even though behavioral theories exist, most educators believe that children learn cognitively.

For example, when teachers introduce new topics by relating those topics to information students are already familiar with or exposed to, they are expecting that students will be able to better integrate new information into their memories by attaching it to something that is already there.

In all of the examples given in this standard, the importance is the application of new learning to something concrete. In essence, what is going on with these examples is that the teacher is slowing building on knowledge or adding knowledge to what students already know. Cognitively, this makes a great deal of sense. Think of a file cabinet. When we already have files for certain things, it's easy for us to find a file and throw new information into it. When we are given something that does not fit into one of the pre-existing files, we struggle to know what to do with it. The same is true with human minds.

The teacher will, of course, have certain expectations regarding where the students will be physically and intellectually when he/she plans for a new class. However, there will be wide variations in the actual classroom. If he/she does not make the extra effort to understand where there are deficiencies and where there are strengths in the individual students, the planning will probably miss the mark, at least for some members of the class. This can be obtained through a review of student records, by observation, and by testing.

For further information on making learning meaningful and relevant, **SEE** Skill 8.3.

Skill 4.2 **Understands that young children think concretely and rely primarily on motor and sensory input and direct experience for development of skills and knowledge and uses this understanding to plan effective, developmentally appropriate learning experiences and assessments**

ADDRESSING YOUNG LEARNERS
Until pre-adolescence, students do not think in abstract forms. Sure, they are able to understand symbols, but deep symbolism is not yet comprehended. For example, language is a symbol, and they can understand that certain words symbolize things, actions, emotions, etc. But they do not yet have the ability to see how symbolism works in a story as well as an adolescent would.

When it is said that young children are concrete thinkers, it means that they are driven by senses. In other words, they are very literal thinkers. If they can see something, hear something, or feel something, they are more likely to believe it—and learn it.

Therefore, the more teachers can utilize this concrete thinking, the better their students will master grade-level standards at this age. Take the example of math. Ever wonder why young children always count with their fingers? This is because, even though they might be able to do it in their heads, seeing it (and feeling it, as they move their fingers) makes it more "real" to them. So, instead of teaching math through words and numbers on a chalkboard, teachers can be more effective at teaching math through manipulatives. By simply putting objects on a table, having students count the objects, taking away a certain number and having them re-count the left-over objects, students are more likely to understand the CONCEPT of subtraction.

Many reading teachers have learned that students can comprehend stories better if they get a chance to dramatize the story. In other words, they "act out" a story, and thereby learn what the words mean more clearly than they could have if they just read it and talked about it.

The whole concept of science laboratory learning in elementary school is founded on the idea that students will be more successful learning concepts if they use their hands, eyes, ears, noses, etc., in the learning process. Many concepts that would otherwise be very difficult for students to learn can be attained very quickly in a laboratory setting.

SEE also Skills 1.1 and 1.6.

Skill 4.3 **Understands that the middle-level years are a transitional stage in which students may exhibit characteristics of both older and younger children, and that these are critical years for developing important skills and attitudes (e.g., working and getting along with others, appreciating diversity, making a commitment to continued schooling)**

ADDRESSING MIDDLE-LEVEL LEARNERS
Middle-level years are very confusing for adults and children alike. Many adolescents may exhibit traits of both children and adults at the same time. Indeed, many adolescents look quite young but have very advanced cognitive abilities; likewise, some look very old but still have not grown out of childhood behaviors.

Thrown into the physical and emotional mix of adolescence is the cognitive ability to think more logically, to have abstract thoughts, and to be more socially aware. The awkwardness sometimes comes into play when one area of development has outgrown another. For example, an adolescent might be a fairly abstract thinker but not have any decent social skills. Most people even out after a few years.

Because of the cognitive, social, and emotional development that takes place so rapidly at this time, it is a time when people start to develop a stronger self-concept. What this means is that adolescents try to determine who they are in the world around them. What this implies is that adolescents develop certain values on their own. They decide what is important to them and what is not important to them. But in the process of determining who they are as people, they look for clues, particularly from adults.

What this means for teachers is that adolescents are making life decisions and they use role models to assist in the process. It is therefore imperative for teachers to note that students are sometimes looking to them to help them decide on their values. They are also looking for guidance in how to deal with peers.

In addition, as they develop self-concepts, they are looking to see how major aspects in their lives fit into their personal characteristics. For example, if an adolescent has not been able to get decent grades, he or she may decide that school is unimportant; this is mainly because that person does not want to look like he or she cares about something that is too difficult. Therefore, teachers must really work to help students feel successful at a variety of things, including academics (even when they really are struggling). This does not mean that teachers should lie to students about their abilities; rather, they should concentrate on helping students find the things that interest them academically with the hope that they will perform better in areas that they enjoy.

In summary, teachers really can be explicit in their teaching of particular life skills. They can help adolescents learn how to get along with those who are unlike themselves. They can teach them how to be more effective with studying. They can also teach them how to identify and engage in areas of personal interest. Doing so will help ease the difficult transition from childhood to adulthood.

TEACHER CERTIFICATION STUDY GUIDE

SEE also Skills 1.1 and 1.6.

Skill 4.4 **Recognizes how characteristics of students at different developmental levels (e.g., limited attention span and need for physical activity and movement for younger children; importance of peers, search for identity, questioning of values and exploration of long-term career and life goals for older students) impact teaching and learning**

NEEDS OF ELEMENTARY STUDENTS

Anyone who has been in an early childhood or elementary school classroom knows that students do not sit still and focus on one thing for too long. Some people joke that the age of a person equals the amount of time the person is willing to sit and listen for any one time. So, a kindergartener, under this premise, would only be able to sit and concentrate on one thing for five to six minutes.

Good teachers know how to capitalize on the need of children to move and change topics. Generally, young children should be changing academic activities every 15-20 minutes. This means that if a teacher wants to fill a block of two hours for literacy learning in the morning, the teacher should have about 6-8 activities planned. Here is an example:

1. Teacher has students write something to access background knowledge; in kindergarten, this might include just a picture, but in grade four, this might include a paragraph
2. Teacher might spend a few minutes asking students what they wrote about in a large group
3. Teacher might introduce a new book by doing a "book walk"—looking at the title, the pictures, etc.
4. Teacher reads book aloud as students follow along
5. Students do a pair-share where they turn to their neighbors to discuss a question
6. Students return to desks to do a comprehension activity on their own
7. Whole class discussion of what they wrote
8. Students go to centers to practice specific skills as teacher works with small groups of students
9. Teacher conducts a vocabulary activity with the whole class

Teachers who switch things around like this are more likely to keep their students' attention, engage their students more, and have a more behaved classroom. When children get bored, they obviously will start to not pay attention, and many will become disruptive. The key is to keep them interested in what they are learning.

NEEDS OF MIDDLE AND HIGH SCHOOL STUDENTS

For information on peers, **SEE** "Role of Peers" in Skill 1.1.

Students at the middle level are continually undergoing physical and emotional changes and development. Young adolescents begin to transition for an adult-driven atmosphere to one where they need to self-motivate. As they gain this independence, adolescents typically begin to question and explore their own identity with thoughts such as, "Who am I?" Teachers, parents, and school counselors play an important role in how young teens navigate the search for their own identity. No matter how well we might try to prepare them for this, they have no point of reference within their own life experiences. Everything that is occurring to them is new and unfamiliar to these students, and often makes them uncomfortable about themselves and in the company of others.

At the middle school level, students often struggle with this gain of independence. A once successful student (under the more managed direction of an elementary teacher) may experience his or her first failure(s) when given more responsibility from a middle school teacher for directing/motivating him or herself. Teachers must provide students with guidance and strategies for how to handle this increased responsibility as it is a critical skill for success in high school. In high school, students will be expected to manage their assignments and learning amongst simultaneously dealing with increased social pressures and stress that comes with the older adolescent years (a job, driving, career or college decisions, increased pressure for risky[ier] behaviors, etc.).

In searching for answers to "Who will I become?" adolescents today face a different world of work than earlier generations. Some 70 years ago, a person may have prepared for a career they kept their entire lives. Today, career paths and specific positions are in a constant state of change, many that follow ongoing changes as technology changes. There are many more people in the workforce today than there were 70 years ago, so teachers and counselors must prepare students with skills that will help them secure gainful employment. In addition to analyzing interests and strengths to find possible career paths, students must learn how to fill out applications, create resumes, and interview effectively.

Skill 4.5 **Applies knowledge of the implications for learning and instruction of the range of thinking abilities found among students in any one grade level and students' increasing ability over time to engage in abstract thinking and reasoning**

MULTIPLE INTELLIGENCES
As children develop into adults, their specific learning abilities and personal interests will become more and more apparent. Particularly in adolescence, students will determine which areas of school they enjoy and which areas they do not. Often, this has to do with the subjects at which they succeed. For example, a common theory used in schools today is "multiple intelligences." While there is a lot of debate on this, the main premise is that there are various types of intelligence that someone can have, so comparing general intelligence between people is unproductive.

Certain types of intelligence might include mathematical, linguistic, kinesthetic, spatial, and interpersonal. If a student has linguistic intelligence, that student might have an easier time with reading comprehension, writing, or learning new languages. If a student has kinesthetic intelligence, he or she might be skilled in art (as many visual arts require good hand-eye movement). If a student has spatial intelligence, he or she might be able to develop a map of a location easily. If a student has strong interpersonal intelligence, he or she might be good at "reading" other people's moods or helping them through problems.

What this means for teachers is that if one type of intelligence or thinking style is prized in the classroom over another, many students will be unsuccessful. This is unfair to students as all types of intelligence are valued in the real world and all types are important. However, when students are judged on their mathematics and reading skills alone, for example, the other areas in which they might excel are ignored.

Addressing Multiple Intelligences
How do teachers demonstrate commitment to all types of intelligences and learning styles? Well, they do not have to design lessons differently for each type of student (because even the categories listed above are only a small portion of categories of intelligences and learning styles that teachers will find in their classrooms). What teachers can do is to first alternate the ways that lessons are taught and knowledge is assessed. If teachers alternate lessons, this allows some students to be very successful at an activity but then exposes other students to that type of thinking.

Secondly, teachers can give students choices. When students are given choices (on how the learn certain things or how they prove that they know something), they further develop the skills of adult thinking. This allows them to assess their knowledge on their own and then assess which style of thinking will best demonstrate mastery. Teachers may be very impressed with how well students perform in this type of environment. Furthermore, it helps to develop responsibility.

It is also crucial to keep in mind that students' abilities to engage in abstract thinking and reasoning develop over time; and, that all students will not develop these skills at exactly the same time. Piaget's theory of cognitive development suggests that it is not until the Formal Operational stage, which begins around age 11 and continues into adulthood, that students begin to think abstractly.

In general, teachers must realize that adolescents are in a stage of life where they are experimenting to determine who they are and what they are best at. Teachers need to encourage this growth and guide them along the way.

Skill 4.6   **Stimulates reflection, critical thinking and inquiry among students (e.g., supports the concept of play as a valid vehicle for young children's learning; provides opportunities for young children to manipulate materials and to test ideas and hypotheses; engages students in structured, hands-on problem-solving activities that are challenging; encourages exploration and risk-taking; creates a learning community that promotes positive contributions, effective communication and the respectful exchange of ideas)**

CRITICAL THINKING

A critical thinking skill is a skill target that teachers help students develop to sustain learning in specific subject areas that can be applied within other subject areas. The effective teacher uses advanced communication skills such as clarification, reflection, perception, and summarization as a means to facilitate communication and a community of learning.

For example, when learning to understand algebraic concepts in solving a math word problem on how much fencing material is needed to build a fence around a backyard area that has an 8-by-12-foot area, a math student must understand the order of numerical expression in how to simplify algebraic expressions. Teachers can provide instructional strategies that show students how to group the fencing measurements into an algebraic word problem that with minor addition, subtraction, and multiplication can produce a simple number equal to the amount of fencing materials needed to build the fence.

Higher Order Thinking Skills

Bloom's taxonomy references six skill levels within the cognitive domain: knowledge, comprehension, application, analysis, synthesis, and evaluation. Higher-order thinking skills, often referred to as HOTS, refer to the top three levels of Bloom's Taxonomy: analysis, synthesis, and evaluation. They are the skills that most apply to critically thinking through information and not simply absorbing it. It is crucial for students to use and refine these skills because they are truly what enable us to learn more sophisticated content and apply our learning to novel situations, skills that apply to life and work success beyond school. For more information on Bloom's Taxonomy, **SEE** Skill 8.2.

Low Order Questioning

Low order questions (recall, knowledge, define, analyze, etc.) are useful to begin the process. They insure the student is focused on the required information and understands what needs to be included in the thinking process. For example, if the objective is for students to be able to read and understand the story "Goldilocks and the Three Bears," the teacher may wish to start with low order questions (i.e., "What are some things Goldilocks did while in the bears home?" [Knowledge] or "Why didn't Goldilocks like the Papa Bear's chair?" [Analysis]).

Students use basic skills to understand things that are read such as a reading passage or a math word problem or directions for a project. However, students should also apply critical thinking skills to fully comprehend how what was read could be applied to their own life or how to make comparatives or choices based on the factual information given.

Using Higher Order Questioning in the Classroom

Most teachers want their educational objectives to use higher level thinking skills, teachers need to direct students to these higher levels on the taxonomy. Questioning is an effective tool to build up students to these higher levels. Through a series of questions, the teacher can move the students up the taxonomy. (For example, "If Goldilocks had come to your house, what are some things she may have used?" [Application], "How might the story differ if Goldilocks had visited the three fishes?" [Synthesis], or "Do you think Goldilocks was good or bad? Why?" [Evaluation]). The teacher through questioning can control the thinking process of the class. As students become more involved in the discussion they are systematically being lead to higher level thinking.

These higher-order thinking skills are called critical thinking skills, as students think in more complex ways and teachers are instrumental in helping students use these skills in everyday activities:

- Analyzing bills for overcharges
- Comparing shopping ads or catalogue deals
- Finding the main idea from readings
- Applying what has been learned to new situations
- Gathering information/data from a diversity of sources to plan a project
- Following a sequence of directions
- Looking for cause and effect relationships
- Comparing and contrasting information in synthesizing information

To develop a critical thinking approach to the world, children need to know enough about valid and invalid reasoning to ask questions. Bringing into the classroom speeches or essays that demonstrate both valid and invalid examples can be useful in helping students develop the ability to question the reasoning of others. These will be published writers or televised speakers, so they can see that they are able even to question ideas that are accepted by some adults and talk about what is wrong in the thinking of those apparently successful communicators.

SEE Skills 4.7 and 8.2 for more information on higher-order thinking skills.

THE ROLE OF PLAY
For more information on the important of play, **SEE** Skill 1.9.

HANDS-ON LEARNING
Learning through multiple modalities enhances the learning experience for all students in the classroom. Teachers using manipulatives can help students to be able to hone their skills in the area of visual processing and can help those students with strength in visual processing learn further about additional concepts and ideas. From as young as infancy, children learn by doing. Play often gives children the opportunity to try things and learn from seeing, doing, and watching. This rudimentary hypothesis testing is carried out throughout schooling, in gradually more formal methods (e.g., a middle or high school science experiment with corresponding lab report).

For information on problem-solving, risk-taking, and critical thinking activities, **SEE** Skill 4.7.

A COMMUNITY OF LEARNERS

The inquiry method is based on students questioning and learning from each other. The teacher plays a pivotal role in fostering a community whereby all student ideas are respected and collaborative ideas bring about overall growth.

SEE also Skill 5.2

REFLECTION
SEE Skill 3.8.

Skill 4.7 **Enhances learning for students by providing age-appropriate instruction that encourages the use and refinement of higher-order thinking skills (e.g., prompting students to explore ideas from diverse perspectives; structuring active learning experiences involving cooperative learning, problem solving, open-ended questioning and inquiry; promoting students' development of research skills)**

ACTIVE LEARNING

Does not all instruction encourage students to think? Well, hopefully, but research tells us that students learn greater aunts when they are engaged in active learning. Active learning derives from the assumptions that (1) learning is by nature an active endeavor and (2) that different people learn in different ways (Meyers and Jones, 1993). Students need to discover, and process, apply, and judge information in order to truly learn. This is achieved through planning a lesson that allows students to talk, listen, read, write, and reflect.

A great in-class activity that promotes active learning is "Think-Pair-Share". Students are given a question or problem to solve. They then "think" independently for a few minutes, discuss their ideas in a "pair" to encourage processing of different perspectives and evaluation of each others' ideas, and then "share" their ideas with the whole class, encouraging synthesis, and further processing and evaluation. Students can incorporate information from text they have read or may be asked to write about the given activity at a later point. Such an activity can be used with classes of all ages and sizes.

OPEN-ENDED QUESTIONING

Other key instructional approaches that utilize HOTS are inquiry-based learning, problem solving and open-ended questioning. The central theme to inquiry-based learning is that learning is driven more so by student questions and elaboration than it is by teacher lessons. Does this sound counter-intuitive? Inquiry-based learning still requires a teacher to have solid goals, objectives, and lesson plans. However, it also relies heavily on creating an environment where students must solve problems, discuss, and analyze. It also requires flexibility and collaborative learning, and most importantly, solid questioning techniques.

TEACHER CERTIFICATION STUDY GUIDE

Open-ended questions require complex thinking and give opportunities for different ways of thinking. The teacher has a responsibility to model good listening and questioning so that the students can utilize the same techniques.

Think about the following "rules for questioning":

- Ask questions that require substantive answers. Avoid yes/no questions.
    o "What do we know about making web pages?" vs. "Has anyone ever made a webpage before?"
- Avoid questions where the answer is a simple fact or a one-word answer.
    o "What year was President Kennedy killed? vs. "What factors played into President Kennedy's assassination?"
- Try to pose contradictions or use phrases such as, "Tell me more about that." or "What will happen as a result of that?" "Explain." "Expand."
- Apply questions to current and real-life situations
    o "What would happen if this situation took place today? How would people react?"

Keeping in mind how to facilitate students' higher-order thinking skills by using the above techniques and instructional methods will make for a dynamic and engaging classroom environment.

For an introductory discussion of critical thinking, **SEE** Skill 4.6.

For information on diverse perspectives, **SEE** Skill 3.7.

For information on cooperative learning, **SEE** Skills 2.5, 5.2, 6.2, and 6.3.

For information on research skills, **SEE** Skill 4.9.

Skill 4.8 **Teaches, models, and monitors organizational and time-management skills at an age-appropriate level (e.g., establishing regular places for classroom toys and materials for young children, keeping related materials together, using organizational tools, using effective strategies for locating information and organizing information systematically)**

TEACHING MANAGEMENT SKILLS

Teachers have a responsibility to help students learn how to manage time and organize their learning environments for maximum effectiveness. Classrooms are great places for children to learn responsibility and good citizenship. Teachers of young children can help students learn how to behave appropriately and take care of their surroundings by providing them with opportunities to practice ownership, chores, and leadership. Many high school and college-aged students reflect on the fact that they were never taught how to do these things in earlier grade levels, and often, they struggle into adulthood without these skills.

Environment

First, teachers should arrange classrooms in ways that students can access materials. However, materials should be arranged in ways that maintain cleanliness. Messy classrooms show students that teachers do not care enough to provide students with clean, safe environment in which to learn. It also presents a negative image to parents, principals, and other teachers.

As children learn to clean up after themselves, they should be taught how to appropriately divide responsibilities (so, if a group of three students are working with blocks together, all three should divide up materials to put away). They should also learn how to put materials back in an organized fashion. So, for example, the first time blocks are put away, the teacher should show how to sort by shapes and size. The teacher can quiz students as a group about which items belong together and which items do not belong together.

Organizing Activities

Teachers can help students by expecting that they keep calendars for themselves. In the calendars, they can write down homework assignments, estimate the amount of time they will need for certain assignments, and plug in important dates. They can also help students organize their learning environments by teaching them how to organize notebooks, desks, etc. It is not unheard of for teachers to do "spot-checks" of notebooks to ensure that students are keeping their materials organized. How effective will a student be at studying for a quiz, for example, if the student shoves all of his or her notes into a backpack? Teachers can help prevent the haphazard methods by which some children decide to "organize" their materials; by doing so, they will help their students become more effective learners.

These skills are important for children to learn. They demonstrate to children how to keep their environments orderly and functional.

For more information on organizing, **SEE** Skills 1.12, 4.9, 5.6 and 6.1.

Skill 4.9   Teaches, models and monitors age-appropriate study skills (e.g., using graphic organizers, outlining, note-taking, summarizing, test-taking) and structures research projects appropriately (e.g., teaches students the steps in research, establishes checkpoints during research projects, helps students use time-management tools)

STUDY SKILLS

Tools and techniques should be introduced at the elementary level and refined throughout the student's educational experience. At all levels, the teacher should plan and provide classroom time for instruction on efficient study methods. The teacher can enable each student to improve his/her study skills through instruction in the acquisition and organization of material, the processing of information, and the use of time/project management techniques. In order to ensure that all students understand and use the same study techniques, the teacher must plan, present, and evaluate student acquisition of the following skills:

- **Underlining**: Keywords, facts, dates, results/solutions. Not entire paragraphs or pages.

- **Note-taking**: In order to take notes effectively and efficiently, a student must know the objective. Anything that is not pertinent to the objective (or is only enhancement, example or further explanation) is not noteworthy unless it directly aids the student in understanding or remembering the information. Note-taking skills must be practiced and evaluated to be developed effectively.
- **Summarizing**: This skill involves relating the essence and significant data of a larger passage or body of work. This skill must also be practiced and evaluated to be developed effectively.
- **Graphic Organizers**: Using graphic organizers and concept web guides that center around a concept and the applications of the concept is an instructional strategy that teachers can use to guide students into further inquiry of the subject matter.
- **Time Management**: Plan what needs to be done and then prioritize the tasks to make sure what needs to be done first is completed. Set a schedule for time to work and time for breaks. Evaluate this schedule for a weekly workload to ensure there is not too much or too little to do each day. Finally, FOCUS! Minimize distractions such as email, texts, IMs, phone calls to be "off limits" during scheduled work time.

TEST TAKING SKILLS

Tests are essential instructional tools. They can greatly influence students' learning and should not be taken lightly nor given without due regard for the importance of preparation. Several studies have been carried out that indicate conclusively that students perform better when they understand what type of test they are going to take and why they are taking the test before they take the test. If students perceive a test to be important or to have relative significance, they will perform better. In a recent study, students who were informed by their teachers as to how their test scores were to be used and who were also urged by their teachers to put forth their best effort scored higher on the Differential Aptitudes Test than students who did not receive this coaching.

Motivation to perform well on tests begins with how well the student wants to do well on an exam. The intrinsic motivation is an internal drive by the student who aspires to do his/her best in school. The extrinsic motivation may be as simple as a student wanting to learn a basic mathematical skill to complete a remedial math class or as complex as a student needing to pass a pre-Calculus class to take an AP (Advanced Placement) Calculus class during senior year to gain college credit and enter Stanford or Harvard University as an early college admission's applicant.

It is also a recognized fact that students will attain higher test scores if they are familiar with the format of the test. It is important for the student to know whether he/she will be taking a multiple-choice test or an essay test. Being prepared for a specific test format can enhance test scores. Teachers can help students boost their test performance by providing them with explicit information in regard to the content of the test. If the focus is on improving student performance on tests, then students must become familiar with the diversity of test taking formats. Students must understand that there are basic study skills and preparations that maximize student performance and learning outcomes.

In researching the effects of sleep deprivation on student learning and test taking, Carlyle Smith, a professor of psychology at Trent University in Ontario, determined that when students are taught a complex logic game of memorization and when one group of volunteers was deprived of sleep the first night, their performance on the logic game decreased by 30 percent. In testing a second group of volunteers who had been deprived of sleep on a second night and another group given a full three nights rest, the results were similar in that their performance on the logic game was similar. For students, the best performance for test taking begins with a good night's sleep.

Effective test taking includes an ability to size up testing formats and quickly eliminate incorrect answers from a listing of possible choices. The good news is that a student has a 25 percent chance of getting the correct answer from a choice of four answers and a 50 percent chance once the decoys and incomplete answers have been eliminated to the final two answers left. Imagine two answers with a 50 percent chance of choosing the correct one. The odds are better if one can get the choices down to the last two remaining answer choices. Knowing how the test is constructed will get a student those better odds.

For more information on types of assessment, **SEE** Skill 3.3.

RESEARCH PROJECTS
Starting in late elementary school, students must be taught how to conduct effective research. This is not an inherent skill and takes a lot of teacher planning. An effective teacher outlines the project and gives clear directions in small steps to guide students through the research process.

Students should have an outline of the purpose of a project or research presentation that includes:

- Purpose - identity the reason for the research information
- Objective - having a clear thesis for a project will allow the students opportunities to be specific on Internet searches
- Preparation - when using resources or collecting data, students should create folders for sorting through the information; providing labels for the folders will create a system of organization that will make construction of the final project or presentation easier and less time consuming
- Procedure - organized folders and a procedural list of what the project or presentation needs to include will create A+ work for students and A+ grading for teachers
- Visuals or artifacts - choose data or visuals that are specific to the subject content or presentation, and make sure that poster boards or Power Point presentations can be visually seen from all areas of the classroom; teachers can provide laptop computers for Power Point presentations.

Here are some more important concepts in outlining a research project:

- **Define and Analyze**: What is to be accomplished? How is it to be done? What are the measures of completeness and correctness? When must it be completed? What information/materials are necessary? How will these be acquired? Is this original?
- **Listing**: Writing down every activity and resource necessary to complete the assignment correctly.
- **Identifying dependencies**: What must be acquired, processed, or learned before something else can be done? In shared assignments, there will be a dependency on other students to provide activities, information, or materials.
- **Deliverables**: What is the final product? When is it due? Will there be segments due for review, at specified times (with longer assignments and class projects, for example)?
- **Feedback and follow up**: How and when will the product (the work) be evaluated? Will there be an opportunity to correct errors? What is the pertinence of skills/knowledge acquired in this assignment to future assignments?

It is crucial for the teacher to continually monitor progress consistently among students. The teacher must also ensure that students have ample in-class (or in-library) time to research. Remember, not every student has access to Internet and computers at home. Teachers must also teach and review bibliography skills with students and provide them with strategies for recording this information as they progress through the project.

Students must then work through the normal writing process with the project and visuals. That is, they gather materials and information, draft, evaluate, revise, add further research if needed, edit and proofread, and produce final products.

TECHNOLOGY AND RESEARCH

The Internet and other research resources provide a wealth of information on thousands of interesting topics for students preparing presentations or projects. Using search engines like Google, Microsoft, and Infotrac, student can search multiple Internet resources on one subject search.

When a teacher models and instructs students in the proper use of search techniques, the teacher can minimize wasted time in preparing projects and wasted paper from students who print every search. In some school districts, students are allowed a maximum number of printed pages per week. Since students have Internet accounts for computer usage, the monitoring of printing is easily done by the school's librarian and teachers in classrooms.

Once the research is completed, use of a desktop publishing program on the computer can produce professional quality books, reports, essays, etc. enhanced by typed text, graphs, clip art, and even photographs downloaded from the World Wide Web. Even primary grade students can use the computer to type and illustrate their stories on simple publishing programs like the Children's Writing and Publishing Center by The Learning Company. Spell check programs and other tools included in these publishing programs can assist students in producing top quality work.

The computer should not replace traditional research and writing skills taught to school-age children but use of the computer as a tool must also be taught to children who live in a technological society. Computers are as much a part of a child's life today as pencils and paper, and the capabilities of computers need to be thoroughly explored to enable students to see computers as much more than a glorified "game machine." A major goal of education is to prepare students for their futures in business and the work place, and if they are not taught how to use the available technology to its fullest advantage, educators will have failed in at least part of that purpose.

For evaluating information, **SEE** Skill 9.3.

Skill 4.10 **Analyzes ways in which teacher behaviors (e.g., teacher expectations, student grouping practices, teacher-student interactions) impact student learning and plans instruction and assessment that minimizes the effects of negative factors and enhance all students' learning**

TEACHER BEHAVIORS

Teachers need to be aware that much of what they say and do can be motivating and may have a positive effect on students' achievement. A teacher's speech skills can be strong motivating elements. Studies have been conducted to determine the impact of teacher behavior on student performance. Surprisingly, a teacher's voice can really make an impression on students. Teachers' voices have several dimensions—volume, pitch, rate, etc. A recent study on the effects of speech rate indicates that both boys and girls prefer to listen at the rate of about 200 words per minute, with boys preferring slower rates overall than girls. This same study indicates that a slower rate of speech directly affects processing ability and comprehension.

Other speech factors such as communication of ideas, communication of emotion, distinctness/pronunciation, quality variation and phrasing, correlate with teaching criterion scores. These scores show that "good" teachers ("good" meaning teachers who positively impact and motivate students) use more variety in speech than do "less effective" teachers.

Body Language

A teacher's body language has an even greater effect on student achievement and ability to set and focus on goals. Teacher smiles provide support and give feedback about the teacher's affective state. A deadpan expression can actually be a detriment to the student's progress. Teacher frowns are perceived by students to mean displeasure, disapproval, and even anger. Studies also show that teacher posture and movement are indicators of the teacher's enthusiasm and energy, which emphatically influence student learning, attitudes, motivation, and focus on goals. Teachers have a greater efficacy on student motivation than any person other than parents.

Affecting Student Behavior

Teachers can also enhance student motivation by planning and directing interactive, "hands-on" learning experiences. Research substantiates that cooperative group projects decrease student behavior problems and increase student on-task behavior. Students who are directly involved with learning activities are more motivated to complete a task to the best of their ability.

Unfortunately, at times misbehavior is the result of specific teacher actions. There is considerable research that indicates that some teacher behavior is upsetting to students and increases the occurrence of student misbehavior. Such teacher behavior may include any action that a child perceives as being unfair, punitive remarks about the child, his behavior or his work, or harsh responses to the child.

Skill 4.11 **Analyzes ways in which factors in the home and community (e.g., parent expectations, availability of community resources, community problems) impact student learning and plans instruction and assessment with awareness of social and cultural factors to enhance all students' learning**

THE TOTAL STUDENT ENVIRONMENT
The student's capacity and potential for academic success within the overall educational experience are products of her or his total environment: classroom and school system; home and family; and neighborhood and community. All of these segments are interrelated and can be supportive, one of the other, or divisive, one against the other. As a matter of course, the teacher will become familiar with all aspects of the system. This would include not only process and protocols but also the availability of resources provided to meet the academic, health and welfare needs of students. It is incumbent upon the teacher to look beyond the boundaries of the school system to identify additional resources as well as issues and situations which will effect (directly or indirectly) a student's ability to succeed in the classroom. These resources include:

- Libraries, museums, zoos, planetariums, etc.
- Clubs, societies and civic organizations, community outreach programs of private businesses and corporations and of government agencies
- Local speakers and presenters
- Departments of social services operating within the local community

These can provide background and program information relevant to social issues which may be impacting individual students. And this can be a resource for classroom instruction regarding life skills, at-risk behaviors, etc. Initial contacts for resources outside of the school system will usually come from within the system itself: from administration, teacher organizations, department heads, and other colleagues.

FACTORS AFFECTING EDUCATION
When considering students from multicultural backgrounds, curriculum objectives and instructional strategies may be inappropriate and unsuccessful when presented in a single format which relies on the student's understanding and acceptance of the values and common attributes of a specific culture which is not his or her own. **SEE** Competency 002 for more information.

TEACHER CERTIFICATION STUDY GUIDE

Family

Family background and influence also plays an important role. Attitude, resources, and encouragement available in the home environment may be attributes for success or failure. Families with higher incomes are able to provide increased opportunities for students. Students from lower income families will need to depend on the resources available from the school system and the community. This should be orchestrated by the classroom teacher in cooperation with school administrators and educational advocates in the community.

Family members with higher levels of education often serve as models for students, and have high expectations for academic success. And families with specific aspirations for children (often, regardless of their own educational background) encourage students to achieve academic success, and are most often active participants in the process.

A family in crisis (caused by economic difficulties, divorce, substance abuse, physical abuse, etc.) creates a negative environment which may profoundly impact all aspects of a student's life, and particularly his or her ability to function academically. The situation may require professional intervention. It is often the classroom teacher who will recognize a family in crisis situation and instigate an intervention by reporting on this to school or civil authorities.

Ensuring Equal Opportunity

Regardless of the positive or negative impacts on the students' education from outside sources, it is the teacher's responsibility to ensure that all students in the classroom have an equal opportunity for academic success. This begins with the teacher's statement of high expectations for every student and develops through planning, delivery, and evaluation of instruction. This instruction should provide for inclusion and ensure that all students have equal access to the resources necessary for successful acquisition of the academic skills being taught and measured in the classroom.

Skill 4.12   Understands the importance of self-directed learning and plans instruction and assessment that promote students' motivation and their sense of ownership of and responsibility for their own learning

If a teacher can help students to take responsibility for their own ideas and thoughts, much has been accomplished. They will only reach that level in a non-judgmental environment, an environment that does not permit criticism of the ideas of others and that accepts any topic for discussion that is in the realm of appropriateness. Success in problem solving boosts students' confidence and makes them more willing to take risks, and the teacher must provide those opportunities for success.

DEVELOP SUCCESS-ORIENTED ACTIVITIES

Success-oriented activities are tasks that are selected to meet the individual needs of the student. During the time a student is learning a new skill, tasks should be selected so that the student will be able to earn a high percentage of correct answers during the teacher questioning and seatwork portions of the lesson. Later, the teacher should also include work that challenges students to apply what they have learned and stimulate their thinking.

TEACHER CERTIFICATION STUDY GUIDE

Skill knowledge, strategy use, motivation, and personal interests are all factors that influence individual student success. The student who cannot be bothered with reading the classroom textbook may be highly motivated to read the driver's handbook for his or her license or the rulebook for the latest video game. Students who did not master their multiplication tables will likely have problems working with fractions.

In the success-oriented classroom, mistakes are viewed as a natural part of the learning process. The teacher can also show that adults make mistakes by correcting errors without getting unduly upset. The students feel safe to try new things because they know that they have a supportive environment and can correct their mistakes.

Activities for Student Success
Activities that promote student success:

1. Are based on useful, relevant content that is clearly specified, and organized for easy learning
2. Allow sufficient time to learn the skill and is selected for high rate of success
3. Allow students the opportunity to work independently, self-monitor, and set goals
4. Provide for frequent monitoring and corrective feedback
5. Include collaboration in group activities or peer teaching

Students with learning problems often attribute their successes to luck or ease of the task. Their failures are often blamed on their supposed lack of ability, difficulty of the task, or the fault of someone else. Successful activities, attribution retraining, and learning strategies can help these students to discover that they can become independent learners. When the teacher communicates the expectation that the students can be successful learners and chooses activities that will help them be successful, achievement is increased.

TEACHER-DIRECTED TO SELF-DIRECTED ACTIVITY

Learning progresses in stages from initial acquisition, when the student needs a lot of teacher guidance and instruction, to adaptation, when the student can apply what he or she has learned to new situations outside the classroom. As students progress through the stages of learning, the teacher gradually decreases the amount of direct instruction and guidance and encourages the student to function independently. The ultimate goal of the learning process is to teach students how to be independent and apply their knowledge.

A summary of these states and their features appears here:

State	Teacher Activity	Emphasis
Initial Acquisition	Provide rationale Guidance Demonstration Modeling Shaping Cueing	Errorless learning Backward Chaining (working from the final product backward through the steps) Forward Chaining

		(proceeding through the steps to a final product)
Advanced Acquisition	Feedback Error correction Specific directions	Criterion evaluation Reinforcement and reward for accuracy
Proficiency	Positive reinforcement Progress monitoring Teach self-management Increased teacher expectations	Increase speed or performance to the automatic level with accuracy Set goals Self-management
Maintenance	Withdraw direct reinforcement Retention and memory Over learning Intermittent schedule of reinforcement	Maintain high level of performance Mnemonic techniques Social and intrinsic reinforcement
Generalization	Corrective feedback	Perform skill in different times and places
Adaptation	Stress independent problem-solving	Independent problem-solving methods No direct guidance or direct instruction

Skill 4.13   Analyzes ways in which various teacher roles (e.g., facilitator, lecturer) and student roles (e.g., active learner, observer, group participant) impact student learning

THE ROLES OF TEACHERS

Teaching consists of a multitude of roles. Teachers must plan and deliver instruction in a creative and innovating way so that students find learning both fun and intriguing. The teacher must also research various learning strategies, decide which to implement in the classroom, and balance that information according to the various learning styles of the students. Teachers must facilitate all aspects of the lesson including preparation and organization of materials, delivery of instruction, and management of student behavior and attention.

Simultaneously, the teacher must also observe for student learning, interactions, and on-task behavior while making mental or written notes regarding what is working in the lesson and how the students are receiving and utilizing the information. This will provide the teacher with immediate feedback as to whether to continue with the lesson, or if it is necessary to slow the instruction or present the lesson in another way. Teachers must also work collaboratively with other adults in the room and utilize them to maximize student learning. The teacher's job requires the teacher to establish a delicate balance among all these factors.

TEACHER CERTIFICATION STUDY GUIDE

Handling the Balance
How the teacher handles this balance depends on the teaching style of the teacher and/or lesson. Cooperative learning will require the teacher to have organized materials ready, perhaps even with instructions for the students as well. The teacher should conduct a great deal of observations during this type of lesson. Direct instruction methods will require the teacher to have an enthusiastic, yet organized, approach to the lesson. When teaching directly to students, the teacher must take care to keep the lesson student-centered and intriguing while presenting accurate information.

For more information, **SEE** Skill 8.1.

Skill 4.14   Incorporates students' different approaches to learning (e.g., auditory, visual, tactile, kinesthetic) into instructional practices

APPROACHING DIFFERENT LEARNING STYLES
As stated in Skills 4.1 and 4.5, Multiple Intelligence theory supports that there are many different approaches to learning and that students learn in many different ways. It is important for teachers to consider these different learning styles so that he may vary activities and instruction so as to touch on all learning styles.

Auditory learners learn by hearing. They like to read to themselves out loud and like to speak in class. These students tend to like music, languages, oral reports, participate in study groups, and follow directions well. To augment instruction for auditory learners, use videos, lecture, group discussion, audiotapes, oral exams, and even recordings of material.

Visual learners learn by seeing, and optimal learning is experience when they see charts, maps, videos, graphs, pictures, etc. For example, visual learners may struggle with an essay exam because it is challenging to recall test material that they heard rather than saw. Visual learners tend to be good at spelling, fashion, math (especially with charts), and sign language to start. For visual learners, it is good for them to draw out maps or charts, make outlines, copy the board, diagram sentences, use color coded notes and highlighters, draw, illustrate, use flashcards, utilize educational videos and have quiet study time.

Kinesthetic learners learn by doing and experiencing. These students like sports, labs, research projects, role playing, adventure stories, model building, music, field trips, and dance. These students also tend to take break often, be a bit fidgety, and have poorer handwriting than others. Some useful strategies to help a kinesthetic learner are for them to study with others, study in short blocks of time, take lab classes, role play, and use games (such as matching games) and manipulatives that tie in to learning.

For more information on Multiple Intelligence Theory, **SEE** Skill 4.1 and 4.5.

DOMAIN II   CREATING A POSITIVE, PRODUCTIVE CLASSROOM ENVIRONMENT

COMPETENCY 005   THE TEACHER KNOWS HOW TO ESTABLISH A CLASSROOM CLIMATE THAT FOSTERS LEARNING, EQUITY AND EXCELLENCE AND USES THIS KNOWLEDGE TO CREATE A PHYSICAL AND EMOTIONAL ENVIRONMENT THAT IS SAFE AND PRODUCTIVE

Skill 5.1   Uses knowledge of the unique characteristics and needs of students at different developmental levels to establish a positive, productive classroom environment (e.g., encourages cooperation and sharing among younger students; provides middle-level students with opportunities to collaborate with peers; encourages older students' respect for the community and the people in it)

Educators play a critical role in an individual's educational experience, ultimately influencing what that person will become in life. Teaching requires many skills beyond subject matter mastery. Interpersonal skills, sensitivity, self-discipline and role modeling are but a few of the extra-curricular qualities which make for a successful teacher. It is in the presentation of skill-based materials, the management of the classroom environment and the facilitation of learning by students as individuals and in groups, that all of the teacher's skills (and eventual experiences) come into play.

ADJUSTING TO STUDENT NEEDS
As noted in Skills 1.1, 1.4, and 1.5, students are continually undergoing physical and emotional changes and development. Everything occurring to them is new, unfamiliar and sometimes uncomfortable. A student undergoing such a change may suddenly exhibit the disorientation and uneasiness more often seen in a child on his/her first day of school. As a result, a student may feel socially awkward, and this may be reflected in schoolwork and especially in classroom participation. The teacher must be sensitive to the issues of a developing child and aware of the impact this may have on student learning, classroom decorum, and the cohesion among classmates that the teacher is trying to foster.

The teacher must be prepared to adapt and control the classroom environment to the degree possible, to ensure a safe and productive learning environment is established and maintained. However, some situations are more readily anticipated and incorporated than controlled or changed. Behavior modification, in the classroom, can often mean simply channeling existing energies and interests (of the students') into acceptable activities that provide a meaningful, educational experience as a positive outcome. This process begins with the teacher.

Varying Student Activities
Students do not respond well to instruction which is singularly formatted (e.g., lectures, audio/video presentations, etc., which expend the entire class period). Multiple formats are preferable, and activities which provide direct involvement by the students are often most successful. It is within these planned activities that the teacher has the best opportunity to instruct on and model the concepts of sharing, cooperative endeavor, social involvement, and

communication skills, and the students have the opportunity to participate and practice these skills.

This, of course, requires continual monitoring by the teacher. While early childhood and elementary students are generally more easily controlled—often appearing better behaved and more responsive to authority—than older students, they still have a tendency to socialize and play just for the sake of play. Younger students benefit from learning centers, small-group activities, journaling, cooperative learning. Social learning in the elementary classrooms encourages a sense of community, sharing, and fun with learning.

Middle and high school-level students have a tendency to socialize, and this can quickly allow the classroom situation to deteriorate, replacing the learning environment with chaos. In middle school, teachers can take advantage of this need to socialize to augment learning if planned well. Peer-reviews, "discussion" journaling, peer edits, and pair and small-group learning all work well at this level as students are ready to work with others and will do so in such a positive environment.

The same can be said for high school students, but at their more sophisticated level, older students can move beyond the simpler peer activities and apply their learning to a larger audience to foster the growing sense of community. At this level, students can engage in learning in a variety of ways such as presentations, discussion groups, complex research projects, experiments, concerts, and more. Such in-depth activities or research projects with real-life applications can direct learning and enhance respect for the larger community. For example, a science unit on engineering might involve the fundamental concepts, as well as experiments, in addition to a community application for a real-life problem to be solved.

FACTORING IN CLASSROOM MANAGEMENT
Allowing for the differing needs of students undergoing physical, emotional, and hormonal changes does not mean abandoning classroom discipline and organized instruction. All students need the reassurance of structure, organization, and discipline. If the appropriate attitudes and responses to structure and discipline are internalized at an early age, they will serve the student throughout his/her educational experience and provide a solid foundation upon which the individual can develop the self-discipline necessary in later life. The teacher who can instill these values in a young student will have earned the gratitude and respect of all the teachers who instruct this student in the future. In middle and/or high school, these students still require discipline in an altered form, and students can still acquire or improve on their self-discipline and benefit from a structured classroom.

It is important to realize that the best time to implement organization and classroom discipline is at the beginning of a semester or school year with the entire class—not at a moment of crisis or chaos. This is an issue that will significantly affect the teacher's ability to teach and the student's ability to learn, day after day. A good deal of thought and preparation, on the part of the classroom teacher, should be devoted to this aspect of the educational experience. There are volumes of text available to the novice teacher, providing criteria and examples for structuring an organized, disciplined, classroom environment.

Specific recommendations for discipline and organization in normal and in unusual classroom situations are available from experienced teachers in journals and on the Internet. Guidelines and structure may be made flexible to allow for certain contingencies, but they must be put into practice with specific limits provided, and the students must be made fully aware of the structure, the guidelines, their responsibilities, and the consequences of their actions should they fail to observe these guidelines.

UPDATING AND STAYING CURRENT
As mentioned in Skill 4.8, it is always beneficial for the teacher to remain current with the studies and findings published in numerous journals related to child and educational psychology and physical and intellectual development in early childhood, pre-adolescence, early adolescence, and adolescence. For classroom use, there are numerous resources (instructional videos, printed materials, instructional games) that provide for controlled interaction among the students and between teacher and students, and address issues of concern to students. They are usually age and/or grade specific, activity-driven, and employ multimedia.

Instructional objectives vary greatly from early childhood, where life skills are introduced through play and activity, into kindergarten and early elementary where the fundamentals of academic subjects are introduced, through elementary, middle, and high school where previously introduced skills are developed and new ones introduced. But it is often possible to include part or all of such instructional materials in a broader lesson plan which incorporates adopting life-skills with learning subject matter. The technology and varieties of media available to the teacher and the students, today, enable the teacher to provide a multifaceted, instructional experience in the classroom. The technology and other tools of the trade will continue to change and improve the means of education. It is the teacher's responsibility to the students to remain aware of these changes and exercise her or his professional judgment as to what is beneficial and when it should be introduced into the classroom environment.

SEE also Skill 5.2.

Skill 5.2 **Establishes a classroom climate that emphasizes collaboration and supportive interactions, respect for diversity and individual differences and active engagement in learning by all students**

CREATING A CLASSROOM CLIMATE
A classroom is a community of learning, and when students learn to respect themselves and the members around them, learning is maximized. Teachers should create a classroom climate that encourages extensive participation from the students. Collaborations and discussions are enhanced when students like and respect each other, and therefore, each student's learning can benefit. This is even truer when students engage in full participation. When everyone's thoughts, perspectives, and ideas are offered, the class can consider each idea carefully in their discussion. The more students' participate, the more learning is gained through a more thorough examination of the topic.

TEACHER CERTIFICATION STUDY GUIDE

To create this environment, teachers must first model how to welcome and consider all points of view for the students. The teacher should then positively affirm and reinforce students for offering their ideas in front of the other students. Even if somewhat amiss, the teacher should receive the idea while perhaps offering a modification or corrected statement (for more factual pieces of information). The idea is for students to feel confident and safe in being able to express their thoughts or ideas. Only then will students be able to engage in independent discussions that consider and respect everyone's statements.

SEE also Skills 1.2, 1.11, 2.3, 2.6, 4.10, 5.1, 6.2 and 6.3.

Skill 5.3   Analyzes ways in which teacher-student interactions and interactions among students impact classroom climate and student learning and development

CALSSROOM INTERACTIONS
Student-student and teacher-student interactions play a significant role in a positive classroom climate. When interactions among classroom members are encouraging, learning becomes a more natural and genuine process. Cold or routine interactions discourage questioning, critical thinking and useful discussion. Teachers should make every effort to be available to their students, as well as provide natural, collaborative opportunities for students in order to strengthen classroom interactions. Reflection, observations, and asking for feedback regarding one's classroom interactions (perhaps during a yearly observation) will help teachers to analyze the effectiveness of their classroom's interactions.

SEE also Skill 4.10

Skill 5.4   Presents instruction in ways that communicate the teacher's enthusiasm for learning

COMMUNICATING ENTHUSIASM
Many studies have demonstrated that the enthusiasm of the teacher is infectious. If students feel that the teacher is ambivalent about a task, they will also catch that attitude. A teacher's enthusiasm can significantly impact a student's desire to learn. If the teacher is droning on about a topic with little personal interest, how are the students expected to enjoy the lesson and learn? Despite a teacher's best efforts to provide important and appropriate instruction, there may be times when a teacher is required to teach a concept, skill, or topic that students may perceive as trivial and irrelevant. These tasks can be effectively presented if the teacher exhibits a sense of enthusiasm and excitement about the content. Teachers can help spark the students' interest by providing anecdotes and interesting digressions. Research indicates that as teachers become significantly more enthusiastic, students exhibit increased on-task behavior.

Not only does the teacher need to be enthusiastic while teaching, he or she needs to model his or her own enthusiasm for gaining knowledge. For example, the teacher should be reading during silent reading time. Or, if a question is asked that the teacher does not know the answer, the teacher should get excited about finding out the right answer while modeling how to do so with the students.

The effective teacher communicates non-verbally with students by using positive body language, expressing warmth, concern, acceptance, and enthusiasm. Effective teachers augment their instructional presentations by using positive non-verbal communication such as smiles, open body posture, movement, and eye contact with students. The energy and enthusiasm of the effective teacher can be amplified through positive body language.

SEE also Skill 1.11.

Skill 5.5 **Uses a variety of means to convey high expectations for all students**

SEE the first half of Skill 1.11 and Skill 6.10.

Skill 5.6 **Knows characteristics of physical spaces that are safe and productive for learning, recognizes the benefits and limitations of various arrangements of furniture in the classroom and applies strategies for organizing the physical environment to ensure physical accessibility and facilitate learning in various instructional contexts**

CLASSROOM SETUP

The physical setting of the classroom contributes a great deal toward the propensity for students to learn. An adequate, well-built, and well-equipped classroom will invite students to learn. This has been called "invitational learning." A classroom must have adequate physical space so students can conduct themselves comfortably. Some students are distracted by windows, pencil sharpeners, doors, etc. Some students prefer the front, middle, or back rows. Classrooms with warmer subdued colors contribute to students' concentration on task items. Neutral hues for coloration of walls, ceiling, and carpet or tile are generally used in classrooms so distraction due to classroom coloration may be minimized.

In the modern classroom, there is a great deal of furniture, equipment, supplies, appliances, and learning aids to help the teacher teach and students learn. The classroom should be provided with furnishings that fit the purpose of the classroom. The kindergarten classroom may have a reading center, a playhouse, a puzzle table, student work desks/tables, a sandbox, and any other relevant learning/interest areas. A middle school or high school classroom may have desks/tables, a content-specific library, a writing station, and a manipulative/project station (particularly for math and science classes).

Whatever the arrangement of furniture and equipment may be the teacher must provide for adequate traffic flow. Rows of desks must have adequate space between them for students to move and for the teacher to circulate. All areas must be open to line-of-sight supervision by the teacher.

ORGANIZATION FOR LEARNING

In the lower grades, an organized system uses a "classroom helper" for effective distribution and collection of books, equipment, supplies, etc. The classroom helpers should be taught to replace the materials in the proper places to obtain them easily for the next time they are used. Periodically, the teacher should inspect to see that all materials are in the proper places and are ready for use as needed.

At higher grade levels, the teacher is concerned with materials such as textbooks, written instructional aides, worksheets, computer programs, etc., which must be produced, maintained, distributed, and collected for future use. One important consideration is the production of sufficient copies of duplicated materials to satisfy classroom needs. Another is the efficient distribution of worksheets and other materials. The teacher may decide to hand out materials as students are in their learning sites (desks, etc.) or to have distribution materials at a clearly specified place (or small number of places) in the classroom. In any case, there should be firmly established procedures, completely understood by student for receiving classroom materials. Special fields such as physical education or media specialists are well schooled in these areas.

SEE also Skills 1.12, 4.8, 6.1 and 6.4.

SAFETY AND MAINTENANCE

In all cases, proper care must be taken to ensure student safety. Furniture and equipment should be situated safely at all times. No equipment, materials, boxes, etc. should be placed where there is danger of falling over. Doors must have entry and exit accessibility at all times.

The teacher has the responsibility to report any items of classroom disrepair to maintenance staff. Broken windows, falling plaster, exposed sharp surfaces, leaks in ceiling or walls, and other items of disrepair present hazards to students. Another factor that must be considered is adequate lighting. Report any inadequacies in classroom illumination. Florescent lights placed at acute angles often burn out faster. A healthy supply of spare tubes is a sound investment.

Local fire and safety codes dictate entry and exit standards. In addition, all corridors and classrooms should be wheelchair accessible for students and others who use them. Older schools may not have this accessibility.

Another consideration is adequate ventilation and climate control. Some classrooms in some states use air conditioning extensively. Sometimes it is so cold as to be considered a distraction. Specialty classes such as science require specialized hoods for ventilation. Physical Education classes have the added responsibility for shower areas and specialized environments that must be heated such as pool or athletic training rooms.

Skill 5.7 **Creates a safe, nurturing, and inclusive classroom environment that addresses students' emotional needs and respects students' rights and dignity**

SEE Skill 5.1 and 5.2.

COMPETENCY 006 THE TEACHER UNDERSTANDS STRATEGIES FOR CREATING AN ORGANIZED AND PRODUCTIVE LEARNING ENVIRONMENT AND FOR MANAGING STUDENT BEHAVIOR

Skill 6.1 Analyzes the effects of classroom routines and procedures on student learning, and knows how to establish and implement age-appropriate routines and procedures to promote an organized and productive learning environment

THE IMPORTANCE OF ROUTINES

There are a number of things that hinder teachers from beginning instruction immediately. Some examples are attendance and discipline (getting students to settle down). Analysts have found that if class is delayed for 10 minutes each day, almost two months of instruction is lost over the school year. Punctuality leads to more on-task time, which results in greater subject matter retention among the students. Therefore, it is very important to begin class on time. Effective teachers have pre-determined plans to deal with these distractions.

Eliminating Wasted Time

Dealing with the daily task of attendance can be done efficiently and quickly with the use of a seating chart. A teacher can spot absentees in seconds by noting the empty seats, rather than calling each student's name, which could take as long as five minutes. Another timesaving technique is to laminate the seating chart. This allows the teacher to make daily notes right on the chart. The teacher may also efficiently keep track of who is volunteering and who is answering questions.

Effective teachers use class time efficiently. This results in higher student subject engagement and will likely result in more subject matter retention. One way teachers use class time efficiently is through a smooth transition from one activity to another; this activity is also known as "management transition." Management transition is defined as "teacher shifts from one activity to another in a systemic, academically oriented way."

Transitions and Sequencing

One factor that contributes to efficient management transition is the teacher's management of instructional material. Effective teachers gather their materials during the planning stage of instruction. Doing this, a teacher avoids flipping through things looking for the items necessary for the current lesson. Momentum is lost and student concentration is broken when this occurs. Smooth transitions can also contribute to increasing student behavior in the classroom. When a teacher handles movement between activities (or to redirect a student who is off-task back to on-task work) well, she decreases opportunities for student inattention and misconduct with her management of student behavior.

Effective teachers deal with daily classroom procedures efficiently and quickly because then students will spend the majority of class time engaged in academic tasks that will likely result in higher achievement. Various studies have shown that the high-achieving classrooms spend less time on off-task behavior. For example, C.W. Fisher, et al, in a 1978 study, found that in the average classroom, students spent about eight minutes per hour engaged in off-task behavior. However, this was reduced to about four minutes in high-achieving classrooms. Therefore, effective teachers spend less time on daily housekeeping chores.

Furthermore, effective teachers maintain a business-like atmosphere in the classroom. This leads to the students getting on-task quickly when instruction begins. There are many ways effective teachers begin instruction immediately. One method is through the use of over-head projectors. The teacher turns-on the overhead the second class begins, and the students begin taking notes. The teacher is then free to circulate for the first few minutes of class and settle down individual students as necessary. Having a routine that is followed regularly at the beginning of class allows the students to begin without waiting for teacher instruction.

Additionally, teachers who keep students informed of the sequencing of instructional activities maintain systematic transitions because the students are prepared to move on to the next activity. For example, the teacher says, "When we finish with this guided practice together, we will turn to page twenty-three and each student will do the exercises. I will then circulate throughout the classroom helping on an individual basis. Okay, let's begin." Following an example such as this will lead to systematic smooth transitions between activities because the students will be turning to page twenty-three when the class finishes the practice without a break in concentration.

Group Fragmentation
Another method that leads to smooth transitions is to move students in groups and clusters rather than one by one. This is called "group fragmentation." For example, if some students do seat work while other students gather for a reading group, the teacher moves the students in pre-determined groups. Instead of calling the individual names of the reading group, which would be time consuming and laborious, the teacher simply says, "Will the blue reading group please assemble at the reading station. The red and yellow groups will quietly do the vocabulary assignment I am now passing out." As a result of this activity, the classroom is ready to move on in a matter of seconds rather than minutes.

Interruptions
Effective teachers have rules that deal with controlled interruptions, such as students who are tardy to class or who do not have their supplies. For example, when a student returns to class after being absent, he or she places his or her parent note in the box on the teacher's desk designated for this. The student then proceeds to the side counter where extra copies of yesterday's work are located. The student takes the work and sits down to begin today's class work. The student is aware that the teacher will deal with individual instructions during seatwork time when it will not disrupt the class momentum.

ORGANIZED MATERIALS
Additionally, effective teachers have highly planned lessons with all materials in order prior to class. If a teacher is going to utilize a chart or a map in a lesson, the chart or map is already prepared and in place in the classroom before class begins. Furthermore, all materials are

copied and in order ready to pass out as needed. This results in the efficient distribution of materials and leads to less off-task time.

These effective organizational and management routines minimize time wasted in the classroom. As discussed above, minimizing distractions, housekeeping and transitions allows for increased instructional time that will positively affect student learning in the classroom.

SEE also Skills 1.12, 4.8, 5.6, 6.4 and 6.6.

Skill 6.2 **Demonstrates an understanding of how young children function in groups and designs group activities that reflect a realistic understanding of the extent of young children's ability to collaborate with others**

USING GROUPS
Young children should be developing social skills coincidentally with other life skills and academic skills. The most logical and practical venue for this development is the classroom. Not only does this afford most children their only, daily opportunity to interact socially with a diverse grouping of peers and adults, it also enables the teacher of young students to ensure that this development is planned, directed, monitored, and evaluated.

All activities the teacher plans for groups of students or the entire class should be age/grade appropriate and provide for the introduction, utilization, and development of social skills as well as academic skills. Each such exercise must have stated and measurable objectives. There are a variety of resources available to the classroom teacher planning such activities. There is a tremendous variety of single medium and multimedia, modular planning and instruction packages available through educational publishers. Not to be overlooked are the programs and activities developed by colleagues within the school system and beyond (via the Internet, for example).

It is beneficial for the teacher to remain current with the studies and findings published in numerous journals related to child and educational psychology and physical and intellectual development in early childhood. For example, several studies—past and present—have shown that girls tend to be more communicative, one with the other, while boys are more prone to be physically active, together, but less responsive to verbal interaction, one with the other. While this is a generalization, it still predicts that an effective grouping will include an approximately equal mix of girls and boys, with the teacher monitoring and encouraging the participation of all in each aspect of the planned activity.

As in this example, awareness of research and findings in the study of childhood development will inform the teacher's application of appropriate groupings and goals for developing teamwork among younger students.

EXAMPLE GROUP ACTIVITIES
The following is a small sampling of teacher-created, team building group activities for elementary school children, available for sharing with colleagues, via the Internet. There are

thousands of similar lesson plans and activities available to address the development of social and academic skills through teamwork, among young children in the classroom setting.

- **Arthur: Group Stories**: An activity where students can create stories as a group. There are several variations available.
- **Spider Web**: In this team building activity, students can get to know each other while creating a unique design.
- **Trading Cards**: Children can share information about themselves by creating personalized trading cards. This could be used as an "ice-breaker" activity.
- **Can You Build It?**: Students can work together toward a common goal in this team activity. It can also be used as an "ice-breaker."
- **Who Am I?**: Children can use this activity to get to know each other by sharing about themselves and working together.

Ideas for Working With Kids: Suggestions for games to help students get to know each other and build group cohesion.
- **Mad Minute Relay**: Students can learn math in a team environment with this timed activity.
- **All of Me**: This activity can help students get to know each other by drawing pictures that show some of the different aspects of their lives, and sharing the pictures with classmates.
- **We're Different/We're Alike**: Students can learn more about each other with this lesson by using Venn diagrams to describe the ways in which they are similar and different.
- **Make a Class Pictogram**: Children can use this activity to help them understand the nature of social groups and their roles as members of various groups.
- **It's Too Loud in Here!**: This lesson plan gives students the opportunity to work as a team and participate in decision-making processes in the classroom.
- **A-Z Teacher's Stuff: Teamwork**: What does it mean to be a team? In this lesson plan, students can learn to define teamwork and work together in groups.

For more information on cooperative learning, **SEE** also Skill 6.3.

Skill 6.3   **Organizes and manages group activities that promote students' ability to work together cooperatively and productively, assume responsible roles and develop collaborative skills and individual accountability**

COOPERATIVE LEARNING
Cooperative learning is one of the best researched and useful teaching strategies in which students are grouped in various ways to engage in learning activities designed to increase their understanding of a subject. Teachers often vary the design of the groups, and the core principle with cooperative learning is that each member of the group is responsible for a specific role. This role entrusts each member to be responsible for their own learning, as well as the other members' learning. When the group is cohesive and each member participates, the idea is that all the students will have a solid understanding of the topic, as well as a sense of worth to the group's success.

Five Elements of Cooperative Learning

Cooperative learning is not just small group work. There are certain elements that must be expected from students in order to obtain the optimum learning results from a cooperative effort. These five elements are:

1. Positive Interdependence: All members' efforts are required for success. The group cannot succeed without the each individual's unique contribution. Each member is indispensable for success.
2. Face-to-Face Interaction: Members must all orally participate and explain their "part" and ensure that the other member's understand and inter-connect their information with the rest of the information.
3. Individual + Group Accountability: Some ways to assess this include:
a. Groups must remain small to ensure all students participate and are accountable for a portion of the work
b. Incorporate some form of individual assessment after each activity or project
c. Frequent observation of groups to monitor participation and learning
d. Have students re-teach the concepts learned in the group to another group
4. Interpersonal & Small-Group Skills: Cooperative learning encourages students to practice their leadership, trust-building, communication, decision-making, and conflict-management skills.
5. Group Processing: Groups should periodically self-assess how their learning is going, how the members are contributing, how their relationships are working, what is working and what is not, and decide what modifications, if any, are needed and ways to implement those changes.

Research supports that cooperative techniques enhance student learning and achievement and retention, increase oral and social skills, and boost social relations, self-esteem, and student involvement. Some examples of cooperative learning include:

- Centers
- Writer's Workshops
- Three-Step Interview
- Think-Pair-Share
- Literature Circles
- Round Robin

Skill 6.4 **Recognizes the importance of creating a schedule for young children that balances restful and active movement activities and that provides large blocks of time for play, projects, and learning centers**

CLASSROOM SCHEDULING

Young children are continually developing physically, emotionally, and intellectually. Even among peers in a classroom setting there can be diverse levels of development. The classroom teacher must plan according to the norm, allowing for exceptions that ensure the inclusion of all students in the education process.

Not only do young children need variety to avoid boredom and remain interested and motivated, but they require a mix of physical and mental activities broken by restful periods where their minds and bodies can adjust and prepare for further activities. As a teacher would not lecture to an early elementary class for an entire hour, she or he would also not expect them to play a game requiring physical exertion for an hour or more. In planning each module of instruction, the teacher must anticipate the physical and intellectual demands necessary for the students to meet the lesson objectives and incorporate limitations which will provide variety in activities and avoid stressing the students' capacity to attend, retain, remain interested and acquire skills.

Guidelines for allocating time by activity type and varying activities within the lesson module may be provided to the teacher within the school system and are usually available at the departmental level. But even guidelines may need to be tempered by common sense and specific classroom experience to ensure that young students are not stressed by demands beyond their current developmental levels and yet are working, learning, and achieving to their full potential.

An organized daily schedule helps children know what to expect during their day, which can reduce confusion in the class and also gives young students the structure they need. Scheduling blocks of time is ideal for large group activities or allowing students to work in reading, science, or math centers. Since many students have short attention spans and are not able to fully concentrate or sit still for long periods of time, scheduling reading activities and group projects into manageable blocks of time is an ideal way to regulate the attention levels of the students.

By having blocks of time set aside for group projects and activity centers, teachers have more time to develop key concepts and incorporate creativity into instruction, and this also allows for more in-depth study time for the students. Teachers that incorporate learning centers into their daily class schedules promote student independence, which causes students to become more responsible, through self-discovery. This also allows time for teachers to work one-on-one with students or in small groups as well.

BLOCK (MODULAR) SCHEDULING
Block scheduling refers to organizing academic days to have fewer, but longer, class periods that allow teachers great amounts of time with which to work students, plan activities that delve deeper, and therefore, boost academic achievement. Block scheduling is typically introduced in the later school years (middle school and higher) but can certainly be utilized, at least for part of the day, in elementary classrooms. For example, regular education teachers who have the same students for the majority of the day could certainly attempt to layout all the Language Arts activities together to create a "Literacy Block" where activities merge reading, writing, and spelling lessons.

Blocks of time devoted to learning centers and group projects may range from 30 minutes to 45 minutes. Students may be unable to fully concentrate if more time is allotted and will become fidgety and lose focus. Teachers should allow a passing time of 10 minutes between each schedule block of learning. Students will need time to re-focus and prepare for the next scheduled activity.

The advantages of block scheduling include teachers having more time with individual students; longer cooperative activities and/or labs can be completed; students have less information to handle at a time so can better focus on and process the information they receive; teachers can vary instruction for students with different abilities; students can retake failed classes; and fewer textbooks are required.

4x4 and A/B Schedules
One common schedule is the 4x4 schedule, where students have four academic classes per day that last for 90 minutes each. Classes meet for one semester, and so there are two 4x4 schedules in a year. An A/B schedule also has four, 90-minute academic classes per day, but has a total of eight classes that are held over the course of two days. An A/B schedule would last an entire academic year. With a trimester schedule, students take two to three core courses each trimester, over 60 days. Within these schedules, most schedules also incorporate traditional amounts of time for lunch, extracurricular activities, and "specials."

A Sample A/B schedule for an elementary school is shown below. Time for lunch, recess and specials are incorporated into additional time for core subjects and would be only a portion of the large block of time.

	Day A	Day B	Day A	Day B	Day A
8:45 - 10:15	Math	Spelling	Math /Library	Spelling	Math
10:15 - 11:45	Science	Reading /Art	Science	Reading	Science /Computers
11:45 - 12:30	Lunch /Recess	Lunch /Recess	Lunch /Recess	Lunch /Recess	Lunch /Recess
12:30 - 2:00	Reading /Gym	History	Reading	History	Reading
2:00 - 3:30	Writing	Lang. Arts	Writing	Math /Music	Writing

Criticism of Block Scheduling
Some critics state not enough research has been conducted to support block scheduling. In addition, some arguments for not relying entirely on block scheduling include:

- Students loose continuity, and possibly a lot of instruction, if a student is absent or if school is out for a holiday
- Poor planning could result in not enough material for the longer time block, and over the course of a year, this could result in a lot of lost instructional time
- Difficult to cover ample material for advanced classes, and on the other side, the long instructional times are difficult for young and/or special needs children

- If a student has an "off" semester (i.e. distracted with a heavy sports schedule, family issue, etc), this could result in that student missing the majority of a subject for the year

Although some educators feel it is not significantly beneficial for students, many educators feel block scheduling heightens moral and encourages the use of innovative teaching methods that perhaps would not be used in a traditional timeframe.

For more information on play, **SEE** Skill 1.9.

Skill 6.5 **Schedules activities and manages time in ways that maximize student learning, including using effective procedures to manage transitions; to manage materials, supplies, and technology; and to coordinate the performance of non-instructional duties (e.g., taking attendance) with instructional activities**

SEE Skill 6.1 and 6.6.

Skill 6.6 **Uses technological tools to perform administrative tasks such as taking attendance, maintaining grade books and facilitating communication**

USING TECHNOLOGICAL TOOLS
Personal, professional time management is as significant for a teacher's effectiveness, today, as classroom management. As new educational programs, services and techniques are continually introduced, demands upon the teacher's time (in and out of the classroom) are increased. Using the available technology to perform (or aid in the performance) of administrative tasks, increasingly becomes a necessity for the modern teacher.

The technology itself will continue to change and, presumably, improve the processes used to access and manipulate a variety of functional tools for the classroom and for administrative use. The teacher should stay informed about these changes and the availability to access new or enhanced technologies through his or her school system. But more significant to the teacher than the types of technology available are the uses for technological tools.

Computers
Whether tied into a school network or not, the teacher will find a portable or home computer to be an asset in planning, grading, communicating, and preparing a variety of materials for professional and classroom use. And access to the Internet enhances all of these capabilities. Individual teachers as well as teacher organizations are on line and available to the teaching community on numerous websites. Today, a teacher with a problem, a question, or an idea to share has virtual access to thousands of peers and mentors.

There are many technological tools and programs for teachers to utilize to minimize housekeeping and increase communication with colleagues, parents, and students. First off, simple teacher record programs can take the place of a handwritten grade book. This can be as simple as a few Excel worksheets or as fancy as using specific computer software or online resources such as www.teacherease.com or www.mygradebook.com. These programs often calculate, weight, and adjust grades and information for easy teacher use. In addition, if given a login, students (and their parents) can view the student's completion of work, attendance, assessment performance, and progress at anytime. For example, teachers can easily notify parents of a poor quiz performance in a simple email, alerting a parent instantly (and eliminating the possibility of that "note" getting lost on the way home).

Web Resources
Many school districts have web applications that collect student data. Teachers should be aware of how to use the programs that interface with these applications in order to maintain daily attendance, student grades, and student portfolios. These web applications are incorporated into classroom management and use these productivity tools on a daily basis. The prerequisites for these are fluent keyboarding skills, knowledge of operating systems, basic word processing abilities, and spreadsheet familiarity.

Teachers can also create individual web sites that show project calendars, homework help information, resources, and useful links to communicate with parents. These can link to homework sites such as www.schoolnotes.com, www.classhomework.com, and www.teacherweb.com, which are also useful for teachers. Here, teachers can make updates to daily homework assignments, as well as usually post a calendar with tests, reports, and projects, so nothing comes as a surprise to students and their parents. Oftentimes, teachers can post instructional notes and homework sheets here to aid students at home. School events, such as conferences or "Back to School" night, can also be noted here to increase parental involvement.

Federal-mandated state standards are now causing educators to find a more efficient and successful means of tracking and evaluating student performance. School districts are now incorporating electronic grading and tracking programs into their curriculum. Many of these programs allow teachers to perform basic housekeeping tasks, such as recording assignments, creating homework assignments, and calculating grades more efficiently than the traditional paper-pencil method. These programs can automatically generate the creation of progress reports which allows schools and parents instant access to their child's school records.

Skill 6.7   Works with volunteers and paraprofessionals to enhance and enrich instruction and applies procedures for monitoring the performance of volunteers and paraprofessionals in the classroom

Depending on the educational situation, team-teaching, or the use of aides or assistants in the classroom, often serves to modify the behavior of students, positively. It is not just the presence of more authority figures but a more diverse environment, more opportunity for individual attention, and a perceived sense of increased security, which engenders a positive attitude among the students.

PARAPROFESSIONALS

A paraprofessional is often brought into a classroom for the benefit of the special needs student. The role of the paraprofessional or any teaching assistant or aide in the classroom must be clearly defined to promote the learning experience for all children and avoid an unnecessary hindrance (or worse, conflict of wills) in the classroom. It is the responsibility of the teacher—often in concert with a team of special education personnel and parents—to clearly define this role.

People skills and management skills are necessary for the teacher to work effectively with assistants in the classroom. These are not unlike the skills necessary to manage a classroom, but the individuals involved will quite likely consider themselves as peers to the teacher. Perceived attitudes and actual interactions will be on a different level than between teacher and student, but there is ultimately one authority in the classroom, and that must be the teacher.

Defining Responsibilities

The primary objective is to determine and define what activities the individual should undertake to support the teacher's mission to provide the highest standards of education for each student and the class as a whole. By appropriate planning and continual monitoring, the teacher can *avoid* the following situations which have been experienced by other teachers:

- Teacher neglect (or "surrender" of responsibility) for a student under the direct care of a paraprofessional
- Allowing an assistant to separate students with disabilities from classmates during a classroom activity although the students' needs and abilities were compatible with classmates regarding the activity
- Allowing an assistant to distract students through activities or discussions which are not related to the current lesson activity
- Allowing a paraprofessional to provide a barrier (intentional or not) between students under the assistant's care and interaction with other classmates
- Allowing an assistant to question or comment upon the teacher's lesson plan, presentation, evaluation methods, etc., in front of the students
- Allowing an assistant to intervene in a matter of classroom disciplined
- Allowing an assistant to initiate and conduct conversations with parents without authority or prior approval

VOLUNTEERS

Having volunteers in the classroom can be beneficial in the classroom. Volunteers can provide extra individualized attention to students while the rest of the class is engaged in other work, or they can offer additional assistance in small group activities. However, as a teacher begins to use the aid of volunteers in their classroom, they will need to devise a plan on how they will be used. Teachers will need to designate time either before or after class to discuss the plans with the volunteers. As the classroom volunteers become acquainted with the needs of the students and the teacher's style of teaching, they will, as a rule, need less clarification of daily activities.

Volunteers are normally required to check in and out at the front office before they enter the classroom. Make sure the name of the volunteer is prominently displayed on the front of the name tag that the volunteer wears. The majority of school districts are now requiring a criminal background check on all volunteers that spend time in the classroom. Be sure that all classroom volunteers are familiar with fire drill procedures and are acquainted with the safety exits in the building.

MONITORING HELP IN THE CLASSROOM
Paraprofessionals and volunteers can be a real help in the classroom, especially since schools now have limited budgets and can rarely afford classroom aides. Setting forth strategies to monitor the help in the classroom may take and effort and once they are in place the results can be positive. However, these plans need to be specific to the paraprofessional or volunteer in the class.

STRATEGIES

- Volunteers should be aware of particular skills students need to practice
- Discuss student and grade confidentiality with the volunteer
- Teacher and volunteer agree upon a daily schedule of events
- Disciplinary measures should be discussed and enforced thoroughly
- Provide encouraging and helpful feedback to volunteers

The effective monitoring of help in the classroom can be a positive experience for the teacher. Teachers can then provide a more enriching experience for their students by using parent, volunteers, and paraprofessionals in their classrooms.

Skill 6.8 **Applies theories and techniques related to managing and monitoring student behavior**

BEHAVIOR MONITORING AND MANAGEMENT
Behavior management techniques should focus on positive procedures that can be used at home as well at school. When an intervention is needed, the least restrictive method should be used first, except in severe situations (i.e., fighting, dangerous behaviors). For example, a child who begins talking instead of working in class would not be immediately placed into time out, because the teacher can use less intrusive techniques to prompt the child to return to task. The teacher could use a signal or verbal prompt to gain the child's attention and then praise him when he is back on task.

Classroom policies should be visible and reviewed, and classroom management plans should be in place when the school year begins, both ideally on the first day of school. Developing a management plan takes a proactive approach—that is, decide what behaviors will be expected of the class as a whole, anticipate possible problems, and teach the behaviors early in the school year. Involving the students in the development of the classroom rules lets the students know the rationale for the rules, allows them to assume responsibility in the rules because they had a part in developing them. For more information on establishing classroom management, **SEE** "Factoring in Classroom Management" in Skill 5.1, as well as Skill 6.10.

Procedures that use social humiliation, withholding of basic needs, pain, or extreme discomfort should never be used in a behavior management plan. Emergency intervention procedures used when the student is a danger to himself or others are not considered behavior management procedures. Throughout the year, the teacher should periodically review the types of interventions being used, and assess the effectiveness of the interventions used in the management plan, and make revisions as needed for the best interests of the child.

BEHAVIOR MANAGEMENT THEORIES

Today, numerous behavioral management programs utilized in modern-day schools are directly influenced by his theories. One of the more influential behavior management theories is from B.F. Skinner. Skinner's theories have been put into practice in school systems in an assortment of ways. However, parents and teachers both have rewarded students for good behavior long before B.F. Skinner's theories were well-known. Skinner believed immediate praise should be offered to students, instantaneous feedback, should be given, and rewards given to encourage proper behavior in the classroom. Teachers wanting to put into action a reinforcement system in their classrooms might possible use strategies such as a "token economy" as an incentive for positive behaviors.

A second theory that is often used in today's classroom is the student-centered approach. This theory encourages independent thinking in order that students choose their own appropriate behavior for the situation. Another behavioral management theory is the moderate approach. In this approach are the combinations of humanist and behaviorists belief systems. Students need to have a sense of belonging and feel important in their environment. This will increase their sense of self-worth in order to improve their behavior, and ultimately their academic achievements.

A final theory is the assertive discipline approach which has a positive discipline system. This system has a clear indication of the rules, frequent reminders of the rules, and clear indication of consequences. This behavioral management method aspires to create a positive discipline system that reinforces the teacher's authority to teach and control in order to guarantee a safe setting which is the best possible environment for student learning.

BEHAVIOR MANAGEMENT TECHNIQUES

Listed below are some behavior management plan strategies for increasing desired behavior:

- **Prompt:** A prompt is a visual or verbal cue that assists the child through the behavior shaping process. In some cases, the teacher may use a physical prompt such as guiding a child's hand. Visual cues include signs or other visual aids. Verbal cues include talking a child through the steps of a task. The gradual removal of the prompt as the child masters the target behavior is called fading.

- **Modeling:** In order for modeling to be effective, the child must first be at a cognitive and developmental level to imitate the model. Teachers are behavior models in the classroom, but peers are powerful models as well, especially in adolescence. A child who does not perceive a model as acceptable will not likely copy the model's behavior. This is why teachers should be careful to reinforce appropriate behavior and not fall into the trap of attending to inappropriate behaviors. Children who see that the students who misbehave get the teacher's constant attention will most likely begin to model those students' behaviors.

- **Contingency Contracting:** Also known as the Premack Principle or "Grandma's Law," this technique is based on the concept that a preferred behavior that frequently occurs can be used to increase a less preferred behavior with a low rate of occurrence. In short, performance of X results in the opportunity to do Y, such as getting 10 minutes of free time for completing the math assignment with 85% accuracy.

Contingency contracts are a process that continues after formal schooling and into the world of work and adult living. Contracts can be individualized, developed with input of the child, and accent positive behaviors. Contingencies can also be simple verbal contracts, such as the teacher telling a child that he or she may earn a treat or special activity for completion of a specific academic activity. Contingency contracts can be simple daily contracts or more formal, written contracts.

Written contracts last for longer periods of time, and must be clear, specific, and fair. Payoffs should be deliverable immediately after the student completes the terms of the contract. An advantage of a written contract is that the child can see and re-affirm the terms of the contract. By being actively involved in the development of the contract with the teacher and/or parent, the child assumes responsibility for fulfilling his share of the deal. Contracts can be renewed and renegotiated as the student progresses toward the target behavior goal.

- **Token Economy:** A token economy mirrors our money system in that the students earn tokens ("money") that are of little value but can be traded for tangible or activity rewards, just as currency can be spent for merchandise. Using stamps, stickers, stars, or point cards instead of items like poker chips decrease the likelihood of theft, loss, and noise in the classroom.

Here are some tips for a token economy:

- Keep the system simple to understand and administer
- Develop a reward "menu" which is deliverable and varied
- Decide on the target behaviors
- Explain the system completely and in positive terms before beginning the economy
- Periodically review the rules
- Price the rewards and costs fairly, and post the menu where it will be easily read
- Gradually fade to a variable schedule of reinforcement

These behavioral management theories are not all inclusive nor do they stand alone. They may overlap or even combine themselves into one cohesive learning theory. Ultimately, each teacher will need to establish the best behavioral management belief system that works for them and their class. Teacher need to keep in mind that each class will be different and behavior management systems will need to be adapted accordingly.

Skill 6.9   Demonstrates awareness of appropriate behavior standards and expectations for students at various developmental levels

COMMUNICATING BEHAVIOR EXPECTATIONS

Behavior management expectations should focus on constructive and encouraging courses of action that can used at school as well as in the student's home environment. When an intervention is needed, the least restrictive method should be implemented first, except in severe situations, such as fighting or destructive behaviors. Student behavior expectations should be taught with the teacher explaining the rules and discussing the consequences of nonconformity. The severity of the consequence should equal the severity of the wrongdoing and must be quickly enforced by the teacher or the principal.

Clear, consistent class rules go a long way to preventing inappropriate behavior. Effective teachers give immediate feedback to students regarding their behavior or misbehavior. If there are consequences, they should be as close as possible to the outside world, especially for adolescents. Consistency, especially with adolescents, reduces the occurrence of power struggles and teaches them that predictable consequences follow for their choice of actions.

Student Involvement

Students enjoy the opportunity to help create the class rules during on the first day of class at school. Allow students to brainstorm what rules should be followed in the classroom, lunchroom, and on the play ground. Students can also offer their opinion on the consequences of breaking the rules. Each classroom will have their own set of behavior standards and expectations, and also the resulting consequences as well. Rules should very concrete and simple for the students to follow.

Listed below are examples of rules of expected behavioral standards at the various developmental levels.

Early Childhood

1. Raise your hand
2. Keep hands and objects to yourself
3. Clean up your area
4. Be kind and show respect
5. Listen carefully

Young Elementary
1. Follow directions the first time given
2. Raise your hand and wait for permission to talk
3. Do not leave seat while the teacher is teaching
4. Stay on task
5. Pay attention

Middle School
1. Raise hand to speak
2. Stay in your seat
3. Speak appropriately to adults and peers
4. No profanity, name calling, or teasing
5. Behave appropriately
6. Keep your hands and feet to yourself
7. No physical or verbal disruption

High School
1. Take an active, positive role in classroom activities
2. Do your own work; do not copy, plagiarize, or cheat
3. Use appropriate language with teachers, staff, and classmates
4. Follow correct dress code rules
5. Do not bring electronic devices into classroom
6. No obscene or profane language
7. No inappropriate displays of affections towards another student

Praise
Teachers should make ample use of praise. When good behavior is noted, these should be noted and acknowledged right away. This can be in the form of a smile, a nod, or even a "thumbs up." Just remember that classroom behavior management expectations are skills that teachers acquire and perfect over time.

Tips to Remember
- The first few days are the most important ones of the year
- Never get into a power struggle with your students
- Not every student will like you
- Do not make any rules for your class with which you are not willing to follow through

Skill 6.10 **Applies effective procedures for managing student behavior and for promoting appropriate behavior and ethical work habits (e.g., academic integrity) in the classroom (e.g., communicating high and realistic behavior expectations, involving students in developing rules and procedures, establishing clear consequences for inappropriate behavior, enforcing behavior standards consistently, encouraging students to monitor their own behavior to use conflict resolution skills, responding appropriately to various types of behavior)**

DEVELOPING CLASSROOM MANAGEMENT
Rules should be established right away when a teacher receives a new group of students. Classroom behavior management plan should be taught with the teacher establishing the rationale and explaining the rules, demonstrating examples and non-examples of the expected behaviors, and guiding the students through practice of the behaviors. In addition to the classroom management plan, a management plan should be developed for special situations, (i.e., fire drills) and transitions (i.e., going to and from the cafeteria). A copy of the classroom plan should be readily available for substitute use, and the classroom aide should also be familiar with the plan and procedures.

Displaying Rules
About four to six classroom rules should be posted where students can easily see and read them. These rules should be stated positively, and describe specific behaviors so they are easy to understand. When the teacher clarifies and models the expected behavior for the students, she is stating the behavior that is expected from students in the classroom. These clear expectations are an excellent way to effectively manage conduct, as well as enhance a positive learning environment. As the students demonstrate the behaviors, the teacher should provide reinforcement and corrective feedback. Periodic review of the rules, as well as modeling and practice, may be conducted as needed, such as after an extended school holiday.

Student Involvement
Students should be involved as much as possible in the formulation of the rules and discuss why the rules are necessary. When students get involved in helping establish the rules, they will be more likely to assume responsibility for following them. Once the rules are established, enforcement and reinforcement for following the rules should begin right away.

Consequences and Rewards
Consequences should be introduced when the rules are introduced, clearly stated, and understood by all of the students. The severity of the consequence should match the severity of the offense and must be enforceable. The teacher must apply the consequence consistently and fairly, so the students will know what to expect when they choose to break a rule.

Like consequences, students should understand what rewards to expect for following the rules. The teacher should never promise a reward that cannot be delivered and should follow through with the reward as soon as possible. Consistency and fairness is also necessary for rewards to be effective. Students will become frustrated and give up if they see that rewards and consequences are not delivered timely and fairly.

SEE also Skills 5.1 and 6.8.

HIGH EXPECTATIONS

Teachers must set the bar high for learning in their classrooms. Academic integrity consists of five core values that are instrumental in managing student behavior and for promoting appropriate behavior in the classroom. Honesty requires truthfulness at all times on the part of the student. Students should be aware of that fact that cheating is not allowed and will not be tolerated in the classroom. Trust is an important issue that should be encouraged between teacher and student. If a problem arises within the classroom, a student should feel comfortable in discussing it with the teacher. Students should treat other students with fairness and understanding. Respect is an extremely important value that needs to be taught to all students concerning race, ethnicity, and diversity. Students should be taught to be understanding of others around them that might hold differing viewpoints than their own. Students should be held responsible and accountable for their actions and deeds.

Students can learn to develop effective work ethics by learning successful study skills. They can also improve reading comprehension by taking time to concentrate on one reading topic at a time. By discovering their own personal study style, students can then learn how to manage their time more efficiently, and eventually choose the best method in which to study for exams. In order for students to develop strong work ethics, teachers need to teach effective time management skills. Students need to stay keep focused on the immediate homework goals, since homework often plays a large factor in the percentage of their grades. Ultimately, it is necessary for students to develop ethical work habits in order to earn a good grade in the class.

For more information on setting high expectations, **SEE** Skill 1.11 and 4.10.

MONITORING AND RESOLVING CONFLICT

Whenever a teacher sees a situation in which two students are involved in a conflict of any sort, immediate action needs to be taken. The students should immediately be removed from each other and from harm's way. The teacher or another third party can then encourage the students to work out their conflict by creating a safe and non-threatening environment, where the problem can be discussed calmly and discreetly. Students should be reminded of the school rules that under no circumstances will this type of behavior be allowed or condoned on school property.

Students need to learn that when they are trying to resolve conflicts, it helps to have a plan in order to solve the problem. There are three basic steps that need to be followed in order to develop strong resolution skills. Students need to define the problem. They can them brainstorm possible solutions for fix the problem. Choosing the best possible answer and then acting on it is the final step in the conflict resolution process. In order for students to monitor their own behavior, they need to be aware of the fact that all parties involved need to agree to work it out in a reasonable manner. There should be no name calling, fist fighting, or arguing between the students. Students need to act calmly and rationally in these types of situations.

By teaching students to use their own conflict resolution skills in handling disagreements in school situations, they can be better prepared to overcome these same types of problems that may occur in their everyday lives.

MODIFYING BEHAVIOR
In an attempt to prevent student misbehaviors the teacher makes clear, concise statements about what is happening in the classroom directing attention to content and the students' accountability for their work rather than focusing the class on the misbehavior. Children believe that their teacher has "eyes in the back of his/her head." When a deviancy occurs in the classroom, the effective teacher knows which student(s) caused the deviancy and swiftly stops the behavior before the deviant conduct spreads to other students or becomes more serious. The teacher must be careful to control his or her voice, both the volume and the tone. Research indicates that soft reprimands are more effective in controlling disruptive behavior than loud reprimands and that when soft reprimands are used fewer are needed.

Verbal techniques, which may be effective in modifying student behavior and setting the classroom tone, include simply stating the student's name, explaining briefly and succinctly what the student is doing that is inappropriate, and what the student should be doing. Verbal techniques for reinforcing behavior include both encouragement and praise delivered by the teacher. In addition, for verbal techniques to positively affect student behavior and learning, the teacher must give clear, concise directives while implying her warmth toward the students.

It is also helpful for the teacher to prominently display the classroom rules. This will serve as a visual reminder of the students' expected behaviors. In a study of classroom management procedures, it was established that the combination of conspicuously displayed rules, frequent verbal references to the rules, and appropriate consequences for appropriate behaviors led to increased levels of on-task behavior.

SEE also Skill 6.8

TEACHER CERTIFICATION STUDY GUIDE

DOMAIN III   IMPLEMENTING EFFECTIVE, RESPONSIVE INSTRUCTION AND ASSESSMENT

COMPETENCY 007   THE TEACHER UNDERSTANDS AND APPLIES PRINCIPLES AND STRATEGIES FOR COMMUNICATING EFFECTIVELY IN VARIED TEACHING AND LEARNING CONTEXTS

Skill 7.1   Demonstrates clear, accurate communication in the teaching and learning process and uses language that is appropriate to students' ages, interests, and backgrounds

Effective teachers are well versed in the areas of cognitive development, which is crucial to presenting ideas and or materials to students at a level appropriate to their developmental maturity. Effective teachers have the ability to use non-verbal and verbal patterns of communications that focus on age-appropriate instructions and materials.

NON-VERBAL COMMUNICATION
The effective teacher communicates non-verbally with students by using positive body language and expressing warmth, concern, acceptance, and enthusiasm. Effective teachers augment their instructional presentations by using positive non-verbal communication such as smiles, open body posture, movement, and eye contact with students. The energy and enthusiasm of the effective teacher can be amplified through positive body language.

A teacher's body language has an even greater effect on student achievement and ability to set and focus on goals. Teacher smiles provide support and give feedback about the teacher's affective state. A deadpan expression can actually be a detriment to the student's progress. Teacher frowns are perceived by students to mean displeasure, disapproval, and even anger. Studies also show that teacher posture and movement are indicators of the teacher's enthusiasm and energy, which emphatically influence student learning, attitudes, motivation, and focus on goals. Teachers have a greater efficacy on student motivation than any person other than parents and therefore it is crucial to be a reflective practitioner, be open to constructive feedback, and be cognizant of the outstanding impact that communication style can have on students. For more information on teacher behavior, **SEE** Skill 5.4.

VERBAL COMMUNICATION
Consistent with Piagean theory of cognitive development, younger children (below age eight) have poor language competencies that result in a poor ability to solve complicated problems. Educational instructions and information should be saturated with simplified language to compensate for the limited language competencies of younger children. Older children (age eight and older) have developed a greater ability to understand language and therefore are capable of solving complex problems. Older children are capable of understanding more advanced instructions and materials that require more advanced language skills.

As the classroom environment increasingly becomes a milieu saturated with cognitive, social, and emotional developmental levels and cultural diversity, the effective teacher must rise to the challenge of presenting ideas and materials appropriate for varying levels of students. Additionally, materials and ideas must be organized, sequenced, and presented to students in a manner consistent with the basic principles of English in a manner relevant to students as a whole.

Barriers to Communication
While teachers should never consider that all student learning is based on teachers communicating to students, much valuable information does occur in the transmission of words between teacher and student. The problem, however, is in dealing with the various types of learning difficulties that students have, as well as all the other environmental factors and learning preferences.

First, various disabilities, including hearing loss, Language-Based Learning Disabilities, Attention Deficit Hyperactivity Disorder, Central Auditory Processing Disorder, and others, can severely impact a student's ability to successfully listen and comprehend what a teacher says. In such cases, teachers should communicate with Special Education and other resource teachers about procedures and practices to follow. But teachers can also place these students in specific classroom locations, give them "partners" who can assist, and periodically check in with them to find out how they are doing. Environmental factors can either aid or inhibit a teacher's communication to students. Often, air conditioners and other room and building noises can impact students' understanding of course content.

Students also have various preferences in how they best understand; some need a lot of teacher explanation and assistance, and others need very little. It is important for the teacher to be very receptive to student comprehension levels and the potential need for further communication (verbal or nonverbal). While one can never judge how much students know from just looking at their expressions, for example, it is possible to get a pretty good idea if a change of communication style or activity is needed—or if they simply need further review.

SEE also Skill 7.2.

Skill 7.2 Engages in skilled questioning and leads effective student discussions, including using questioning and discussion to engage all students in exploring content; extends students' knowledge; and fosters active student inquiry, higher-order thinking, problem solving and productive, supportive interactions, including appropriate wait time

DISCUSSION AND QUESTIONING
Beginning-teacher training explains that the focus of the classroom discussion should be on the subject matter and controlled by teacher-posed questions. When a student response is correct, it is not difficult to maintain academic focus. However, when the student response is incorrect, this task is a little more difficult. The teacher must redirect the discussion to the task at hand, and at the same time not devalue the student response. It is more difficult for the teacher to avoid digression when a student poses a non-academic question.

For example, during the classroom discussion of *Romeo and Juliet*, the teacher asks "Who told Romeo Juliet's identity?" A student raises his or her hand and asks, "May I go to the rest room?" The teacher could respond in one of two ways. If the teacher did not feel this was a genuine need, he or she could simply shake his or her head no while repeating the question, "Who told Romeo Juliet's identity?" If the teacher felt this was a genuine need and could not have waited until a more appropriate time, he or she may hold up the index finger indicating "just a minute" and illicit a response to the academic question from another student. Then, during the next academic question's pause time, the teacher could hand the student the bathroom pass.

Encouraging Participation
It is risky for students to respond to questions in a classroom. If a student is ridiculed or embarrassed by an incorrect response, the student may shut down and not participate thereafter in classroom discussion. One way to respond to an incorrect answer is to ask the child, "Show me from your book why you think that." This gives the student a chance to correct the answer and redeem him or herself.

Another possible response from the teacher is to use the answer as a non-example. For example, after discussing the characteristics of warm-blooded and cold-blooded animals, the teacher asks for some examples of warm-blooded animals. A student raises his or her hand and responds, "A snake." The teacher could then say, "Remember, snakes lay eggs; they do not have live birth. However, a snake is a good non-example of a mammal." The teacher then draws a line down the board and under a heading of "non-example" writes "snake." This action conveys to the child that even though the answer was wrong, it still contributed positively to the class discussion. Notice how the teacher did not digress from the task of listing warm-blooded animals, which in other words is maintaining academic focus and at the same time allowed the student to maintain dignity.

Learning is increased when the teacher acknowledges and amplifies the student responses. Additionally, this can be even more effective if the teacher takes one student's response and directs it to another student for further comment. When this occurs, the students acquire greater subject matter knowledge. This is due to a number of factors. One is that the student feels that he or she is a valuable contributor to the lesson. Another is that all students are forced to pay attention because they never know when they will be called on, which is known as group alert.

Group Alert and Wait-Time
The teacher achieves group alert by stating the question, allowing for a pause time for the students to process the question and formulate an answer, and then calling on someone to answer. If the teacher calls on someone before stating the question, the rest of the students tune-out because they know they are not responsible for the answer. Teachers are advised to also alert the non-performers to pay attention because they may be called on to elaborate on the answer. Non-performers are defined as all the students not chosen to answer.

One part of the questioning process is wait-time, the time between the question and either the student response or teacher follow-up. Many teachers vaguely recommend some general amount of wait-time (approximately five seconds or until the student starts to get uncomfortable or is clearly perplexed), but the focus here is on wait-time as a specific and powerful communicative tool that speaks through its structured silences. Embedded in wait-time are subtle clues about the judgments of a student's abilities and the expectations of individuals and groups. For example, the more time that a student is allowed to mull through a question, the more the teacher trusts his or her ability to answer that question without getting flustered. As a rule, the practice of prompting is not a problem. Giving support and helping students reason through difficult conundrums is part of being an effective teacher.

Incorporating Student Responses
The idea of directing the student comment to another student is a valuable tool for engaging the lower achieving student. If the teacher can illicit even part of an answer from a lower-achieving student and then move the spotlight off of that student onto another student, the lower achieving student will be more likely to engage in the class discussion the next time. This is because they were not put "on the spot" for very long, and they successfully contributed to the class discussion.

Additionally, the teacher shows more acceptance and value to student responses, not by correcting, but by acknowledging, amplifying, discussing, or restating the comment or question. If student responses are allowed, even if it is blurted out, the response must be acknowledged, and the student should be told the quality of the response.

For example, the teacher asks, "Is chalk a noun?" During the pause time a student says, "Oh, so my bike is a noun." Without breaking the concentration of the class, the teacher looks to the student, nods and then places his or her index finger to the lips as a signal for the student not to speak out of turn and then calls on someone to respond to the original question. If the blurted-out response is incorrect or needs further elaboration, the teacher may just hold up his or her index finger as an indication to the student that the class will address that in a minute when the class is finished with the current question.

A teacher acknowledges a student response by commenting on it. For example, the teacher states the definition of a noun and then asks for examples of nouns in the classroom. A student responds, "My pencil is a noun." The teacher answers, "Okay, let us list that on the board." By this response and the action of writing "pencil" on the board, the teacher has just incorporated the student's response into the lesson. A teacher may also amplify the student response through another question directed to either the original student or to another student. For example, the teacher may probe the response by saying, "Okay," giving the student feedback on the quality of the answer, and then adding, "What do you mean by 'run' when you say the battery runs the radio?"

Another way of showing acceptance and value of student response is to discuss the student response. For example, after a student responds, the teacher would say, "Class, let us think along that line. What is some evidence that proves what Susie just stated?" And finally, the teacher may restate the response. For example, the teacher might say, "So you are saying, the seasons are caused by the tilt of the earth. Is this what you said?"

Therefore, a teacher keeps students involved by utilization of group alert. Additionally, the teacher shows acceptance and value of student responses by acknowledging, amplifying, discussing, or restating the response. This contributes to maintaining academic focus.

SEE also Skill 4.6.

Skill 7.3 **Communicates directions, explanations and procedures effectively and uses strategies for adjusting communication to enhance student understanding (e.g., by providing examples, simplifying complex ideas, using appropriate communication tools)**

ENHANCING STUDENT UNDERSTANDING
Generally speaking, complex concepts can be taught in two manners: deductively or inductively. In a deductive manner, the teacher gives a definition along with one or two examples and one or two non-examples. As a means of checking understanding, the teacher will ask the students to give additional examples or non-examples and perhaps to repeat the definition. In an inductive manner, the students will derive the definition from examples and non-examples provided by the teacher. The students will test these examples and non-examples to ascertain if they possess the attributes that meet the criteria of the definition.

Using Definitions
It cannot be assumed that students are gaining meaning through definitions. It is quite possible that some students are able to memorize definitions without actually understanding the concept. If students understand concepts and gain meaning from definitions, they will be able to apply this information by giving both examples and non-examples. Students will further be able to list attributes and recognize related concepts. Research indicates that when students gain knowledge through instruction that includes a combination of giving definitions, examples, non-examples, and by identifying attributes, they are more likely to grasp complicated concepts than by other instructional methods.

Using Examples and Non-Examples
To help simplify complex ideas, the teacher can help define the concept more clearly for students by providing both examples of the concept, as well as non-examples. Several studies have been carried out to determine the effectiveness of giving examples as well as the difference in effectiveness of various types of examples. It was found conclusively that the most effective method of concept presentation included giving a definition along with examples and non-examples and also providing an explanation of the examples and non-examples. These same studies indicate that boring examples were just as effective as interesting examples in promoting learning.

Additional studies have been conducted to determine the most effective number of examples that will result in maximum student learning. These studies concluded that a few thoughtfully selected examples are just as effective as several examples. It was determined that the actual number of examples necessary to promote student learning was relative to the learning characteristics of the learners. It was again ascertained that learning is facilitated when examples are provided along with the definition.

Using Critical Attributes
Learning is further enhanced when critical attributes are listed along with a definition, examples, and non-examples. Classifying attributes is an effective strategy for both very young students and older students. According to Piaget's pre-operational phase of development, children learn concepts informally through experiences with objects just as they naturally acquire language. It is during this stage that students' language develops, as well as an ability to understand symbols and classifications. One of the most effective learning experiences with objects is learning to classify objects by a single obvious feature or attribute. Children classify objects typically, often without any prompting or directions. This natural inclination to classify objects carries over to classifying attributes of a particular concept and contributes to the student's understanding of concepts.

In order to scaffold students to learn at increasingly higher levels, it is crucial to initially simplify complex ideas. This is important for all students and especially important for students with learning disabilities, for whom research reinforces the need for simplifying ideas and concepts. Strategies to simplify complex ideas include utilizing visual and/or tactile aids to help students make connections, breaking ideas into smaller manageable parts (potentially over several days) and relating new ideas to background knowledge and a central, unifying idea.

Using Communication Tools
Often the ability to simplify and effectively communicate information is related to the communication tools that a teacher is using to instruct on the targeted lesson. Research reinforces the need for multi-sensory instruction for learning. Providing a visual or tactile learning experience, in addition to a verbal definition or an example, can often be the key in helping a student make connections. Appropriate visuals can include pictures, graphs, videos, or demonstrations. Tactile experiences can be as simple as touching an object or as complex as building a model or completing an experiment. Taking into account the multiple intelligences that are present in a classroom means that a teacher must consider communicating in a variety of modalities.

Extensive research highlights the fact that new learning occurs when novel information is integrated with that which the learner already knows. The act of activating background knowledge to enhance student understanding often relates back to providing and obtaining examples from students. The process of relating those examples and background knowledge to a central unifying idea is what helps students make the cognitive leap to learning new, and complex, information.

Skill 7.4 **Practices effective communication techniques and interpersonal skills (including both verbal and nonverbal skills and electronic communication) for meeting specified goals in various contexts**

SEE Skill 7.1, 7.3, 9.4 and 9.5.

TEACHER CERTIFICATION STUDY GUIDE

COMPETENCY 008   THE TEACHER PROVIDES APPROPRIATE INSTRUCTION THAT ACTIVELY ENGAGES STUDENTS IN THE LEARNING PROCESS

Skill 8.1   Employs various instructional techniques (e.g., discussion, inquiry, problem solving) and varies teacher and student roles in the instructional process and provides instruction that promotes intellectual involvement and active student engagement and learning

There are a variety of ways a teacher can plan to implement instruction to enhance student learning. Hands-on lessons that keep students engaged are ideal for maintaining students' interest. The way a teacher groups and arranges students for such lessons is important to keeping students engaged.

Students can be taught the skills that lead to factual recall, and beginning to teach those skills at even very early grades will result in more successful students. It is important for teachers to vary their instructional techniques because experiencing a fact or an idea in several different ways or through multiple senses increases the ability to recall it. For further information on the Multiple Intelligence Theory, **SEE** Skills 4.1 and 4.5.

VARYING INSTRUCTIONAL STRATEGIES
Classrooms have begun to drift away from being entirely composed of lectures (or direct instruction). By varying presentation of material, teachers increase learning in their classrooms. There are literally hundreds of instructional techniques that can be used at many levels from early childhood through advanced high school courses. A good glossary of these strategies can be viewed at http://glossary.plasmalink.com/glossary.html.

Discussions
One excellent, and common, strategy is classroom discussion. This strategy encourages respect, open thinking, and an atmosphere of a community when used effectively in a classroom. Typically, teachers begin a discussion by stating or suggesting a goal for the group(s). This can be done by posting a question, asking an opinion about a topic, quoting a statistic or current research, or having the students come up with their own topic. Nowadays, discussions can take the form of small group, large group, online via web boards, cross classroom, debate, and more.

For discussions to be effective, teachers must set clear expectations for discussion sessions, as well as inform students on how they will be evaluated on their participation. Teachers must also control and use their classroom space strategically, as well as to be sure to actively monitor student groups when they are working together. If the teacher is leading a large group discussion, he or she must ask good, direct questions, as well as call on individual students.

Inquiry
Inquiry is another common instructional strategy. This technique encourages students to ask questions in order to form a possible answer or hypothesis to solve a problem. Through their

questioning, students are typically expected to collect and/or analyze data to support their solution, which is derived from their inquiries. This strategy is especially useful in providing feedback to both teachers and students. It also provides direct connections between the teachers and students, as well as between students as a group.

Problem Solving
Inquiry is related to another strong instructional strategy—problem solving. Whether individually, in pairs, or in groups, students are given problems for which they are to present solutions. In the best scenarios, teachers will present real-world problems to students who will utilize inquiry and other critical-thinking skills to arrive at possible solutions. Another variation is for teachers to ask students to develop one or multiple problem scenarios to perhaps present to other students or groups.

Bringing It All Together
Many types of instructional strategies, including discussions, inquiry, and problem solving mentioned here, can be incorporated or implemented with cooperative learning strategies (**SEE** Skills 6.2 and 6.3), as well as differentiated instructional strategies (**SEE** Skill 2.5). Some, but certainly not all, other ways to vary instruction are listed below:

- Activating Prior Knowledge
- Brainstorming
- Analogies
- Evaluating Cause and Effect
- Venn Diagrams or other Visuals
- Chronological Sequencing
- Circles or Centers
- Journaling
- Dramatization
- Write, Pair, Share

ROLES IN THE CLASSROOM
In today's classrooms, the role of the teacher has evolved to more of a facilitator of learning, rather than the old-fashioned direct source of all information. In a learner-centered classroom, the teacher fosters learning by creating an information-rich atmosphere that is safe, structured, and organized. The teacher is still the leader, but in a different way than in the past—not in the sense that they *literally* lead the class each day, but that they lead the students, including their parents, to success.

So if the teacher's role has changed so much, it is expected that the student's role has changed as well. Students today are expected to do more than sit in silence and simply listen. In the mini-community effective teachers establish, the student now must take on the role of an active participant responsible for their own learning. The students are the researchers, the discussion leaders, the problem solvers, the question askers, the writers, the readers, the presenters, in the classroom today, which drastically impacts a higher level of learning and overall knowledge. Obviously, this role is smaller with the younger students, but good school systems will develop this student independence through staff development. Thus, it is a gradual shift to increased student independence as the years progress.

For more information, **SEE** Skill 4.13.

Skill 8.2 **Applies various strategies to promote student engagement and learning (e.g., by structuring lessons effectively, using flexible instructional groupings, pacing lessons flexibly in response to student needs, including wait time)**

Once long-range goals have been identified and established, it is important to ensure that all goals and objectives are also in conjunction with student ability and needs. Some objectives may be too basic for a higher level student, while others cannot be met with a student's current level of knowledge. There are many forms of evaluating student needs to ensure that all goals set are challenging yet achievable.

SEE also Skill 8.1

FLEXIBLE GROUPING
For information on flexible instructional groupings, **SEE** Skill 2.5, 6.2, 6.3, and 8.1.

STRUCTURING LESSONS
When organizing and sequencing objectives the teacher needs to remember that skills are building blocks. Because most goals are building blocks, all necessary underlying skills should be determined and a teacher must evaluate if the student has demonstrated these abilities. For example, to do mathematical word problems, students must have a sufficiently high enough level of reading to understand the problem.

Many teachers adhere to Bloom's Taxonomy of thinking skills. Bloom identified six levels of thinking within the cognitive domain (from low to high):

- Knowledge (define, list, organize, recall, label)
- Understanding (classify, explain, identify, review, discuss)
- Application (illustrate, apply, practice, solve, write)
- Analysis (categorize, compare, criticize, examine, question)
- Synthesis (arrange, collect, compose, create, propose, design, develop)
- Evaluation (argue, assess, defend, estimate, predict, support)

Bloom's research showed that 95 percent of how students were required to think was at the lowest level, knowledge, with tasks such as recall and memorizing used the most. Today, teachers are encouraged to develop instruction that requires thinking at the higher levels.

Ordering Thinking Skills
Educational objectives can be helpful to construct and organize objectives. Knowledge of material, such as memorizing definitions or famous quotes, is low on the taxonomy of learning

and should be worked with early in the sequence of teaching. Eventually, objectives should be developed to include higher-level thinking such as comprehension (i.e., being able to use a definition); application (i.e., being able to apply the definition to other situations); synthesis (i.e., being able to add other information); and evaluation (i.e., being able to judge the value of something).

As a teacher, it is important to be aware of the skills and information that are pertinent to the subject area being taught. Teachers need to determine what information a student should carry with them at the end of a term. The teacher should also be aware of skills needed to complete any objective for that subject area and determine how skilled their students are at using them.

Long-Range vs. Short-Range Objectives
Once the desired knowledge, skills, and attitudes have been established, a teacher must develop short-range objectives designed to help in the achievement of these outcomes. An objective is a specific learning outcome that is used to achieve long-range goals. Objectives should be stated in observable terms such as: to state, to demonstrate, to list, to complete or to solve. Objectives should be clear and concise (i.e. students will be able to state five causes of World War II). It should also be stated in the lesson plan which curriculum objectives are met with each lesson and how it relates to course goals.

A list of the materials needed for the lesson is needed which should be followed by the specific methodologies and/or activities for the lesson. Effective teachers always include a unique activity or anticipatory set to kick off the lesson— something that hooks the students to ensure their engagement. Then the lesson is introduced and the activity(ies) begin. Since most classrooms have varied learning abilities, the teacher should prepare some activities in this list that allow for differentiated instruction.

Closing a Lesson
Lessons should close with a closing activity, review, recap, or summarizing activity. The teacher should also include how the students are to be or were assessed during the activities, as well as how the teacher assesses his own instruction and what can be added or changed for next time. Finally, enrichment extensions should be listed for any student who is looking for more.

SEE also "Emergent Curriculum" in Skill 2.5.

PACING LESSONS
How, when, and the pace at which lessons are presented is also important. A teacher should be flexible and diverse in how they arrange and present lessons. Teachers should be sure to provide information through a variety of contexts, in a myriad of ways, and in a logical sequence. When an assortment of material is diverse and connected to the world around the students, the material has more impact and meaning to the students.

Focusing on the needs evident in almost any classroom population, the teacher will want to use textbooks that include some of the activities and selections to challenge the most advanced students as well as those who have difficulty in mastering the material at a moderate pace.

Some of the exercises may be eliminated altogether for faster learners, while students who have difficulty may need to have material arranged into brief steps or sections.

TEACHER OBSERVATIONS

The value of teacher observations cannot be underestimated. It is through the use of observations that the teacher is able to informally assess the needs of the students during instruction. These observations will drive the lesson and determine the direction that the lesson will take based on student activity and behavior. After a lesson is carefully planned, teacher observation is the single most important component of an instructional presentation. If the teacher observes that a particular student is not on-task, she will change the method of instruction accordingly. She may change from a teacher-directed approach to a more interactive approach. Questioning will increase in order to increase the participation of the students. If appropriate, the teacher will introduce manipulative materials to the lesson. In addition, teachers may switch to a cooperative group activity, thereby removing the responsibility of instruction from the teacher and putting it on the students.

SEE also Skills 3.2, 3.6, 3.7

Skill 8.3 **Presents content to students in ways that are relevant and meaningful and that link with students' prior knowledge and experience**

LINKING PRIOR KNOWLEDGE WITH CURRENT LESSONS

Most young students come to school ready and eager to learn, but as the grades pass, many students become bored and uninterested in school. By middle school, many students simply complete assignments for the sake of doing so, rather than with an understanding as to why that particular learning was important. Most teachers would agree that in order to truly engage students, the students must be genuinely motivated to learn. In many classrooms, it can be quite a challenge to present subjects in a way that motivates everyone at one time. This challenge is greater when the students feel that what they are learning has no connection or use in their own lives. As a result, their attention decreases, resulting in lower student achievement. Educators are finding, however, that if students are motivated to learn, they will invest more effort in participation and classroom assignments if they feel there is a purpose to the work.

Strategies for Classroom Motivation

Motivational researchers have found several strategies work to help increase classroom motivation. First off, it is recommended that teachers stimulate student curiosity by asking thought-provoking questions. When there is a gap between what students know and what they want to know, teachers will be able to utilize the natural curiosity which arises as a result of that gap by having students explore this discrepancy. With young children, this need to explore is inherent, and so these students can use manipulatives, games, and play to explore their topics.

A common tool used to activate and record prior knowledge for the class is a KWL chart. KWL charts consist of three columns, each with a letter heading, K, W, and L. These charts help organize what students know (K), what they want to know (W), and (later) what they have learned (L).

Secondly, connections to what they are learning should be made to both the students' prior experience (if possible) as well as to their emotions. When links to memory and emotion are provoked in learning, the brain can relate, retain, and store the information more effectively than if it was presented in isolation. When connected to something the student remembers, likes, enjoys, is curious about, etc., the student is better able to make connections between the old and new material, therefore making better sense of the world around them and the new information they are receiving.

For example, teachers could ask young students, "What is wrong with our playground?" This question will provoke emotion for a place the students typically like, pinpoint a discrepancy with what is there and what they might want, and pose a problem they could problem solve. Depending on responses and teacher direction, lessons in economics, language, environmental, physics, citizenship, and more could evolve as a result. Not only are these topics now interrelated, they are also relevant to the students. For information on interdisciplinary teaching, **SEE** Skill 3.7.

As students enter middle and high school levels, a more sophisticated question could be asked, but still, these strategies can be utilized in addition to research projects, topics that tie in to their community, and cooperative learning units and presentations can increase motivation.

SEE also Skills 4.1, 8.6, and 8.7.

Skill 8.4 **Applies criteria for evaluating the appropriateness of instructional activities, materials, resources and technologies for students with varied characteristics and needs**

Today's educator must address the needs of diverse learners within a single classroom. In addition, the teacher must attain materials that may be necessary for the majority of the regular education students and some of the special needs children and, more and more frequently, one individual student. The "effective" teacher knows that there are currently hundreds of adaptive materials that could be used to help these students increase achievement and develop skills.

DETERMINING INSTRUCTIONAL ACTIVITIES
A teacher's job would be relatively easy if simply instructing students in current curriculum objectives was his/her primary responsibility. Today's educator must first assure that the students are able to come to school, are able to attend to the curriculum, have individual learning styles met, and are motivated to work to their fullest capacity. To determine appropriateness of instructional activities, teachers should have a good understanding of the age group with which they are working. For information on the stages of development, **SEE** Skills 1.1, 1.3, 1.4, 1.5, and 1.6.

Once the teacher is clear on the general abilities of his or her age group (accounting for individual differences, of course), the teacher should begin by informing herself of what the students did the prior year and what they are expected to do the following year. In an organized district, this will provide the teacher with a framework of where to work.

For example, teachers in early childhood education know that three- and four-year olds should be working on early writing skills. Does this mean that three-year-olds are sitting with pencils all day forced to write letters? Of course not, an effective teacher will also know that activities such as forming letters in sand, playing with play-doh, and crawling on the floor (in the form of a game at this age) will all aid in the development of fine motor skills used in writing later on and are age appropriate.

In another example, take the use of picture books in a sixth-grade classroom. Picture books, traditionally placed in young classrooms, are being utilized more and more with older students. However, they should still be evaluated for age appropriateness. A picture book on the Holocaust for instance would not likely be used in a first grade classroom but could be used if appropriate in an older classroom as an introduction to a unit or to the children's novel *Number the Stars* (perhaps, fifth grade) or *The Diary of Ann Frank* (perhaps grade eight or nine).

Teachers must also keep in mind the needs for special needs students when evaluating activities. Most special needs students have an Individual Educational Plan or a 504 Plan. These documents clearly state the students' educational objectives and learning needs as well as persons responsible for meeting these objectives. A well-written Individual Educational Plan will contain evidence that the student is receiving resources from the school and the community that will assist in meeting the physical, social, and academic needs of the student.

The challenges of meeting the needs of all students in the classroom require that the teacher is a lifelong learner. Ongoing participation in professional staff development, attendance at local, state, and national conferences, and continuing education classes help teachers grow in many ways including an awareness of resources available for students.

For more information on the teacher's self-evaluation, **SEE** Skill 3.3.

For more information on the effectiveness of these activities, **SEE** Skill 8.5.

INSTRUCTIONAL MATERIALS & RESOURCES
Student-centered classrooms contain not only textbooks, workbooks, and literature materials but also rely heavily on a variety of audio-visual equipment and computers. There are tape recorders, language masters, filmstrip projectors, and laser disc players to help meet the learning styles of the students.

Although most school centers cannot supply all the materials that special needs students require, each district more than likely has a resource center where teachers can check out special equipment.

Regardless of what the material is, teachers must make sure that the materials used in their classrooms are:

- Accurate
- Age-appropriate

- Useful
- Current (relatively); if mandated materials are somewhat outdated, it is possible to supplement them with other learning materials that offer more current perspectives
- Readable
- Easy to use (especially software, videos, and websites)
- Has connections to the curriculum

These questions can help a teacher evaluate the materials from the teacher's point of view, but be sure to also evaluate from the student's perspective. Some questions to consider are:

- Will this interest my students?
- Will this offer a new perspective?
- Does this promote critical thinking?
- Does this promote interdisciplinary learning?
- What types of learning strategies are involved?
- Does this touch upon multiple intelligences?
- Is learning interactive and hands-on?

Most communities support agencies which offer assistance in providing the necessities of special needs people including students. Teachers must know how to obtain a wide range of materials including school supplies, medical care, clothing, food, adaptive computers and books (such as Braille), eye glasses, hearing aids, wheelchairs, counseling, transportation, etc.

EVALUATING TECHNOLOGY
SEE Skill 9.1 and 9.3.

Skill 8.5 Engages in continuous monitoring of instructional effectiveness

SEE Skills 3.3 and 12.9.

Skill 8.6 Applies knowledge of different types of motivation (i.e., internal, external) and factors affecting student motivation

INTRINSIC AND EXTRINSIC MOTIVATION
Extrinsic motivation is motivation that comes from the expectation of rewards or punishments. The rewards and punishments can be varied. For example, in social situations, most human beings are extrinsically motivated to behave in common, socially-accepted ways. The punishment for NOT doing so might be embarrassment or ridicule. The reward for doing so might be the acceptance of peers. In the classroom, rewards might be grades, candy, or special privileges. Punishments might be phone calls to parents, detention, suspension, or poor grades.

Intrinsic motivation is motivation that comes from within. For example, while some children only read if given extrinsic rewards (e.g., winning an award for the most pages read), other children read because they enjoy it.

There are benefits and drawbacks of both methods of motivation. In reality, it should be noted that in an ideal world, all motivation would be intrinsic. But this is not the case. Consider having to clean an apartment, dorm room, or house. The "reward" of a clean living space at the end of the activity is appreciated, but most people do not particularly enjoy the process of cleaning and only put up with it for the end result.

Those who work in education of course want all students to be intrinsically motivated. They want students to not care about grades or prizes as much as they might want them to do their work, listen attentively, and read just because they want to learn. And while all teachers should work tirelessly to ensure that they develop intrinsic motivation as much as possible within their students, everyone knows that for certain students and subjects, extrinsic motivators must be used.

Extrinsic Motivators in the Classroom
What extrinsic motivators are useful in the classroom? Well, to start, if things like candy and prizes are always used to get students to pay attention in class, soon, they will expect these things and possibly not pay attention in their absence. Specific praise is another good motivator. Instead of simply stating, "Nice painting, Mary," for an art class, specific praise notes good behavior or achievement. For example, one could say "Excellent job, Mary. Your use of color emphasizes a happy mood." Specific praise highlights exactly what the student is doing well and clearly emphasizes what the student did well that met expectations.

Likewise, if punishment is always used as a motivator, students may be more consumed with fear than with the frame of mind that is most conducive to learning. So, while grades can consume many students, having benchmarks and standards are indeed useful for many teachers. Punishments, if they are reasonable and if students know what to expect (with consistent application), can be useful in making sure students behave appropriately. The best punishments, though, are ones in which a whole school has decided will be consistently used from classroom to classroom and grade level to grade level.

Factors That Affect Motivation
Motivating students becomes even a greater challenge as the students get older. With high school students, the factors that affect motivation change slightly. Students at this higher level are less interested in small and fun group games. Instead, they begin to value the process of learning, realizing its potential, and therefore, are motivated in a different manner.

Some factors that affect older students' motivation include:

- High expectations set by the instructor
- Clear objectives about how to succeed in the class
- Varied instructional strategies are utilized
- The value of learning is emphasized rather than just grades
- Assignments are given in a timely manner with respect/consideration for outside commitments like jobs, sports, or other extracurricular activities
- Teacher cares genuinely for student success

- Desire to boost self-confidence
- Teachers who are easy to understand, fair, experienced, organized, interested, and passionate

In general, teachers must walk a careful line with motivation. They must utilize extrinsic motivators when all possible intrinsic motivators have failed to work.

SEE also Skills 8.3 and 8.7.

Skill 8.7   Employs effective motivational strategies and encourages students' self-motivation

Motivation is an internal state that activates, guides, and sustains behavior. Educational psychology research on motivation is concerned with the volition or will that students bring to a task, their level of interest and intrinsic motivation, the personally held goals that guide their behavior, and their belief about the causes of their success or failure.

STRATEGIES FOR INCREASING MOTIVATION
Effective teachers encourage students to develop small practices that they can utilize each day to increase motivation. There are many techniques teachers can implement in their class and/or with individual students to help increase their motivation. First off, teachers can enhance student motivation by planning and directing interactive, "hands-on" learning experiences. Research substantiates that teamwork and/or cooperative group projects decrease student behavior problems and increase student on-task behavior. Students who are directly involved with learning activities are more motivated to complete a task to the best of their ability.

Another strategy is to have students create daily and unit lists or goals for learning. Students could also create "dream boards"—poster boards that are collages of pictures that depict what successes they will find with their learning.

A third strategy is to break larger tasks into more manageable steps. In higher-ordered learning atmospheres, sometimes the projects can appear too challenging. Sometimes students are overwhelmed and prematurely give up on a project when it is presented as a huge, looming assignment. If the teacher helps the students see the smaller steps ("baby steps"), they can take to handle it one piece at a time, their confidence will increase, as well as their motivation to do a good job. Students will also find more confidence and maintain motivation if they check off the items they have accomplished; this allows students to visually see their progress. Be sure to give positive feedback on work, participation, behaviors that are found to be satisfying and do this early in the project and frequently, so that students start off strong and with the correct expectations.

A fourth strategy is to have students identify their connections with the assignments. Make it personal. When a student feels the connection to the work, he or she can relate to the material better, they become personally invested and are more motivated to do good work when they see the learning as valuable. Therefore, personal meaning and connection can be a positive motivational strategy.

A fifth strategy is to give students control. This especially will help with students becoming more self-motivated. When the student or student groups sense they are leading the assignment, that sense of control empowers them to take hold of their own learning.

With students who are especially difficult to motivate, the sixth strategy of using incentives and rewards programs can be effective, but be sure to be sparing with such rewards and make sure rewards are given out only for successful completion—not just for participating.

A seventh strategy is to create a positive learning environment where the teacher genuinely cares about each participant. Teachers should ensure that all students feel like a valued member of this authentic learning community.

Motivation is one of the most important factors that affects student learning, and it is imperative that today's teacher focus on ensuring all of their students are properly motivated and set up for successful learning.

SEE also Skills 8.3 and 8.6.

TEACHER CERTIFICATION STUDY GUIDE

COMPETENCY 009   **THE TEACHER INCORPORATES THE EFFECTIVE USE OF TECHNOLOGY TO PLAN, ORGANIZE, DELIVER, AND EVALUATE INSTRUCTION FOR ALL STUDENTS**

Skill 9.1   **Demonstrates knowledge of basic terms and concepts of current technology (e.g., hardware, software applications and functions, input/output devices, networks)**

The computer system can be divided into two main parts—the hardware and the software. Hardware can be defined as all the physical components that make up the machine. Software includes the programs (sets of instructions) that enable that machine to do a particular job.

HARDWARE
Input devices are those parts of the computer that accept information from the user. The most common input devices are the keyboard and the mouse. Other more specialized input devices might include joysticks, light pens, touch pads, graphic tablets, voice recognition devices, and optical scanners.

Output devices are the parts of the computer that display the results of processing for the user. These commonly include the monitor and printers, but a computer might also output information to plotters and speech synthesizers. Monitors and printers can vary greatly in the quality of the output displayed. Monitors are classified according to their resolution (dpi = dots per square inch).

Printers
Printers vary in the way they produce "hard copy" as well as in the quality of the resultant product. With market prices coming down, they are becoming much more affordable. The best hard copies are produced by laser printers, but laser printers are also the most expensive. They are usually found in offices where volume is not high but the best quality is desired.

Hard Drives
Storage devices enable computers to save documents and other important files for future editing. Hard drives are built into most computers for the storage of the large programs used today. As programs increase in size and complexity to make use of the enhanced graphic and sound capabilities of today's computers, the amount of storage space on a hard drive has become increasingly important. An option that adds portability for students to move small files from one computer to another is a flash drive. For example, this device allows students to bring in a paper from home to print up in the school's computer lab.

CDs and DVDs
Many schools avoid the limitations imposed by the hard drive's storage space by using networks to deliver programs to the individual systems. The CD-ROM drives of multimedia computers that can access CD-ROM disks containing large amounts of information and usually including sound, graphics, and even video clips. For even larger files, a Digital Video Disk/Rewriteable (DVD R/W) can be used for storing of data, music, movies and other large files. They can be

used repeatedly to be updated and store the information that is needed at the time. Another option is for students to use an external hard drive which adds portability to move around stored data, as well as to use as a backup system.

One way to take advantage of the computer's ability to store vast amounts of data is to utilize them in the classroom as a research tool. Entire encyclopedias, whole classical libraries, specialized databases in history, science, and the arts can be obtained on CD-ROM disks to allow students to complete their research from the classroom computer. With the "Search" feature of these programs, students can type in a one or two word description of the desired topic and the computer will actually locate all articles that deal with that topic. The student can either read the articles on the computer monitor or print them out.

CPU and Motherboard

The last hardware component of a computer system is the Central Processing Unit, or CPU, along with all the memory chips on the motherboard. This "brain" of the computer is responsible for receiving input from the input or storage devices, placing it in temporary storage (RAM or Random Access Memory), performing any processing functions required by the program (like mathematical equations or sorting) and eventually retrieving the information from storage and displaying it by means of an output device.

SOFTWARE

Software consists of all the programs containing instructions for the computer and is stored on the hard drive, CD-ROM disks, or can be downloaded with proper permissions. Programs fall into two major groups: operating systems and application programs. Operating system programs contain instructions that allow the computer to function. Applications are all the jobs that a user might wish to perform on the computer. These might include word processors, databases, spreadsheets, educational and financial programs, games, and telecommunications programs.

Educational Software

With a surplus of educational software on the market, it is important for an educator to be able to evaluate a program before purchasing it. There are three general steps to follow when evaluating a software program. First, one must read the instructions thoroughly to familiarize oneself with the program, its hardware requirements, and its installation. Once the program is installed and ready to run, the evaluator should first run the program as it would be run by a successful student, without deliberate errors but making use of all the possibilities available to the student. Thirdly, the program should be run making deliberate mistakes to test the handling of errors. One should try to make as many different kinds of mistakes as possible, including those for incorrect keyboard usage and the validity of user directions.

Many school districts have addressed the overwhelming number of educational software products by publishing a list of approved software titles for each grade level in much the same way that they publish lists of approved text books and other classroom materials. In addition, most districts have developed a software evaluation form to be used by any instructor involved in the purchase of software that is not already on the "approved" list.

TEACHER CERTIFICATION STUDY GUIDE

NETWORKS

A network is composed of two or more computers, linked together. More specifically, a computer network is a data communications system made up of hardware and software that transmits data from one computer to another. In part, a computer network includes physical infrastructure like wires, cables, fiber optic lines, undersea cables, and satellites. The other part of a network is the software to keep it running. Computer networks can connect to other computer networks to create a vast computer network.

There are numerous configurations for computer networks, including:

- Local-area networks (LANS)—the computers are all contained within the same building
- Wide-area networks (WANS)—the computers are at a distance and are connected through telephone lines or radio waves
- Campus-area networks (CANs)—the computers are within a specific, geographic area, such as a school campus or military base
- Metropolitan-area networks (MANs)—a data network developed for a specific town or city
- Home-area networks (HANs)—a network contained within a private home which connects all the digital devices
- Internet—the communicating and sharing of data via shared routers and servers using common protocols

Depending on the type of network access, the teacher has productivity and instructional information and communications capabilities available from the next office or around the world.

Skill 9.2   Understands issues related to the appropriate use of technology in society and follows guidelines for the legal and ethical use of technology and digital information (e.g., privacy guidelines, copyright laws, acceptable use policies)

APPROPRIATE USE OF TECHNOLOGY

Students must exercise responsibility and accountability in adhering to technology usage during the school day. Internet usage agreements define a number of criteria of technology use that a students must agree to in order to have access to school computers. Students who violate any parts of the computer usage agreement are subject to have all access to school computers or other educational technology denied or blocked, which, for the student needing to print a paper using the school computer and printer, could make the difference in handing assignments in on time or receiving a lower grade for late assignments.

District and school policies are developed to provide a consistent language of expectation for students using school technology with an acceptable use policy. Districts are liable for the actions of students and teachers in school communities who use publicly funded and legislatively funded technology. The standards of usage for school computers are created to maximize student use for educational purposes and to minimize student surfing for non-educational sites that minimize learning during class times. The timeframes for computer usage are limited for students, since the numbers of computers being used in school communities are minimal to the users.

Technology use has policies that transcend from the district to school communities to students and staff. Federal and state funding to districts also carry technology expectations as conditions of funding, so the chain of expectation starts from top management to school communities. Given the predator nature of users on the Internet, the policies and procedures for school usage are necessary to keep students safe when they are using computers for educational purposes.

OTHER ELECTRONIC DEVICES

Beyond computer usage in schools, the use of other electronics like I-pods, Walkmans, and cell phones are prohibited in classrooms. The constant distractions of phones beeping, emitting loud noises, along with the choice of music that each generation listens to on a daily basis impede the educational access for students struggling to maintain focus on the lesson objectives. A student having trouble with inference in a reading passage could be easily distracted with the constant phone noises and electronic music coming from student earphones or computer downloads. An effective teacher underscores in the classroom that the focus on learning will be exclusive of electronic distractions and inappropriate computer use.

Students who have their computer privileges revoked due to abuse of the Internet agreements or general computer policies may find that academic progress may be jeopardized, especially if the students do not own computers or have Internet access beyond the classrooms. Teachers should monitor the activities of students who are using computers and actively respond to students who misuse public technology intended to enhance the learning process and access for all students.

Skill 9.3 **Applies procedures for acquiring, analyzing and evaluating electronic information (e.g., locating information on networks, accessing and manipulating information from secondary storage and remote devices, using online help and other documentation, evaluating electronic information for accuracy and validity)**

Resources and materials for instruction are everywhere—in schools, on the web, in bookstores, and in adopted school programs. How does one decide where to get materials for instruction? And how does one evaluate materials for use in instruction?

DEALING WITH ELECTRONIC RESOURCES

If the classroom computer has Internet access, the research possibilities are unlimited. When hooked up to the World Wide Web, students can actually talk to people from other parts of the globe or access libraries and journals from all over the world.

For example, if students are studying weather, they might go on-line with students who live in different weather zones to discuss how weather affects their lives. Then they might access global weather reports and print out weather maps and discuss their research with meteorologists—and all from a single computer station.

Guest Experts

Having the school's librarian or technology expert as a guest speaker in a classroom provides another method of sharing and modeling proper presentation preparation using technology. Teachers can also appoint technology experts from the students in a classroom to work with students on projects and presentations. In high schools, technology classes provide students with upper-class teacher assistants who fill the role of technology assistants. The wealth of resources for teachers and students seeking to incorporate technology and structured planning for student presentations and projects is as diverse as the presentations. There is an expert in every classroom who is always willing to offer advice and instruction. In school communities, that expert starts with the teacher.

Shared Electronic Resources

Many school districts have shared drives that contain multiple files of lesson and unit plans, curriculum maps, pacing guides, and assessment ideas. While these can be very beneficial, it is always a good idea to determine the intended use for such files and documents. The best place to start is identifying the required materials that should be used in instruction. After that, many websites contain lesson plans and instructional ideas. Be careful, though, as some websites do not monitor the information places on their servers. While a lesson may have a creative title and purpose, it may not always serve the best purpose for your instructional agenda.

When looking through shared drives, remote devices, and other online databases, it is important to understand who has posted information and what the intended use of the information is. Often times, it might be for specialized programs within the district. It is always safest to ask.

ACCURACY AND VALIDITY

The Internet contains a tremendously wide variety of information that ranges in accuracy and validity. Unlike newspapers and books that undergo a fact checker or editor, the Internet is an open forum for websites, blogs, posts, opinions and information. Students must first be made aware of this fact alone (that material posted on the Internet may or may not have been approved for content before it was available to all). For example, please make students aware that Wikipedia can be a good source of information, but that it is not edited or approved prior to publication. Then, students will need to evaluate the material for accuracy, validity, and if it suits his or her needs.

Before the lesson is introduced, information should be screened. At younger levels, students should be directed and contained to pre-selected sites, and then at older levels, students should be given possible options for sites to help in the assignment. Not only does this help save the students time from wasted searches (as they hone this skill); it keeps them on track to safe sites. Of course, even though districts typically have filters in line to keep students on safe sites, students should be closely monitored at all times when browsing the Internet.

Students should take part in the discussion of what types of sites would be considered reliable before they begin searching. Are they looking for surveys, opinions, text, or media? Then students should consider what sites are likely to be credible? In a research project on the colonization of America, would a student rather view a site from the New World Encyclopedia, PBS, and/or Joe Smith, Age 8, third grade project?

Once browsing, students should find the author's credentials (job, institution, training, etc) of each site as a first step in determining credibility. Another factor to consider is when it was written. For certain research, time will be sensitive. A third factor would be to consider for whom it was written. Knowing an author's audience will provide insight into the material that is provided. The students should also consider how comprehensive the information is, as well as how reasonable the information is when considering accuracy. Finally, students should consider utilizing multiple good quality sites to "cross check" and merge information when appropriate.

For more information on Reliability and Validity, **SEE** Skill 13.5.

Skill 9.4 **Knows how to use task-appropriate tools and procedures to synthesize knowledge, create and modify solutions and evaluate results to support the work of individuals and groups in problem-solving situations and project-based learning activities (e.g., planning, creating and editing word processing documents, spreadsheet documents and databases; using graphic tools; participating in electronic communities as learner, initiator and contributor; sharing information through online communication)**

Technological tools are varied, and to ensure that the ones selected for use in the classroom are effective at providing students with good instruction, teachers will want to think about the relationship between instructional objectives and the technological tools. Instructional technology tools can easily be divided into three primary categories: (a) instruction/practice/assessment, (b) creation, and (c) research.

INSTRUCTION/PRACTICE/ASSESSMENT TOOLS
The first category, broadly labeled instruction/practice/assessment, refers to instructional or assessment programs that students typically work on individually, sometimes in relationship to wider class activities, but often as "extra" work. This might include reading programs where all students would spend a certain amount of time per week on a particular reading practice program that may have short formative assessments. Or it could be an accelerated program or a program that is meant for students who finish assignments early. While these types of programs can have multiple benefits, they do not necessarily teach students *about* technology, as the programs are very user-friendly and straightforward.

CREATION TOOLS
The second category, creation, refers to activities where students use word processing tools, spreadsheet tools, graphic tools, or multi-media tools to either demonstrate proficiency with the technology, or more likely, to demonstrate (or practice) proficiency with a skill that can be evidenced through technology. This sounds confusing, but think of it this way: typing an essay on a word processing program is seemingly all about the task of writing (composition, grammar, etc.), but in reality, students would need to know how the technology works and how it can assist in the production of the writing. Often, graphic and multi-media programs are used in

ways that allow students to demonstrate proficiency in certain subjects in alternative or unconventional ways.

RESEARCH TOOLS
The final category would be research. This is where students use the internet, databases, or software programs to find new information. While many students are proficient with the Internet, teachers should not assume that students know how to properly research a topic online. In fact, one of the most important technological *and* literacy skills is the evaluation of written material. For example, students need to be taught how to decide whether a website on the topic they are researching is valid information or not.

USING ALL TOOLS
Bringing all these skills together in the classroom is a very tricky thing for teachers. Of course, teachers must strategize to deal with the fact that most classrooms will not have one computer per student, but that works to the advantage of a good teacher. Many of these skills can be taught in collaborative, group settings.

Finally, because the world of electronic communication is so prolific, and because the world is inter-connected, teachers have the incredible advantage of using web-based tools for communication between students all around the world—for the purpose of sharing work, asking questions, and learning in new and unique environments.

Skill 9.5 **Knows how to use productivity tools to communicate information in various formats (e.g., slide show, multimedia presentation, newsletter) and applies procedures for publishing information in various ways (e.g., printed copy, monitor display, Internet document, video)**

The tools teachers have available to them to present information to students are growing. Where just 10 years ago teachers needed to only know how to use word processing programs, grading programs, and overhead projectors, today, electronic slideshows (most people think of Power Point) are becoming the new "norm," and other methods of information distribution are expected by principals, parents, and students alike.

USING TOOLS TO COMMUNICATE
Many instructional programs include short video clips for students to help exemplify ideas. For example, many science programs include very short clips to demonstrate scientific principles. Literature programs might include short dramatizations of stories or background information on a literature selection. These tools are particularly helpful to activate "prior knowledge" for students before embarking on new topics, and they are especially important for students who are strong visual learners.

In many schools, electronic and print information from teachers is necessary for communicating things to parents. For example, since many students' parents are at work all day long, it is more efficient for parents to look online for homework assignments rather than discuss certain homework issues online. Many schools have instituted homework hotlines where teachers record homework for parents or absent students to call in and access.

In general, it is known that the more a teacher communicates with parents, the more likely parents will trust the teacher and assist the teacher in his or her methods and strategies. And parents are impressed by teachers who take the time to put together something in a professional manner. So, teachers will earn much more respect from families by providing information in a timely and professional manner.

Many teachers now also have websites where they post assignments, as well as exemplary student work, helpful websites, and other useful information. While this is a good thing, teachers will want to double-check to ensure that sensitive student information is not included on the web. Although most people would say that it is fine to include possibly a picture of the students at work in the classroom, schools are finding that having NO pictures of students—individually or in a group—is better for the protection of students.

Teachers who do now know how to use these various tools have multiple learning options. Many districts offer training seminars, community colleges offer classes that specifically teach these skills, and many websites are available with video-based tutorials.

Skill 9.6 **Knows how to incorporate the effective use of current technology; use technology applications in problem-solving and decision-making situations; implement activities that emphasize collaboration and teamwork; and use developmentally appropriate instructional practices, activities and materials to integrate the Technology Applications TEKS into the curriculum**

INCORPORATING TECHNOLOGY
Incorporating technology effectively into a fully content- and skill-based curriculum requires a good understanding of lesson objectives and how those objectives can be met with the technology. While teachers should definitely consider technological integration as an important aspect of their work in any subject and at any grade level, teachers should not include technology simply for the sake of technology. The best approach, considering all subjects can in certain ways be enhanced with technology, is for the teacher to consider a variety of lessons and units and decide which focus areas can be enhanced with technological tools.

UTILIZING COMPUTERS FOR INSTRUCTION
When dealing with large class sizes and at the same time trying to offer opportunities for students to use computers, it is often necessary to use a lot of ingenuity. If the number of computers available for student use is limited, the teacher must take a tip from elementary school teachers who are skilled at managing centers. Students can be rotated singly or in small groups to the computer centers as long as they are well oriented in advance to the task to be accomplished and with the rules to be observed. Rules for using the computer should be emphasized with the whole class prior to individual computer usage in advance and then prominently posted.

If a computer lab is available for use by the curriculum teacher, the problem of how to give each student the opportunity to use the computer as an educational tool might be alleviated, but a whole new set of problems must be dealt with. Again the rules to be observed in the computer lab should be discussed before the class ever enters the lab and students should have a thorough understanding of the assignment. When a large group of students is visiting a computer lab, it is very easy for the expensive hardware to suffer from accidental or deliberate harm if the teacher is not aware of what is going on at all times. Students need to be aware of the consequences for not following the rules because it is so tempting to experiment and show off to their peers.

Dealing with Varying Experience Levels
Unfortunately, students who have access to computers outside of school often feel like they know everything already and are reluctant to listen to instruction on lab etiquette or program usage. The teacher must be constantly on guard to prevent physical damage to the machines from foreign objects finding their way into disk drives, key caps from disappearing from keyboards (or being rearranged), or stray pencil or pen marks from appearing on computer systems.

Highly experienced students might be tempted to engage in technological activities that affect the productivity of the computers, causing the district's technology team time and energy (for example, saving games on hard drives, moving files into new directories or eliminating them altogether, creating passwords to prevent others from using machines, etc.). At the same time, the other students need a lot of assistance to prevent accidents caused by their inexperience. It is possible to pair inexperienced students with more capable ones to alleviate some of the problem. Teachers must constantly rotate around the room and students must be prepared before their arrival in the lab so that they know exactly what to do when they get there to prevent them from exercising their creativity.

COLLABORATING AND PROBLEM SOLVING
Practically, most teachers cannot assign one computer to each student in the class whenever the teacher would like to utilize computers in the classroom. But that should not matter. As technological tools are complicated and complex, pair and small group work better facilitates stronger, social-based learning. Even though teachers may assume all students know how to use various technological tools, they need to remember two very important things: First, not ALL students are proficient. Even though some highly proficient students lead teachers to believe that the entire generation of kids in schools today already understands technology, many students actually never learned it at home, and some actually do not have the tools at home due to the high costs and therefore have no opportunity to practice.

Second, not all technology skills transfer. While one student may navigate the web easily, he or she may not be able to use a word processing program with a similar level of expertise. Social opportunities to learn technology will help students to engage in a more productive, friendly, and help-centered fashion. Learning together, particularly in technology, can indeed reduce any anxiety or fear a student may have.

Teachers can consider technology learning as a method to also teach cooperation, decision-making skills, and problem-solving skills. For example, as a small group of students work together on a project on a computer, they must decide together how they will proceed and create. Teachers can instruct students in good cooperative decision-making skills to make the process easier. Students can also engage in activities where they are required to solve problems, build real-life solutions to situations, and create real-world products. Doing so will only enhance content-area instruction.

Finally, it is important to remember that as with all other learning, technological learning must be developmentally appropriate. First, realize that while very young students can perform various functions on the computer, by virtue of development level, the time required for a particular activity may be greatly increased. Also, various technological tools are simply too advanced, too fast, and too complex for very young students. It may be best to introduce basic elements of technology in the earlier grades.

SEE also Skills 5.2, 6.2, and 6.3.

Skill 9.7 **Knows how to evaluate students' technologically produced products and projects using established criteria related to design, content delivery, audience and relevance to assignment**

EVALUATING STUDENT PERFORMANCE WITH TECHNOLOGY

When teachers ask students to produce something with technology, typically to practice—and then prove proficiency—with a particular content-based skill or area of knowledge, they are giving students the opportunity to be creative with new learning. Furthermore, they are giving students the chance to utilize knowledge in authentic situations.

As with any "open-ended" assignment, teachers will be more objective in their evaluations, as well as be more specific about expectations to students, if they develop scoring criteria, rubrics, or other evaluation guides. The following elements should be considered.

Design
This is the format that the product takes. Teachers can (considering developmental level) expect that students will present information in a way that is organized, clear, and straightforward. However, with design, non-language elements, such as graphics, pictures, sounds, video, etc., students can demonstrate an added element of creativity. Furthermore, it can help to add a symbolic touch that conveys more than words can. While clarity is important, even in this regard, the use of non-linguistic material must not confuse the viewer.

Content Delivery
This refers to the method of technology used. Often, the teacher should make it clear to students what program an assignment should be completed in. For example, an essay would be better completed in a word processing program. A more creative piece should be done in a multi-media program format. Teachers can evaluate the ways in which the tool is used. So, for example, if the teacher asks students to produce something in a multi-media program, content

must be taught (say for a history lesson). But the teacher would also have to teach students how to use the program, itself. Students will end up demonstrating knowledge of the content (history), as well as the method of content delivery (the computer program).

AUDIENCE
When students focus on audience, they consider what the audience will need to comprehend. So, while a very creative student may have fun with a program and use it to do very unusual things, the student will not be evaluated highly in this regard as it does not focus on presenting information in a clear manner to the anticipated audience. Teachers do not always have to be the "audience," though. Either teachers can ask students to produce something for hypothetical situations, or they can suggest to students that their audience is the rest of the class.

RELEVANCE
This could actually be the most important element. Students may demonstrate incredible proficiency with the technological tool, but if they do not demonstrate how it was used to prove proficiency on the content, then the activity was done for the sake of the technological tool only. Teachers want to encourage students to view technology as a tool for learning, research, and presentation.

Skill 9.8   Identifies and addresses equity issues related to the use of technology

There are two primary areas of equity issues related to technology. One is the level at which students come to school with proficiency in technology. The other is the fair distribution of technology exposure to all students in a class.

TECHNOLOGICAL BACKGROUND
The first area, the level at which students come to school with a background in technology, is particularly important. First, teachers will need to understand that they have a variety of ability levels in their classrooms. Second, a lack of technological proficiency may actually be an embarrassment to students. Usually, not having technology skills can indicate that the student does not have much money—or even that the student is living in poverty.

When students come to school with a wide variety of skills, teachers need to find unique ways to provide students who have fewer skills more opportunities to learn without compromising the ability of other students to still grow in their understandings of technology. Often, group-based work can be very helpful.

ENSURING FAIR OPPORTUNITY FOR TECHNOLOGY USE
The second level of equity is ensuring that all students have similar opportunities to use technology, particularly as the students with the least home exposure will need more time. Again, a good way of dealing with this is by having students work in groups. Specific rules should be put in place to ensure that students share actual keyboard/mouse control.

TEACHER CERTIFICATION STUDY GUIDE

COMPETENCY 010 THE TEACHER MONITORS STUDENT PERFORMANCE AND ACHIEVEMENT; PROVIDES STUDENTS WITH TIMELY, HIGH-QUALITY FEEDBACK; AND RESPONDS FLEXIBLY TO PROMOTE LEARNING FOR ALL STUDENTS

Skill 10.1 Demonstrates knowledge of the characteristics, uses, advantages and limitations of various assessment methods and strategies, including technological methods and methods that reflect real-world applications

ASSESSMENTS

Assessment is observing an event and making a judgment about its status of success. There are seven purposes of assessment:

- To assist student learning
- To identify students' strengths and weaknesses
- To assess the effectiveness of a particular instructional strategy
- To assess and improve the effectiveness of curriculum programs
- To assess and improve teaching effectiveness
- To provide data that assists in decision making
- To communicate with and involve parents

There are various kinds of assessments:

1. Observation: noticing someone and judging their action
2. Informal continuous assessment:
   A. Less structured: informal continuous assessment is informal because it is informal, not formal like a test or exam; it is continuous because it occurs periodically, on a daily or weekly basis
   B. More structured: setting up assessment situations periodically; an assessment situation is an activity you organize so that the learners could be assessed—it could be a quiz, or it could also be a group activity, where the participants will be assessed
3. Formal assessment: a structured, infrequent measure of learner achievement that involves the use of test and exam; exams are used to measure the learner's progress

FORMAL ASSESSMENT

A formal assessment is highly structured, keeping the learner in mind. It must be done at regular intervals, and if the progress is not satisfactory, parent involvement is absolutely essential. An achievement test or exam measures the broader picture of knowledge acquired from cumulative learning experiences, and this type of test is a good example of formal assessment. A science project is also a formal assessment.

Whether a teacher is using criterion-referenced, norm-referenced, or performance-based data to inform and impact student learning and achievement, the more important objective is ensuring that teachers know how to effectively use the data to improve and reflect upon existing teaching instructions. The goal of identifying ways for teachers to use the school data is simple, "Is the teacher's instructional practice improving student learning goals and academic success?"

School data can include demographic profiling, cultural and ethnic academic trends, state and/or national assessments, portfolios, academic subject pre-post assessment and weekly assessments, projects, and disciplinary reports. By looking at trends and discrepancies in school data, teachers can ascertain whether they are meeting the goals and objectives of the state, national, and federal mandates for school improvement reform and curriculum implementation.

Objective Tests
Most objective tests will include multiple-choice, matching, and true/false questions that include a selection of answer choices. The correct answer can be found using a simple process of elimination of decoy or incomplete answers. Helping students review material needed for the tests and providing them sample practice questions will increase student-testing performance. Listed below are basic strategies for taking multiple choice tests such as the SAT, ACT, state tests, and class assessment:

- Read the questions and the answers thoroughly
- Look for decoy or partial answers and eliminate them
- Make an educated guess from the answers that remain
- For true/false answers, if any part of the answer given is false, then the entire answer is false, so you have a 50-50 chance of getting a correct response from true/false
- Answer the easy questions first and spend more time on the harder questions
- Listen to your gut instinct on tests; usually your first instinct is correct, but don't be afraid to second guess your gut if you know for a fact that part of the answer that you've chosen has a false component embedded in the answer

Subjective Tests
Subjective tests put the student in the driver's seat. These types of assessments usually consist of short answer, longer essays, or problem-solving questions that involve critical thinking skills and require definitive proof from the short reading passages to support your answer. Sometimes teachers provide rubrics that include assessment criteria for high-scoring answers and projects. The bottom line is studying and preparing for any type of tests will equate to better student performance and achievement on tests.

Disadvantages of Formal Assessment
There are some disadvantages to formal assessment that need to be considered. Formal assessments do not always provide a full picture of a student's capabilities. They tend have multiple choice questions and/or some written format, and they rarely challenge the student to originate their own answer, showing their depth of understanding. These tests require strict rules and circumstances for implementation, and they are difficult for students who have a hard time sitting for long periods. They are unlikely to show oral, visual, or creative abilities in students, and some experts consider these tests culturally biased. In addition, these tests can neglect the students who have solid potential but need a little support to make the most of their

education. Teachers must keep in mind that formal assessment is one component of assessment and must be combined with other types of assessment for a more accurate representation of students' abilities.

While the efficacy of the standardized tests that are being used nationally has come under attack recently, they are actually the only device for comparing where an individual student stands with a wide range of peers. They also provide a measure for a program or a school to evaluate how their own students are doing as compared to the populace at large. Even so, they should not be the only measure upon which decisions are made or evaluations drawn. There are many other instruments for measuring student achievement that the teacher needs to consult and take into account.

INFORMAL & AUTHENTIC ASSESSMENT

The purpose of informal assessment is to help students learn better. This form of assessment helps the teacher to how well the learners are learning and progressing. Informal assessment can be applied to home work assignments, field journals, and daily class work, which are good indicators of student progress and comprehension.

Authentic assessments are a type of assessment that presents students with a real-world task that they must solve by applying their knowledge and skills. Students are typically provided with a rubric or structured outline of how they will be graded. Rubrics tend to focus on performance, skills, and demonstration of knowledge, not just if a student can select a correct answer from four choices.

Informal Evaluations

At the beginning of each school term the teacher should conduct some informal evaluations in order to obtain a general awareness of his/her students. These informal evaluations should be the result of a learning activity rather than a "test" and may include classroom observations, collections of reading and writing samples, and notations about the students' cognitive abilities as demonstrated by classroom discussions and participation including the students' command of language. The value of these informal evaluations cannot be underestimated. These evaluations, if utilized effectively, will drive instruction and facilitate learning.

One of the simplest most efficient ways for the teacher to get to know his/her students is to conduct an entry survey. This is a record that provides useful background information about the students as they enter a class or school. Collecting information through an entry survey will give valuable insights into a student's background knowledge and experience. Teachers can customize entry surveys according to the type of information considered valuable. Some of the information that may be incorporated include student's name and age, family members, health factors, special interests, strengths, needs, fears, etc., parent expectations, languages spoken in the home, what the child likes about school, etc.

Disadvantages of Informal Assessment

Informal assessments do provide a picture of abilities across different formats; however, informal assessments may not measure specific retention and achievement. Informal assessments tend to be subjective and therefore are affected by the people involved. For example, if the teacher misses something in an observation or is in a bad mood when grading an essay, this may affect the outcome of the assessment. Although unprofessional, these tendencies can occur. Some informal assessments, such as reading through journals weekly, long essays, and large lab projects, are timely to score/assess.

Reading Records
A simple-to-administer, information-rich evaluation of a child's reading strengths and weaknesses is the running reading record. "This technique for recording reading behavior is the most insightful, informative, and instructionally useful assessment procedure you can use for monitoring a child's progress in learning to read" (Traill, 1993). The teacher uses a simple coding system to record what a child does while reading text out loud. At a later time, the teacher can go back to the record and assess what the child knows about reading and what the teacher needs to address in an effort to help the student become a better reader.

In later grades (fourth grade and above), a running record will not provide all of the information necessary for a teacher in understanding the ability of a student to use text for learning. It is at this point that assessment of comprehension (for both narrative and expository text) is essential. Again, commercially designed assessments can often be very effective. It is certainly possible, however, to provide students with grade-appropriate passages to informally gather information about a student's ability to understand concrete and abstract text relationships.

If the teacher is evaluating a child's writing, it is a good idea to discourage the child from erasing his/her errors and to train the child to cross out errors with a single line so that the teacher can actually see the process that the student went through to complete a writing assignment. This writing becomes an important means of getting to know about students' writing and is an effective, valuable writing evaluation. As students grow to learn more about the writing process, it is extremely valuable for the teacher to utilize all components of the writing process (i.e., brainstorming, outlining, drafting, revision and editing) when evaluating and grading students. There is much information to be gained from these steps regarding organization of thoughts and ideas, and knowledge and application of grammar, sentence, and paragraph construction.

Mathematic and Informal Evaluations
Mathematics skills can be evaluated informally by observing students as they work at their seats or perform at the board. Teachers can see if the students know basic computation skills, if they understand place value, or if they transpose numbers simply by watching them as they solve computation problems. Teachers will also see if a student struggles more or less with word problems, when a greater language component is added to the computations of mathematics. Some teachers may prefer to administer some basic computation "tests" to determine a student's mathematics strengths and weaknesses. Although these "tests" are not as effective or thorough in assessing students, they are quick and easy to administer.

CLASSROOM OBSERVATION
One of the most valuable and effective assessment tools available to any teacher is the classroom observation. As instructional decision makers, teachers must base their instructional strategies upon students' needs. An astute observer of student behaviors and performance is

most capable of choosing instructional strategies that will best meet the needs of the learners. Classroom observations take place within the context of the learning environment thus allowing the observer the opportunity to notice natural behaviors and performances.

Classroom observations should be sensitive and systematic in order to permit a constant awareness of student progress. One of the shortcomings of classroom observations is that they are often performed randomly and frequently are focused on those students whose behaviors are less than desirable. If the teacher establishes a focused observation process then observations become more valuable. It has been suggested that a teacher focus his/her observations on five or six students at a time for a period of one to two weeks.

In order for observations to truly be useful, teachers must record the information obtained from observations. When doing a formal behavioral observation, the teacher will write what the child is doing for a designated time period. At times, the teacher will tally the occurrences of specific behaviors within a designated time period. When making focused observations that are ongoing, the teacher may simply use a blank piece of paper with only the student's name and date written on it and space for the teacher to write anecdotal notes. Other teachers might write on post-it notes and put the information in a student's file. If it is not possible to record the information as it occurs and is observed, it is critical that it be recorded as soon as possible in order to maintain accuracy.

Sometimes it is helpful to do an observation simply to watch for frequency of a specific behavior. An observation can answer questions such as: is the student on-task during independent work time? Is the student interacting appropriately with peers? Is the student using materials appropriately? These behaviors can be tallied on a piece of paper with the student's name and date of observation.

Classroom observations can provide the teacher with one of the most comprehensive means of knowing their students. Teachers can observe students to see how they interact with their peers, to see which activities they choose, what they like to read, and how frequently they choose to work alone. "Everything you hear a child say and see a child do is a glimpse into a mind and a source of information to 'know' from" (Traill, 1993).

ALTERNATIVE ASSESSMENTS

Alternative assessment is an assessment where students create an answer or a response to a question or task, as opposed to traditional, inflexible assessments where students choose a prepared response from among a selection of responses, such as matching, multiple-choice or true/false. When implemented effectively, an alternative assessment approach will exhibit these characteristics, among others:

- Requires higher-order thinking and problem-solving
- Provides opportunities for student self-reflection and self-assessment
- Uses real world applications to connect students to the subject
- Provides opportunities for students to learn and examine subjects on their own, as well as to collaborate with their peers

- Encourages students to continuing learning beyond the assignment requirements
- Clearly defines objective and performance goals

TESTING MODIFICATIONS

The intent of testing modifications is to minimize the effect of a student's disability or learning challenge and to provide an equal opportunity to participate in assessments to demonstrate and express knowledge and ability. Testing modifications should be identified in the student's IEP, be consistently implemented, and should be used to the least extent possible. Types of testing modifications include:

- **Flexible Scheduling**: Providing time extensions, breaks, or altering testing duration
- **Flexible Setting**: Using special lighting or acoustics, minimizing distractions (e.g., testing the student in a separate location), using adaptive equipment.
- **Alternate Test Format**: Using large print or Braille, increasing the space allocated for student response, realigning the format of question and answer selections (e.g., vertically rather than horizontally).
- **Use of Mechanical Aids**: Using tape recorders, word processors, visual and auditory magnification devices, calculators, spell check and grammar check software (where spelling and grammar are not the focus of assessment)

For technological assessment information, **SEE** Skill 9.7

Skill 10.2 **Creates assessments that are congruent with instructional goals and objectives and communicates assessment criteria and standards to students based on high expectations for learning**

CREATING ASSESSMENTS

The purpose for testing the students is to determine the extent to which the instructional objectives have been met. Therefore, the test items must be constructed to achieve the desired outcome from the students. Gronlund and Linn advise that effective tests begin with a test plan that includes the instructional objectives and subject matter to be tested, as well as the emphasis each item should have. Having a test plan will result in valid interpretation of student achievement.

Objective Questions

After determining the content of the test, a teacher selects appropriate test items. The test items used in typical classroom tests are either objective questions or essay questions. In an objective question, the student must either supply the answer or select the answer from a number of choices. In the supply answer type of objective question, the student typically writes a short answer. For example, "_____is the author of Moby Dick" or "Who is the author of Moby Dick?" is a short answer question. The drawback to this test item is the possible ambiguity of student-supplied answers.

Another common form of objective question is the true/false test item. Gronlund and Linn point out some limitations to this test item is its susceptibility to guessing, the difficulty involved in constructing a true/false item that is valid, and the limited specific learning outcomes it can measure. However, they also point out its usefulness in identifying cause and effect relationships as well as distinguishing fact and opinion.

A third form of test item is the matching exercise. An advantage of this type of test item is its ability to test large blocks of material in a short time. The major problem with this type of test item is its emphasis on memorization. Kenneth H. Hoover does not favor this type of test item and points out that it can be appropriate when the exercise contains at least 5, but not more than 12 items, uses only homogeneous items, and contains at least three extra answers to choose from.

The most commonly used objective question where the student chooses an answer is the multiple-choice question. The multiple-choice test item consists of a stem and a list of responses, of which only one is the best answer.

The responses that are not the correct answer are called distracters. Gronlund and Linn point out that multiple-choice test items are most useful for specific learning outcomes that utilize the student's ability to understand or interpret factual information. Since the multiple-choice test item can be adopted to most subject matter, and because of its versatile nature, it is the most commonly used item on standardized tests. However, as Gronlund and Linn point out, the multiple-choice test item cannot test the ability to organize and present ideas.

Essays
The best way to test the student's ability to organize and present ideas is with the essay test item. This type of test item also utilizes the student's ability to think and problem solve. However, the main drawbacks to this type of question are the unreliability of scoring and the amount of time necessary to score the item. Nevertheless, it is valuable when the specific learning outcomes cannot be measured any other way.

Therefore, it is true that all test items have useful purposes as well as drawbacks. It is important to keep the specific learning outcome and the subject matter covered in mind when constructing each item. The effective teacher evaluates and re-evaluates each test item with each test presentation.

Skill 10.3   **Uses appropriate language and formats to provide students with timely, effective feedback that is accurate, constructive, substantive and specific**

THE IMPORTANCE OF FEEDBACK
In the old days, students expected that teachers would put a letter grade at the top of their papers and perhaps make grammatical corrections to written work. Those days are over. Teachers now are expected to provide feedback that actually helps students learn more.

The amount of time that teachers spent grading work yielded little new learning for students. The fear of a low grade alone is not viewed as sufficient to let students know what they have done well and what they need additional work on. Students need deeper interaction, particularly as areas of knowledge and skills taught are becoming more complex.

Aspects of Good Feedback

How can a teacher provide good feedback so that students will learn from their assessments? First, language should be helpful and constructive. Critical language does not necessarily help students learn. They may become defensive or hurt, and therefore, they may be more focused on the perceptions than the content. Language that is constructive and helpful will guide students to specific actions and recommendations that would help them improve in the future.

In addition, language should be specific. Specific feedback is particularly important. Comments like, "This should be clearer" and "Your grammar needs to be worked on" provide information that students may already know. They may already know they have a problem with clarity. What they can benefit from is commentary that provides very specific actions students could take to make something more clearly or to improve his or her grammar.

Teachers should also provide feedback promptly. When teachers provide timely feedback, they increase the chance that students will reflect on their thought-processes as they originally produced the work. When feedback comes weeks after the production of an assignment, the student may not remember what it is that caused him or her to respond in a particular way.

When teachers provide feedback on a set of assignments, for example, they enhance their students' learning by teaching students how to use the feedback. For example, returning a set of papers can actually do more than provide feedback to students on their initial performance. Teachers can ask students to do additional things to work with their original products, or they can even ask students to take small sections and rewrite based on the feedback. While written feedback will enhance student learning, having students do something with the feedback encourages even deeper learning and reflection.

Experienced teachers may be reading this and thinking, "When will I ever get the time to provide so much feedback?" Although detailed and timely feedback is important—and necessary—teachers do not have to provide it all the time to increase student learning. They can also teach students how to use scoring guides and rubrics to evaluate their own work, particularly before they turn it in. One particularly effective way of doing this is by having students examine models and samples of proficient work. Over years, teachers should collect samples, remove names and other identifying factors and show these to students so that they understand what is expected of them. Often, when teachers do this, they will be surprised to see how much students gain from this in terms of their ability to assess their own performance.

Finally, teachers can help students develop plans for revising and improving upon their work, even if it is not evaluated by the teacher in the preliminary stages. For example, teachers can have students keep track of words they commonly misspell, or they can have students make personal lists of areas they feel on which they need to focus.

Skill 10.4 **Knows how to promote students' ability to use feedback and self-assessment to guide and enhance their own learning**

For information on feedback, **SEE** Skill 10.3.

For information on self-assessment, **SEE** Skill 3.8.

Skill 10.5 **Responds flexibly to various situations (e.g., lack of student engagement in an activity, the occurrence of an unanticipated learning opportunity) and adjusts instructional approaches based on ongoing assessment of student performance**

ADJUSTING TO ENSURE OPTIMAL LEARNING
A teacher's ultimate goal is ensuring that students learn, and because student learning depends on many factors, including the engagement students have in a lesson, specific "teachable" moments, and other issues that arise in the learning environment, it is important that teachers pay close attention for things that might reduce optimal learning. While assessment is thought of as an official or structured activity (such as a test or an assignment), teachers must be aware of what is going on in their classrooms to promote informal and ongoing assessments.

Examples
Here's an example: say that a science teacher has prepared a lesson on a very difficult science concept. Knowing that the concept is not simple, the teacher develops a lesson that she believes is very engaging. However, half-way through the lesson, the teacher notices that students are either puzzled or bored. Realizing that continuing the lesson "as is" will not promote deep learning, the teacher immediately changes the situation and alters the lesson to promote better engagement and understanding.

Or, say that the science teacher notices that a particular student question draws great interest among other students. The question is sparked by the content, related to science, but not part of the teacher's learning objective. That teacher would be irresponsible to just move forward and ignore the question. To ignore it would be to say to students that learning is supposed to be boring and that school is not supposed to feed the intellectual interests of students. Assessing a sense of curiosity in the students, the teacher engages students in a brief answer to the question.

In another example, say the science teacher incorporated a brief experiment as a learning exercise for her particular learning objectives in that lesson. Walking around watching students, she notices that students are making incorrect attributions to the things they are finding in their experiments. The science teacher pauses the experiment and re-teaches a simple concept. Students can then proceed to finish the experiment.

Finally, say the science teacher gives a quiz on the key concepts of the past three days of experiment and the majority of students struggled with the concepts on the assessment. The teacher should revisit the confusing concepts; presenting the material in the same as well as an alternative way to help students better internalize the concept.

These examples demonstrate how an expert teacher adjusts lessons to meet the learning needs of students on an on-going basis. It proves that any well-planned lesson still may need adjustment. It also shows that the good teacher should look out for ways to make a good lesson better—even if it is in the middle of the lesson delivery.

TEACHER CERTIFICATION STUDY GUIDE

DOMAIN IV   FULFILLING PROFESSIONAL ROLES AND RESPONSIBILITIES

COMPETENCY 011   THE TEACHER UNDERSTANDS THE IMPORTANCE OF FAMILY INVOLVEMENT IN CHILDREN'S EDUCATION AND KNOWS HOW TO INTERACT AND COMMUNICATE EFFECTIVELY WITH FAMILIES

Skill 11.1   Applies knowledge of appropriate ways (including electronic communication) to work and communicate effectively with families in various situations

COMMUNICATING WITH STUDENT FAMILIES

Teachers possess a variety of methods to communicate with families. Many early childhood and elementary teachers choose to start off the year (or end the summer) with a friendly letter welcoming the students to her classroom, in addition to introducing herself to the students and their families. Many teachers choose to include their school phone number, as well as email, so parents can reach out at their earliest desire or need. In the higher grades, teachers typically provide at least a handout with their course content and contact information as a reference for parents and students. This communication sets an open and positive tone with the families so they know how to reach the teacher and that she is willing to communicate.

Another good form of communication is to set up a weekly avenue of communication. Advances in technology have made communication with parents even easier. Email can be a source of quick and effective communication (and eliminates the "I lost the note" response from students). Some teachers maintain classroom websites that list a class calendar, and sometimes even test dates, project due dates and other helpful information. Other teachers utilize online classroom management systems where attendance, grades, notes, assignments, class calendars, and more are all available in one place through a login.

SEE Skill 6.6 for information on utilizing electronic communication.

SEE also Skill 11.4 for routine communication ideas.

SEE Skill 11.5 for more information on conferences.

Skill 11.2   Engages families, parents, guardians and other legal caregivers in various aspects of the educational program

ENGAGING STUDENT FAMILIES

Research proves that the more a family is involved in a child's educational experience, the more that child will succeed academically. The problem is that often teachers assume that involvement in education simply means that the parents show up to help at school events or participate in parental activities on campus. With this belief, many teachers devise clever strategies to increase parental involvement at school. Parents are invited in to assist with workshops, attend class trips, participate as a room parents, organize special events, read to the class, speak of an occupation, help with classroom housekeeping, and more. Parents can also be involved by volunteering for the PTO/A, library help, office help, and other tasks. Some teachers plan a few events a year in the classroom for special parties, presentations and events.

However, just because a parent shows up to school and assists with an activity does not mean that the child will learn more. Many parents work all day long and cannot assist in the school. Teachers, therefore, have to think of different ways to encourage parental and family involvement in the educational process.

Communication
Quite often, teachers have great success within involving families by just informing families of what is going on in the classroom. Newsletters are particularly effective at this. Parents love to know what is going on in the classroom, and this way, they will feel included. In newsletters, for example, teachers can provide suggestions on how parents can help with the educational goals of the school. For example, teachers can recommend that parents read with their children for 20 minutes per day. To add effectiveness to that, teachers can also provide suggestions on what to do when their children come across difficult words or when they ask a question about comprehension. This gives parents practical strategies.

Parents often equate phone calls from teachers with news about misbehaviors of their children. Teachers can change that tone by calling parents with good news. Or they can send positive notes home with students. By doing this, if and when negative phone calls need to be made, teachers will have greater success.

Teachers can also provide very specific suggestions to individual parents. For example, say a student needs additional assistance in a particular subject. The teacher can provide tips to parents to encourage and increase deeper understandings in the subject outside of class.

Skill 11.3   Interacts appropriately with all families, including those that have diverse characteristics, backgrounds and needs

INTERACTING WITH STUDENT FAMILIES
Teachers today will deal with an increasingly diverse group of cultures in their classrooms. And while this is an exciting prospect for most teachers, it creates new challenges in dealing with a variety of family expectations for school and teachers. First, teachers must show respect to all parents and families. They need to set the tone that suggests that their mission is to develop students into the best people they can be. And then they need to realize that various cultures have different views of how children should be educated. **SEE** Competency 002 for further information regarding cultural differences and the implications they can have on learning and communicating.

Second, teachers will have better success when they talk personally about each student. Even though teachers may have many students, when they share personal things about each student, parents will feel more confident that their child will be "in the right hands." Third, it is very important that teachers act like they are partners in the children's education and development. Parents know their children best, and it is important to get feedback, information, and advice from them.

Finally, teachers will need to be patient with difficult families, realizing that certain methods of criticism (including verbal attacks, etc.) are unacceptable. Such circumstances would require the teacher to get assistance from an administrator. This situation, however, is very unusual, and most teachers will find that when they really attempt to be friendly and personal with parents, the parents will reciprocate and assist in the educational program.

Skill 11.4   Communicates effectively with families on a regular basis (e.g., to share information about students' progress) and responds to their concerns

THE IMPORTANT OF REGULAR COMMUNICATION

The support of the parent is an invaluable aid in the educational process. It is in the best interests of child, parent, and teacher for there to be cooperation and mutual support between parent and teacher. One of the teacher's professional responsibilities is to establish and maintain effective communication with parents. A few basic techniques to pursue are oral communication (phone calls), written communication in the form of general information classroom newsletters, notes to the parent of a particular child, and parent-teacher conferences.

Teachers should share items of interest with parents, including but not limited to, classroom rules and policies, class schedules and routines, homework expectations, communication procedures, conferences plans, and other similar information. Much of this can be done in a newsletter format sent home early in the school year. It is imperative that all such written communications be error free. It is a good idea to have another teacher read the letter before it is sent out. Good writing and clear communication are learned skills and require time and effort to develop.

When it is necessary to communicate (whether by phone, letter, or in person) with a parent regarding a concern about a student, allow a "cooling off" period before making contact with the parent. It is important to remain professional and objective. The purpose for contacting the parent is to elicit support and additional information that may have a bearing on the student's behavior or performance. Be careful to not demean the child and do not appear antagonistic or confrontational. It is also a nice courtesy to notify parents of positive occurrences with their children. The teacher's communication with parents should not be limited to negative items.

Be aware that the parent is likely to be quite uncomfortable with the bad news and will respond best if a cooperative, problem-solving approach to the issue is taken. It is also a nice courtesy to notify parents of positive occurrences with their children. The teacher's communication with parents should not be limited to negative items.

When parents contact the teacher with concerns, the teacher should respond professionally and promptly. Be sure to keep a copy of, print up, or save all correspondence with parents in the event it is needed for future reference.

Skill 11.5   Conducts effective conferences with parents, guardians and other legal caregivers

The parent-teacher conference is generally for one of three purposes. First, the teacher may wish to share information with the parents concerning the performance and behavior of the child. Second, the teacher may be interested in obtaining information from the parents about the child. Such information may help answer questions or concerns that the teacher has. A third purpose may be to request parent support or involvement in specific activities or requirements. In many situations, more than one of the purposes may be involved.

PLANNING THE CONFERENCE
When a conference is scheduled, whether at the request of the teacher or parent, the teacher should allow sufficient time to prepare thoroughly. Collect all relevant information, samples of student work, records of behavior, and other items needed to help the parent understand the circumstances. It is also a good idea to compile a list of questions or concerns you wish to address. Arrange the time and location of the conference to provide privacy and to avoid interruptions.

CONDUCTING THE CONFERENCE
Begin the conference by putting the parents as ease. Take the time to establish a comfortable mood, but do not waste time with unnecessary small talk. Begin the discussion with positive comments about the student. Identify strengths and desirable attributes but do not exaggerate.

As issues or areas of concern are addressed, be sure to focus on observable behaviors and concrete results or information. Do not make judgmental statements about parent or child. Share specific work samples, anecdotal records of behavior, etc., which demonstrate clearly the concerns you about the student. Be a good listener and hear the parent's comments and explanations. Such background information can be invaluable in understanding the needs and motivations of the child.

Finally, end the conference with an agreed plan of action between parents and teacher (and, when appropriate, the student). Bring the conference to a close politely but firmly, and thank the parents for their involvement.

AFTER THE CONFERENCE
A day or two after the conference, it is a good idea to send a follow-up note to the parents. In this note, briefly and concisely reiterate the plan or step agreed to in the conference. Be polite and professional; avoid the temptation to be too informal or chatty. If the issue is a long-term one, such as the behavior or on-going work performance of the student, make periodic follow-up contacts to keep the parents informed of the progress.

Skill 11.6 **Effectively uses family support resources (e.g., community, interagency) to enhance family involvement in student learning**

According to Campbell, Campbell, and Dickinson (1992) "Teaching and Learning Through Multiple Intelligences," "The changing nature of demographics is one of the strongest rationales for multicultural education in the United States." The Census Bureau predicts a changing demographic for the American population and school communities that will include a forecast between 1990 and 2030, that "while the white population will increase by 25%, the African American population will increase by 68%, the Asian-American, Pacific Island, and American Indian by 79%, and the Hispanic-American population by 187%." Reinforcing the learning beyond the classroom must include a diversity of instructional and learning strategies for any adult role models in a student's life.

TECHNOLOGY AND MENTORING

Mentoring has become an instrumental tool in addressing student achievement and access to learning. Adult mentors work individually with identified students on specific subject areas to reinforce the learning through tutorial instruction and application of knowledge. Providing students with adult role models to reinforce the learning has become a crucial instructional strategy for teachers seeking to maximize student learning beyond the classroom. Students who work with adult mentors from culturally diverse backgrounds are given a multicultural aspect of learning that is cooperative and multi-modal in personalized instruction.

The interpersonal use of technology provides a mentoring tutorial support system and different conceptual learning modalities for students seeking to understand classroom material. Technology provides a networking opportunity for students to find study buddies and peer study groups, along with free academic support to problem-solve and develop critical thinking skills that are imperative in acquiring knowledge and conceptual learning. Distance Learning is a technological strategy that keeps students and teachers interactively communicating about issues in the classroom and beyond. Students will communicate more freely using technology to ask teacher or adult mentors clarity questions than they will in a classroom of peers and the typical insecurities that typify teenage development and learning acquisition.

Connecting with community resources will also provide viable avenues of support in helping students who need additional academic remediation access learning. There are diverse programs that are offered through the local universities and community agencies that connect college students or working adults with subject areas and classrooms in need of additional student interns/adult volunteers to support the academic programs in school communities.

THE COMMUNITY AS A RESOURCE

The community is a vital link to increasing learning experiences for students. Community resources can supplement the minimized and marginal educational resources of school communities. With state and federal educational funding becoming increasingly subject to legislative budget cuts, school communities welcome the financial support that community resources can provide in terms of discounted prices on high end supplies (e.g. computers, printers, and technology supplies), along with providing free notebooks, backpacks, and student supplies for low-income students who may have difficulty obtaining the basic supplies for school.

Community stores can provide cash rebates and teacher discounts for educators in struggling school districts and compromised school communities. Both professionally and personally, communities can enrich the student learning experiences by including the following support strategies:

- Provide programs that support student learning outcomes and future educational goals
- Create mentoring opportunities that provide adult role models in various industries to students interested in studying in that industry
- Provide financial support for school communities to help low-income or homeless students begin the school year with the basic supplies
- Develop paid internships with local university students to provide tutorial services for identified students in school communities who are having academic and social difficulties processing various subject areas
- Provide parent-teen-community forums to create public voice of change in communities
- Offer parents without computer or Internet connection stipends to purchase technology to create equitable opportunities for students to do research and complete word.doc paper requirements
- Stop in classrooms and ask teachers and students what's needed to promote academic progress and growth

Community resources are vital in providing that additional support to students, school communities, and families, particularly those struggling to remain engaged or in declining educational institutions competing for federal funding and limited district funding. The commitment that a community shows to its educational communities is a valuable investment in the future. Community resources that are able to provide additional funding for tutors in marginalized classrooms or help schools reduce classrooms of students needing additional remedial instruction directly impact educational equity and facilitation of teaching and learning for both teachers and students.

PROMOTING A SENSE OF COMMUNITY
The bridge to effective learning for students begins with a collaborative approach by all stakeholders that support the educational needs of students. Underestimating the power and integral role of the community institutions in impacting the current and future goals of students can carry high stakes for students beyond the high school years who are competing for college access, student internships, and entry level jobs in the community. Researchers have shown that school involvement and connections with community institutions yield greater retention rates of students graduating and seeking higher education experiences. The current disconnect and autonomy that has become commonplace in today's society must be reevaluated in terms of promoting tomorrow's citizens.

When community institutions provide students and teachers with meaningful connections and input, the commitment is apparent in terms of volunteering, loyalty and professional promotion.

Providing students with placements in leadership positions such as the ASB (Associated Student Body); the PTSA (Parent Teacher Student Association); school boards; neighborhood sub-committees addressing political or social issues; or government boards that impact and influence school communities creates an avenue for students to explore ethical, participatory, collaborative, transformational leadership that can be applied to all areas of a student's educational and personal life.

Community liaisons provide students with opportunities to experience accountability and responsibility so that students learn about life and how organizations work with effective communication and teams working together to accomplish goals and objectives. Teaching students skills of inclusion and social and environmental responsibility and creating public forums that represent student voice and vote foster student interest and access to developing and reflecting on individual opinions and understanding the dynamics of the world around them.

When a student sees that the various support systems are in place and consistently working as a team to effectively provide resources and avenues of academic promotion and accountability, students have no fear of taking risks to grow by becoming a teen voice on a local committee about "Teen Violence" or volunteering in a local hospice for young children with terminal diseases. The linkages of community institutions provide role-models of a world in which the student will soon become an integral and vital member, so being a part of that world as a student makes the transition easier as a young adult.

COMPETENCY 012 THE TEACHER ENHANCES PROFESSIONAL KNOWLEDGE AND SKILLS BY EFFECTIVELY INTERACTING WITH OTHER MEMBERS OF THE EDUCATIONAL COMMUNITY AND PARTICIPATING IN VARIOUS TYPES OF PROFESSIONAL ACTIVITIES

Skill 12.1 Interacts appropriately with other professionals in the school community (e.g., vertical teaming, horizontal teaming, team teaching, mentoring)

PROFESSIONAL GROWTH

Part of being an effective teacher is to not only get students to grow educationally but to allow oneself to grow as well. Working with other members of the school community—peers, supervisors, and other staff—will give provide the grounding needed to increase skills and knowledge sets. Identifying possible mentors, such as respected teachers and ones that should be emulated, is one step. Search out other teachers who have had an amount of success in the desired areas. Ask them questions and for advice on brushing up lesson plans. Talk to a supervisor or the principal when experiencing difficulties or when there is more to be learned. They may know of development training seminars, books, journals, or other resources that might help.

Vertical Teaming

Many school districts have implemented teaming systems that encourage teachers working interactively with each other and the other professional in the schools. One example of this is vertical teaming where groups of educators of the same discipline but from different grade levels work cooperatively to plan curriculum, units, and lessons across multiple grade levels to ensure an effective flow of instruction. For example, a team of middle school science teachers would team together, at least one from each grade level, to develop, plan, organize, and implement the science curriculum for students' entire "stay" at that school building. This planning eliminates repeat of material and encourages all teachers to utilize higher-ordered and critical thinking skills throughout each year of the curriculum.

Horizontal Teaming

Another teaming example is horizontal teaming. In this system, teachers in one grade level work to integrate all of the subjects taught across the grade. For example, in a team of four fifth grade teachers, teachers may collaborate to find the connections between language arts, science, math, and social studies to present interdisciplinary instruction across the entire fifth grade level. Then, each teacher implements instruction by teaching one of the subjects to all four sections of fifth grade. This system cuts down on planning for each teacher and encourages solid educational connections between subjects and material, therefore enhancing the real-life applications of the material, as well as student interest.

Team Teaching

Team teaching is another teaming option. Team teaching consists of two or more teachers involved in the classroom instruction. In this system, teachers share the roles of instructor, monitor, and additional supporter, etc. to share the instructional workload and increase individual student achievement. In this model, teachers must be clear with one another regarding objectives, roles, and assessment so each teacher can conduct his or her role most effectively.

Mentoring Systems

Mentoring systems are another important element in schools. New teachers tend to be overwhelmed with the start of their first few school years and having guidance from an experienced teacher can help them navigate their new responsibilities. Mentors can offer guidance in all areas including classroom setup, materials, organization, classroom management, curriculum implementation, planning, and events such as "Back To School" night, staff responsibilities, and emotional support. Research supports that implementing strong and effective mentoring programs benefits the new teachers, as well as the student achievement in the new teacher's classroom.

Teachers should remember that they are part of a team of professionals, and that their personal success is part of a greater success that everyone hopes to achieve.

Skill 12.2   Maintains supportive, cooperative relationships with professional colleagues and collaborates to support students' learning and to achieve campus and district goals

The teacher is the manager of his classroom. If teachers are sharing the same student, they can, together, develop a strategy for dealing with that student. The same is true of parents. That relationship must not be adversarial unless there is no other way to handle the student and the situation. In communications with other teachers, administration, and parents, respectful, reciprocal communication solves many problems.

COLLABORATION

Collaboration is a powerful tool to build a professional learning community. When teachers work together on lesson and unit planning, they learn new techniques, test ideas on each other, and develop stronger instructional methods. Many researchers say that collaborating can be more powerful in instructional practice than attending professional development. This is because people learn in a more natural setting and can get assistance from those who give them the new ideas.

SEE also Skills 12.1 and 12.3.

Skill 12.3   Knows the roles and responsibilities of specialists and other professionals at the building and district levels (e.g., department chairperson, principal, board of trustees, curriculum coordinator, technology coordinator, special education professional)

While teachers often find that they spend considerable time in their classrooms with children, schools are organized in such a way that many groups of people have important and powerful roles. Some people are specialists and are meant to assist teachers in their work. Specialists are certified teachers who specialize in certain learning needs. Others are administrators (or various levels of administrators) that run the school programs. And others are board members or district officials that oversee all schools in the district. This section will look at each group in particular.

SPECIAL EDUCATION & CHILD STUDY TEAMS
Special education teachers are specialists with students who may have learning or physical disabilities. Reading specialists focus on students who need additional assistance in reading. Special education teachers work with regular education teachers, as well as other school staff, to develop, implement, and evaluate students with special needs. Special education teachers play an important role in the development and implementation of each student's 504 plan or Individualized Education Plan (IEP). These plans are legal documents stating the educational, behavioral, objectives, and goals for each student.

Gifted and talented teachers are included in this group, as they oversee the individual needs of students with specific, advanced abilities.

Many schools have Child Study Teams made up of additional professionals who aid students with various needs. These often include the students' teachers, parents, and the inclusion of necessary professionals which could include occupational therapists, special education teachers, speech therapists, guidance counselors, and school psychologists.

CURRICULUM COORDINATOR
Curriculum coordinators serve as the leader in the development and implementation of a subject. These professionals work with teachers who are involved in instruction of a particular subject. For example, the Language Arts Curriculum Coordinator would ensure that all the teachers who teach language arts understand the curriculum, have the materials to implement the curriculum, plan and conduct professional development, update curriculum, and so on.

TECHNOLOGY COORDINATOR
Technology coordinators either work entirely at one school, or they work for a variety of schools within a district. These people develop programs and assist teachers in the use of technology or curricular programs.

ADMINISTRATORS
While most people might be able to identify the principal or assistant principal, some people hold more specific administrative positions. Sometimes, schools will hire people to administer programs such as Title I (additional resources for students who live in impoverished conditions). Or an "instructional coach" might have administrative duties, while also assisting teachers with particular areas of instruction. Department chairs, particularly in junior highs/middle schools and high schools, carry some administrative weight, as they have to organize and manage all the teachers in large departments of teachers.

NOTE: Some schools consider instructional coaches and department chairs as administrators, while some consider them to be specialists. Some schools even consider them in a totally separate function, volunteers.

The district will have various administrators (for example, the superintendent) and board members. While the administrators of the district are in charge of all schools in the district—and all principals—they also want to ensure that parents and community members are satisfied with the local school system.

The Board of Education (Board of Trustees) is responsible for working with the school in matters concerning the "business" of running a school. It is typically comprised of elected community members who are involved matters regarding school governance, administration and personnel, fiscal management, educational programming, and school-community relations. Board members are voted on in regular elections. Often, they represent parents or community members. Their goal is ensuring that the schools operate in a way that reflects community wishes. If the schools do not operate as the community desires, they do not get re-elected.

PARENT-TEACHER ORGANIZATIONS

Most schools have some form of a parent-teacher organization (PTO, PTA, etc) where active parents volunteer for various events and needs at the school and are dedicated to promoting the well-being of the students at the school. Typically, PTO members organize fundraising, school events, and social events for students, educational speakers, book fairs, and more. These volunteers are often organized to help volunteer in the library, office, classrooms or where they are needed.

Skill 12.4   Understands the value of participating in school activities and contributes to school and district (e.g., by participating in decision making and problem solving, sharing ideas and expertise, serving on committees, volunteering to participate in events and projects)

SCHOOL COMMUNITY INVOLVEMENT

Schools are communities of learners. Gone are the days when teachers are considered to be the people with all the knowledge and students to be the people who have limited amounts of knowledge. Today, schools attempt to be "professional learning communities" where teachers, parents, administrators, and specialists work together to learn about new and exciting methods of instruction and better ways of addressing student needs. For a school to be considered a professional learning community, teachers need to see their environment not just as the classroom but as the entire school. Many school administrators do depend on teachers working together to make decisions. Not because they need extra people to make decisions but because they believe that when teachers are invested in their schools, teachers will work more productively to make their schools powerful places of learning for all students.

When teachers get involved in the operations of the school by serving on committees, volunteering for projects, and participating in problem solving and decision making, they influence the direction of the school in terms of the needs the teachers see for the school. As teachers are the ones dealing with students on a daily basis, they see what needs to be done to assist the school in providing the best educational opportunities for their students. By being so involved, they will bring new ideas and effective strategies to help the whole school develop into an extremely effective organization.

Skill 12.5   Uses resources and support systems effectively (e.g., mentors, service centers, state initiatives, universities) to address professional development needs

PROFESSIONAL DEVELOPMENT
The level of knowledge available to teachers to improve practice is unprecedented. New knowledge is widely available in instructional methods, content, and child development. Teachers could continue to learn more and more and still be far behind the most current understandings of educational practice. To make the most of all this new knowledge, particularly as teachers have limited time, teachers should be strategic about how they pursue new knowledge and support.

The implementation of an integrated approach to professional development is a critical component to ensuring success of programs for students. It involves teachers, parents, and other community members working together to develop appropriate programs to ensure students are receiving the necessary instruction to be successful in the future workforce.

In addition to coaches, mentors can be assigned to teachers to provide suggestions and feedback outside of the classroom. While the mentor may not be in the actual classroom, he or she can still review lesson strategies, provide new techniques, and be a critical listener. For more information on mentors, **SEE** Skill 12.1.

Development Outside of the School
Outside of the school, service centers provide professional development opportunities. Often, teachers can get this information through principals and other school administrators. Usually, these service centers will provide workshops on specific instructional topics. While teachers may need to get permission to attend, these types of workshops can be very effective at giving teachers good strategies to use in their classrooms.

State initiatives often provide unique ways of approaching common educational problems. For example, many schools get extra funding for reading programs, community service learning programs, and math programs. These programs typically involve intensive teacher learning.

Finally, universities often are looking for schools and classrooms to experiment in. When teachers get opportunities to participate, they will definitely be amazed at what can happen. Usually, universities are hoping to test new strategies and activities with students. While teachers learn new techniques, the universities get terrific data.

In general, teachers really need to consider themselves as life-long learners. As a teacher, there is no end to learning.

SEE also Skill 12.8.

Skill 12.6 Recognizes characteristics, goals and procedures associated with teacher appraisal and uses appraisal results to improve teaching skills

TEACHER EVALUATIONS

Often, teachers are fearful about being evaluated by their principals. However, most principals are not out to criticize teachers or find fault with their methods. They simply want to help all teachers be successful in their jobs. A teacher appraisal is merely a method of "assessing" a teacher and providing them with feedback to help them improve practice.

Usually, the process begins with principals working on particular goals and objectives that teachers will work to attain throughout the year. These goals and objectives typically are the things that principals will look to see improvement on within the school year.

Some key recommendations for teacher appraisal will help to alleviate the concern teachers have about the process, and it will help them get the most out of the process. Second, teachers should consider areas that the principal can be of assistance in. For example, if a teacher feels uncomfortable with something that the principal will observe, the teacher may see an appraisal as a perfect opportunity to ask to attend professional development activities. Principals will most likely see such a request as a good thing. It shows initiative and desire to improve.

Finally, teachers should be proactive about getting support from other teachers, mentors, and instructional coaches when they feel they have areas in which they need significant work.

Skill 12.7 Works productively with supervisors, mentors and other colleagues to address issues and to enhance professional knowledge and skills

SEE Skills 12.1, 12.5 and 12.8.

Skill 12.8 Understands and uses professional development resources (e.g., mentors and other support systems, conferences, online resources, workshops, journals, professional associations, coursework) to enhance knowledge, pedagogical skills and technological expertise

PROFESSIONAL DEVELOPMENT OPPORTUNITIES

Professional development opportunities for teacher performance improvement or enhancement in instructional practices are essential for creating comprehensive learning communities. In order to promote the vision, mission, and action plans of school communities, teachers must be given the toolkits to maximize instructional performances. The development of student-centered learning communities that foster the academic capacities and learning synthesis for all students should be the fundamental goal of professional development for teachers.

The level of professional development may include traditional district workshops that enhance instructional expectations for teachers or the more complicated multiple day workshops given by national and state educational organizations to enhance the federal accountability of skill and professional development for teachers. Most workshops on the national and state level provide clock hours that can be used to renew certifications for teachers every five years. Typically, 150 clock hours is the standard certification number needed to provide a five-year certification renewal, so teachers must attend and complete paperwork for a diversity of workshops that range from 1–50 clock hours according to the timeframe of the workshops.

Most districts and schools provide in-service professional development opportunities for teachers during the school year dealing with district objectives/expectations and relevant workshops or classes that can enhance the teaching practices for teachers. Clock hours are provided with each class or workshop, and the type of professional development being offered to teachers determines clock hours. Each year, schools are required to report the number of workshops, along with the participants attending the workshops to the superintendent's office for filing. Teachers collecting clock hour forms are required to file the forms to maintain certification eligibility and job eligibility.

School data can include demographic profiling, cultural and ethnic academic trends, state and/or national assessments, portfolios, academic subject pre-post assessment and weekly assessments, projects, and disciplinary reports. By looking at trends and discrepancies in school data, teachers can ascertain whether they are meeting the goals and objectives of the state, national, and federal mandates for school improvement reform and curriculum implementation.

When a teacher is involved in the process of self-reflection and self-assessment, one of the common outcomes is that the teacher comes to identify areas of skill or knowledge that require more research or improvement on her part. She may become interested in overcoming a particular weakness in her performance or may decide to attend a workshop or consult with a mentor to learn more about a particular area of concern.

For information on mentors, **SEE** Skill 12.1

For information on conferences, **SEE** Skill 11.5.

For information on online resources, **SEE** Skill 9.6.

For more information on professional development, **SEE** Skill 12.5.

Skill 12.9   **Engages in reflection and self-assessment to identify strengths, challenges and potential problems; improve teaching performance; and achieve professional goals**

It is important for teachers to involve themselves in constant periods of reflection and self-reflection to ensure they are meeting the needs of the students.

SEE Skill 3.3.

TEACHER CERTIFICATION STUDY GUIDE

COMPETENCY 013 **THE TEACHER UNDERSTANDS AND ADHERES TO LEGAL AND ETHICAL REQUIREMENTS FOR EDUCATORS AND IS KNOWLEDGEABLE OF THE STRUCTURE OF EDUCATION IN TEXAS**

Skill 13.1 Knows legal requirements for educators (e.g., those related to special education, students' and families' rights, student discipline, equity, child abuse) and adheres to legal guidelines in education-related situations

KNOWLEDGE OF STUDENT RESOURCES

One of the first things that a teacher learns is how to obtain resources and help for his/her students. All schools have guidelines for receiving this assistance especially since the implementation of the Americans with Disabilities Act. The first step in securing help is for the teacher to approach the school's administration or exceptional education department for direction in attaining special services or resources for qualifying students. Many schools have a committee designated for addressing these needs such as a Child Study Team or Core Team. These teams are made up of both regular and exceptional education teachers, school psychologists, guidance counselors, and administrators. The particular student's classroom teacher usually has to complete some initial paper work and will need to do some behavioral observations.

The teacher will take this information to the appropriate committee for discussion and consideration. The committee will recommend the next step to be taken. Often subsequent steps include a complete psychological evaluation along with certain physical examinations such as vision and hearing screening and a complete medical examination by a doctor.

The referral of students for this process is usually relatively simple for the classroom teacher and requires little more than some initial paper work and discussion. The services and resources the student receives as a result of the process typically prove to be invaluable to the student with behavioral disorders.

Going Beyond the School System

At times, the teacher must go beyond the school system to meet the needs of some students. An awareness of special services and resources and how to obtain them is essential to all teachers and their students. When the school system is unable to address the needs of a student, the teacher often must take the initiative and contact agencies within the community. Frequently there is no special policy for finding resources. It is simply up to the individual teacher to be creative and resourceful and to find whatever help the student needs. Meeting the needs of all students is certainly a team effort that is most often spearheaded by the classroom teacher.

FAMILY INVOLVEMENT

Under the IDEA, parent/guardian involvement in the development of the student's IEP is required and absolutely essential for the advocacy of the disabled student's educational needs. IEPs must be tailored to meet the student's needs, and no one knows those needs better than the parent/guardian and other significant family members. Optimal conditions for a disabled student's education exist when teachers, school administrators, special education professionals, and parents/guardians work together to design and execute the IEP.

DUE PROCESS
Under the IDEA, Congress provides safeguards for students against schools' actions, including the right to sue in court, and encourages states to develop hearing and mediation systems to resolve disputes. No student or their parents/guardians can be denied due process because of disability.

INCLUSION, MAINSTREAMING, AND LEAST RESTRICTIVE ENVIRONMENT
Inclusion, mainstreaming, and least restrictive environment are interrelated policies under the IDEA, with varying degrees of statutory imperatives.

- Inclusion is the right of students with disabilities to be placed in the regular classroom
- Least restrictive environment is the mandate that children be educated to the maximum extent appropriate with their non-disabled peers
- Mainstreaming is a policy where disabled students can be placed in the regular classroom, as long as such placement does not interfere with the student's educational plan

ASPECTS OF DEALING WITH STUDENT NEEDS
Listed below are some important areas to keep in mind when addressing student needs and resources.

Services and Physical accommodations

- Services needed by the student are available (e.g. health, physical, occupational, or speech therapy).
- Accommodations to the physical plant and equipment are adequate to meet the students' needs (e.g. toys, building and playground facilities, learning materials, assistive devices).

School Support

- The principal understands the needs of students with disabilities
- Adequate numbers of personnel, including aides and support personnel, are available
- Adequate staff development and technical assistance, based on the needs of the school personnel, are being provided (e.g. information on disabilities, instructional methods, awareness and acceptance activities for students and team-building skills)
- Appropriate policies and procedures for monitoring individual student progress, including grading and testing are in place

Collaboration

- Special educators are part of the instructional or planning team
- Teaming approaches are used for program implementation and problem solving
- Regular teachers, special education teachers, and other specialists collaborate (e.g. co-teach, team teach, work together on teacher assistance teams)

Instructional Methods

- Teachers have the knowledge and skills needed to select and adapt curricular and instructional methods according to individual student needs
- A variety of instructional arrangements is available (e.g. team teaching, cross-grade grouping, peer tutoring, teacher assistance teams)
- Teachers foster a cooperative learning environment and promote socialization

ABUSE SITUATIONS

The child who is undergoing the abuse is the one whose needs must be served first. A suspected case gone unreported may destroy a child's life, and their subsequent life as a functional adult. It is the duty of any citizen who suspects abuse and neglect to make a report to their administrator/child protective services (an organization which identifies and handles cases of abuse), and it is especially important and required for state licensed and certified persons to make a report. All reports can be kept confidential if required, but it is best to disclose one's identity in case more information is required. This is a personal matter that has no impact on qualifications for license or certification. Failure to make a report when abuse or neglect is suspected is punishable by revocation of certification and license, a fine, and criminal charges.

It is the right of any accused individual to have counsel and make a defense, as in any matter of law. The procedure for reporting makes clear the rights of the accused, who stands before the court innocent until proven guilty, with the right to representation, redress and appeal, as in all matters of United States law. The state is cautious about receiving spurious reports but investigates any that seem real enough. Some breaches of standards of decency are not reportable offenses, such as possession of pornography that is not hidden from children. But teachers should make the report, and let the counselor make the decision. In this case, a teacher's conscience is clear, and they will have followed all procedures that keep them from liability. The obligation to report is immediate when abuse is suspected.

There is no time given as an acceptable or safe period of time to wait before reporting, so hesitation to report may be a cause for action. One should not wait once suspicion is firm. Reasonable suspicion is all that is needed, not actual proof, which is the job for the investigators.

EMOTIONAL DISTURBANCES

Many safe and helpful interventions are available to the classroom teacher when dealing with a student who is suffering serious emotional disturbances. First, and foremost, the teacher must maintain open communication with the parents and other professionals who are involved with the student whenever overt behavior characteristics are exhibited. Students with behavior disorders need constant behavior modification, which may involve two-way communication between the home and school on a daily basis.

The teacher should also initiate a behavior modification program for any student that might show emotional or behavioral disorders. Such behavior modification plans can be effective means of preventing deviant behavior. If deviant behavior does occur, the teacher should have arranged for a safe and secure time-out place where the student can go for a respite and an opportunity to regain self-control. Often when a behavior disorder is more severe, the student must be involved in a more concentrated program aimed at alleviating deviant behavior such as psychotherapy. In such instances, the school psychologist, guidance counselor, or behavior specialist is directly involved with the student and provides counseling and therapy on a regular basis. Frequently, they are also involved with the student's family.

As a last resort, many families are turning to drug therapy. Once viewed as a radical step, administering drugs to children to balance their emotions or control their behavior has become a widely used form of therapy. Of course, only a medical doctor can prescribe such drugs. Great care must be exercised when giving pills to children in order to change their behavior, especially since so many medicines have undesirable side effects. It is important to know that these drugs relieve only the symptoms of behavior and do not get at the underlying causes. Parents and teachers need to be educated as to the side effects of these medications.

Skill 13.2 **Knows and adheres to legal and ethical requirements regarding the use of educational resources and technologies (e.g., copyright, Fair Use, data security, privacy, acceptable use policies)**

KNOWLEDGE OF COPYRIGHT LAWS

The advent of technology that made copying print and non-print media efficient poses serious concern for educators who unwittingly or otherwise violate copyright law on a regular basis. Regardless of their intentions to provide their students access to materials that may be too costly for mass purchase, educators must understand the reasons for copyright protection, and they must, by example, ensure the upholding of that protection.

There are many fine publications that clarify copyright law for educators. In many instances, school districts endorse these publications or provide their own concise summaries for reference. Though all educators should be cognizant of the law, it becomes the responsibility of the school library media specialist to help inform colleagues and monitor the proper application of the law.

Actually, educators have the benefit of greater leeway in copying than any other group. Many print instructional materials carry statements that allow production of multiple copies for classroom use, provided they adhere to the "Guidelines for Classroom Copying in Nonprofit Educational Institutions." Teachers may duplicate enough copies to provide one per student per course, provided that they meet the tests of brevity, spontaneity, and cumulative effect.

Brevity Test
These are the brevity requirements for materials that can be copied.

- **Poetry**: suggested maximum 250 words
- **Prose**: one complete essay, story, or article less than 2500 words <u>or</u> excerpts of no more than 1000 words or 10% of the work, whichever is less (Children's books with text under 2500 words may not be copied in their entirety; no more than two pages containing 10% of the text may be copied.
- **Illustration**: charts, drawings, cartoons, etc. are limited to one per book or periodical article

Spontaneity Test
Normally copying that does not fall under the brevity test requires publisher's permission for duplication. However, allowances are made if "the inspiration and decision to use the work" occur too soon prior to classroom use for permission to be sought in writing.

Cumulative Effect Test
Even in the case of short poems or prose, it is preferable to make only one copy. However, three short items from one work are allowable during one class term. Reuse of copied material from term to term is expressly forbidden. Compilation of works into anthologies to be used in place of purchasing texts is prohibited.

HISTORY OF COPYRIGHT AND FAIR USE LAWS
Copyright legislation has existed in the United States for more than 100 years. Conflicts over copyright were settled in the courts. The Copyright Act, especially section 107 dealing with Fair use, created legislative criteria to follow based on judicial precedents. In 1978, when the law took effect, it set regulations for duration and scope of copyright, specified author rights, and set monetary penalties for infringement. The statutory penalty may be waived by the court for an employee of a non-profit educational institution where the employee can prove fair use intent.

Fair use, especially important to educators, is meant to create a balance between copyright protection and the needs of learners for access to protected material. Fair use is judged by the purpose of the use, the nature of the work (whether creative or informational), the quantity of the work for use, and the market effect. In essence, if a <u>portion</u> of a work is used to benefit the learner with no intent to deprive the author of his profits, fair use is granted.

Recently, Fair Use has been challenged most in cases of videotaping off-air of television programs. Guidelines, too numerous to delineate here, affect copying audio-visual materials and computer software. Most distributors place written regulations in the packaging of these products. Allowances for single back-up copies in the event of damage to the original are granted.

Section 108 is pertinent to libraries in that it permits reproducing a single copy of an entire work if no financial gain is derived, if the library is public or archival, and if the copyright notice appears on all copies.

In any event in which violation of the law is a concern, the safest course of action is to seek written permission from the publisher of the copyrighted work. If permission is granted, a copy of that permission should accompany any duplicates.

COURSE OF ACTION REGARDING A VIOLATION OF COPYRIGHT

When a suspected infringement of copyright is brought to the attention of the school library media specialist, certain procedures should be followed.

1. Determine if a violation has in effect occurred. Never accuse or report alleged instances to a higher authority without verification.
2. If an instance is verified, tactfully inform the violator of the specific criteria to use so that future violations can be avoided. Presented properly, the information will be accepted as constructive.
3. If advice is unheeded and further infractions occur, bring them to the attention of the teacher's supervisor (a team leader or department chair) who can handle the matter as an evaluation procedure.
4. Inform the person who has reported the alleged violation of the procedures being used.

JUDICIAL RULINGS THAT HAVE IMPACTED LIBRARY MEDIA ISSUES

Copyright and Fair Use

Judicial rulings have come in the area of copyright issues. The 1975 ruling in the case of Williams & Wilkins Co. v. U.S. provided guidance to legislators in preparing the fair use provisions of the 1976 Copyright Act. It ruled that entire articles may be mass-duplicated for use, which advances the public welfare without doing economic harm to the publishers. This ruling provides encouragement to educators that fair use may be interpreted more liberally.

In 1984, the ruling in the Sony Corp. of America v. Universal City Studios, Inc. placed the burden of proving infringement on the plaintiff. The Supreme Court upheld the right of individuals to off-air videotape television programs for non-commercial use. Thus, a copyright holder must prove that the use of videotaped programming is intentionally harmful. Civil suits against educators would require the plaintiff to prove that the existing or potential market would be negatively affected by use of these programs in a classroom setting.

Current fair use practice specifies that a videotaped copy must be shown within 10 days of its airing and be kept no longer than 45 days for use in constructing supplemental teaching materials related to the programming.

Censorship

Court rulings have ambiguously addressed the issue of censorship. In 1972, the U.S. Court of Appeals for the Second Circuit (President's Council v. Community School Board No. 25, New York City) ruled in favor of the removal of a library book, reasoning that its removal did not oppose or aid religion.

TEACHER CERTIFICATION STUDY GUIDE

In 1976, the Court of Appeals for the Sixth Circuit (Minarcini v. Strongsville City School District) ruled against the removal of Joseph Heller's *Catch 22* and two Kurt Vonnegut novels on the grounds that removal of books from a school library is a burden on the freedom of classroom discussion and an infringement of the First Amendment's guarantee of an individual's "right to know." The Board of the City of Chelsea ordered the school board to return to the high school library a poetry anthology which contained "objectionable and filthy" language. The court asserted that the school had control over curriculum but not library collections.

Three cases in the 1980s dealt with challenging the removal of materials from high school libraries. The first two, in circuit courts, condemned the burning of banned books (Zykan v. Warsaw Community School Corporation, Indiana) and the removal of books of considerable literary merit. The case of Board of Education, Island Trees Union Free School District 26 (New York) v. Pico reached the Supreme Court in 1982 after the U.S. Court of Appeals for the Second Circuit had reversed a lower court ruling granting the school board the right to remove nine books which had been deemed "anti-American, anti-Semitic, anti-Christian and just plain filthy." The Supreme Court, in a 5-4 ruling, upheld the Court of Appeals ruling, and the nine books were returned.

The dissenting opinion, however, continued to foster ambiguity claiming that, if the intent was to deny free access to ideas, it was an infringement of the First Amendment, but if the intent was to remove pervasively vulgar material, the board had just cause. Ultimately, the issue hinged on a school board's authority in determining the selection of optional rather than required reading. Library books, being optional, should not be denied to users.

Skill 13.3 **Applies knowledge of ethical guidelines for educators in Texas (e.g., those related to confidentiality, interactions with students and others in the school community), including policies and procedures described in the *Code of Ethics and Standard Practices for Texas Educators***

KNOWLEDGE OF STATE OF TEXAS GUIDELINES

In 2002, the state of Texas released its *Code of Ethics and Standard Practices for Texas Educators*, a series of codes divided into three categories. The categories include:

- Professional Ethical Conduct, Practices and Performance
- Ethical Conduct Toward Professional Colleagues
- Ethical Conduct Toward Students

Each of the three categories has between seven and eight standards. The standards describe the legal requirements of being a teacher in the state of Texas. For example, in the first section, Professional Ethical Conduct, educators are told that they must behave in a manner consistent with the honest operation of the schools.

So, for example, all board and state policies must be followed; fraudulent activity is barred; and so on. In the second section, Ethical Conduct Toward Professional Colleagues, educators are reminded that they must not discriminate, that they must not reveal confidential information, and

so on. In the final section, Ethical Conduct Toward Students, educators are reminded that they must not act in a way toward or with students that would cause students any harm. While there are many "dos and do nots" in any profession, this document should be viewed by educators as the "bottom line." For more information, please see
http://www.tcta.org/capital/sbec/codeapproved.htm.

The ultimate goal of teachers when they enter the profession of teaching is to provide a comprehensive education for all students by providing challenging curriculum and setting high expectations for learning. In an ideal classroom, the mechanisms for providing the perfect teaching climate and instruction are the norm and not the exception. Given the diversity of learners from a multitude of cultural, ethnic, intellectual, socioeconomic, and grade level– prepared backgrounds, the reality is that teachers are confronted with classrooms that are infused with classroom management issues and differentiated learning among learners who are either positively engaged in the learning process or negatively removed from all aspects of learning.

Researchers have shown that for new teachers entering the profession, the two greatest obstacles are dealing with increasing behavioral issues in the classroom and dealing with student minimally engaged in their own learning process. The goal of teachers is to maintain a toolkit of resources to deal with an ever-changing landscape of learners and classroom environments. The educator's primary professional concern will always be for the student and for the development of the student's potential. The educator will therefore strive for professional growth and will seek to exercise the best professional judgment and integrity.

The ethical conduct of an educator has undergone extensive scrutiny in today's classrooms. Teachers are under intense rules and regulations to maintain the highest degree of conduct and professionalism in the classroom. Current court cases in Florida have examined ethical violations of teachers engaged in improper communication and abuse with students, along with teachers engaged in drug violations and substance abuse in classrooms. It is imperative that teachers educating today's young people have the highest regard for professionalism and be proper role models for students in and out of the classrooms.

Skill 13.4   Follows procedures and requirements for maintaining accurate student records

STUDENT RECORDS
The student permanent record is a file of the student's cumulative educational history. It contains a profile of the student's academic background as well as the student's behavioral and medical background. The purpose of the permanent record is to provide applicable information about the student so that the student's individual educational needs can be met. If any specialized testing has been administered, the results are noted in the permanent record. Any special requirements that the student may have are indicated in the permanent record. Highly personal information, including court orders regarding custody, is filed in the permanent record as is appropriate. The importance and value of the permanent record cannot be underestimated. It offers a comprehensive knowledge of the student.

Other pertinent individual information contained in the permanent record includes the student's attendance, grade averages, and schools attended. Personal information such as parents' names and addresses, immunization records, child's height and weight, and narrative information about the child's progress and physical and mental well being is an important aspect of the permanent record. All information contained within the permanent record is strictly confidential and is only to be discussed with the student's parents or other involved school personnel.

Maintaining the Student Record
The current teacher is responsible for maintaining the student's permanent record. All substantive information in regard to testing, academic performance, the student's medical condition, and personal events are placed in the permanent record file. Updated information in regard to the student's grades, attendance, and behavior is added annually. These files are kept in a locked fireproof room or file cabinet and cannot be removed from this room unless the person removing them signs a form acknowledging full responsibility for the safe return of the complete file. Again, only the student's parents (or legal guardians), the teacher or other concerned school personnel may view the contents of the permanent record file.

The permanent record file follows the student as he/she moves through the school system with information being updated along the way. Anytime the student leaves a school, the permanent record is transferred with the student. The permanent record is regarded as legal documentation of a student's educational experience.

The contents of any student records should be indicative of the student's academic aptitude and/or achievement. The information contained should never be in any way derogatory or potentially damaging. It is important to keep in mind that others who view the contents of the records may form an opinion of the student based on the information in the student's record or file. Anyone who places information in a student's record must make every effort to give an accurate reflection of the student's performance while maintaining a neutral position as to the student's potential for future success or failure.

Confidentiality
The most essential fact to remember in regard to students' records is that the information within is confidential. Although specific policies may vary from one school or district to another, confidentiality remains constant and universal. Teachers never discuss any student or his/her progress with anyone other than the student's parents or essential school personnel. Confidentiality applies to all student information whether it is a student's spelling test, portfolio, standardized test information, report card, or the contents of the permanent record file.

The significance of the student's records is not to be taken lightly. In many instances, teachers have access to a student's records before actually meeting the student. It is important for the teacher to have helpful information about the student without developing any preconceived biases about the student.

Careful regard must be given to all information that is added to a student's file without diluting the potential effectiveness of that information. It is also important to be cognizant of the fact that the primary function of student records is that they are intended to be used as a means of developing a better understanding of the students' needs and to generate a more effective plan for meeting these needs.

Skill 13.5   Understands the importance of and adheres to required procedures for administering state- and district-mandated assessments

STATE AND DISTRICT ASSESSMENTS

State and federal law requires that public schools administer various assessments. Furthermore, most districts have additional assessments. While all assessments can provide information for teachers so that they can modify and improve instruction, all required assessments also provide the district, the state, and the federal government with information regarding the academic growth of students. Therefore, policies and procedures for administering tests must be followed carefully and thoroughly.

Reliability

Whenever procedures are not followed carefully, the reliability and validity of the test scores is put into jeopardy. Reliability refers to the extent that assessments are consistent over time and setting. This essentially means that an assessment given at different times of day, on different days, in different classrooms, and by different administrators should all yield the same result. It is crucial that all teachers follow the same procedures so that all students get the same experiences, and the test scores can also be deemed reliable. By doing so, there is much less chance that differences in test scores occur because of conditions outside of what students know.

Validity

Validity, as stated by the *Joint technical standards for educational and psychological testing* (APA, AERA, NCME, 1985), is "the most important consideration in test evaluation. The concept refers to the appropriateness, meaningfulness and usefulness of *the specific inferences made from test scores*. Test validation is the process of accumulating evidence to support such inferences. A variety of inferences may be made from scores produced by a given test, and there are many ways of accumulating evidence to support any particular inference.

Validity, however, is a unitary concept. Although evidence may be accumulated in many ways, validity always refers to the degree to which that evidence supports the inferences that are made from test scores." This means that in order for a test to be valid, the content needs to match the instructional objective and the scores need to support the external criterion (e.g., statewide assessments). Once again, if test administrators do not follow the set-upon procedures, test validity can be called into question.

While schools will provide clear and specific information on test procedures, it is always worth asking for assistance when a procedure does not make sense. Common directions may include time limitations, allowances or bans of assistive tools (e.g., calculator, ruler), break regulations,

TEACHER CERTIFICATION STUDY GUIDE

or seating/space restrictions. For more information on validity and accuracy, **SEE** Skill 9.3.

Skill 13.6 **Uses knowledge of the structure of the state education system, including relationships among campus, local and state components, to seek information and assistance**

THE SYSTEM OF EDUCATION
The entire state system of education works to support each school, each classroom, and each teacher. The general structure, including the federal, U.S. Department of Education system, is the following:

- At the top is the U.S. Department of Education. The Secretary of this department is appointed by the President of the United States. While significant amounts of money do get distributed from this department for various projects and needs, its primary role, at least in this day and age, is to enforce No Child Left Behind.
- Under the U.S. Department of Education are various research and "service" centers. Scattered around the country, these centers conduct research in education and distribute it to school systems around the country. Often, the research is posted online. See http://ies.ed.gov/ncee/edlabs/ for more information.
- The next level is the state level. The state is the primary controller for public education. Each state has a set of laws and requirements for public education. All public schools in the state must follow these laws. In addition, the state sets standards for student learning and mandates and oversees achievement testing.
- Under the state are local service centers. Usually, these are operated by counties. These service centers provide professional development to teachers and administrators, provide additional student services, and set instructional tones for all districts within the region.
- Under these centers are the school districts themselves. Districts are set up to run the day-to-day operations of schools. They deal with the hiring of teachers, the management of bus and food services, the facilities of schools, and many more things. Under the districts are the schools. So while a teacher may work at a particular school, the teacher is really an employee of the district.

So, what does this all mean for teachers? First, when there is a simple advice question, teachers should go to their colleagues in their own school. However, for professional development, teachers may want to contact their local service centers. For large-scale research, the teacher may want to investigate which federal research laboratory is closest to the district. Having these multiple layers of support is extremely beneficial to teachers looking for the best, most pertinent instructional information.

Skill 13.7 **Advocates for students and for the profession in various situations**

BEING A STUDENT ADVOCATE
As an individual who spends a great deal of time with his or her students, the teacher is one who truly understands what students and schools need. It is important for teachers to vocalize

concerns, issues, and/or problems regarding their students, class, school and district. With that being said, knowing the proper channels to voice concerns or issues is also crucial. All teachers have a responsibility of understanding the hierarchy within their school and district (e.g., mentor, teacher team, principal) and knowing the appropriate teams (e.g., Child Study Team) that work to explore and solve learning problems for students within a school. Advocating for students within these channels and volunteering time and efforts can help to ensure that all students have the opportunity to succeed.

The teachers' ability to be a good student advocate is also tied to the ability to speak coherently and intellectually regarding many educational domains. Teachers must maintain the highest professional standards for themselves. To do so, teachers must utilize the practices of this book and their state's educational resources, including professional development, collaboration with peers, continuing higher education, professional organizations, community resources, and other resources to stay current in the profession of teaching. It is through these resources that teachers become, and remain, knowledgeable enough to be effective advocates for their students and their profession.

TEACHER CERTIFICATION STUDY GUIDE

TExES PEDAGOGY AND PROFESSIONAL RESPONSIBILITIES EC-12

TEACHER CERTIFICATION STUDY GUIDE

SAMPLE TEST

Directions: Read each item and select the best response.

1. **What developmental patterns should a professional teacher assess to meet the needs of the student?**
   (Average)

   A. Academic, regional, and family background
   B. Social, physical, and cognitive
   C. Academic, physical, and family background
   D. Physical, family, and ethnic background

2. **According to Piaget, what stage is characterized by the ability to think abstractly and to use logic?**
   (Easy)

   A. Concrete operations
   B. Pre-operational
   C. Formal operations
   D. Conservative operational

3. **At approximately what age is the average child able to define abstract terms such as honesty and justice?**
   (Rigorous)

   A. 10–12 years old
   B. 4–6 years old
   C. 14–16 years old
   D. 6–8 years old

4. **What would improve planning for instruction?**
   (Average)

   A. Describe the role of the teacher and student
   B. Evaluate the outcomes of instruction
   C. Rearrange the order of activities
   D. Give outside assignments

5. **What is the most significant development emerging in children at age two?**
   (Easy)

   A. Immune system develops
   B. Socialization occurs
   C. Language develops
   D. Perception develops

6. **You are leading a substance abuse discussion for health class. The students present their belief that marijuana is not harmful to their health. What set of data would refute their claim?**
   (Rigorous)

   A. It is more carcinogenic than nicotine, lowers resistance to infection, worsens acne, and damages brain cells
   B. It damages brain cells, causes behavior changes in prenatally exposed infants, leads to other drug abuse, and causes short-term memory loss
   C. It lowers tolerance for frustration, causes eye damage, increases paranoia, and lowers resistance to infection
   D. It leads to abusing alcohol, lowers white blood cell count, reduces fertility, and causes gout

7. Bobby, a nine-year-old, has been caught stealing frequently in the classroom. What might be a factor contributing to this behavior?
   (Average)

   A. Need for the items stolen
   B. Serious emotional disturbance
   C. Desire to experiment
   D. A normal stage of development

8. What strategy can teachers incorporate in their classrooms that will allow students to acquire the same academic skills even though the students are at various learning levels?
   (Rigorous)

   A. Create learning modules
   B. Apply concrete rules to abstract theories
   C. Incorporate social learning skills
   D. Follow cognitive development progression

9. The process approach is a three-phase model approach that aims directly at the enhancement of self concept among students. Which of the following are components of this process approach?
   (Rigorous)

   A. Sensing function, transforming function, acting function
   B. Diversity model, ethnicity model, economic model
   C. Problem approach, acting function, diversity model
   D. Ethnicity approach, sensing model, problem approach

10. Andy shows up to class abusive and irritable. He is often late, sleeps in class, sometimes slurs his speech, and has an odor of drinking. What is the first intervention to take?
    (Rigorous)

    A. Confront him, relying on a trusting relationship you think you have
    B. Do a lesson on alcohol abuse, making an example of him
    C. Do nothing, it is better to err on the side of failing to identify substance abuse
    D. Call administration, avoid conflict, and supervise others carefully

11. What is a good strategy for teaching ethnically diverse students?
    (Average)

    A. Do not focus on the students' culture
    B. Expect them to assimilate easily into your classroom
    C. Imitate their speech patterns
    D. Include ethnic studies in the curriculum

12. Which of the following is an accurate description of an English Language Learner student?
    (Average)

    A. Remedial students
    B. Exceptional education students
    C. Are not a homogeneous group
    D. Feel confident in communicating in English when with their peers

13. What is an effective way to help an English Language Learner student succeed in class? *(Average)*

    A. Refer the child to a specialist
    B. Maintain an encouraging, success-oriented atmosphere
    C. Help them assimilate by making them use English exclusively
    D. Help them cope with the content materials you presently use

14. Johnny, a middle-schooler, comes to class uncharacteristically tired, distracted, withdrawn, and sullen and cries easily. What should be the teacher's first response? *(Average)*

    A. Send him to the office to sit
    B. Call his parents
    C. Ask him what is wrong
    D. Ignore his behavior

15. What should be considered when evaluating textbooks for content? *(Easy)*

    A. Type of print used
    B. Number of photographs used
    C. Free of cultural stereotyping
    D. Outlines at the beginning of each chapter

16. What steps are important in the review of subject matter in the classroom? *(Rigorous)*

    A. A lesson-initiating review, topic, and a lesson-end review
    B. A preview of the subject matter, an in-depth discussion, and a lesson-end review
    C. A rehearsal of the subject matter and a topic summary within the lesson
    D. A short paragraph synopsis of the previous day's lesson and a written review at the end of the lesson

17. What are critical elements of the instructional process? *(Rigorous)*

    A. Content, goals, teacher needs
    B. Means of getting money to regulate instruction
    C. Content, materials, activities, goals, learner needs
    D. Materials, definitions, assignments

18. The teacher states that the lesson the students will be engaged in will consist of a review of the material from the previous day, a demonstration of the scientific principles of an electronic circuit, and small group work on setting up an electronic circuit. What has the teacher demonstrated?
    (Rigorous)

    A. The importance of reviewing
    B. Giving the general framework for the lesson to facilitate learning
    C. Giving students the opportunity to leave if they are not interested in the lesson
    D. Providing momentum for the lesson

19. What is one component of the instructional planning model that must be given careful evaluation?
    (Rigorous)

    A. Students' prior knowledge and skills
    B. The script the teacher will use in instruction
    C. Future lesson plans
    D. Parent participation

20. How many stages of intellectual development does Piaget define?
    (Average)

    A. Two
    B. Four
    C. Six
    D. Eight

21. Who developed the theory of multiple intelligences?
    (Average)

    A. Bruner
    B. Gardner
    C. Kagan
    D. Cooper

22. What is an example of a low order question?
    (Easy)

    A. "Why is it important to recycle items in your home?"
    B. "Compare how glass and plastics are recycled"
    C. "What items do we recycle in our county?"
    D. "Explain the importance of recycling in our county"

23. Bloom's taxonomy references six skill levels within the cognitive domain. The top three skills are known as higher-order thinking skills (HOTS). Which of the following are the three highest order skills?
    (Rigorous)

    A. Comprehension, application, analysis
    B. Knowledge, comprehension, evaluation
    C. Application, synthesis, comprehension
    D. Analysis, synthesis, and evaluation

TEACHER CERTIFICATION STUDY GUIDE

24. **Teachers have a responsibility to help students learn how to organize their classroom environments. Which of the following is NOT an effective method of teaching responsibility to students?**
    (Rigorous)

    A. Dividing responsibilities among students
    B. Doing "spot-checks" of notebooks
    C. Cleaning up after students leave the classroom
    D. Expecting students to keep weekly calendars

25. **How can students use a computer desktop publishing center?**
    (Easy)

    A. To set up a classroom budget
    B. To create student made books, reports, essays, and more
    C. To design a research project
    D. To create a classroom behavior management system

26. **Which of the following is considered a study skill?**
    (Average)

    A. Using graphs, tables, and maps
    B. Using a desktop publishing program
    C. Explaining important vocabulary words
    D. Asking for clarification

27. **According to research, what can be a result of specific teacher actions on behavior?**
    (Rigorous)

    A. Increase in student misconduct
    B. Increase in the number of referrals
    C. Decrease in student participation
    D. Decrease in student retentions

28. **When using a kinesthetic approach, what would be an appropriate activity?**
    (Average)

    A. List
    B. Match
    C. Define
    D. Debate

29. **How can the teacher establish a positive climate in the classroom?**
    (Average)

    A. Help students see the unique contributions of individual differences
    B. Use whole group instruction for all content areas
    C. Help students divide into cooperative groups based on ability
    D. Eliminate teaching strategies that allow students to make choices

30. **How can the teacher help students become more work-oriented and less disruptive?**
    (Rigorous)

    A. Seek their input for content instruction
    B. Challenge the students with a task and show genuine enthusiasm for it
    C. Use behavior modification techniques with all students
    D. Make sure lesson plans are complete for the week

31. **What has been established to increase student originality, intrinsic motivation, and higher-order thinking skills?**
    (Rigorous)

    A. Classroom climate
    B. High expectations
    C. Student choice
    D. Use of authentic learning opportunities

32. **Which of the following is NOT a component of the invitational learning theory?**
    (Rigorous)

    A. Proper arrangement of classroom furniture
    B. Adequate ventilation and classroom lighting
    C. The regular use of substitute teachers
    D. Neutral hues for coloration of walls

33. **How can student misconduct be redirected at times?**
    (Easy)

    A. The teacher threatens the students
    B. The teacher assigns detention to the whole class
    C. The teacher stops the activity and stares at the students
    D. The teacher effectively handles changing from one activity to another

34. **The concept of efficient use of time includes which of the following?**
    (Rigorous)

    A. Daily review, seatwork, and recitation of concepts
    B. Lesson initiation, transition, and comprehension check
    C. Review, test, and review
    D. Punctuality, management transition, and wait time avoidance

35. **Reducing off-task time and maximizing the amount of time students spend attending to academic tasks is closely related to which of the following?**
    (Rigorous)

    A. Using whole class instruction only
    B. Business-like behaviors of the teacher
    C. Dealing only with major teaching functions
    D. Giving students a maximum of two minutes to come to order

36. What do cooperative learning methods all have in common?
    (Rigorous)

    A. Philosophy
    B. Cooperative task/cooperative reward structures
    C. Student roles and communication
    D. Teacher roles

37. The use of volunteers and paraprofessionals within a classroom enriches the setting by:
    (Easy)

    A. Providing more opportunity for individual student attention
    B. Offering a perceived sense of increased security for students
    C. Modifying the behavior of students
    D. All of the above

38. What is the definition of proactive classroom management?
    (Rigorous)

    A. Management that is constantly changing
    B. Management that is downplayed
    C. Management that gives clear and explicit instructions and rewards compliance
    D. Management that is designed by the students

39. Which of the following significantly increases appropriate behavior in the classroom?
    (Average)

    A. Monitoring the halls
    B. Having class rules
    C. Having class rules, giving feedback, and having individual consequences
    D. Having class rules, and giving feedback

40. What have recent studies regarding effective teachers concluded?
    (Average)

    A. Effective teachers let students establish rules
    B. Effective teachers establish routines by the sixth week of school
    C. Effective teachers state their own policies and establish consistent class rules and procedures on the first day of class
    D. Effective teachers establish flexible routines

41. What is one way of effectively managing student conduct?
    (Average)

    A. State expectations about behavior
    B. Let students discipline their peers
    C. Let minor infractions of the rules go unnoticed
    D. Increase disapproving remarks

42. **When is utilization of instructional materials most effective?**
    (Average)

    A. When the activities are organized and sequenced
    B. When the materials are prepared weeks in advance
    C. When the students choose the pages to work on
    D. When the students create the instructional materials

43. **Why is it important for a teacher to pose a question before calling on students to answer?**
    (Rigorous)

    A. It helps manage student conduct
    B. It keeps the students as a group focused on the class work
    C. It allows students time to collaborate
    D. It gives the teacher time to walk among the students

44. **Wait-time has what effect?**
    (Average)

    A. Gives structure to the class discourse
    B. Fewer chain and low-level questions are asked with more high-level questions included
    C. Gives the students time to evaluate the response
    D. Gives the opportunity for in-depth discussion about the topic

45. **What is one benefit of amplifying a student's response?**
    (Rigorous)

    A. It helps the student develop a positive self-image
    B. It is helpful to other students who are in the process of learning the reasoning or steps in answering the question
    C. It allows the teacher to cover more content
    D. It helps to keep the information organized

46. **What is not a way that teachers show acceptance and give value to a student response?**
    (Rigorous)

    A. Acknowledging
    B. Correcting
    C. Discussing
    D. Amplifying

47. **What is an effective amount of wait-time?**
    (Easy)

    A. 1 second
    B. 5 seconds
    C. 15 seconds
    D. 10 seconds

48. **Ms. Smith says, "Yes, exactly what do you mean by 'It was the author's intention to mislead you'" What does this illustrate?**
    (Rigorous)

    A. Digression
    B. Restates response
    C. Probes a response
    D. Amplifies a response

49. The teacher responds, "Yes, that is correct" to a student's answer. What is this an example of?
    (Average)

    A. Academic feedback
    B. Academic praise
    C. Simple positive response
    D. Simple negative response

50. When are students more likely to understand complex ideas?
    (Rigorous)

    A. If they do outside research before coming to class
    B. Later when they write out the definitions of complex words
    C. When they attend a lecture on the subject
    D. When they are clearly defined by the teacher and are given examples and non-examples of the concept

51. What are the two ways concepts can be taught?
    (Easy)

    A. Factually and interpretively
    B. Inductively and deductively
    C. Conceptually and inductively
    D. Analytically and facilitatively

52. According to Piaget, when does the development of symbolic functioning and language take place?
    (Average)

    A. Concrete operations stage
    B. Formal operations stage
    C. Sensorimotor stage
    D. Preoperational stage

53. What should a teacher do when students have not responded well to an instructional activity?
    (Average)

    A. Reevaluate learner needs
    B. Request administrative help
    C. Continue with the activity another day
    D. Assign homework on the concept

54. How could a KWL chart be used in instruction?
    (Average)

    A. To motivate students to do a research paper
    B. To assess prior knowledge of the students
    C. To assist in teaching skills
    D. To put events in sequential order

55. Which of the following is an example of a synthesis question according to Bloom's taxonomy?
    (Rigorous)

    A. "What is the definition of _____?"
    B. "Compare _____ to _____."
    C. "Match column A to column B."
    D. "Propose an alternative to _____."

56. **Which statement is an example of specific praise?**
    (Average)

    A. "John, you are the only person in class not paying attention"
    B. "William, I thought we agreed that you would turn in all of your homework"
    C. "Robert, you did a good job staying in line. See how it helped us get to music class on time?"
    D. "Class, you did a great job cleaning up the art room"

57. **Mrs. Grant is providing her students with many extrinsic motivators in order to increase their intrinsic motivation. Which of the following best explains this relationship?**
    (Rigorous)

    A. This is a good relationship and will increase intrinsic motivation
    B. The relationship builds animosity between the teacher and the students
    C. Extrinsic motivation does not in itself help to build intrinsic motivation
    D. There is no place for extrinsic motivation in the classroom

58. **Which of the following is NOT a factor in student self-motivation?**
    (Rigorous)

    A. Breaking larger tasks into more manageable steps
    B. Permitting students to turn in assignments late
    C. Offering students control over the assignment
    D. Allowing students to create dream boards

59. **Which of the following is NOT a part of the hardware of a computer system?**
    (Easy)

    A. Storage device
    B. Input devices
    C. Software
    D. Central Processing Unit

60. **When pulling educational information from shared drives what is the MOST important factor to consider?**
    (Rigorous)

    A. What is the intended use of the information
    B. What age group is the information best suited for
    C. Where the information came from
    D. Who the author of the information is

61. **Which of the following are the three primary categories of instructional technology tools?**
    (Rigorous)

    A. Creation/design/implementation
    B. Research/implementation/assessment
    C. Assessment/creation/research
    D. Design/research/usage

62. **When a teacher is evaluating a student's technologically produced product, which of the following is considered the MOST important factor to consider?**
    (Rigorous)

    A. Content
    B. Design
    C. Audience
    D. Relevance

63. **You are a classroom teacher in a building that does not have a computer lab for your class to use. However, knowing that you enjoy incorporating technology into the classroom, your principal has worked to find computers for your room. They are set up in the back of your classroom and have software loaded, but have no access to the intranet or internet within your building. Which of the following is NOT an acceptable method for using these computers within your classroom instruction?**
    (Rigorous)

    A. Rotating the students in small groups through the computers as centers
    B. Putting students at the computers individually for skill-based review or practice
    C. Dividing your classroom into three groups and putting each group at one computer and completing a whole class lesson
    D. Using the computers for students to complete their writing assignments with an assigned sign-up sheet, so the students know the order in which they will type their stories

64. **What are three steps, in the correct order, for evaluating software before purchasing it for use within the classroom?**
(Rigorous)

   A. Read the instructions to ensure it will work with the computer you have, try it out as if you were a student, and examine how the program handles errors or mistakes the student may make
   B. Try the computer program as if you were a student, read any online information about the program, have a student use the program and provide feedback
   C. Read the instructions and load it onto your computer, try out the program yourself as if you were a student, have a student use the program and provide feedback
   D. Read the instructions, have a student use the program, try it out yourself

65. **When a teacher wants to utilize an assessment that is subjective in nature, which of the following is the most effective method for scoring?**
(Easy)

   A. Rubric
   B. Checklist
   C. Alternative assessment
   D. Subjective measures should not be utilized

66. **What is an example of formative feedback?**
(Average)

   A. The results of an intelligence test
   B. Correcting the tests in small groups
   C. Verbal behavior that expresses approval of a student response to a test item
   D. Scheduling a discussion prior to the test

67. **Norm-referenced tests:**
(Rigorous)

   A. Give information only about the local samples results
   B. Provide information about how the local test takers did compared to a representative sampling of national test takers
   C. Make no comparisons to national test takers
   D. None of the above

68. **What is the best definition for an achievement test?**
(Average)

   A. It measures mechanical and practical abilities
   B. It measures broad areas of knowledge that are the result of cumulative learning experiences
   C. It measures the ability to learn to perform a task
   D. It measures performance related to specific, recently acquired information

69. **How are standardized tests useful in assessment?**
    (Average)

    A. For teacher evaluation
    B. For evaluation of the administration
    C. For comparison from school to school
    D. For comparison to the population on which the test was normed

70. **Mr. Brown wishes to improve his parent communication skills. Which of the following is a strategy he can utilize to accomplish this goal?**
    (Easy)

    A. Hold parent-teacher conferences
    B. Send home positive notes
    C. Have parent nights where the parents are invited into his classroom
    D. All of the above

71. **When communicating with parents for whom English is not the primary language, you should:**
    (Easy)

    A. Provide materials whenever possible in their native language
    B. Use an interpreter
    C. Provide the same communication as you would to native English speaking parents
    D. All of the above

72. **Which statement best reflects why family involvement is important to a student's educational success?**
    (Easy)

    A. Reading the class newsletter constitutes strong family involvement
    B. Family involvement means to attend graduation
    C. There are limited ways a parent can be active in their child's education
    D. The more family members are involved, the more success a student is likely to experience

73. **Which of the following is NOT an appropriate method for teachers to interact with families of diverse backgrounds?**
    (Easy)

    A. Show respect to parents
    B. Share personal stories concerning the student
    C. Display patience with parents
    D. Disregard culture of student

74. A parent has left an angry message on the teacher's voicemail. The message relates to a concern about a student and is directed at the teacher. The teacher should:
 (Average)

   A. Call back immediately and confront the parent
   B. Cool off, plan what to discuss with the parent, then call back
   C. Question the child to find out what set off the parent
   D. Ignore the message, since feelings of anger usually subside after a while

75. Which is NOT considered a good practice when conducting parent-teacher conferences?
 (Average)

   A. Ending the conference with an agreed plan of action
   B. Figure out questions for parents during the conference
   C. Prepare work samples, records of behavior, and assessment information
   D. Prepare a welcoming environment, set a good mood, and be an active listener

76. Which of the following should NOT be a purpose of a parent-teacher conference?
 (Average)

   A. To involve the parent in their child's education
   B. To establish a friendship with the child's parents
   C. To resolve a concern about the child's performance
   D. To inform parents of positive behaviors by the child

77. Which of the following is a technological strategy that keeps students and teachers interactively communicating about issues in the classroom and beyond?
 (Rigorous)

   A. Distance learning
   B. Mentoring support system
   C. Conceptual learning modalities
   D. Community resources

78. In the past, teaching has been viewed as _____ while in more current society it has been viewed as _____.
 (Rigorous)

   A. isolating…collaborative
   B. collaborative…isolating
   C. supportive…isolating
   D. isolating…supportive

79. Which of the following is a good reason to collaborate with a pee? *(Easy)*

    A. To increase your knowledge in areas where you feel you are weak, but the peer is strong
    B. To increase your planning time and that of your peer by combining the classes and taking more breaks
    C. To have fewer lesson plans to write
    D. To teach fewer subjects

80. Which of the following is responsible for working with the school in matters concerning the business of running a school? *(Rigorous)*

    A. Curriculum coordinators
    B. Administrators
    C. Board of Education
    D. Parent-Teacher organizations

81. What would happen if a school utilized an integrated approach to professional development? *(Average)*

    A. All stakeholders needs are addressed
    B. Teachers and administrators are on the same page
    C. High-quality programs for students are developed
    D. Parents drive the curriculum and instruction

82. Which is true of child protective services? *(Rigorous)*

    A. They have been forced to become more punitive in their attempts to treat and prevent child abuse and neglect
    B. They have become more a means for identifying cases of abuse and less an agent for rehabilitation due to the large volume of cases
    C. They have become advocates for structured discipline within the school
    D. They have become a strong advocate in the court system

83. What is a benefit of frequent self-assessment? *(Average)*

    A. Opens new venues for professional development
    B. Saves teachers the pressure of being observed by others
    C. Reduces time spent on areas not needing attention
    D. Offers a model for students to adopt in self-improvement

84. Mrs. Graham has taken the time to reflect, completed observations, and asked for feedback about the interactions between her and her students from her principal. It is obvious by seeking this information out that Mrs. Graham understands which of the following?
    (Rigorous)

    A. The importance of clear communication with the principal
    B. She needs to analyze her effectiveness of classroom interactions
    C. She is clearly communicating with the principal
    D. She cares about her students

85. Which of the following are ways a professional can assess his/her teaching strengths and weaknesses?
    (Rigorous)

    A. Examining how many students were unable to understand a concept
    B. Asking peers for suggestions or ideas
    C. Self-evaluation/reflection of lessons taught
    D. All of the above

86. In successful inclusion of students with disabilities:
    (Average)

    A. A variety of instructional arrangements are available
    B. School personnel shift the responsibility for learning outcomes to the student
    C. The physical facilities are used as they are
    D. Regular classroom teachers have sole responsibility for evaluating student progress

87. Teachers may duplicate copies of informational materials provided that they meet the following requirement/s:
    (Rigorous)

    A. Brevity
    B. Spontaneity
    C. Cumulative effect
    D. All of the above

88. Which of the following is one of the greatest obstacles that new teachers face when first entering the profession?
    (Rigorous)

    A. Dealing with behavioral issues in the classroom
    B. Monitoring daily student success
    C. Developing rapport with parents and caretakers
    D. Creating weekly lesson plans

89. **How can a teacher use a student's permanent record?**
    (Average)

    A. To develop a better understanding of the needs of the student
    B. To record all instances of student disruptive behavior
    C. To brainstorm ideas for discussing with parents at parent-teacher conferences
    D. To develop realistic expectations of the student's performance early in the year

90. **To what does the validity of a test refer?**
    (Rigorous)

    A. Its consistency
    B. Its usefulness
    C. Its accuracy
    D. The degree of true scores it provide

TEACHER CERTIFICATION STUDY GUIDE

Answer Key

1.	B	31.	C	61.	C
2.	C	32.	C	62.	D
3.	A	33.	D	63.	C
4.	B	34.	D	64.	A
5.	C	35.	B	65.	A
6.	B	36.	B	66.	C
7.	B	37.	D	67.	B
8.	A	38.	C	68.	B
9.	A	39.	C	69.	D
10.	D	40.	C	70.	D
11.	D	41.	A	71.	D
12.	C	42.	A	72.	D
13.	B	43.	B	73.	D
14.	C	44.	B	74.	B
15.	C	45.	B	75.	B
16.	A	46.	B	76.	B
17.	C	47.	B	77.	A
18.	B	48.	C	78.	A
19.	A	49.	C	79.	A
20.	B	50.	D	80.	C
21.	B	51.	B	81.	C
22.	C	52.	D	82.	B
23.	D	53.	A	83.	A
24.	C	54.	B	84.	B
25.	B	55.	D	85.	D
26.	A	56.	C	86.	A
27.	A	57.	C	87.	D
28.	B	58.	B	88.	A
29.	A	59.	C	89.	A
30.	B	60.	A	90.	B

Rigor Table

Easy
2, 5, 15, 22, 25, 33, 37, 47, 51, 59, 65, 70, 71, 72, 73, 79

Average
1, 4, 7, 11, 12, 13, 14, 20, 21, 26, 28, 29, 39, 40, 41, 42, 44, 49, 52, 53, 54, 56, 66, 68, 69, 74, 75, 76, 81, 83, 86, 89

Rigorous
3, 6, 8, 9, 10, 16, 17, 18, 19, 23, 24, 27, 30, 31, 32, 34, 35, 36, 38, 43, 45, 46, 48, 50, 55, 57, 58, 60, 61, 62, 63, 64, 67, 77, 78, 80, 82, 84, 85, 87, 88, 90

TEACHER CERTIFICATION STUDY GUIDE

SAMPLE TEST WITH RATIONALES

Directions: Read each item and select the best response.

1. What developmental patterns should a professional teacher assess to meet the needs of the student?
   (Average)

   A. Academic, regional, and family background
   B. Social, physical, and cognitive
   C. Academic, physical, and family background
   D. Physical, family, and ethnic background

Answer: B. Social, physical, and cognitive
The effective teacher applies knowledge of physical, social, and cognitive developmental patterns and of individual differences to meet the instructional needs of all students in the classroom. The most important premise of child development is that all domains of development (physical, social, and academic) are integrated. The teacher has a broad knowledge and thorough understanding of the development that typically occurs during the students' current period of life. More importantly, the teacher understands how children learn best during each period of development. An examination of the student's file coupled with ongoing evaluation assures a successful educational experience for both teacher and students.

2. According to Piaget, what stage is characterized by the ability to think abstractly and to use logic?
   (Easy)

   A. Concrete operations
   B. Pre-operational
   C. Formal operations
   D. Conservative operational

Answer: C. Formal operations
The four development stages are described in Piaget's theory as follows:

   1. Sensorimotor stage: from birth to age 2 years (children experience the world through movement and senses)
   2. Preoperational stage: from ages 2 to 7 (acquisition of motor skills)
   3. Concrete operational stage: from ages 7 to 11 (children begin to think logically about concrete events)
   4. Formal operational stage: after age 11 (development of abstract reasoning)

TEACHER CERTIFICATION STUDY GUIDE

These chronological periods are approximate and, in light of the fact that studies have demonstrated great variation between children, cannot be seem as rigid norms. Furthermore, these stages occur at different ages, depending upon the domain of knowledge under consideration. The ages normally given for the stages reflect when each stage tends to predominate even though one might elicit examples of two, three, or even all four stages of thinking at the same time from one individual, depending upon the domain of knowledge and the means used to elicit it.

3. **At approximately what age is the average child able to define abstract terms such as honesty and justice?**
   (Rigorous)

   A. 10–12 years old
   B. 4–6 years old
   C. 14–16 years old
   D. 6–8 years old

Answer: A. 10–12 years old
The usual age for the fourth stage (the formal operational stage) as described by Piaget is from 10 to 12 years old. It is in this stage that children begin to be able to define abstract terms.

4. **What would improve planning for instruction?**
   (Average)

   A. Describe the role of the teacher and student
   B. Evaluate the outcomes of instruction
   C. Rearrange the order of activities
   D. Give outside assignments

Answer: B. Evaluate the outcomes of instruction
Important as it is to plan content, materials, activities, and goals taking into account learner needs and to base what goes on in the classroom on the results of that planning, it makes no difference if students are not able to demonstrate improvement in the skills being taught. An important part of the planning process is for the teacher to constantly adapt all aspects of the curriculum to what is actually happening in the classroom. Planning frequently misses the mark or fails to allow for unexpected factors. Evaluating the outcomes of instruction regularly and making adjustments accordingly will have a positive impact on the overall success of a teaching methodology.

TEACHER CERTIFICATION STUDY GUIDE

5. **What is the most significant development emerging in children at age two?**
   (Easy)

   A. Immune system develops
   B. Socialization occurs
   C. Language develops
   D. Perception develops

   Answer: C. Language develops
   Language begins to develop in an infant not long after birth. Chomsky claims that children teach themselves to speak using the people around them for resources. Several studies of the sounds infants make in their cribs seem to support this. The first stage of meaningful sounds is the uttering of a word that obviously has meaning for the child, for example "bird," when the child sees one flying through the air. Does the development of real language begin when the noun is linked with a verb ("bird fly")? When language begins and how it develops has been debated for a long time. It is useful for a teacher to investigate those theories and studies.

6. **You are leading a substance abuse discussion for health class. The students present their belief that marijuana is not harmful to their health. What set of data would refute their claim?**
   (Rigorous)

   A. It is more carcinogenic than nicotine, lowers resistance to infection, worsens acne, and damages brain cells
   B. It damages brain cells, causes behavior changes in prenatally exposed infants, leads to other drug abuse, and causes short-term memory loss
   C. It lowers tolerance for frustration, causes eye damage, increases paranoia, and lowers resistance to infection
   D. It leads to abusing alcohol, lowers white blood cell count, reduces fertility, and causes gout

   Answer: B. It damages brain cells, causes behavior changes in prenatally exposed infants, leads to other drug abuse, and causes short-term memory loss
   The student tending toward the use of drugs and/or alcohol will exhibit losses in social and academic functional levels that were previously attained. He may begin to experiment with substances. The adage "Pot makes a smart kid average and an average kid dumb" is right on the mark. There exist not a few families where pot smoking is a known habit of the parents. The children start their habit by stealing from the parents, making it almost impossible to convince the child that drugs and alcohol are not good for them. Parental use is hampering national efforts to clean up America. The school may be the only source for the real information that children need in order to make intelligent choices about drug use. It's important to remember that if children start

using drugs early, it will interfere with their accomplishing developmental tasks and will likely lead to a lifetime of addiction.

7. **Bobby, a nine-year-old, has been caught stealing frequently in the classroom. What might be a factor contributing to this behavior?**
   (Average)

   A. Need for the items stolen
   B. Serious emotional disturbance
   C. Desire to experiment
   D. A normal stage of development

Answer: B. Serious emotional disturbance
Lying, stealing, and fighting are atypical behaviors that most children may exhibit occasionally, but if a child lies, steals, or fights regularly or blatantly, these behaviors may be indicative of emotional distress. Emotional disturbances in childhood are not uncommon and take a variety of forms. Usually these problems show up in the form of uncharacteristic behaviors. Most of the time, children respond favorably to brief treatment programs of psychotherapy. At other times, disturbances may need more intensive therapy and are harder to resolve. All stressful behaviors need to be addressed, and any type of chronic antisocial behavior needs to be examined as a possible symptom of deep-seated emotional upset.

8. **What strategy can teachers incorporate in their classrooms that will allow students to acquire the same academic skills even though the students are at various learning levels?**
   (Rigorous)

   A. Create learning modules
   B. Apply concrete rules to abstract theories
   C. Incorporate social learning skills
   D. Follow cognitive development progression

Answer: A. Create learning modules
Teachers should be aware of the fact that each student develops cognitively, mentally, emotionally, and physically at different levels. Each student is a unique person and may require individualized instruction. This may require teachers to adapt their lesson plans according to a student's developmental progress.

9. **The process approach is a three-phase model approach that aims directly at the enhancement of self concept among students. Which of the following are components of this process approach?**
   (Rigorous)

   A. Sensing function, transforming function, acting function
   B. Diversity model, ethnicity model, economic model
   C. Problem approach, acting function, diversity model
   D. Ethnicity approach, sensing model, problem approach

Answer: A. Sensing function, transforming function, acting function
This three-phase approach can be simplified into the words by which the model is usually known: reach, touch, and teach. The sensing function integrates information. The transforming function conceptualizes and provides meaning and value to perceived information. The acting function chooses actions from several different alternatives to be acted upon. This three-phase approach can be applied to any situation.

10. **Andy shows up to class abusive and irritable. He is often late, sleeps in class, sometimes slurs his speech, and has an odor of drinking. What is the first intervention to take?**
    (Rigorous)

    A. Confront him, relying on a trusting relationship you think you have
    B. Do a lesson on alcohol abuse, making an example of him
    C. Do nothing, it is better to err on the side of failing to identify substance abuse
    D. Call administration, avoid conflict, and supervise others carefully

Answer: D. Call administration, avoid conflict, and supervise others carefully
Educators are not only likely to, but often do, face students who are high on something. Of course, they are not only a hazard to their own safety and those of others, but their ability to be productive learners is greatly diminished, if not non-existent. They show up instead of skip, because it is not always easy or practical for them to spend the day away from home but not in school. Unless they can stay inside they are at risk of being picked up for truancy. Some enjoy being high in school, getting a sense of satisfaction by putting something over on the system. Some just do not take drug use seriously enough to think usage at school might be inappropriate. The first responsibility of the teacher is to assure the safety of all of the children. Avoiding conflict with the student who is high and obtaining help from administration is the best course of action.

TEACHER CERTIFICATION STUDY GUIDE

11. **What is a good strategy for teaching ethnically diverse students?**
    (Average)

    A. Do not focus on the students' culture
    B. Expect them to assimilate easily into your classroom
    C. Imitate their speech patterns
    D. Include ethnic studies in the curriculum

    Answer: D. Include ethnic studies in the curriculum
    Exploring a student's own culture increases their confidence levels in the group. It is also a very useful tool when students are struggling to develop identities that they can feel comfortable with. The bonus is that this is good training for living in the world.

12. **Which of the following is an accurate description of an English Language Learner student?**
    (Average)

    A. Remedial students
    B. Exceptional education students
    C. Are not a homogeneous group
    D. Feel confident in communicating in English when with their peers

    Answer: C. Are not a homogenous group
    Because ELL students are often grouped in classes that take a different approach to teaching English than those for native speakers, it is easy to assume that they are all present with the same needs and characteristics. Nothing could be further from the truth, even in what they need when it comes to learning English. It is important that their backgrounds and personalities be observed just as with native speakers. It was very surprising several years ago when Vietnamese children began arriving in American schools with little training in English and went on to excel in their classes, often even beyond their American counterparts. In many schools, there were Vietnamese merit scholars in the graduating classes.

TEACHER CERTIFICATION STUDY GUIDE

13. **What is an effective way to help an English Language Learner student succeed in class?**
    (Average)

    A. Refer the child to a specialist
    B. Maintain an encouraging, success-oriented atmosphere
    C. Help them assimilate by making them use English exclusively
    D. Help them cope with the content materials you presently use

    Answer: B. Maintain an encouraging, success-oriented atmosphere
    Anyone who is in an environment where his language is not the standard one feels embarrassed and inferior. The student who is in that situation expects to fail. Encouragement is even more important for these students. They need many opportunities to succeed.

14. **Johnny, a middle-schooler, comes to class uncharacteristically tired, distracted, withdrawn, and sullen and cries easily. What should be the teacher's first response?**
    (Average)

    A. Send him to the office to sit
    B. Call his parents
    C. Ask him what is wrong
    D. Ignore his behavior

    Answer: C. Ask him what is wrong
    If a teacher has developed a trusting relationship with a child, the reasons for the child's behavior may come out. It might be that the child needs to tell someone what is going on and is seeking a confidant, and a trusted teacher can intervene. If the child is unwilling to talk to the teacher about what is going on, the next step is to contact the parents, who may or may not be willing to explain why the child is the way he/she is. If they simply do not know, then it is time to add a professional physician or counselor to the mix.

15. **What should be considered when evaluating textbooks for content?**
    (Easy)

    A. Type of print used
    B. Number of photographs used
    C. Free of cultural stereotyping
    D. Outlines at the beginning of each chapter

    Answer: C. Free of cultural stereotyping
    While textbook writers and publishers have responded to the need to be culturally diverse in recent years, a few texts are still being offered that do not meet these

standards. When teachers have an opportunity to be involved in choosing textbooks, they can be watchdogs for the community in keeping the curriculum free of matter that reinforces bigotry and discrimination.

16. **What steps are important in the review of subject matter in the classroom?** *(Rigorous)*

    A. A lesson-initiating review, topic, and a lesson-end review
    B. A preview of the subject matter, an in-depth discussion, and a lesson-end review
    C. A rehearsal of the subject matter and a topic summary within the lesson
    D. A short paragraph synopsis of the previous day's lesson and a written review at the end of the lesson

Answer: A. A lesson-initiating review, topic, and a lesson-end review
The effective teacher utilizes all three of these together with comprehension checks to make sure the students are processing the information. Lesson-end reviews are restatements (by the teacher or teacher and students) of the content of discussion at the end of a lesson. Subject matter retention increases when lessons include an outline at the beginning of the lesson and a summary at the end of the lesson. This type of structure is utilized in successful classrooms. Moreover, when students know what is coming next and what is expected of them, they feel more a part of their learning environment, and deviant behavior is lessened.

17. **What are critical elements of the instructional process?** *(Rigorous)*

    A. Content, goals, teacher needs
    B. Means of getting money to regulate instruction
    C. Content, materials, activities, goals, learner needs
    D. Materials, definitions, assignments

Answer: C. Content, materials, activities, goals, learner needs
Goal-setting is a vital component of the instructional process. The teacher will, of course, have overall goals for her class, both short-term and long-term. However, perhaps even more important than that is the setting of goals that take into account the individual learner's needs, background, and stage of development. Making an educational program child-centered involves building on the natural curiosity children bring to school and asking children what they want to learn. Student-centered classrooms contain not only textbooks, workbooks, and literature but also rely heavily on a variety of audiovisual equipment and computers. There are tape recorders, language masters, filmstrip projectors, and laser disc players to help meet the learning styles of the students. Planning for instructional activities entails identification or selection of the activities the teacher and students will engage in during a period of instruction.

TEACHER CERTIFICATION STUDY GUIDE

18. The teacher states that the lesson the students will be engaged in will consist of a review of the material from the previous day, a demonstration of the scientific principles of an electronic circuit, and small group work on setting up an electronic circuit. What has the teacher demonstrated?
    (Rigorous)

    A. The importance of reviewing
    B. Giving the general framework for the lesson to facilitate learning
    C. Giving students the opportunity to leave if they are not interested in the lesson
    D. Providing momentum for the lesson

Answer: B. Giving the general framework for the lesson to facilitate learning
If children know where they're going, they're more likely to be engaged in getting there. It's important to give them a road map whenever possible for what is coming in their classes.

19. What is one component of the instructional planning model that must be given careful evaluation?
    (Rigorous)

    A. Students' prior knowledge and skills
    B. The script the teacher will use in instruction
    C. Future lesson plans
    D. Parent participation

Answer: A. Students' prior knowledge and skills
The teacher will, of course, have certain expectations regarding where the students will be physically and intellectually when he/she plans for a new class. However, there will be wide variations in the actual classroom. If he/she does not make the extra effort to understand where there are deficiencies and where there are strengths in the individual students, the planning will probably miss the mark, at least for some members of the class. This can be obtained through a review of student records, by observation, and by testing.

TEACHER CERTIFICATION STUDY GUIDE

20. **How many stages of intellectual development does Piaget define?**
    (Average)

    A. Two
    B. Four
    C. Six
    D. Eight

Answer: B. Four
The stages are:

1. Sensorimotor stage: from birth to age 2 years (children experience the world through movement and senses)
2. Preoperational stage: from ages 2 to 7 (acquisition of motor skills)
3. Concrete operational stage: from ages 7 to 11 (children begin to think logically about concrete events)
4. Formal operational stage: after age 11 (development of abstract reasoning)

21. **Who developed the theory of multiple intelligences?**
    (Average)

    A. Bruner
    B. Gardner
    C. Kagan
    D. Cooper

Answer: B. Gardner
Howard Gardner's most famous work is probably *Frames of Mind*, which details seven dimensions of intelligence (visual/spatial intelligence, musical intelligence, verbal intelligence, logical/mathematical intelligence, interpersonal intelligence, intrapersonal intelligence, and bodily/kinesthetic intelligence). Gardner's claim that pencil and paper IQ tests do not capture the full range of human intelligences has garnered much praise within the field of education but has also met criticism, largely from psychometricians. Since the publication of *Frames of Mind*, Gardner has additionally identified the 8th dimension of intelligence: naturalist intelligence, and is still considering a possible ninth—existentialist intelligence.

TEACHER CERTIFICATION STUDY GUIDE

22. **What is an example of a low order question?**
    (Easy)

    A. "Why is it important to recycle items in your home?"
    B. "Compare how glass and plastics are recycled"
    C. "What items do we recycle in our county?"
    D. "Explain the importance of recycling in our county"

Answer: C. "What items do we recycle in our county?"
Remember that the difference between specificity and abstractness is a continuum. The most specific is something that is concrete and can be seen, heard, smelled, tasted, or felt, like cans, bottles, and newspapers. At the other end of the spectrum is an abstraction like importance. Lower-order questions are on the concrete end of the continuum; higher-order questions are on the abstract end.

23. **Bloom's taxonomy references six skill levels within the cognitive domain. The top three skills are known as higher-order thinking skills (HOTS). Which of the following are the three highest order skills?**
    (Rigorous)

    A. Comprehension, application, analysis
    B. Knowledge, comprehension, evaluation
    C. Application, synthesis, comprehension
    D. Analysis, synthesis, and evaluation

Answer: D. Analysis, synthesis, and evaluation
The six skill levels of Bloom's taxonomy are: knowledge, comprehension, application, analysis, synthesis, and evaluation. Key instructional approaches that utilize HOTS are inquiry-based learning, problem solving, and open-ended questioning. It is crucial for students to use and refine these skills in order to apply them to everyday life and situations outside of school.

TEACHER CERTIFICATION STUDY GUIDE

24. Teachers have a responsibility to help students learn how to organize their classroom environments. Which of the following is NOT an effective method of teaching responsibility to students?
    (Rigorous)

    A. Dividing responsibilities among students
    B. Doing "spot-checks" of notebooks
    C. Cleaning up after students leave the classroom
    D. Expecting students to keep weekly calendars

Answer: C. Cleaning up after students leave the classroom
Teachers of young children can help students learn how to behave appropriately and take care of their surroundings by providing them with opportunities to practice ownership, chores, and leadership. Allowing students to leave a messy and disorganized class at the end of the day does not teach them responsibility.

25. How can students use a computer desktop publishing center?
    (Easy)

    A. To set up a classroom budget
    B. To create student made books, reports, essays, and more
    C. To design a research project
    D. To create a classroom behavior management system

Answer: B. To create student made books, reports, essays, and more
By creating a book, students gain new insights into how communication works. Suddenly, the concept of audience for what they write and create becomes real. They also have an opportunity to be introduced to graphic arts, an exploding field. In addition, just as computers are a vital part of the world they will be entering as adults, so is desktop publishing. It is universally used by businesses of all kinds.

26. Which of the following is considered a study skill?
    (Average)

    A. Using graphs, tables, and maps
    B. Using a desktop publishing program
    C. Explaining important vocabulary words
    D. Asking for clarification

Answer: A. Using graphs, tables, and maps
In studying, it is certainly true that "a picture is worth a thousand words." Not only are these devices useful in making a point clear, they are excellent mnemonic devices for remembering facts.

TEACHER CERTIFICATION STUDY GUIDE

27. According to research, what can be a result of specific teacher actions on behavior?
    (Rigorous)

    A. Increase in student misconduct
    B. Increase in the number of referrals
    C. Decrease in student participation
    D. Decrease in student retentions

Answer: A. Increase in student misconduct
Unfortunately, at times, misbehavior is the result of specific teacher actions. There is considerable research that indicates that some teacher behavior is upsetting to students and increases the occurrence of student misbehavior. Such teacher behavior may include any action that a child perceives as being unfair; punitive remarks about the child, his behavior, or his work; or harsh responses to the child.

28. When using a kinesthetic approach, what would be an appropriate activity?
    (Average)

    A. List
    B. Match
    C. Define
    D. Debate

Answer: B. Match
Brain lateralization theory emerged in the 1970s and demonstrated that the left hemisphere appeared to be associated with verbal and sequential abilities whereas the right hemisphere appeared to be associated with emotions and with spatial, holistic processing. Although those particular conclusions continue to be challenged, it is clear that people concentrate, process, and remember new and difficult information under very different conditions. For example, auditory and visual perceptual strengths, passivity, and self-oriented or authority-oriented motivation often correlate with high academic achievement, whereas tactual and kinesthetic strengths, a need for mobility, nonconformity, and peer motivation often correlate with school underachievement (Dunn & Dunn, 1992, 1993). Understanding how students perceive the task of learning new information differently is often helpful in tailoring the classroom experience for optimal success.

TEACHER CERTIFICATION STUDY GUIDE

29. **How can the teacher establish a positive climate in the classroom?**
    (Average)

    A. Help students see the unique contributions of individual differences
    B. Use whole group instruction for all content areas
    C. Help students divide into cooperative groups based on ability
    D. Eliminate teaching strategies that allow students to make choices

Answer: A. Help students see the unique contributions of individual differences
In the first place, an important purpose of education is to prepare students to live successfully in the real world, and this is an important insight and understanding for them to take into that world. In the second place, the most fertile learning environment is one in which all viewpoints and backgrounds are respected and where everyone has equal respect.

30. **How can the teacher help students become more work-oriented and less disruptive?**
    (Rigorous)

    A. Seek their input for content instruction
    B. Challenge the students with a task and show genuine enthusiasm for it
    C. Use behavior modification techniques with all students
    D. Make sure lesson plans are complete for the week

Answer: B. Challenge the students with a task and show genuine enthusiasm for it
Many studies have demonstrated that the enthusiasm of the teacher is infectious. If students feel that the teacher is ambivalent about a task, they will also catch that attitude.

31. **What has been established to increase student originality, intrinsic motivation, and higher-order thinking skills?**
    (Rigorous)

    A. Classroom climate
    B. High expectations
    C. Student choice
    D. Use of authentic learning opportunities

Answer: C. Student choice
While all of the descriptors are good attributes for students to demonstrate, it has been shown through research that providing student choice can increase all of the described factors.

32. Which of the following is NOT a component of the invitational learning theory?
   (Rigorous)

   A. Proper arrangement of classroom furniture
   B. Adequate ventilation and classroom lighting
   C. The regular use of substitute teachers
   D. Neutral hues for coloration of walls

Answer: C. The regular use of substitute teachers
The physical environment is one of the main principles of the invitational learning theory. The teacher can create and design their classroom to cultivate a warm and caring environment for their students. This thoughtful atmosphere can create positive learning experiences for their students.

33. How can student misconduct be redirected at times?
   (Easy)

   A. The teacher threatens the students
   B. The teacher assigns detention to the whole class
   C. The teacher stops the activity and stares at the students
   D. The teacher effectively handles changing from one activity to another

Answer: D. The teacher effectively handles changing from one activity to another
Appropriate verbal techniques include a soft non-threatening voice void of undue roughness, anger, or impatience regardless of whether the teacher is instructing, providing student alerts, or giving a behavior reprimand. Verbal techniques that may be effective in modifying student behavior include simply stating the student's name, explaining briefly and succinctly what the student is doing that is inappropriate and what the student should be doing. Verbal techniques for reinforcing behavior include both encouragement and praise delivered by the teacher. In addition, for verbal techniques to positively affect student behavior and learning, the teacher must give clear, concise directives while implying her warmth toward the students.

TEACHER CERTIFICATION STUDY GUIDE

34. The concept of efficient use of time includes which of the following?
    (Rigorous)

    A. Daily review, seatwork, and recitation of concepts
    B. Lesson initiation, transition, and comprehension check
    C. Review, test, and review
    D. Punctuality, management transition, and wait time avoidance

Answer: D. Punctuality, management transition, and wait time avoidance
The "benevolent boss" concept applies here. One who succeeds in managing a business follows these rules; so does the successful teacher.

35. Reducing off-task time and maximizing the amount of time students spend attending to academic tasks is closely related to which of the following?
    (Rigorous)

    A. Using whole class instruction only
    B. Business-like behaviors of the teacher
    C. Dealing only with major teaching functions
    D. Giving students a maximum of two minutes to come to order

Answer: B. Business-like behaviors of the teacher
The effective teacher continually evaluates his/her own physical/mental/social/emotional well-being with regard to the students in his/her classroom. There is always the tendency to satisfy social and emotional needs through relationships with the students. A good teacher genuinely likes his/her students, and that is a positive thing. However, if students are not convinced that the teacher's purpose for being there is to get a job done, the atmosphere in the classroom becomes difficult to control. This is the job of the teacher. Maintaining a business-like approach in the classroom yields many positive results. It is a little like a benevolent boss.

36. What do cooperative learning methods all have in common?
    (Rigorous)

    A. Philosophy
    B. Cooperative task/cooperative reward structures
    C. Student roles and communication
    D. Teacher roles

Answer: B. Cooperative task/cooperative reward structures
Cooperative learning situations, as practiced in today's classrooms, grew out of searches conducted by several groups in the early 1970s. Cooperative learning situations can range from very formal applications such as STAD (Student Teams-Achievement Divisions) and CIRC (Cooperative Integrated Reading and Composition) to

TEACHER CERTIFICATION STUDY GUIDE

less formal groupings known variously as "group investigation," "learning together," and "discovery groups." Cooperative learning as a general term is now firmly recognized and established as a teaching and learning technique in American schools. Since cooperative learning techniques are so widely diffused in the schools, it is necessary to orient students in the skills by which cooperative learning groups can operate smoothly, and thereby enhance learning. Students who cannot interact constructively with other students will not be able to take advantage of the learning opportunities provided by the cooperative learning situations and will furthermore deprive their fellow students of the opportunity for cooperative learning.

37. **The use of volunteers and paraprofessionals within a classroom enriches the setting by:**
    (Easy)

    A. Providing more opportunity for individual student attention
    B. Offering a perceived sense of increased security for students
    C. Modifying the behavior of students
    D. All of the above

Answer: D. All of the above
Research has shown that volunteers and paraprofessionals involvement in the educational process positively impacts the attitude and conduct of children in the classroom. Always be cautious in choosing classroom helpers that you trust and are competent.

38. **What is the definition of proactive classroom management?**
    (Rigorous)

    A. Management that is constantly changing
    B. Management that is downplayed
    C. Management that gives clear and explicit instructions and rewards compliance
    D. Management that is designed by the students

Answer: C. Management that gives clear and explicit instructions and rewards compliance
Classroom management plans should be in place when the school year begins. Developing a management plan takes a proactive approach—that is, decide what behaviors will be expected of the class as a whole, anticipate possible problems, and teach the behaviors early in the school year. Involving the students in the development of the classroom rules lets the students know the rationale for the rules and allows them to assume responsibility in the rules because they had a part in developing them.

TEACHER CERTIFICATION STUDY GUIDE

39. **Which of the following significantly increases appropriate behavior in the classroom?**
    (Average)

    A. Monitoring the halls
    B. Having class rules
    C. Having class rules, giving feedback, and having individual consequences
    D. Having class rules, and giving feedback

Answer: C. Having class rules, giving feedback, and having individual consequences

Clear, consistent class rules go a long way to preventing inappropriate behavior. Effective teachers give immediate feedback to students regarding their behavior or misbehavior. If there are consequences, they should be as close as possible to the outside world, especially for adolescents. Consistency, especially with adolescents, reduces the occurrence of power struggles and teaches them that predictable consequences follow for their choice of actions.

40. **What have recent studies regarding effective teachers concluded?**
    (Average)

    A. Effective teachers let students establish rules
    B. Effective teachers establish routines by the sixth week of school
    C. Effective teachers state their own policies and establish consistent class rules and procedures on the first day of class
    D. Effective teachers establish flexible routines

Answer: C. Effective teachers state their own policies and establish consistent class rules and procedures on the first day of class

The teacher can get ahead of the game by stating clearly on the first day of school in her introductory information for the students exactly what the rules are. These should be stated firmly but unemotionally. When one of those rules is broken, he/she can then refer to the rules, rendering enforcement much easier to achieve. It is extremely difficult to achieve goals with students who are out of control. Establishing limits early and consistently enforcing them enhances learning. It is also helpful for the teacher to display prominently the classroom rules. This will serve as a visual reminder of the students' expected behaviors. In a study of classroom management procedures, it was established that the combination of conspicuously displayed rules, frequent verbal references to the rules, and appropriate consequences for appropriate behaviors led to increased levels of on-task behavior.

TEACHER CERTIFICATION STUDY GUIDE

41. **What is one way of effectively managing student conduct?**
    (Average)

    A. State expectations about behavior
    B. Let students discipline their peers
    C. Let minor infractions of the rules go unnoticed
    D. Increase disapproving remarks

Answer: A. State expectations about behavior
The effective teacher demonstrates awareness of what the entire class is doing and is in control of the behavior of all students even when the teacher is working with only a small group of the children. In an attempt to prevent student misbehaviors the teacher makes clear, concise statements about what is happening in the classroom directing attention to content and the students' accountability for their work rather than focusing the class on the misbehavior. It is also effective for the teacher to make a positive statement about the appropriate behavior that is observed. If deviant behavior does occur, the effective teacher will specify who the deviant is, what he or she is doing wrong, and why this is unacceptable conduct or what the proper conduct would be. This can be a difficult task to accomplish as the teacher must maintain academic focus and flow while addressing and desisting misbehavior. The teacher must make clear, brief statements about the expectations without raising his/her voice and without disrupting instruction.

42. **When is utilization of instructional materials most effective?**
    (Average)

    A. When the activities are organized and sequenced
    B. When the materials are prepared weeks in advance
    C. When the students choose the pages to work on
    D. When the students create the instructional materials

Answer: A. When the activities are organized and sequenced
Most assignments will require more than one educational principle. It is helpful to explain to students the proper order in which these principles must be applied to complete the assignment successfully. Subsequently, students should also be informed of the nature of the assignment (i.e., cooperative learning, group project, individual assignment, etc). This is often done at the start of the assignment.

43. **Why is it important for a teacher to pose a question before calling on students to answer?**
    (Rigorous)

    A. It helps manage student conduct
    B. It keeps the students as a group focused on the class work
    C. It allows students time to collaborate
    D. It gives the teacher time to walk among the students

Answer: B. It keeps the students as a group focused on the class work
It does not take much distraction for a class's attention to become diffused. Once this happens, effectively teaching a principle or a skill is very difficult. The teacher should plan presentations that will keep students focused on the lesson. A very useful tool is effective, well thought-out, pointed questions.

44. **Wait-time has what effect?**
    (Average)

    A. Gives structure to the class discourse
    B. Fewer chain and low-level questions are asked with more high-level questions included
    C. Gives the students time to evaluate the response
    D. Gives the opportunity for in-depth discussion about the topic

Answer: B. Fewer chain and low-level questions are asked with more high-level questions included
One part of the questioning process for the successful teacher is *wait-time*: the time between the question and either the student response or a follow-up. Many teachers vaguely recommend some general amount of wait-time (until the student starts to get uncomfortable or is clearly perplexed), but here the focus is on wait-time as a specific and powerful communicative tool that speaks through its structured silences. Embedded in wait-time are subtle clues about judgments of a student's abilities and expectations of individuals and groups. For example, the more time a student is allowed to mull through a question, the more the teacher trusts his or her ability to answer that question without getting flustered. As a rule, the practice of prompting is not a problem. Giving support and helping students reason through difficult conundrums is part of being an effective teacher.

TEACHER CERTIFICATION STUDY GUIDE

45. **What is one benefit of amplifying a student's response?**
    (Rigorous)

    A. It helps the student develop a positive self-image
    B. It is helpful to other students who are in the process of learning the reasoning or steps in answering the question
    C. It allows the teacher to cover more content
    D. It helps to keep the information organized

Answer: B. It is helpful to other students who are in the process of learning the reasoning or steps in answering the question
Not only does the teacher show acceptance and give value to student responses by acknowledging, amplifying, discussing, or restating the comment or question, she also helps the rest of the class learn to reason. If a student response is allowed, even if it is blurted out, it must be acknowledged and the student made aware of the quality of the response. A teacher acknowledges a student response by commenting on it. For example, the teacher states the definition of a noun, and then asks for examples of nouns in the classroom. A student responds, "My pencil is a noun." The teacher answers, "Okay, let us list that on the board." By this response and the action of writing "pencil" on the board, the teacher has just incorporated the student's response into the lesson.

46. **What is not a way that teachers show acceptance and give value to a student response?**
    (Rigorous)

    A. Acknowledging
    B. Correcting
    C. Discussing
    D. Amplifying

Answer: B. Correcting
There are ways to treat every answer as worthwhile even if it happens to be wrong. The objective is to keep students involved in the dialogue. If their efforts to participate are "rewarded" with what seems to them to be a rebuke or that leads to embarrassment, they will be less willing to respond the next time.

TEACHER CERTIFICATION STUDY GUIDE

47. What is an effective amount of wait-time?
    (Easy)

    A. 1 second
    B. 5 seconds
    C. 15 seconds
    D. 10 seconds

Answer: B. 5 seconds
See rationale for question 44.

48. Ms. Smith says, "Yes, exactly what do you mean by 'It was the author's intention to mislead you'" What does this illustrate?
    (Rigorous)

    A. Digression
    B. Restates response
    C. Probes a response
    D. Amplifies a response

Answer: C. Probes a response
From ancient times, notable teachers such as Socrates have employed oral-questioning to enhance their discourse, to stimulate thinking, and/or to stir emotion among their audiences. Educational researchers and practitioners virtually all agree that teachers' effective use of questioning promotes student learning. Effective teachers continually develop their questioning skills.

49. The teacher responds, "Yes, that is correct" to a student's answer. What is this an example of?
    (Average)

    A. Academic feedback
    B. Academic praise
    C. Simple positive response
    D. Simple negative response

Answer: C. Simple positive response
The reason for praise in the classroom is to increase the desirable in order to eliminate the undesirable. This refers to both conduct and academic focus. It further states that effective praise should be authentic, it should be used in a variety of ways, and it should be low-keyed. Academic praise is a group of specific statements that give information about the value of the response or its implications. For example, a teacher using academic praise would respond, "That is an excellent analysis of Twain's use of the river

in Huckleberry Finn." Whereas a simple positive response to the same question would be, "That's correct."

50. **When are students more likely to understand complex ideas?**
    (Rigorous)

    A. If they do outside research before coming to class
    B. Later when they write out the definitions of complex words
    C. When they attend a lecture on the subject
    D. When they are clearly defined by the teacher and are given examples and non-examples of the concept

Answer: D. When they are clearly defined by the teacher and are given examples and non-examples of the concept
Several studies have been carried out to determine the effectiveness of giving examples as well as the difference in effectiveness of various types of examples. It was found conclusively that the most effective method of concept presentation included giving a definition along with examples and non-examples and also providing an explanation of them. These same studies indicate that boring examples were just as effective as interesting examples in promoting learning. Additional studies have been conducted to determine the most effective number of examples that will result in maximum student learning. These studies concluded that a few thoughtfully selected examples are just as effective as many examples. It was determined that the actual number of examples necessary to promote student learning was relative to the learning characteristics of the learners. It was again ascertained that learning is facilitated when examples are provided along with the definition.

51. **What are the two ways concepts can be taught?**
    (Easy)

    A. Factually and interpretively
    B. Inductively and deductively
    C. Conceptually and inductively
    D. Analytically and facilitatively

Answer: B. Inductively and deductively
Induction is reasoning from the particular to the general—that is, looking at a feature that exists in several examples and drawing a conclusion about that feature. Deduction is the reverse; it is the statement of the generality and then supporting it with specific examples.

TEACHER CERTIFICATION STUDY GUIDE

52. According to Piaget, when does the development of symbolic functioning and language take place?
    (Average)

    A. Concrete operations stage
    B. Formal operations stage
    C. Sensorimotor stage
    D. Preoperational stage

Answer: D. Preoperational stage
Although there is no general theory of cognitive development, the most historically influential theory was developed by Jean Piaget, a Swiss psychologist (1896-1980). His theory provided many central concepts in the field of developmental psychology. His theory concerned the growth of intelligence, which for Piaget meant the ability to more accurately represent the world and perform logical operations on representations of concepts grounded in the world. His theory concerns the emergence and acquisition of schemata - schemes of how one perceives the world - in "developmental stages," times when children are acquiring new ways of mentally representing information.

His theory is considered "constructivist," meaning that, unlike nativist theories (which describe cognitive development as the unfolding of innate knowledge and abilities) or empiricist theories (which describe cognitive development as the gradual acquisition of knowledge through experience), asserts that we construct our cognitive abilities through self-motivated action in the world. For his development of the theory, Piaget was awarded the Erasmus Prize.

53. What should a teacher do when students have not responded well to an instructional activity?
    (Average)

    A. Reevaluate learner needs
    B. Request administrative help
    C. Continue with the activity another day
    D. Assign homework on the concept

Answer: A. Reevaluate learner needs
The value of teacher observations cannot be underestimated. It is through the use of observations that the teacher is able to informally assess the needs of the students during instruction. These observations will drive the lesson and determine the direction that the lesson will take based on student activity and behavior. After a lesson is carefully planned, teacher observation is the single most important component of an instructional presentation. If the teacher observes that a particular student is not on task, she will change the method of instruction accordingly. She may change from a teacher-directed approach to a more interactive approach. Questioning will increase in order to

increase the participation of the students. If appropriate, the teacher will introduce manipulative materials to the lesson. In addition, teachers may switch to a cooperative group activity, thereby removing the responsibility of instruction from the teacher and putting it on the students.

54. How could a KWL chart be used in instruction?
    (Average)

    A. To motivate students to do a research paper
    B. To assess prior knowledge of the students
    C. To assist in teaching skills
    D. To put events in sequential order

Answer: B. To assess prior knowledge of the students
To understand information, not simply repeat it, students must connect it to their previous understanding. Textbooks cannot do that. Instead, teachers—the people who know students best—have to find out what they know and how to build on that knowledge. In science, having students make predictions before conducting experiments is an obvious way of finding out what they know and having them compare their observations to those predictions helps connect new knowledge and old. In history, teachers can also ask students what they know about a topic before they begin studying it or ask them to make predictions about what they will learn. KWL charts, in which students discuss what they know, what they want to know, and (later), what they have learned, are one way to activate this prior knowledge.

55. Which of the following is an example of a synthesis question according to Bloom's taxonomy?
    (Rigorous)

    A. "What is the definition of_____?"
    B. "Compare ____ to ____."
    C. "Match column A to column   B."
    D. "Propose an alternative to_____."

Answer: D. "Propose an alternative to_____"
There are six levels to the taxonomy: knowledge, comprehension, application, analysis, synthesis, and evaluation. Synthesis is compiling information together in a different way by combining elements in a new pattern or proposing alternative solutions to produce a unique communication, plan, or proposed set of operations or to derive a set of abstract relations.

TEACHER CERTIFICATION STUDY GUIDE

56. Which statement is an example of specific praise?
    (Average)

    A. "John, you are the only person in class not paying attention"
    B. "William, I thought we agreed that you would turn in all of your homework"
    C. "Robert, you did a good job staying in line. See how it helped us get to music class on time?"
    D. "Class, you did a great job cleaning up the art room"

Answer: C. "Robert, you did a good job staying in line. See how it helped us get to music class on time?"
Praise is a powerful tool in obtaining and maintaining order in a classroom. In addition, it is an effective motivator. It is even more effective if the positive results of good behavior are included.

57. Mrs. Grant is providing her students with many extrinsic motivators in order to increase their intrinsic motivation. Which of the following best explains this relationship?
    (Rigorous)

    A. This is a good relationship and will increase intrinsic motivation
    B. The relationship builds animosity between the teacher and the students
    C. Extrinsic motivation does not in itself help to build intrinsic motivation
    D. There is no place for extrinsic motivation in the classroom

Answer: C. Extrinsic motivation does not in itself help to build intrinsic motivation
There are some cases where it is necessary to utilize extrinsic motivation; however, the use of extrinsic motivation is not alone a strategy to use to build intrinsic motivation. Intrinsic motivation comes from within the student themselves, while extrinsic motivation comes from outside parties.

58. Which of the following is NOT a factor in student self-motivation?
    (Rigorous)

    A. Breaking larger tasks into more manageable steps
    B. Permitting students to turn in assignments late
    C. Offering students control over the assignment
    D. Allowing students to create dream boards

Answer: B. Permitting students to turn in assignments late
Student motivation in the classroom is an essential component of teaching. Highly motivated students actively engage more in the learning process than less motivated students. Teachers should have a firm understanding of the diverse aspects that

TEACHER CERTIFICATION STUDY GUIDE

influence student motivation and then incorporate strategies for encouraging motivation in the classroom.

59. **Which of the following is NOT a part of the hardware of a computer system?**
    (Easy)

    A. Storage device
    B. Input devices
    C. Software
    D. Central Processing Unit

Answer: C. Software
Software is not a part of the hardware of a computer but instead consists of all of the programs which allow the computer to run. Software is either an operating system or an application program.

60. **When pulling educational information from shared drives what is the MOST important factor to consider?**
    (Rigorous)

    A. What is the intended use of the information
    B. What age group is the information best suited for
    C. Where the information came from
    D. Who the author of the information is

Answer: A. What is the intended use of the information
The concept of using shared drives is well established and as with most educational network operating systems, retrieving information is relatively straightforward. However, it is fundamentally important to know that not all information is the best suited for classroom instruction. Each lesson will need to be tailored and adjusted to students' needs.

TEACHER CERTIFICATION STUDY GUIDE

61. Which of the following are the three primary categories of instructional technology tools?
    (Rigorous)

    A. Creation/design/implementation
    B. Research/implementation/assessment
    C. Assessment/creation/research
    D. Design/research/usage

Answer: C. Assessment/creation/research
Assessment programs may not necessarily teach students about technology but are very clear-cut and simple programs to use. Creation is the category where students can practice their technology skills. Teachers can permit students to utilize their researching skills by allowing classroom time to research the topics they are studying. This also allows them to keep them abreast of technological advances.

62. When a teacher is evaluating a student's technologically produced product, which of the following is considered the MOST important factor to consider?
    (Rigorous)

    A. Content
    B. Design
    C. Audience
    D. Relevance

Answer: D. Relevance
All of the above are important; however, relevance is of utmost importance. It is imperative that students are aware of how to design a technologically based assignment and also to incorporate effective content. However, if the content is not relevant and pertinent to the topic studied, it is not considered an effective learning strategy.

63. You are a classroom teacher in a building that does not have a computer lab for your class to use. However, knowing that you enjoy incorporating technology into the classroom, your principal has worked to find computers for your room. They are set up in the back of your classroom and have software loaded, but have no access to the intranet or internet within your building. Which of the following is NOT an acceptable method for using these computers within your classroom instruction?
(Rigorous)

   A. Rotating the students in small groups through the computers as centers
   B. Putting students at the computers individually for skill-based review or practice
   C. Dividing your classroom into three groups and putting each group at one computer and completing a whole class lesson
   D. Using the computers for students to complete their writing assignments with an assigned sign-up sheet, so the students know the order in which they will type their stories

Answer: C. Dividing your classroom into three groups and putting each group at one computer and completing a whole class lesson
Three computers are not enough for a typical class size across the country. This would involve too many students at one computer and could result in behavioral issues. Additionally, it would be difficult for the students to all have the ability to interact in a meaningful way with the software. If you would like to complete a whole class lesson using the technology, it would be best to find a projector that connects to the computer so all students have equal opportunity to participate and see.

TEACHER CERTIFICATION STUDY GUIDE

64. **What are three steps, in the correct order, for evaluating software before purchasing it for use within the classroom?**
    (Rigorous)

    A. Read the instructions to ensure it will work with the computer you have, try it out as if you were a student, and examine how the program handles errors or mistakes the student may make
    B. Try the computer program as if you were a student, read any online information about the program, have a student use the program and provide feedback
    C. Read the instructions and load it onto your computer, try out the program yourself as if you were a student, have a student use the program and provide feedback
    D. Read the instructions, have a student use the program, try it out yourself

Answer: A. Read the instructions to ensure it will work with the computer you have, try it out as if you were a student, and examine how the program handles errors or mistakes the students may make

You should not have students use the program until you have read all of the material related to the use, tried it out yourself as if you were a student and made many different types of mistakes when using it. You should try to make as many different types of errors as possible, so that you can see how the program responds and ensure it is how you want your student's errors handled.

65. **When a teacher wants to utilize an assessment that is subjective in nature, which of the following is the most effective method for scoring?**
    (Easy)

    A. Rubric
    B. Checklist
    C. Alternative assessment
    D. Subjective measures should not be utilized

Answer: A. Rubric
Rubrics are the most effective tool for assessing items that can be considered subjective. They provide the students with a clearer picture of teacher expectations and provide the teacher with a more consistent method of comparing this type of assignment.

TEACHER CERTIFICATION STUDY GUIDE

66. **What is an example of formative feedback?**
    (Average)

    A. The results of an intelligence test
    B. Correcting the tests in small groups
    C. Verbal behavior that expresses approval of a student response to a test item
    D. Scheduling a discussion prior to the test

Answer: C. Verbal behavior that expresses approval of a student response to a test item
Standardized testing is currently under great scrutiny, but educators agree that any test that serves as a means of gathering and interpreting information about children's learning and that can provide accurate, helpful input for nurturing children's further growth is acceptable. All testing must be formative in nature. Formative evaluation is the basic, everyday kind of assessment that teachers continually do to understand students' growth and to help them learn further.

67. **Norm-referenced tests:**
    (Rigorous)

    A. Give information only about the local samples results
    B. Provide information about how the local test takers did compared to a representative sampling of national test takers
    C. Make no comparisons to national test takers
    D. None of the above

Answer: B. Provide information about how the local test takers did compared to a representative sampling of national test takers
This is the definition of a norm-referenced test.

68. **What is the best definition for an achievement test?**
    (Average)

    A. It measures mechanical and practical abilities
    B. It measures broad areas of knowledge that are the result of cumulative learning experiences
    C. It measures the ability to learn to perform a task
    D. It measures performance related to specific, recently acquired information

Answer: B. It measures broad areas of knowledge that are the result of cumulative learning experiences
The ways that a teacher uses test data is a meaningful aspect of instruction and may increase the motivation level of the students especially when this information is available in the form of feedback to the students. This feedback should indicate to the students

what they need to do in order to improve their achievement. Frequent testing and feedback is most often an effective way to increase achievement.

69. **How are standardized tests useful in assessment?**
    (Average)

    A. For teacher evaluation
    B. For evaluation of the administration
    C. For comparison from school to school
    D. For comparison to the population on which the test was normed

Answer: D. For comparison to the population on which the test was normed
While the efficacy of the standardized tests that are being used nationally has come under attack recently, they are actually the only device for comparing where an individual student stands with a wide range of peers. They also provide a measure for a program or a school to evaluate how their own students are doing as compared to the populace at large.

70. **Mr. Brown wishes to improve his parent communication skills. Which of the following is a strategy he can utilize to accomplish this goal?**
    (Easy)

    A. Hold parent-teacher conferences
    B. Send home positive notes
    C. Have parent nights where the parents are invited into his classroom
    D. All of the above

Answer: D. All of the above
Increasing parent communication skills is important for teachers. All of the listed strategies are methods a teacher can utilize to increase his skills.

TEACHER CERTIFICATION STUDY GUIDE

71. **When communicating with parents for whom English is not the primary language, you should:**
    (Easy)

    A. Provide materials whenever possible in their native language
    B. Use an interpreter
    C. Provide the same communication as you would to native English speaking parents
    D. All of the above

Answer: D. All of the above
When communicating with non-English speaking parents, it is important to treat them as you would any other parent and utilize any means necessary to ensure they have the ability to participate in their child's educational process.

72. **Which statement best reflects why family involvement is important to a student's educational success?**
    (Easy)

    A. Reading the class newsletter constitutes strong family involvement
    B. Family involvement means to attend graduation
    C. There are limited ways a parent can be active in their child's education
    D. The more family members are involved, the more success a student is likely to experience

Answer: D. The more family members are involved, the more success a student is likely to experience
Although reading the class newsletter and coming to graduation are obvious parts of parental involvement, it is not the sole involvement for which teachers hope. Unlike the statement in choice C, there are many unique ways parents can participate and share talents toward their child's education. Parents are invited in to assist with workshops, attend class trips, participate as room parents, organize special events, read to the class, speak of an occupation, help with classroom housekeeping, and more. Parents can also be involved by volunteering for the PTO/A, library help, office help, and other tasks. Some teachers plan a few events a year in the classroom for special parties, presentations and events.

TEACHER CERTIFICATION STUDY GUIDE

73. **Which of the following is NOT an appropriate method for teachers to interact with families of diverse backgrounds?**
    (Easy)

    A. Show respect to parents
    B. Share personal stories concerning the student
    C. Display patience with parents
    D. Disregard culture of student

Answer: D. Disregard culture of student
The culture of the student must be taken into account when interacting with families of diverse backgrounds. Teachers must show respect to all parents and families, and they need to realize that various cultures have different views of how children should be educated—this must be taken into consideration when dealing with families.

74. **A parent has left an angry message on the teacher's voicemail. The message relates to a concern about a student and is directed at the teacher. The teacher should:**
    (Average)

    A. Call back immediately and confront the parent
    B. Cool off, plan what to discuss with the parent, then call back
    C. Question the child to find out what set off the parent
    D. Ignore the message, since feelings of anger usually subside after a while

Answer: B. Cool off, plan what to discuss with the parent, then call back
It is professional for a teacher to keep her head in the face of emotion and respond to an angry parent in a calm and objective manner. The teacher should give herself time to cool off and plan the conversation with the parents with the purpose of understanding the concern and resolving it, rather than putting the parent in his or her place. Above all, the teacher should remember that parent-teacher interactions should aim to benefit the student.

TEACHER CERTIFICATION STUDY GUIDE

75. **Which is NOT considered a good practice when conducting parent-teacher conferences?**
    (Average)

    A. Ending the conference with an agreed plan of action
    B. Figure out questions for parents during the conference
    C. Prepare work samples, records of behavior, and assessment information
    D. Prepare a welcoming environment, set a good mood, and be an active listener

Answer: B. Figure out questions for parents during the conference
Choices A, C, and D all reflect effective practices for holding a successful parent teacher conference. Teachers should prepare questions and comments for parents prior to the conference so they are optimally prepared.

76. **Which of the following should NOT be a purpose of a parent-teacher conference?**
    (Average)

    A. To involve the parent in their child's education
    B. To establish a friendship with the child's parents
    C. To resolve a concern about the child's performance
    D. To inform parents of positive behaviors by the child

Answer: B. To establish a friendship with the child's parents
The purpose of a parent-teacher conference is to involve parents in their child's education, address concerns about the child's performance, and share positive aspects of the student's learning with the parents. It would be unprofessional to allow the conference to degenerate into a social visit to establish a friendship.

77. **Which of the following is a technological strategy that keeps students and teachers interactively communicating about issues in the classroom and beyond?**
    (Rigorous)

    A. Distance learning
    B. Mentoring support system
    C. Conceptual learning modalities
    D. Community resources

Answer: A. Distance learning
Distance learning is the process of creating educational experiences for students outside the classroom. This growing technological tool is becoming widely used in schools and

institutions around the country. With the recent trend of technological advances, distance learning is becoming highly appreciated as an effective learning strategy.

78. **In the past, teaching has been viewed as _____ while in more current society it has been viewed as _____.**
    (Rigorous)

    A. isolating…collaborative
    B. collaborative…isolating
    C. supportive…isolating
    D. isolating…supportive

Answer: A. isolating…collaborative
In the past, teachers often walked into their own classrooms and closed the door. They were not involved in any form of collaboration and were responsible for only the students within their classrooms. However, in today's more modern schools, teachers work in collaborative teams and are responsible for all of the children in a school setting.

79. **Which of the following is a good reason to collaborate with a peer?**
    (Easy)

    A. To increase your knowledge in areas where you feel you are weak, but the peer is strong
    B. To increase your planning time and that of your peer by combining the classes and taking more breaks
    C. To have fewer lesson plans to write
    D. To teach fewer subjects

Answer: A. To increase your knowledge in areas where you feel you are weak, but the peer is strong
One of the best reasons to collaborate is to share and develop your knowledge base.

80. **Which of the following is responsible for working with the school in matters concerning the business of running a school?**
    (Rigorous)

    A. Curriculum coordinators
    B. Administrators
    C. Board of Education
    D. Parent-Teacher organizations

Answer: C. Board of Education
The Board of Education is elected by the district to offer direction for the students and their schools. Among its many responsibilities, the Board establishes a long-term vision

for the district and designs their policies and goals. The administrator carries out the school district's policies and manages the day-to-day operations of the school.

81. **What would happen if a school utilized an integrated approach to professional development?**
    (Average)

    A. All stakeholders needs are addressed
    B. Teachers and administrators are on the same page
    C. High-quality programs for students are developed
    D. Parents drive the curriculum and instruction

Answer: C. High-quality programs for students are developed
The implementation of an integrated approach to professional development is a critical component to ensuring success of programs for students. It involves teachers, parents, and other community members working together to develop appropriate programs to ensure students are receiving the necessary instruction to be successful in the future workforce.

82. **Which is true of child protective services?**
    (Rigorous)

    A. They have been forced to become more punitive in their attempts to treat and prevent child abuse and neglect
    B. They have become more a means for identifying cases of abuse and less an agent for rehabilitation due to the large volume of cases
    C. They have become advocates for structured discipline within the school
    D. They have become a strong advocate in the court system

Answer: B. They have become more a means for identifying cases of abuse and less an agent for rehabilitation due to the large volume of cases
Child protective serves is the agency a teacher/school district would contact for suspected child abuse in a student.

TEACHER CERTIFICATION STUDY GUIDE

83. **What is a benefit of frequent self-assessment?**
    (Average)

    A. Opens new venues for professional development
    B. Saves teachers the pressure of being observed by others
    C. Reduces time spent on areas not needing attention
    D. Offers a model for students to adopt in self-improvement

Answer: A. Opens new venues for professional development
When a teacher is involved in the process of self-reflection and self-assessment, one of the common outcomes is that the teacher comes to identify areas of skill or knowledge that require more research or improvement on her part. She may become interested in overcoming a particular weakness in her performance or may decide to attend a workshop or consult with a mentor to learn more about a particular area of concern.

84. **Mrs. Graham has taken the time to reflect, completed observations, and asked for feedback about the interactions between her and her students from her principal. It is obvious by seeking this information out that Mrs. Graham understands which of the following?**
    (Rigorous)

    A. The importance of clear communication with the principal
    B. She needs to analyze her effectiveness of classroom interactions
    C. She is clearly communicating with the principal
    D. She cares about her students

Answer: B. She needs to analyze her effectiveness of classroom interactions
By utilizing reflection, observations, and feedback from peers or supervisors, teachers can help to build their own understanding of how they interact with students. In this way, they can better analyze their effectiveness at building appropriate relationships with students.

85. **Which of the following are ways a professional can assess his/her teaching strengths and weaknesses?**
    (Rigorous)

    A. Examining how many students were unable to understand a concept
    B. Asking peers for suggestions or ideas
    C. Self-evaluation/reflection of lessons taught
    D. All of the above

Answer: D. All of the above
It is important for teachers to involve themselves in constant periods of reflection and self-reflection to ensure they are meeting the needs of the students.

TEACHER CERTIFICATION STUDY GUIDE

86. **In successful inclusion of students with disabilities:**
    (Average)

    A. A variety of instructional arrangements are available
    B. School personnel shift the responsibility for learning outcomes to the student
    C. The physical facilities are used as they are
    D. Regular classroom teachers have sole responsibility for evaluating student progress

Answer: A. A variety if instructional arrangements are available
Here are some support systems and activities that are in evidence where successful inclusion has occurred: attitudes and beliefs

- The regular teacher believes the student can succeed
- School personnel are committed to accepting responsibility for the learning outcomes of students with disabilities
- School personnel and the students in the class have been prepared to receive a student with disabilities

87. **Teachers may duplicate copies of informational materials provided that they meet the following requirement/s:**
    (Rigorous)

    A. Brevity
    B. Spontaneity
    C. Cumulative effect
    D. All of the above

Answer: D. All of the above
Copyright is a type of protection provided by the United States to an author's literary works which also includes dramatic, musical, artistic, and other intellectual works. The conscientious use of these requirements will protect teachers and students from accusations of educational copyright infringement.

88. **Which of the following is one of the greatest obstacles that new teachers face when first entering the profession?**
   (Rigorous)

   A. Dealing with behavioral issues in the classroom
   B. Monitoring daily student success
   C. Developing rapport with parents and caretakers
   D. Creating weekly lesson plans

Answer: A. Dealing with behavioral issues in the classroom
Dealing with behavioral problems is one of the major concerns that teachers in the classroom face today. Disruptive behavior results in lost curriculum time and creates a classroom environment that is not always conducive to learning. Teachers should be proactive in dealing with behavioral issues at the time of the occurrence.

89. **How can a teacher use a student's permanent record?**
   (Average)

   A. To develop a better understanding of the needs of the student
   B. To record all instances of student disruptive behavior
   C. To brainstorm ideas for discussing with parents at parent-teacher conferences
   D. To develop realistic expectations of the student's performance early in the year

Answer: A. To develop a better understanding of the needs of the student
The purpose of a student's permanent record is to give the teacher a better understanding of the student's educational history and provide her with relevant information to support the student's learning. Permanent records may not be used to arrive at preconceived judgments or to build a case against the student. Above all, the contents of a student's permanent record are confidential.

90. **To what does the validity of a test refer?**
   (Rigorous)

   A. Its consistency
   B. Its usefulness
   C. Its accuracy
   D. The degree of true scores it provide

Answer: B. Its usefulness
The *Joint Technical Standards for Educational and Psychological Testing* APA, AERA, NCME, 1985) states: "Validity is the most important consideration in test evaluation. The concept refers to the appropriateness, meaningfulness and usefulness of *the specific*

inferences made from test scores. Test validation is the process of accumulating evidence to support such inferences. A variety of inferences may be made from scores produced by a given test, and there are many ways of accumulating evidence to support any particular inference. Validity, however, is a unitary concept. Although evidence may be accumulated in many ways, validity always refers to the degree to which that evidence supports the inferences that are made from test scores."

TEACHER CERTIFICATION STUDY GUIDE

THEA
TEXAS HIGHER EDUCATION ASSESSMENT

TEACHER CERTIFICATION STUDY GUIDE

READING SAMPLE TEST

Read the following paragraph, and answer the questions that follow.

This writer has often been asked to tutor hospitalized children with cystic fibrosis. While undergoing all the precautionary measures to see these children (i.e., scrubbing thoroughly and donning sterilized protective gear—for the children's protection), she has often wondered why their parents subject these children to the pressures of schooling and trying to catch up on what they have missed because of hospitalization, a normal part of cystic fibrosis patients' lives. These children undergo so many tortuous treatments a day that it seems cruel to expect them to learn as normal children do, especially with their life expectancies as short as they are.

1. **What is meant by the word "precautionary" in the second sentence?**
   (Easy)

   A. Careful
   B. Protective
   C. Medical
   D. Sterilizing

2. **What is the main idea of this passage?**
   (Average)

   A. There is a lot of preparation involved in visiting a patient of cystic fibrosis.
   B. Children with cystic fibrosis are incapable of living normal lives.
   C. Certain concessions should be made for children with cystic fibrosis.
   D. Children with cystic fibrosis die young.

3. **What is the author's purpose?**
   (Average)

   A. To inform
   B. To entertain
   C. To describe
   D. To narrate

4. **What is the author's tone?**
   (Rigorous)

   A. Sympathetic
   B. Cruel
   C. Disbelieving
   D. Cheerful

5. **What type of organizational pattern is the author using?**
   (Rigorous)

   A. Classification
   B. Explanation
   C. Compare and contrast
   D. Cause and effect

6. **How is the author so familiar with the procedures used when visiting a child with cystic fibrosis?**
   (Easy)

   A. She has read about it.
   B. She works in a hospital.
   C. She is the parent of one.
   D. She often tutors them.

7. **What kind of relationship is found within the last sentence that starts with "These children undergo..." and ends with "...as short as they are"?**
   (Rigorous)

   A. Addition
   B. Explanation
   C. Generalization
   D. Classification

8. **Does the author present an argument that is valid or invalid concerning the schooling of children with cystic fibrosis?**
   (Easy)

   A. Valid
   B. Invalid

9. **The author states that it is "cruel" to expect children with cystic fibrosis to learn as "normal" children do. Is this a fact or an opinion?**
   (Easy)

   A. Fact
   B. Opinion

10. **Is there evidence of bias in this paragraph?**
    (Rigorous)

    A. Yes
    B. No

Read the following passage, and answer the questions that follow.
Disciplinary practices have been found to affect diverse areas of child development such as moral values, obedience to authority, and performance at school. Even though the dictionary has a specific definition for the word "discipline," it is still open to interpretation by people of different cultures.

There are four types of disciplinary styles: assertion of power, withdrawal of love, reasoning, and permissiveness. Assertion of power involves the use of force to discourage unwanted behavior. Withdrawal of love involves making the love of a parent conditional on children's good behavior. Reasoning involves persuading children to behave one way rather than another. Permissiveness involves allowing children to do as they please and face the consequences of their actions.

11. **What is the meaning of the word "diverse" in the first sentence?**
    (Average)

    A. Many
    B. Related to children
    C. Disciplinary
    D. More

12. **What is the main idea of this passage?**
    (Easy)

    A. Different people have different ideas of what discipline is.
    B. Permissiveness is the most widely used disciplinary style.
    C. Most people agree on their definition of discipline.
    D. There are four disciplinary styles.

13. **Name the four types of disciplinary styles.**
    (Easy)

    A. Reasoning, power assertion, morality, and permissiveness
    B. Morality, reasoning, permissiveness, and withdrawal of love
    C. Withdrawal of love, permissiveness, assertion of power, and reasoning
    D. Permissiveness, morality, reasoning, and power assertion

14. **What does the technique of reasoning involve?**
    (Average)

    A. Persuading children to behave in a certain way
    B. Allowing a child to do as he or she pleases
    C. Using force to discourage unwanted behavior
    D. Making love conditional on good behavior

15. **What organizational structure is used in the first sentence of the second paragraph?**
    (Rigorous)

    A. Addition
    B. Explanation
    C. Definition
    D. Simple listing

16. **What is the author's purpose in writing this?**
    (Average)

    A. To describe
    B. To narrate
    C. To entertain
    D. To inform

17. **What is the author's tone?**
    (Rigorous)

    A. Disbelieving
    B. Angry
    C. Informative
    D. Optimistic

18. **What is the overall organizational pattern of this passage?**
    (Rigorous)

    A. Generalization
    B. Cause and effect
    C. Addition
    D. Summary

Read the following passage, and answer the questions that follow.

One of the most difficult problems plaguing American education is the assessment of teachers. No one denies that teachers ought to be answerable for what they do, but what exactly does that mean? *The Oxford American Dictionary* defines accountability as the obligation to give a reckoning or explanation for one's actions.

Do students have to learn, for teaching to have taken place? Historically, teaching has not been defined in this restrictive manner; teachers were thought to be responsible for the quantity and quality of material covered and for the way in which it was presented. However, some definitions of teaching now imply that students must learn in order for teaching to have taken place.

As a teacher who tries my best to keep current on all the latest teaching strategies, I believe that those teachers who do not bother to read an educational journal every once in a while should be kept under close watch. There are many teachers out there who have been teaching for decades and refuse to change their ways, although research has proven that their methods are outdated and ineffective. There is no place in the profession of teaching for these types of individuals. It is time that the American educational system clean house, for the sake of our children.

19. **From reading this passage we can conclude that**
    (Average)

    A. The author is a teacher.
    B. The author has many children.
    C. The author has written a book about discipline.
    D. The author has done a lot of research on discipline.

20. **The author states that "assertion of power involves the use of force to discourage unwanted behavior." Is this a fact or an opinion?**
    (Average)

    A. Fact
    B. Opinion

21. **Is this passage biased?**
    (Rigorous)

    A. Yes
    B. No

22. What is the meaning of the word "reckoning" in the third sentence?
    (Easy)

    A. Thought
    B. Answer
    C. Obligation
    D. Explanation

23. What is meant by the word "plaguing" in the first sentence?
    (Average)

    A. Causing problems
    B. Causing illness
    C. Causing anger
    D. Causing failure

24. Where does the author get her definition of "accountability?"
    (Average)

    A. *Webster's Dictionary*
    B. *Encyclopedia Britannica*
    C. *Oxford Dictionary*
    D. *World Book Encyclopedia*

25. What is the main idea of the passage?
    (Average)

    A. Teachers should not be answerable for what they do.
    B. Teachers who do not do their job should be fired.
    C. The author is a good teacher.
    D. Assessment of teachers is a serious problem in society today.

26. The author states that teacher assessment is a problem for
    (Average)

    A. Elementary schools
    B. Secondary schools
    C. American education
    D. Families

27. What is the author's purpose in writing this?
    (Average)

    A. To entertain
    B. To narrate
    C. To describe
    D. To persuade

28. The author's tone is one of
    (Rigorous)

    A. Disbelief
    B. Excitement
    C. Support
    D. Concern

29. Is there evidence of bias in this passage?
    (Rigorous)

    A. Yes
    B. No

30. What is the organizational pattern of the second paragraph?
    (Rigorous)

    A. Cause and effect
    B. Classification
    C. Addition
    D. Explanation

31. **From the passage, one can infer that**
    (Average)

    A. The author considers himself or herself to be a good teacher.
    B. Poor teachers should be fired.
    C. Students have to learn for teaching to take place.
    D. The author will be fired.

32. **Is this a valid argument?**
    (Easy)

    A. Yes
    B. No

33. **Teachers who do not keep current on educational trends should be fired. Is this a fact or an opinion?**
    (Easy)

    A. Fact
    B. Opinion

34. **What is the best summary for the passage?**
    (Average)

    A. Teachers need to be more accountable.
    B. Today's teachers must be responsible for student learning.
    C. Older teachers have no place in the classroom.
    D. Teachers are responsible for the quantity they teach, not the quality.

Read the following paragraph, and answer the questions that follow.

Mr. Smith gave instructions for the painting to be hung on the wall. And then it leaped forth before his eyes: the little cottages on the river, the white clouds floating over the valley, and the green of the towering mountain ranges which were seen in the distance. The painting was so vivid that it seemed almost real. Mr. Smith was now absolutely certain that the painting had been worth the money.

35. **What is the meaning of the word "vivid" in the third sentence?**
    (Easy)

    A. Lifelike
    B. Dark
    C. Expensive
    D. Big

36. **What does the author mean by the expression "it leaped forth before his eyes"?**
    (Average)

    A. The painting fell off the wall.
    B. The painting appeared so real it was almost three-dimensional.
    C. The painting struck Mr. Smith in the face.
    D. Mr. Smith was hallucinating.

37. **What is the main idea of this passage?**
    (Average)

    A. The painting that Mr. Smith purchased is expensive.
    B. Mr. Smith purchased a painting.
    C. Mr. Smith was pleased with the quality of the painting he had purchased.
    D. The painting depicted cottages and valleys.

38. **The author's purpose is to**
    (Average)

    A. Inform
    B. Entertain
    C. Persuade
    D. Narrate

39. **From the last sentence, one can infer that**
    (Rigorous)

    A. The painting was expensive.
    B. The painting was cheap.
    C. Mr. Smith was considering purchasing the painting.
    D. Mr. Smith thought the painting was too expensive and decided not to purchase it.

40. **Is this passage biased?**
    (Rigorous)

    A. Yes
    B. No

TEACHER CERTIFICATION STUDY GUIDE

Answer Key

1.	B		21.	B
2.	C		22.	D
3.	C		23.	A
4.	A		24.	C
5.	B		25.	D
6.	D		26.	C
7.	B		27.	D
8.	B		28.	D
9.	B		29.	A
10.	A		30.	D
11.	A		31.	A
12.	A		32.	B
13.	C		33.	B
14.	A		34.	B
15.	D		35.	A
16.	D		36.	B
17.	C		37.	C
18.	C		38.	D
19.	D		39.	A
20.	A		40.	B

Rigor Table

Easy
1, 6, 8, 9, 12, 13, 22, 32, 33, 35

Average
2, 3, 11, 14, 16, 19, 20, 23, 24, 25, 26, 27, 31, 34, 36, 37, 38

Rigorous
4, 5, 7, 10, 15, 17, 18, 21, 28, 29, 30, 39, 40

TEACHER CERTIFICATION STUDY GUIDE

READING SAMPLE TEST WITH RATIONALES

Read the following paragraph, and answer the questions that follow.
This writer has often been asked to tutor hospitalized children with cystic fibrosis. While undergoing all the precautionary measures to see these children (i.e., scrubbing thoroughly and donning sterilized protective gear—for the children's protection), she has often wondered why their parents subject these children to the pressures of schooling and trying to catch up on what they have missed because of hospitalization, a normal part of cystic fibrosis patients' lives. These children undergo so many tortuous treatments a day that it seems cruel to expect them to learn as normal children do, especially with their life expectancies as short as they are.

1. **What is meant by the word "precautionary" in the second sentence?**
   (Easy)

   A. Careful
   B. Protective
   C. Medical
   D. Sterilizing

Answer: B. Protective
The writer uses expressions such as "protective gear" and "child's protection" to emphasize this.

2. **What is the main idea of this passage?**
   (Average)

   A. There is a lot of preparation involved in visiting a patient of cystic fibrosis.
   B. Children with cystic fibrosis are incapable of living normal lives.
   C. Certain concessions should be made for children with cystic fibrosis.
   D. Children with cystic fibrosis die young.

Answer: C. Certain concessions should be made for children with cystic fibrosis
The author states that she wonders "why parents subject these children to the pressures of schooling," and that "it seems cruel to expect them to learn as normal children do." In making these statements, she appears to be expressing the belief that these children should not have to do what "normal" children do. They have enough to deal with—their illness itself.

TEACHER CERTIFICATION STUDY GUIDE

3. What is the author's purpose?
   (Average)

   A. To inform
   B. To entertain
   C. To describe
   D. To narrate

Answer: C. To describe
The author is simply describing her experience in working with children with cystic fibrosis.

4. What is the author's tone?
   (Rigorous)

   A. Sympathetic
   B. Cruel
   C. Disbelieving
   D. Cheerful

Answer: A. Sympathetic
The author states that "it seems cruel to expect them to learn as normal children do," thereby indicating that she feels sorry for them.

5. What type of organizational pattern is the author using?
   (Rigorous)

   A. Classification
   B. Explanation
   C. Compare and contrast
   D. Cause and effect

Answer: B. Explanation
The author mentions tutoring children with cystic fibrosis in her opening sentence and goes on to "explain" some of these issues that are involved with her job.

TEACHER CERTIFICATION STUDY GUIDE

6. How is the author so familiar with the procedures used when visiting a child with cystic fibrosis?
   (Easy)

   A. She has read about it.
   B. She works in a hospital.
   C. She is the parent of one.
   D. She often tutors them.

Answer: D. She often tutors them.
The writer states this fact in the opening sentence.

7. What kind of relationship is found within the last sentence that starts with "These children undergo..." and ends with "...as short as they are"?
   (Rigorous)

   A. Addition
   B. Explanation
   C. Generalization
   D. Classification

Answer: B. Explanation
In mentioning that their life expectancies are short, she is explaining by giving one reason why it is cruel to expect them to learn as normal children do.

8. Does the author present an argument that is valid or invalid concerning the schooling of children with cystic fibrosis?
   (Easy)

   A. Valid
   B. Invalid

Answer: B. Invalid
Even though to most readers, the writer's argument makes good sense, it is biased and lacks real evidence.

TEACHER CERTIFICATION STUDY GUIDE

9. The author states that it is "cruel" to expect children with cystic fibrosis to learn as "normal" children do. Is this a fact or an opinion?
   (Easy)

   A. Fact
   B. Opinion

Answer: B. Opinion
The fact that she states that it "seems" cruel indicates that there is no evidence to support this belief.

10. Is there evidence of bias in this paragraph?
    (Rigorous)

    A. Yes
    B. No

Answer: A. Yes
The writer clearly feels sorry for these children and gears her writing in that direction.

Read the following passage, and answer the questions that follow.
Disciplinary practices have been found to affect diverse areas of child development such as moral values, obedience to authority, and performance at school. Even though the dictionary has a specific definition for the word "discipline," it is still open to interpretation by people of different cultures.

There are four types of disciplinary styles: assertion of power, withdrawal of love, reasoning, and permissiveness. Assertion of power involves the use of force to discourage unwanted behavior. Withdrawal of love involves making the love of a parent conditional on children's good behavior. Reasoning involves persuading children to behave one way rather than another. Permissiveness involves allowing children to do as they please and face the consequences of their actions.

11. What is the meaning of the word "diverse" in the first sentence?
    (Average)

    A. Many
    B. Related to children
    C. Disciplinary
    D. More

Answer: A. Many
Any of the other choices would be redundant in this sentence.

TEACHER CERTIFICATION STUDY GUIDE

12. **What is the main idea of this passage?**
    (Easy)

    A. Different people have different ideas of what discipline is.
    B. Permissiveness is the most widely used disciplinary style.
    C. Most people agree on their definition of discipline.
    D. There are four disciplinary styles.

Answer: A. Different people have different ideas of what discipline is.
Choice C is not true; the opposite is stated in the passage. Choice B could be true, but we have no evidence of this. Choice D is just one of the many facts listed in the passage.

13. **Name the four types of disciplinary styles.**
    (Easy)

    A. Reasoning, power assertion, morality, and permissiveness
    B. Morality, reasoning, permissiveness, and withdrawal of love
    C. Withdrawal of love, permissiveness, assertion of power, and reasoning
    D. Permissiveness, morality, reasoning, and power assertion

Answer: C. Withdrawal of love, permissiveness, assertion of power, and reasoning
This is directly stated in the second paragraph.

14. **What does the technique of reasoning involve?**
    (Average)

    A. Persuading children to behave in a certain way
    B. Allowing a child to do as he or she pleases
    C. Using force to discourage unwanted behavior
    D. Making love conditional on good behavior

Answer: A. Persuading children to behave in a certain way
This fact is directly stated in the second paragraph.

15. What organizational structure is used in the first sentence of the second paragraph?
    (Rigorous)

    A. Addition
    B. Explanation
    C. Definition
    D. Simple listing

Answer: D. Simple listing
The author simply states the types of disciplinary styles.

16. What is the author's purpose in writing this?
    (Average)

    A. To describe
    B. To narrate
    C. To entertain
    D. To inform

Answer: D. To inform
The author is providing the reader with information about disciplinary practices.

17. What is the author's tone?
    (Rigorous)

    A. Disbelieving
    B. Angry
    C. Informative
    D. Optimistic

Answer: C. Informative
The author appears to simply be stating the facts.

18. What is the overall organizational pattern of this passage?
    (Rigorous)

    A. Generalization
    B. Cause and effect
    C. Addition
    D. Summary

Answer: C. Addition
The author has taken a subject, in this case discipline, and developed it point by point.

TEACHER CERTIFICATION STUDY GUIDE

19. **From reading this passage we can conclude that**
    (Average)

    A. The author is a teacher.
    B. The author has many children.
    C. The author has written a book about discipline.
    D. The author has done a lot of research on discipline.

Answer: D. The author has done a lot of research on discipline.
Given all the facts mentioned in the passage, this is the only inference one can make.

20. **The author states that "assertion of power involves the use of force to discourage unwanted behavior." Is this a fact or an opinion?**
    (Average)

    A. Fact
    B. Opinion

Answer: A. Fact
The author appears to have done extensive research on this subject.

21. **Is this passage biased?**
    (Rigorous)

    A. Yes
    B. No

Answer: B. No
If the reader were so inclined, he could research discipline and find this information.

Read the following passage, and answer the questions that follow.
One of the most difficult problems plaguing American education is the assessment of teachers. No one denies that teachers ought to be answerable for what they do, but what exactly does that mean? *The Oxford American Dictionary* defines accountability as the obligation to give a reckoning or explanation for one's actions.

Do students have to learn, for teaching to have taken place? Historically, teaching has not been defined in this restrictive manner; teachers were thought to be responsible for the quantity and quality of material covered and for the way in which it was presented. However, some definitions of teaching now imply that students must learn in order for teaching to have taken place.

As a teacher who tries my best to keep current on all the latest teaching strategies, I believe that those teachers who do not bother to read an educational journal every once in a while should be kept under close watch. There are many teachers out there who have been teaching for decades and refuse to change their ways, although research has proven that their methods are outdated and ineffective. There is no place in the profession of teaching for these types of individuals. It is time that the American educational system clean house, for the sake of our children.

22. What is the meaning of the word "reckoning" in the third sentence? *(Easy)*

    A. Thought
    B. Answer
    C. Obligation
    D. Explanation

Answer: D. Explanation
The meaning of this word is directly stated in the same sentence.

23. What is meant by the word "plaguing" in the first sentence? *(Average)*

    A. Causing problems
    B. Causing illness
    C. Causing anger
    D. Causing failure

Answer: A. Causing problems
The first paragraph makes this definition clear.

TEACHER CERTIFICATION STUDY GUIDE

24. **Where does the author get her definition of "accountability?"**
    (Average)

    A. *Webster's Dictionary*
    B. *Encyclopedia Britannica*
    C. *Oxford Dictionary*
    D. *World Book Encyclopedia*

Answer: C. *Oxford Dictionary*
This is directly stated in the third sentence of the first paragraph.

25. **What is the main idea of the passage?**
    (Average)

    A. Teachers should not be answerable for what they do.
    B. Teachers who do not do their job should be fired.
    C. The author is a good teacher.
    D. Assessment of teachers is a serious problem in society today.

Answer: D. Assessment of teachers is a serious problem in society today.
Most of the passage is dedicated to elaborating on why teacher assessment is such a problem.

26. **The author states that teacher assessment is a problem for**
    (Average)

    A. Elementary schools
    B. Secondary schools
    C. American education
    D. Families

Answer: C. American education
This fact is directly stated in the first paragraph.

TEACHER CERTIFICATION STUDY GUIDE

27. What is the author's purpose in writing this?
    (Average)

    A. To entertain
    B. To narrate
    C. To describe
    D. To persuade

Answer: D. To persuade
The author does some describing, but the majority of her statements seemed geared towards convincing the reader that teachers who are lazy or who do not keep current should be fired.

28. The author's tone is one of
    (Rigorous)

    A. Disbelief
    B. Excitement
    C. Support
    D. Concern

Answer: D. Concern
The author appears concerned with the future of education.

29. Is there evidence of bias in this passage?
    (Rigorous)

    A. Yes
    B. No

Answer: A. Yes
The entire third paragraph is the author's opinion on the matter.

30. What is the organizational pattern of the second paragraph?
    (Rigorous)

    A. Cause and effect
    B. Classification
    C. Addition
    D. Explanation

Answer: D. Explanation
The author further explains what she meant by "...what exactly does that mean?" in the first paragraph.

TEACHER CERTIFICATION STUDY GUIDE

31. **From the passage, one can infer that**
    (Average)

    A. The author considers himself or herself to be a good teacher.
    B. Poor teachers should be fired.
    C. Students have to learn for teaching to take place.
    D. The author will be fired.

Answer: A. The author considers himself or herself to be a good teacher.
The first sentence of the third paragraph alludes to this.

32. **Is this a valid argument?**
    (Easy)

    A. Yes
    B. No

Answer: B. No
In the third paragraph, the author appears to be resentful of lazy teachers.

33. **Teachers who do not keep current on educational trends should be fired. Is this a fact or an opinion?**
    (Easy)

    A. Fact
    B. Opinion

Answer: B. Opinion
There may be those who feel they can be good teachers by using old methods.

34. **What is the best summary for the passage?**
    (Average)

    A. Teachers need to be more accountable.
    B. Today's teachers must be responsible for student learning.
    C. Older teachers have no place in the classroom.
    D. Teachers are responsible for the quantity they teach, not the quality.

Answer: B. Today's teachers must be responsible for student learning.
The one idea that applies to the whole passage is Choice B.

TEACHER CERTIFICATION STUDY GUIDE

Read the following paragraph, and answer the questions that follow.
Mr. Smith gave instructions for the painting to be hung on the wall. And then it leaped forth before his eyes: the little cottages on the river, the white clouds floating over the valley, and the green of the towering mountain ranges which were seen in the distance. The painting was so vivid that it seemed almost real. Mr. Smith was now absolutely certain that the painting had been worth the money.

35. What is the meaning of the word "vivid" in the third sentence?
(Easy)

- A. Lifelike
- B. Dark
- C. Expensive
- D. Big

Answer: A. Lifelike
This is reinforced by the second half of the same sentence.

36. What does the author mean by the expression "it leaped forth before his eyes"?
(Average)

- A. The painting fell off the wall.
- B. The painting appeared so real it was almost three-dimensional.
- C. The painting struck Mr. Smith in the face.
- D. Mr. Smith was hallucinating.

Answer: B. The painting appeared so real it was almost three-dimensional
This is almost directly stated in the third sentence.

37. What is the main idea of this passage?
(Average)

- A. The painting that Mr. Smith purchased is expensive.
- B. Mr. Smith purchased a painting.
- C. Mr. Smith was pleased with the quality of the painting he had purchased.
- D. The painting depicted cottages and valleys.

Answer: C. Mr. Smith was pleased with the quality of the painting he had purchased.
Every sentence in the paragraph alludes to this fact.

TEACHER CERTIFICATION STUDY GUIDE

38. **The author's purpose is to**
    (Average)

    A. Inform
    B. Entertain
    C. Persuade
    D. Narrate

Answer: D. Narrate
The author is simply narrating or telling the story of Mr. Smith and his painting.

39. **From the last sentence, one can infer that**
    (Rigorous)

    A. The painting was expensive.
    B. The painting was cheap.
    C. Mr. Smith was considering purchasing the painting.
    D. Mr. Smith thought the painting was too expensive and decided not to purchase it.

Answer: A. The painting was expensive.
Choice B is incorrect because, had the painting been cheap, chances are that Mr. Smith would not have considered his purchase. Choices C and D are ruled out by the fact that the painting had already been purchased. The author makes this clear when she says, "...the painting had been worth the money."

40. **Is this passage biased?**
    (Rigorous)

    A. Yes
    B. No

Answer: B. No
The author appears merely to be telling what happened when Mr. Smith had his new painting hung on the wall.

MATHEMATICS SAMPLE TEST

1. $\left(\dfrac{-4}{9}\right) + \left(\dfrac{-7}{10}\right) =$
   (Rigorous)

   A. $\dfrac{23}{90}$

   B. $\dfrac{-23}{90}$

   C. $\dfrac{103}{90}$

   D. $\dfrac{-103}{90}$

2. $0.74 =$
   (Easy)

   A. $\dfrac{74}{100}$

   B. 7.4%

   C. $\dfrac{33}{50}$

   D. $\dfrac{74}{10}$

3. $-9\dfrac{1}{4}$ ☐ $-8\dfrac{2}{3}$
   (Average)

   A. =
   B. <
   C. >
   D. ≤

4. 303 is what percent of 600?
   (Average)

   A. 0.505%
   B. 5.05%
   C. 505%
   D. 50.5%

5. An item that sells for $375 is put on sale at $120. What is the percent of decrease?
   (Average)

   A. 25%
   B. 28%
   C. 68%
   D. 34%

6. Two mathematics classes have a total of 410 students. The 8:00 am class has 40 more than the 10:00 am class. How many students are in the 10:00 am class?
   (Average)

   A. 123.3
   B. 370
   C. 185
   D. 330

PPR EC-12 BONUS EDITION

TEACHER CERTIFICATION STUDY GUIDE

7. A restaurant employs 465 people. There are 280 waiters and 185 cooks. If 168 waiters and 85 cooks receive pay raises, what percent of the waiters will receive a pay raise?
 (Average)

 A. 36.13%
 B. 60%
 C. 60.22%
 D. 40%

8. $\dfrac{7}{9} + \dfrac{1}{3} \div \dfrac{2}{3} =$
 (Average)

 A. $\dfrac{5}{3}$

 B. $\dfrac{3}{2}$

 C. 2

 D. $\dfrac{23}{18}$

9. Choose the statement that is true for all real numbers.
 (Rigorous)

 A. $a = 0, b \neq 0$, then $\dfrac{b}{a} =$ undefined.

 B. $^-(a + {^-a}) = 2a$

 C. $2(ab) = {^-(2a)b}$

 D. $^-a(b+1) = ab - a$

10. The price of gas was $3.27 per gallon. Your tank holds 15 gallons of fuel. You are using two tanks a week. How much will you save weekly if the price of gas goes down to $2.30 per gallon?
 (Average)

 A. $26.00
 B. $29.00
 C. $15.00
 D. $17.00

11. In a sample of 40 full-time employees at a particular company, 35 were also holding down a part-time job requiring at least 10 hours/week. If this proportion holds for the entire company of 25000 employees, how many full-time employees at this company are actually holding down a part-time job of at least 10 hours per week?
    (Rigorous)

    A. 714
    B. 625
    C. 21,875
    D. 28,571

12. A sofa sells for $520. If the retailer makes a 30% profit, what was the wholesale price?
    (Average)

    A. $400
    B. $676
    C. $490
    D. $364

13. A car gets 25.36 miles per gallon. The car has been driven 83,310 miles. What is a reasonable estimate for the number of gallons of gas used?
    (Average)

    A. 2,087 gallons
    B. 3,000 gallons
    C. 1,800 gallons
    D. 164 gallons

14. What unit of measurement could we use to report the distance traveled walking around a track?
    (Easy)

    A. degrees
    B. square meters
    C. kilometers
    D. cubic feet

15. What unit of measurement would describe the spread of a forest fire in a unit time?
    (Average)

    A. 10 square yards per second
    B. 10 yards per minute
    C. 10 feet per hour
    D. 10 cubic feet per hour

16. Express .0000456 in scientific notation.
    (Easy)

    A. 4.56×10^{-4}
    B. 45.6×10^{-6}
    C. 4.56×10^{-6}
    D. 4.56×10^{-5}

17. A student organization is interested in determining how strong the support is among registered voters in the United States for the president's education plan. Which of the following procedures would be most appropriate for selecting a statistically unbiased sample?
(Average)

   A. Having viewers call in to a nationally broad-cast talk show and give their opinions.
   B. Survey registered voters selected by blind drawing in the three largest states.
   C. Select regions of the country by blind drawing and then select people from the voter's registration list by blind drawing.
   D. Pass out survey forms at the front entrance of schools selected by blind drawing and ask people entering and exiting to fill them in.

18. The following chart shows the yearly average number of international tourists visiting Palm Beach for 1990-1994. How many more international tourists visited Palm Beach in 1994 than in 1991?
(Easy)

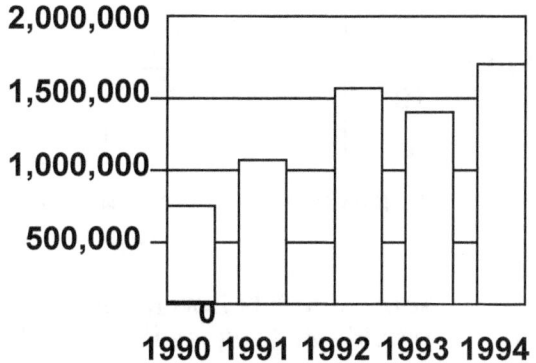

   A. 100,000
   B. 600,000
   C. 1,600,000
   D. 8,000,000

19. Consider the graph of the distribution of the length of time it took individuals to complete an employment form.
(Average)

Approximately how many individuals took less than 15 minutes to complete the employment form?

A. 35
B. 28
C. 7
D. 4

20. Which statement is true about George's budget?
(Easy)

A. George spends the greatest portion of his income on food.
B. George spends twice as much on utilities as he does on his mortgage.
C. George spends twice as much on utilities as he does on food.
D. George spends the same amount on food and utilities as he does on mortgage.

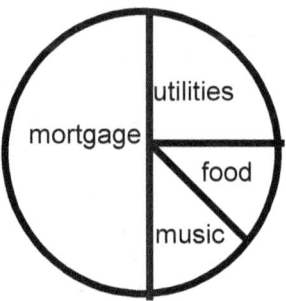

21. Corporate salaries are listed for several employees. Which is the best measure of central tendency?
(Average)

$24,000 $24,000 $26,000
$28,000 $30,000 $120,000

A. Mean
B. Median
C. Mode
D. No difference

TEACHER CERTIFICATION STUDY GUIDE

22. Compute the median for the following data set:
    (Easy)

    {12, 19, 13, 16, 17, 14}

    A. 14.5
    B. 15.17
    C. 15
    D. 16

23. State the domain of the function $f(x) = \dfrac{3x-6}{x^2-25}$
    (Rigorous)

    A. $x \neq 2$
    B. $x \neq 5, -5$
    C. $x \neq 2, -2$
    D. $x \neq 5$

24. Which graph represents the equation of $y = x^2 + 3x$?
    (Rigorous)

    A.   B.

    C.   D.

25. Choose the equation that is equivalent to the following:
    (Rigorous)

    $$\dfrac{3x}{5} - 5 = 5x$$

    A. $3x - 25 = 25x$
    B. $x - \dfrac{25}{3} = 25x$
    C. $6x - 50 = 75x$
    D. $x + 25 = 25x$

26. If $4x - (3 - x) = 7(x - 3) + 10$, then
    (Rigorous)

    A. $x = 8$
    B. $x = -8$
    C. $x = 4$
    D. $x = -4$

27. Solve for x.
    $$3x - \dfrac{2}{3} = \dfrac{5x}{2} + 2$$
    (Rigorous)

    A. $5\dfrac{1}{3}$

    B. $\dfrac{17}{3}$

    C. 2

    D. $\dfrac{16}{2}$

28. Given the formula *d =rt*, (where *d* = distance, *r* =rate, and *t* =time), calculate the time required for a vehicle to travel 585 miles at a rate of 65 miles per hour.
    (Average)

    A. 8.5 hours
    B. 6.5 hours
    C. 9.5 hours
    D. 9 hours

29. Solve the system of equations for x, y and z.
    (Rigorous)

    $$3x + 2y - z = 0$$
    $$2x + 5y = 8z$$
    $$x + 3y + 2z = 7$$

    A. (−1, 2, 1)
    B. (1, 2, −1)
    C. (−3, 4, −1)
    D. (0, 1, 2)

30. What is the equation that expresses the relationship between x and y in the table below?
    (Average)

x	y
-2	4
-1	1
0	-2
1	-5
2	-8

    A. y = −x − 2
    B. y = −3x − 2
    C. y = 3x − 2
    D. $y = \frac{1}{3}x - 1$

31. Choose the expression that is not equivalent to 5x + 3y + 15z:
    (Average)

    A. 5(x + 3z) + 3y
    B. 3(x + y + 5z)
    C. 3y + 5(x + 3z)
    D. 5x + 3(y + 5z)

32. Simplify: $\sqrt{27} + \sqrt{75}$
    (Average)

    A. $8\sqrt{3}$
    B. 34
    C. $34\sqrt{3}$
    D. $15\sqrt{3}$

33. What is the equation of the graph below?
    (Rigorous)

    A. $2x + y = 2$
    B. $2x - y = -2$
    C. $2x - y = 2$
    D. $2x + y = -2$

    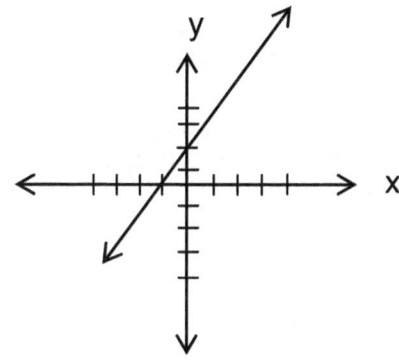

34. $f(x) = 3x - 2;\ f^{-1}(x) =$
    (Rigorous)

    A. $3x + 2$
    B. $x/6$
    C. $2x - 3$
    D. $(x + 2)/3$

35. What is the area of a square whose side is 13 feet?
    (Easy)

    A. 169 feet
    B. 169 square feet
    C. 52 feet
    D. 52 square feet

36. The trunk of a tree has a 2.1 meter radius. What is its circumference?
    (Easy)

    A. 2.1π square meters
    B. 4.2π meters
    C. 2.1π meters
    D. 4.2π square meters

37. The figure below shows a running track and the shape of an inscribed rectangle with semicircles at each end.
    (Rigorous)

    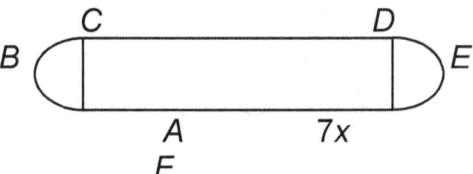

    Calculate the distance around the track. (r = 1.5y)

    A. $6\pi y + 14x$
    B. $3\pi y + 7x$
    C. $6\pi y + 7x$
    D. $3\pi y + 14x$

38. What type of triangle is triangle ABC?
    (Easy)

    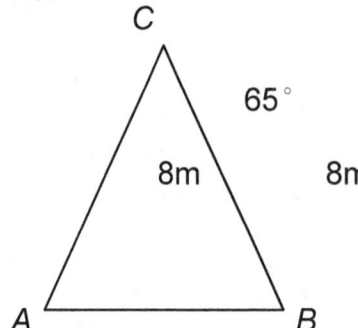

    A. right
    B. equilateral
    C. scalene
    D. isosceles

39. What is the area of this triangle?
    (Easy)

    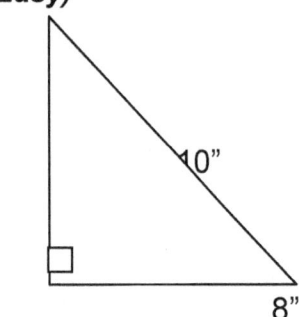

    A. 80 square inches
    B. 20 square inches
    C. 40 square inches
    D. 30 square inches

40. For the following statements
    (Average)

    I. All parallelograms are rectangles
    II. Some rhombi are squares

    A. Both statements are correct
    B. Both statements are incorrect
    C. Only II is correct
    D. Only I is correct

41. Find the surface area of a box which is 3 feet wide, 5 feet tall, and 4 feet deep.
    (Average)

    A. 47 sq. ft.
    B. 60 sq. ft.
    C. 94 sq. ft
    D. 188 sq. ft.

42. The owner of a rectangular piece of land 40 yards in length and 30 yards in width wants to divide it into two parts. She plans to join two opposite corners with a fence as shown in the diagram below. The cost of the fence will be approximately $25 per linear foot. What is the estimated cost for the fence needed by the owner?
    (Rigorous)

    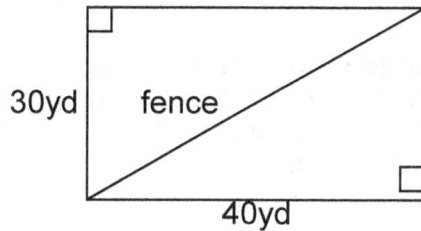

    A. $1,250
    B. $62,500
    C. $5,250
    D. $3,750

43. Which term most accurately describes two coplanar lines without any common points? *(Average)*

    A. perpendicular
    B. parallel
    C. intersecting
    D. skew

44. Set A, B, C, and U are related as shown in the diagram. *(Rigorous)*

    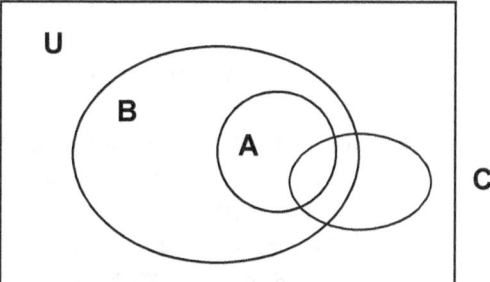

    Which of the following is true, assuming not one of the six regions is empty?

    A. Any element that is a member of set B is also a member of set A.
    B. No element is a member of all three sets A, B, and C.
    C. Any element that is a member of set U is also a member of set B.
    D. None of the above statements is true.

45. Select the statement that is the negation of the statement, "If the weather is cold, then the soccer game will be played." *(Rigorous)*

    A. If the weather is not cold, then the soccer game will be played.
    B. The weather is cold and the soccer game was not played.
    C. If the soccer game is played, then the weather is not cold.
    D. The weather is cold and the soccer game will be played.

46. Select the statement below that is logically equivalent to "If Mary works late, then Bill will prepare lunch."
    (Rigorous)

    A. Bill prepares lunch or Mary does not work late.
    B. If Bill does not prepare lunch, then Mary did not work late.
    C. If Bill prepares lunch, then Mary works late.
    D. Mary does not work late or Bill prepares lunch.

47. Select the rule of logical equivalence that directly (in one step) transforms the statement (i) into statement (ii),
    (Average)

    i. Not all the students have books.
    ii. Some students do not have books.

    A. "If p, then q" is equivalent to "if not q, then b."
    B. "Not all are p" is equivalent to "some are not p."
    C. "Not q" is equivalent to "p."
    D. "All are not p" is equivalent to "none are p"

48. Given that:

    i. No athletes are weak.
    ii. All football players are athletes.

    Determine which conclusion can be logically deduced.
    (Average)

    A. Some football players are weak.
    B. All football players are weak.
    C. No football player is weak.
    D. None of the above is true.

49. Study the information given below. If a logical conclusion is given, select that conclusion.
    (Rigorous)

    Bob eats donuts or he eats yogurt. If Bob eats yogurt, then he is healthy. If Bob is healthy, then he can run the marathon. Bob does not eat yogurt.

    A. Bob does not eat donuts.
    B. Bob is healthy.
    C. If Bob runs the marathon then he eats yogurt.
    D. None of the above is warranted.

50. Given $K(-4, y)$ and $M(2, -3)$ with midpoint $L(x, 1)$, determine the values of x and y.
    (Rigorous)

    A. $x = -1, y = 5$
    B. $x = 3, y = 2$
    C. $x = 5, y = -1$
    D. $x = -1, y = -1$

TEACHER CERTIFICATION STUDY GUIDE

Answer Key

1.	D	26.	C
2.	A	27.	A
3.	B	28.	D
4.	D	29.	A
5.	C	30.	B
6.	C	31.	B
7.	B	32.	A
8.	D	33.	B
9.	A	34.	D
10.	B	35.	B
11.	C	36.	B
12.	A	37.	D
13.	B	38.	D
14.	C	39.	C
15.	A	40.	C
16.	D	41.	C
17.	C	42.	D
18.	B	43.	B
19.	C	44.	D
20.	C	45.	B
21.	B	46.	B
22.	C	47.	B
23.	B	48.	C
24.	C	49.	D
25.	A	50.	A

TEACHER CERTIFICATION STUDY GUIDE

Rigor Table

Easy
2, 14, 16, 18, 20, 22, 35, 36, 38, 39

Average
3, 4, 5, 6, 7, 8, 10, 12, 13, 15, 17, 19, 21, 28, 30, 31, 32, 40, 41, 43, 47, 48

Rigorous
1, 9, 11, 23, 24, 25, 26, 27, 29, 33, 34, 37, 42, 44, 45, 46, 49, 50

TEACHER CERTIFICATION STUDY GUIDE

MATHEMATICS SAMPLE TEST WITH RATIONALES

1. $\left(\dfrac{-4}{9}\right) + \left(\dfrac{-7}{10}\right) =$

   (Rigorous)

   A. $\dfrac{23}{90}$

   B. $\dfrac{-23}{90}$

   C. $\dfrac{103}{90}$

   D. $\dfrac{-103}{90}$

Answer: D. $\dfrac{-103}{90}$

Find the LCD of $\dfrac{-4}{9}$ and $\dfrac{-7}{10}$. The LCD is 90, so you get $\dfrac{-40}{90} + \dfrac{-63}{90} = \dfrac{-103}{90}$

TEACHER CERTIFICATION STUDY GUIDE

2. 0.74 =
   (Easy)

   A. $\dfrac{74}{100}$

   B. 7.4%

   C. $\dfrac{33}{50}$

   D. $\dfrac{74}{10}$

Answer: A. $\dfrac{74}{100}$

0.74 ⑧ the 4 is in the hundredths place, so the answer is $\dfrac{74}{100}$

3. $-9\dfrac{1}{4}\ \square\ -8\dfrac{2}{3}$

   (Average)

   A. =
   B. <
   C. >
   D. ≤

Answer: B. <
The larger the absolute value of a negative number, the smaller the negative number is. The absolute value of $-9\dfrac{1}{4}$ is $9\dfrac{1}{4}$ which is larger than the absolute value of $-8\dfrac{2}{3}$, which is $8\dfrac{2}{3}$. Therefore, the relationship should be $-9\dfrac{1}{4} < -8\dfrac{2}{3}$

4. 303 is what percent of 600?
   (Average)

   A. 0.505%
   B. 5.05%
   C. 505%
   D. 50.5%

Answer: D. 50.5%
Use x for the percent. $600x = 303$. $\dfrac{600x}{600} = \dfrac{303}{600} \to x = 0.505 = 50.5\%$

5. An item that sells for $375 is put on sale at $120. What is the percent of decrease?
   (Average)

   A. 25%
   B. 28%
   C. 68%
   D. 34%

Answer: C. 68%
Use $(1 - x)$ as the discount. $375x = 120$.
$375(1 - x) = 120 \to 375 - 375x = 120 \to 375x = 255 \to x = 0.68 = 68\%$

6. Two mathematics classes have a total of 410 students. The 8:00 am class has 40 more than the 10:00 am class. How many students are in the 10:00 am class?
   (Average)

   A. 123.3
   B. 370
   C. 185
   D. 330

Answer: C. 185
Let x = # of students in the 8 am class and $x - 40$ = # of students in the 10 am class. $x + (x - 40) = 410 \to 2x - 40 = 410 \to 2x = 450 \to x = 225$. So there are 225 students in the 8 am class, and $225 - 40 = 185$ in the 10 am class.

TEACHER CERTIFICATION STUDY GUIDE

7. A restaurant employs 465 people. There are 280 waiters and 185 cooks. If 168 waiters and 85 cooks receive pay raises, what percent of the waiters will receive a pay raise?
   (Average)

   A. 36.13%
   B. 60%
   C. 60.22%
   D. 40%

Answer: B. 60%
The total number of waiters is 280 and only 168 of them get a pay raise.
Divide the number getting a raise by the total number of waiters to get the percent.
$$\frac{168}{280} = 0.6 = 60\%$$

8. $\dfrac{7}{9} + \dfrac{1}{3} \div \dfrac{2}{3} =$
   (Average)

   A. $\dfrac{5}{3}$

   B. $\dfrac{3}{2}$

   C. 2

   D. $\dfrac{23}{18}$

Answer: D. $\dfrac{23}{18}$
First, do the division.
$$\frac{1}{3} \div \frac{2}{3} = \frac{1}{3} \times \frac{3}{2} = \frac{1}{2}$$
Add.
$$\frac{7}{9} + \frac{1}{2} = \frac{14}{18} + \frac{9}{18} = \frac{23}{18}$$

TEACHER CERTIFICATION STUDY GUIDE

9. **Choose the statement that is true for all real numbers.**
   (Rigorous)

   A. $a = 0, b \neq 0$, then $\dfrac{b}{a}$ = undefined.

   B. $^-(a + (^-a)) = 2a$

   C. $2(ab) =^- (2a)b$

   D. $^-a(b+1) = ab - a$

Answer: A. $a = 0, b \neq 0$, then $\dfrac{b}{a}$ = undefined.
A is the correct answer because any number divided by 0 is undefined.

10. **The price of gas was $3.27 per gallon. Your tank holds 15 gallons of fuel. You are using two tanks a week. How much will you save weekly if the price of gas goes down to $2.30 per gallon?**
    (Average)

    A. $26.00
    B. $29.00
    C. $15.00
    D. $17.00

Answer: B. $29.00
15 gallons x 2 tanks = 30 gallons a week
= 30 gallons x $3.27 = $98.10
30 gallons x $2.30 = $69.00
$98.10 - $69.00 = $29.10 is approximately $29.00.

TEACHER CERTIFICATION STUDY GUIDE

11. In a sample of 40 full-time employees at a particular company, 35 were also holding down a part-time job requiring at least 10 hours/week. If this proportion holds for the entire company of 25,000 employees, how many full-time employees at this company are actually holding down a part-time job of at least 10 hours per week?
    (Rigorous)

    A. 714
    B. 625
    C. 21,875
    D. 28,571

Answer: C. 21, 875

$\frac{35}{40}$ full time employees have a part time job also. Out of 25,000 full time employees, the number that also have a part time job is

$\frac{35}{40} = \frac{x}{25000} \rightarrow 40x = 875000 \rightarrow x = 21875$, so 21875 full time employees also have a part time job.

12. A sofa sells for $520. If the retailer makes a 30% profit, what was the wholesale price?
    (Average)

    A. $400
    B. $676
    C. $490
    D. $364

Answer: A. $400
$400; Let x be the wholesale price, then x + .30x = 520, 1.30x = 520. divide both sides by 1.30.

TEACHER CERTIFICATION STUDY GUIDE

13. A car gets 25.36 miles per gallon. The car has been driven 83,310 miles. What is a reasonable estimate for the number of gallons of gas used?
    (Average)

    A. 2,087 gallons
    B. 3,000 gallons
    C. 1,800 gallons
    D. 164 gallons

Answer: B. 3,000 gallons
Divide the number of miles by the miles per gallon to determine the approximate number of gallons of gas used. $\dfrac{83310 \text{ miles}}{25.36 \text{ miles per gallon}} = 3285$ gallons. This is approximately 3,000 gallons.

14. What unit of measurement could we use to report the distance traveled walking around a track?
    (Easy)

    A. degrees
    B. square meters
    C. kilometers
    D. cubic feet

Answer: C. kilometers
Degrees measures angles, square meters measures area, cubic feet measure volume, and kilometers measures length. Kilometers is the only reasonable answer.

15. What unit of measurement would describe the spread of a forest fire in a unit time?
    (Average)

    A. 10 square yards per second
    B. 10 yards per minute
    C. 10 feet per hour
    D. 10 cubic feet per hour

Answer: A. 10 square yards per second
The only appropriate answer is one that describes "an area" of forest consumed per unit time. All answers are not units of area measurement except answer A.

TEACHER CERTIFICATION STUDY GUIDE

16. **Express .0000456 in scientific notation.**
    (Easy)

    A. 4.56×10^{-4}
    B. 45.6×10^{-6}
    C. 4.56×10^{-6}
    D. 4.56×10^{-5}

Answer: D. 4.56×10^{-5}
In scientific notation, the decimal point belongs to the right of the 4, the first significant digit. To get from 4.56×10^{-5} back to 0.0000456, we would move the decimal point 5 places to the left.

17. **A student organization is interested in determining how strong the support is among registered voters in the United States for the president's education plan. Which of the following procedures would be most appropriate for selecting a statistically unbiased sample?**
    (Average)

    A. Having viewers call in to a nationally broad-cast talk show and give their opinions.
    B. Survey registered voters selected by blind drawing in the three largest states.
    C. Select regions of the country by blind drawing and then select people from the voter's registration list by blind drawing.
    D. Pass out survey forms at the front entrance of schools selected by blind drawing and ask people entering and exiting to fill them in.

Answer: C. Select regions of the country by blind drawing and then select people from the voter's registration list by blind drawing.
C is the best answer because it is random and it surveys a larger population.

18. The following chart shows the yearly average number of international tourists visiting Palm Beach for 1990-1994. How many more international tourists visited Palm Beach in 1994 than in 1991?
   (Easy)

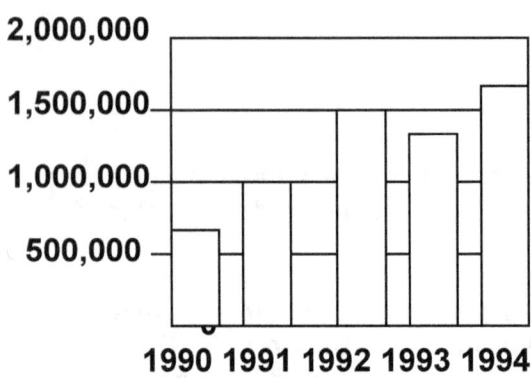

   A. 100,000
   B. 600,000
   C. 1,600,000
   D. 8,000,000

Answer: B. 600,000
The number of tourists in 1991 was 1,000,000 and the number in 1994 was 1,600,000. Subtract to get a difference of 600,000.

19. Consider the graph of the distribution of the length of time it took individuals to complete an employment form.
(Average)

Approximately how many individuals took less than 15 minutes to complete the employment form?

A. 35
B. 28
C. 7
D. 4

Answer: C. 7
According to the chart, the number of people who took under 15 minutes is 7.

TEACHER CERTIFICATION STUDY GUIDE

20. **Which statement is true about George's budget?**
    (Easy)

    A. George spends the greatest portion of his income on food.
    B. George spends twice as much on utilities as he does on his mortgage.
    C. George spends twice as much on utilities as he does on food.
    D. George spends the same amount on food and utilities as he does on mortgage.

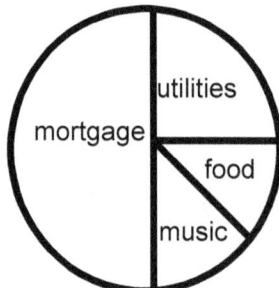

Answer: C. George spends twice as much on utilities as he does on food.
The wedge representing utilities is twice as large as the wedge representing food.

21. **Corporate salaries are listed for several employees. Which is the best measure of central tendency?**
    (Average)

    $24,000 $24,000 $26,000 $28,000 $30,000 $120,000

    A. Mean
    B. Median
    C. Mode
    D. No difference

Answer: B. Median
The median provides the best measure of central tendency in this case where the mode is the lowest number and the mean is disproportionately skewed by the outlier $120,000.

TEACHER CERTIFICATION STUDY GUIDE

22. Compute the median for the following data set:
(Easy)

{12, 19, 13, 16, 17, 14}

A. 14.5
B. 15.17
C. 15
D. 16

Answer: C. 15
Arrange the data in ascending order: 12,13,14,16,17,19. The median is the middle value in a list with an odd number of entries. When there is an even number of entries, the median is the mean of the two center entries. Here the average of 14 and 16 is 15.

23. State the domain of the function $f(x) = \dfrac{3x-6}{x^2-25}$

(Rigorous)

A. $x \neq 2$
B. $x \neq 5, -5$
C. $x \neq 2, -2$
D. $x \neq 5$

Answer: B. $x \neq 5, -5$
The values of 5 and –5 must be omitted from the domain of all real numbers because if x took on either of those values, the denominator of the fraction would have a value of 0, and therefore the fraction would be undefined.

24. Which graph represents the equation of $y = x^2 + 3x$?
    (Rigorous)

    A.   B.

    C.   D.

    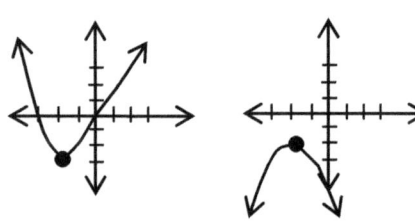

Answer: C.
B is not the graph of a function. D is the graph of a parabola where the coefficient of x^2 is negative. A appears to be the graph of $y = x^2$. To find the x-intercepts of $y = x^2 + 3x$, set y = 0 and solve for x: $0 = x^2 + 3x = x(x + 3)$ to get $x = 0$ or $x = -3$. Therefore, the graph of the function intersects the x-axis at x=0 and x=-3.

TEACHER CERTIFICATION STUDY GUIDE

25. Choose the equation that is equivalent to the following:
    (Rigorous)

    $$\frac{3x}{5} - 5 = 5x$$

    A. $3x - 25 = 25x$

    B. $x - \frac{25}{3} = 25x$

    C. $6x - 50 = 75x$

    D. $x + 25 = 25x$

Answer: A. $3x - 25 = 25x$
A is the correct answer because it is the original equation multiplied by 5. The other choices alter the answer to the original equation.

26. If $4x - (3 - x) = 7(x - 3) + 10$, then
    (Rigorous)

    A. $x = 8$
    B. $x = -8$
    C. $x = 4$
    D. $x = -4$

Answer: C. $x = 4$
Solve for x.

$$4x - (3 - x) = 7(x - 3) + 10$$
$$4x - 3 + x = 7x - 21 + 10$$
$$5x - 3 = 7x - 11$$
$$5x = 7x - 11 + 3$$
$$5x - 7x = {}^-8$$
$${}^-2x = {}^-8$$
$$x = 4$$

27. Solve for x.
$$3x - \frac{2}{3} = \frac{5x}{2} + 2$$
(Rigorous)

A. $5\frac{1}{3}$

B. $\frac{17}{3}$

C. 2

D. $\frac{16}{2}$

Answer: A. $5\frac{1}{3}$

$3x(6) - \frac{2}{3}(6) = \frac{5x}{2}(6) + 2(6)$ 6 is the LCD of 2 and 3

$18x - 4 = 15x + 12$

$18x = 15x + 16$

$3x = 16$

$x = \frac{16}{3} = 5\frac{1}{3}$

28. Given the formula $d = rt$, (where d = distance, r = rate, and t = time), calculate the time required for a vehicle to travel 585 miles at a rate of 65 miles per hour.
(Average)

    A. 8.5 hours
    B. 6.5 hours
    C. 9.5 hours
    D. 9 hours

Answer: D. 9 hours
We are given $d = 585$ miles and $r = 65$ miles per hour and $d = rt$. Solve for t.
$585 = 65t \rightarrow t = 9$ hours.

TEACHER CERTIFICATION STUDY GUIDE

29. **Solve the system of equations** for x, y and z.
    (Rigorous)

    $3x + 2y - z = 0$
    $2x + 5y = 8z$
    $x + 3y + 2z = 7$

    A. $(-1, 2, 1)$
    B. $(1, 2, -1)$
    C. $(-3, 4, -1)$
    D. $(0, 1, 2)$

Answer: A. $(-1, 2, 1)$
Multiplying equation 1 by 2, and equation 2 by –3, and then adding together the two resulting equations gives -11y + 22z = 0. Solving for y gives y = 2z. In the meantime, multiplying equation 3 by –2 and adding it to equation 2 gives –y – 12z = -14. Then substituting 2z for y, yields the result z = 1. Subsequently, one can easily find that y = 2, and x = -1.

30. **What is the equation that expresses the relationship between x and y in the table below?**
    (Average)

x	y
-2	4
-1	1
0	-2
1	-5
2	-8

    A. y = -x – 2
    B. y = -3x – 2
    C. y = 3x – 2
    D. $y = \frac{1}{3}x - 1$

Answer: B. y = -3x - 2
Solve by plugging the values of x and y into the equations to see if they work. The answer is B because it is the only equation for which the values of x and y are correct.

31. Choose the expression that is not equivalent to
    5x + 3y + 15z:
    (Average)

    A. 5(x + 3z) + 3y
    B. 3(x + y + 5z)
    C. 3y + 5(x + 3z)
    D. 5x + 3(y + 5z)

Answer: B. 3(x + y +5z)

5x + 3y + 15z = (5x + 15z) + 3y = 5(x + 3z) + 3y   A. is true
            = 5x + (3y + 15z) = 5x + 3(y + 5z)   D. is true
            = 3y + (5x + 15z) = 3y + 5(x + 3z)   C. is true

We can solve all of these using the associative property and then factoring. However, in B 3(x + y + 5z) by distributive property = 3x + 3y + 15z, which does not equal 5x + 3y + 15z.

32. Simplify: $\sqrt{27} + \sqrt{75}$
    (Average)

    A. $8\sqrt{3}$
    B. 34
    C. $34\sqrt{3}$
    D. $15\sqrt{3}$

Answer: A. $8\sqrt{3}$
Simplifying radicals gives $\sqrt{27} + \sqrt{75} = 3\sqrt{3} + 5\sqrt{3} = 8\sqrt{3}$.

33. **What is the equation of the graph below?**
    (Rigorous)

    A. $2x + y = 2$
    B. $2x - y = -2$
    C. $2x - y = 2$
    D. $2x + y = -2$

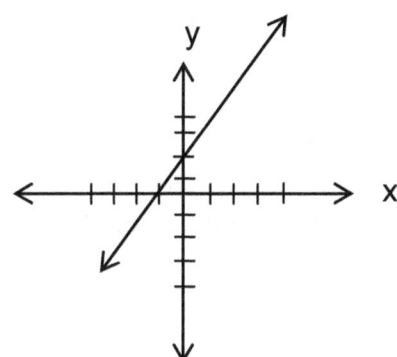

Answer: B. $2x - y = -2$

By observation, we see that the graph has a y-intercept of 2 and a slope of 2/1 = 2. Therefore its equation is y = mx + b = 2x + 2. Rearranging the terms gives 2x – y = -2.

34. $f(x) = 3x - 2;\ f^{-1}(x) =$
    (Rigorous)

    A. $3x + 2$
    B. $x/6$
    C. $2x - 3$
    D. $(x+2)/3$

Answer: D. $(x+2)/3$

To find the inverse, f⁻¹(x), of the given function, reverse the variables in the given equation, y = 3x – 2, to get x = 3y – 2. Then solve for y as follows:
x+2 = 3y, and y = $\dfrac{x+2}{3}$.

TEACHER CERTIFICATION STUDY GUIDE

35. What is the area of a square whose side is 13 feet?
    (Easy)

    A. 169 feet
    B. 169 square feet
    C. 52 feet
    D. 52 square feet

Answer: B. 169 square feet
Area = length times width (*lw*).
Length = 13 feet
Width = 13 feet (square, so length and width are the same).
Area = $13 \times 13 = 169$ square feet.
Area is measured in square feet.

36. The trunk of a tree has a 2.1 meter radius. What is its circumference?
    (Easy)

    A. 2.1π square meters
    B. 4.2π meters
    C. 2.1π meters
    D. 4.2π square meters

Answer: B. 4.2π meters
Circumference is $2\pi r$, where r is the radius. The circumference is $2\pi 2.1 = 4.2\pi$ meters (not square meters because we are not measuring area).

37. The figure below shows a running track and the shape of an inscribed rectangle with semicircles at each end.
(Rigorous)

Calculate the distance around the track (r = 1.5y).

A. $6\pi y + 14x$
B. $3\pi y + 7x$
C. $6\pi y + 7x$
D. $3\pi y + 14x$

Answer: D. $3\pi y + 14x$

The two semicircles of the track create one circle with a diameter 3y. The circumference of a circle is $C = \pi d$ so $C = 3\pi y$. The length of both sides of the track is 7x each side, so the total circumference around the track is $3\pi y + 7x + 7x = 3\pi y + 14x$

38. What type of triangle is triangle ABC?
    (Easy)

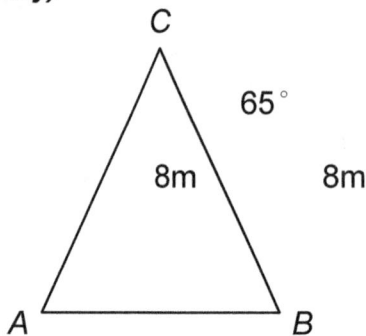

A. right
B. equilateral
C. scalene
D. isosceles

Answer: D. isosceles

Two of the sides are the same length, so we know the triangle is either equilateral or isosceles. ∡CAB and ∡CBA are equal, because their sides are. Therefore, $180° - 65° - 2x = \frac{115°}{2} = 57.5°$. Because all three angles are not equal, the triangle is isosceles.

39. What is the area of this triangle?
    (Easy)

    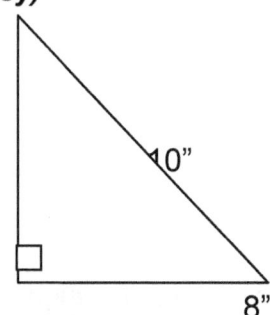

    A. 80 square inches
    B. 20 square inches
    C. 40 square inches
    D. 30 square inches

Answer: C. 40 square inches

The area of a triangle is $\frac{1}{2}bh$.

$\frac{1}{2} \times 8 \times 10 = 40$ square inches.

40. For the following statements
    (Average)

    I. **All parallelograms are rectangles**
    II. **Some rhombi are squares**

    A. Both statements are correct
    B. Both statements are incorrect
    C. Only II is correct
    D. Only I is correct

Answer: C. Only II is correct

I is false because only some parallelograms are rectangles. II is true. So only II is correct.

41. Find the surface area of a box which is 3 feet wide, 5 feet tall, and 4 feet deep.
(Average)

   A. 47 sq. ft.
   B. 60 sq. ft.
   C. 94 sq. ft
   D. 188 sq. ft.

Answer: C. 94 sq. ft.
Let's assume the base of the rectangular solid (box) is 3 by 4, and the height is 5. Then the surface area of the top and bottom together is 2(12) = 24. The sum of the areas of the front and back are 2(15) = 30, while the sum of the areas of the sides are 2(20)=40. The total surface area is therefore 94 square feet.

42. The owner of a rectangular piece of land 40 yards in length and 30 yards in width wants to divide it into two parts. She plans to join two opposite corners with a fence as shown in the diagram below. The cost of the fence will be approximately $25 per linear foot. What is the estimated cost for the fence needed by the owner?
(Rigorous)

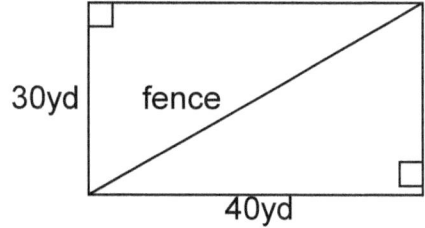

   A. $1,250
   B. $62,500
   C. $5,250
   D. $3,750

Answer: D. $3,750
Find the length of the diagonal by using the Pythagorean theorem. Let x be the length of the diagonal.

$$30^2 + 40^2 = x^2 \rightarrow 900 + 1600 = x^2$$
$$2500 = x^2 \rightarrow \sqrt{2500} = \sqrt{x^2}$$
$$x = 50 \text{ yards}$$

Convert to feet.
50 yards x 3 feet per yard = 150 feet
It cost $25.00 per linear foot, so the cost is (150 ft) ($25) = $3750.

TEACHER CERTIFICATION STUDY GUIDE

43. **Which term most accurately describes two coplanar lines without any common points?**
    (Average)

    A. perpendicular
    B. parallel
    C. intersecting
    D. skew

Answer: B. parallel
By definition, parallel lines are coplanar lines without any common points.

44. **Set A, B, C, and U are related as shown in the diagram.**
    (Rigorous)

    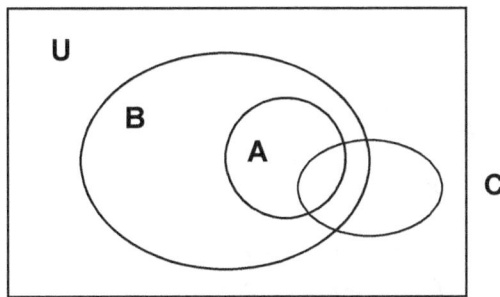

    Which of the following is true, assuming not one of the six regions is empty?

    A. Any element that is a member of set B is also a member of set A.
    B. No element is a member of all three sets A, B, and C.
    C. Any element that is a member of set U is also a member of set B.
    D. None of the above statements is true.

Answer: D. None of the above statements is true.
Answer A is incorrect because not all members of set B are also in set A. Answer B is incorrect because there are elements that are members of all three sets A, B, and C. Answer C is incorrect because not all members of set U are members of set B. This leaves answer D, which states that none of the above choices are true.

TEACHER CERTIFICATION STUDY GUIDE

45. **Select the statement that is the negation of the statement, "If the weather is cold, then the soccer game will be played."**
    (Rigorous)

    A. If the weather is not cold, then the soccer game will be played.
    B. The weather is cold and the soccer game was not played.
    C. If the soccer game is played, then the weather is not cold.
    D. The weather is cold and the soccer game will be played.

    Answer: B. The weather is cold and the soccer game was not played.
    Negation of "if p, then q" is "p and (not q)". So the negation of the given statement is "The weather is cold and the soccer game was not played ".

46. **Select the statement below that is logically equivalent to "If Mary works late, then Bill will prepare lunch."**
    (Rigorous)

    A. Bill prepares lunch or Mary does not work late.
    B. If Bill does not prepare lunch, then Mary did not work late.
    C. If Bill prepares lunch, then Mary works late.
    D. Mary does not work late or Bill prepares lunch.

    Answer: B. If Bill does not prepare lunch, then Mary did not work late.
    The contrapositive of a statement is always logically equivalent to the statement. The contrapositive of "if p then q" is "if not q then not p". Since statement B is the contrapositive of the given statement, it is logically equivalent.

    The other answer choices assume that if Mary does not work late then Bill does not prepare lunch. This is not a valid deduction from the original statement which merely states that Bill prepares lunch when Mary works late. It does not eliminate the possibility that Bill prepares lunch when Mary does not work late. Hence these statements are not logically equivalent to the given statement.

47. **Select the rule of logical equivalence that directly (in one step) transforms the statement (i) into statement (ii),**
(Average)

   i. Not all the students have books.
   ii. Some students do not have books.

   A. "If p, then q" is equivalent to "if not q, then b."
   B. "Not all are p" is equivalent to "some are not p."
   C. "Not q" is equivalent to "p."
   D. "All are not p" is equivalent to "none are p"

Answer: B. "Not all are p" is equivalent to "some are not p."
If we assume that the statement p is "students have books", then "not p" is "students do not have books". It is clear that statements (i) and (ii) are equivalent to the choice B.

48. **Given that:**

   i. No athletes are weak.
   ii. All football players are athletes.

   Determine which conclusion can be logically deduced.
   (Average)

   A. Some football players are weak.
   B. All football players are weak.
   C. No football player is weak.
   D. None of the above is true.

Answer: C. No football player is weak.
According to the law of syllogism, "if p then q and if q then r" implies "if p then r".
We can rephrase the statements above to read:

i. If a person is a football player, he or she is an athlete.
ii. If a person is an athlete, he or she is not weak.

Then, using the law of syllogism, we can conclude:
If a person is a football player, he or she is not weak.
This statement is equivalent to the one in choice C.

TEACHER CERTIFICATION STUDY GUIDE

49. Study the information given below. If a logical conclusion is given, select that conclusion.
   (Rigorous)

   Bob eats donuts or he eats yogurt. If Bob eats yogurt, then he is healthy. If Bob is healthy, then he can run the marathon. Bob does not eat yogurt.

   A. Bob does not eat donuts.
   B. Bob is healthy.
   C. If Bob runs the marathon then he eats yogurt.
   D. None of the above is warranted.

   Answer: D. None of the above is warranted.
   Statement A is not warranted since "Bob eats donuts or he eats yogurt" and "Bob does not eat yogurt" implies that "Bob eats donuts".

   Statement B is not warranted since according to the given statements, Bob does not eat yogurt and Bob is healthy if he eats yogurt. The statements do not say anything about Bob's health if he does not eat yogurt.

   Statement C is not warranted since Bob may run the marathon even if he does not eat yogurt. The given statements do not say anything about Bob's ability to run the marathon if he does not eat yogurt. It merely implies that he can run the marathon if he does eat yogurt.

50. Given $K(-4, y)$ and $M(2, -3)$ with midpoint $L(x, 1)$, determine the values of x and y.
   (Rigorous)

   A. $x = -1, y = 5$
   B. $x = 3, y = 2$
   C. $x = 5, y = -1$
   D. $x = -1, y = -1$

   Answer: A. $x = -1, y = 5$
   The formula for finding the midpoint (a,b) of a segment passing through the points (x_1, y_1) and (x_2, y_2) is $(a, b) = (\frac{x_1 + x_2}{2}, \frac{y_1 + y_2}{2})$. Setting up the corresponding equations from this information gives us $x = \frac{-4 + 2}{2}$, and $1 = \frac{y - 3}{2}$. Solving for x and y gives x = -1 and y = 5.

ELEMENTS OF COMPOSITION SAMPLE TEST

Directions: The passage below contains many errors. Read the passage. Then, answer each test item by choosing the option that corrects an error in the underlined portion(s). No more than one underlined error will appear in each item. If no error exists, choose "No change is necessary."

Climbing to the top of Mount Everest is an adventure. One which everyone--whether physically fit or not--seems eager to try. The trail stretches for miles, the cold temperatures are usually frigid and brutal.

Climbers must endure severel barriers on the way, including other hikers, steep jagged rocks, and lots of snow. Plus, climbers often find the most grueling part of the trip is their climb back down, just when they are feeling greatly exhausted. Climbers who take precautions are likely to find the ascent less arduous than the unprepared. By donning heavy flannel shirts, gloves, and hats, climbers prevented hypothermia, as well as simple frostbite. A pair of rugged boots is also one of the necesities. If climbers are to avoid becoming dehydrated, there is beverages available for them to transport as well.

Once climbers are completely ready to begin their lengthy journey, they can comfortable enjoy the wonderful scenery. Wide rock formations dazzle the observers eyes with shades of gray and white, while the peak forms a triangle that seems to touch the sky.

Each of the climbers are reminded of the splendor and magnificence of God's great Earth.

1. If climbers are to avoid <u>becoming</u> dehydrated, there <u>is</u> beverages available for <u>them</u> to transport as well.
   (Rigorous)

   A. becomming
   B. are
   C. him
   D. No change is necessary.

2. **Each of the climbers <u>are</u> reminded of the splendor and <u>magnificence</u> of <u>God's</u> great Earth.**
   (Rigorous)

   A. is
   B. magnifisence
   C. Gods
   D. No change is necessary.

3. **Climbing to the top of Mount Everest is an <u>adventure. One</u> which everyone <u>—whether</u> physically fit or not—<u>seems</u> eager to try.**
   (Average)

   A. adventure, one
   B. everyone, whether
   C. seem
   D. No change is necessary.

4. A pair of rugged boots is also one of the necesities.
   (Average)

   A. are
   B. also, one
   C. necessities
   D. No change is necessary.

5. Plus, climbers often find the most grueling part of the trip is their climb back down, just when they are feeling greatly exhausted.
   (Rigorous)

   A. his
   B. down; just
   C. were
   D. No change is necessary.

6. By donning heavy flannel shirts, boots, and hats, climbers prevented hypothermia, as well as simple frostbite.
   (Average)

   A. hats climbers
   B. can prevent
   C. hypothermia;
   D. No change is necessary.

7. Climbers must endure severel barriers on the way, including other hikers, steep jagged rocks, and lots of snow.
   (Average)

   A. several
   B. on the way: including
   C. hikers'
   D. No change is necessary.

8. Climbers who take precautions are likely to find the ascent less difficult than the unprepared.
   (Easy)

   A. Climbers, who
   B. least difficult
   C. then
   D. No change is necessary.

9. Once climbers are completely prepared for their lengthy journey, they can comfortable enjoy the wonderful scenery.
   (Easy)

   A. they're
   B. journey; they
   C. comfortably
   D. No change is necessary.

10. Wide rock formations dazzle the observers eyes with shades of gray and white, while the peak forms a triangle that seems to touch the sky.
    (Average)

    A. observers' eyes
    B. white; while
    C. formed
    D. No change is necessary.

11. The trail stretches for miles, the cold temperatures are usually frigid and brutal.
    (Rigorous)

    A. trails
    B. miles;
    C. usual
    D. No change is necessary.

Directions: The passage below contains several errors. Read the passage. Then, answer each test item by choosing the option that corrects an error in the underlined portion(s). No more than one underlined error will appear in each item. If no error exists, choose "No change is necessary."

Every job places different kinds of demands on their employees. For example, whereas such jobs as accounting and bookkeeping require mathematical ability; graphic design requires creative/artistic ability.

Doing good at one job does not usually guarantee success at another. However, one of the elements crucial to all jobs are especially notable: the chance to accomplish a goal.

The accomplishment of the employees varies according to the job. In many jobs, the employees become accustom to the accomplishment provided by the work they do every day.

In medicine, for example, every doctor tests him self by treating badly injured or critically ill people. In the operating room, a team of Surgeons, is responsible for operating on many of these patients. In addition to the feeling of accomplishment that the workers achieve, some jobs also give a sense of identity to the employees'. Profesions like law, education, and sales offer huge financial and emotional rewards. Politicians are public servants: who work for the federal and state governments. President obama is basically employed by the American people to make laws and run the country.

Finally; the contributions that employees make to their companies and to the world cannot be taken for granted. Through their work, employees are performing a service for their employers and are contributing something to the world.

12. **Every job places different kinds of demands on their employees.**
    (Average)

    A. place
    B. its
    C. employes
    D. No change is necessary.

13. **However, one of the elements crucial to all jobs are especially notable: the accomplishment of a goal.**
    (Average)

    A. However
    B. is
    C. notable;
    D. No change is necessary.

14. **The accomplishment of the employees varies according to the job.**
    (Average)

    A. accomplishment,
    B. employee's
    C. vary
    D. No change is necessary.

15. <u>Profesions</u> like law, <u>education,</u> and sales <u>offer</u> huge financial and emotional rewards.
    (Easy)

    A. Professions
    B. education;
    C. offered
    D. No change is necessary.

16. Doing <u>good</u> at one job does not <u>usually</u> guarantee <u>success</u> at another.
    (Average)

    A. well
    B. usualy
    C. succeeding
    D. No change is necessary.

17. In many jobs, the employees <u>become</u> <u>accustom</u> to the accomplishment <u>provided</u> by the work they do every day.
    (Rigorous)

    A. became
    B. accustomed
    C. provides
    D. No change is necessary.

18. In medicine, for example, every doctor <u>tests</u> <u>him self</u> by treating badly-injured and <u>critically</u> ill people.
    (Easy)

    A. test
    B. himself
    C. critical
    D. No change is necessary.

19. In addition to the feeling of accomplishment that the workers <u>achieve</u>, some jobs also <u>give</u> a sense of self-identity to the <u>employees'</u>.
    (Average)

    A. acheve
    B. gave
    C. employees
    D. No change is necessary.

20. <u>For example, whereas</u> such jobs as accounting and bookkeeping require mathematical <u>ability;</u> graphic design requires creative/artistic ability.
    (Rigorous)

    A. For example
    B. whereas,
    C. ability,
    D. No change is necessary.

21. In the <u>operating room,</u> a team of <u>Surgeons, is</u> responsible for operating on many of <u>these</u> patients.
    (Easy)

    A. operating room:
    B. surgeons is
    C. those
    D. No change is necessary.

22. Politicians <u>are</u> public servants: <u>who</u> <u>work</u> for the federal and state governments.
    (Average)

    A. were
    B. servants who
    C. worked
    D. No change is necessary.

23. President obama is basically employed <u>by</u> the American people to <u>make</u> laws and run the country.
    (Easy)

    A. Obama
    B. to
    C. made
    D. No change is necessary.

24. <u>Finally;</u> the contributions that employees make to <u>their</u> companies and to the world cannot be <u>taken</u> for granted.
    (Average)

    A. Finally,
    B. thier
    C. took
    D. No change is necessary.

Directions: For the underlined sentence(s), choose the option that expresses the meaning with the most fluency and the clearest logic within the context. If the underlined sentence should not be changed, choose Option A, which shows no change.

25. Which of the following sentences logically and correctly expresses the comparison?
    (Rigorous)

    A. The Empire State Building in New York is taller than buildings in the city.
    B. The Empire State Building in New York is taller than any other building in the city.
    C. The Empire State Building in New York is tallest than other buildings in the city.

26. **Treating patients for drug and/or alcohol abuse is a sometimes difficult process. <u>Even though there are a number of different methods for helping the patient overcome a dependency, there is no way of knowing which is best in the long run.</u>**
    (Rigorous)

    A. Even though there are a number of different methods for helping the patient overcome a dependency, there is no way of knowing which is best in the long run.
    B. Even though different methods can help a patient overcome a dependency, there is no way to know which is best in the long run.
    C. Even though there is no way to know which way is best in the long run, patients can overcome their dependencies when they are helped.
    D. There is no way to know which method will help the patient overcome a dependency in the long run, even though there are many different ones.

27. **Selecting members of a President's cabinet can often be an aggravating process. <u>Either there are too many or too few qualified candidates for a certain position, and then they have to be confirmed by the Senate, where there is the possibility of rejection.</u>**
    (Rigorous)

    A. Either there are too many or too few qualified candidates for a certain position, and then they have to be confirmed by the Senate, where there is the possibility of rejection.
    B. Qualified candidates for certain positions face the possibility of rejection, when they have to be confirmed by the Senate.
    C. The Senate has to confirm qualified candidates, who face the possibility of rejection.
    D. Because the Senate has to confirm qualified candidates; they face the possibility of rejection.

28. Many factors account for the decline in the quality of public education. <u>Overcrowding, budget cutbacks, and societal deterioration which have greatly affected student learning</u>.
 (Rigorous)

   A. Overcrowding, budget cutbacks, and societal deterioration which have greatly affected student learning.
   B. Student learning has been greatly affected by overcrowding, budget cutbacks, and societal deterioration.
   C. Due to overcrowding, budget cutbacks, and societal deterioration, student learning has been greatly affected.
   D. Overcrowding, budget cutbacks, and societal deterioration have affected students learning greatly.

Directions: Choose the most effective word within the context of the sentence.

29. Many of the clubs in Boca Raton are noted for their _____ elegance.
 (Average)

   A. vulgar
   B. tasteful
   C. ordinary

30. When a student is expelled from school, the parents are usually _____ in advance.
 (Easy)

   A. rewarded
   B. congratulated
   C. notified

31. Before appearing in court, the witness was _____ the papers requiring her to show up.
 (Easy)

   A. condemned
   B. served
   C. criticized

Directions: Choose the underlined word or phrase that is unnecessary within the context of the passage.

32. <u>Considered by many to be</u> one of the worst <u>terrorist</u> incidents <u>on American soil</u> was the bombing of the Oklahoma City Federal Building, which will be remembered <u>for years to come</u>.
 (Rigorous)

   A. considered by many to be
   B. terrorist
   C. on American soil
   D. for years to come

33. The flu epidemic struck most of the respected faculty and students of The Woolbright School, forcing the Boynton Beach School Superintendent to close it down for two weeks. *(Rigorous)*

    A. flu
    B. most of
    C. respected
    D. for two weeks

34. The expanding number of television channels has prompted cable operators to raise their prices, even though many consumers do not want to pay a higher increased amount for their service. *(Average)*

    A. expanding
    B. prompted
    C. even though
    D. increased

Directions: The passage below contains several errors. Read the passage. Then, answer each test item by choosing the option that corrects an error in the underlined portion(s). No more than one underlined error will appear in each item. If no error exists, choose "No change is necessary."

The discovery of a body at Paris Point marina in Boca Raton shocked the residents of Palmetto Pines, a luxury condominium complex located next door to the marina.

The victim is a thirty-five year old woman who had been apparently bludgeoned to death and dumped in the ocean late last night. Many neighbors reported terrible screams, gunshots: as well as the sound of a car backfiring loudly to Boca Raton Police shortly after midnight. The woman had been spotted in the lobby of Palmetto Pines around ten thirty, along with an older man, estimated to be in his fifties, and a younger man, in his late twenties.

"Apparently, the victim had been driven to the complex by the older man and was seen arguing with him when the younger man intervened," said Sheriff Fred Adams, "all three of them left the building together and walked to the marina, where gunshots rang out an hour later." Deputies found five bullets on the sidewalk and some blood, along with a steel pipe that is assumed to be the murder weapon. Two men were seen fleeing the scene in a red Mercedes shortly after, rushing toward the Interstate. The Palm Beach County Coroner, Melvin Watts, said he concluded the victim's skull had been crushed by a blunt tool, which resulted in a brain hemorrhage. As of now, there is no clear motive for the murder.

35. **The victim is a thirty-five-year-old who had been apparently bludgeoned to death and dumped in the ocean late last night.**
    (Rigorous)

    A. was
    B. bludgoned
    C. ocean: late
    D. No change is necessary.

36. **The discovery of a body at Paris Point marina in Boca Raton shocked the residents of Palmetto Pines, a luxury condominium complex located next door to the marina.**
    (Rigorous)

    A. Marina
    B. residence
    C. condominnium
    D. No change is necessary.

37. **Deputies found five bullets on the sidewalk and some blood, along with a steel pipe that is assumed to be the murder weapon.**
    (Rigorous)

    A. blood;
    B. assuming
    C. to have been
    D. No change is necessary.

38. Many neighbors reported terrible screams, gunshots: as well as the sound of a car, backfiring loudly to Boca Raton Police shortly after midnight.
    (Average)

    A. nieghbors
    B. gunshots, as
    C. loud
    D. No change is necessary.

39. The woman had been spotted in the lobby of Palmetto Pines around ten thirty, along with an older man, estimated to be in his fifties, and a younger man in his late twenties.
    (Average)

    A. has
    B. thirty;
    C. man estimated
    D. No change is necessary.

40. "Apparently, the victim had been driven to the complex by the older man and was seen arguing with him when the younger man intervened," said Sheriff Fred Adams, "all three of them left the building together and walked to the marina, where gunshots rang out an hour later."
    (Rigorous)

    A. sheriff Fred Adams, "all
    B. sheriff Fred Adams, "All
    C. Sheriff Fred Adams. "All
    D. No change is necessary.

TEACHER CERTIFICATION STUDY GUIDE

Answer Key

1.	B		21.	B
2.	A		22.	B
3.	A		23.	A
4.	C		24.	A
5.	D		25.	B
6.	B		26.	B
7.	A		27.	C
8.	D		28.	B
9.	C		29.	B
10.	A		30.	C
11.	B		31.	B
12.	B		32.	A
13.	B		33.	C
14.	C		34.	D
15.	A		35.	A
16.	A		36.	A
17.	B		37.	C
18.	B		38.	B
19.	C		39.	C
20.	C		40.	C

TEACHER CERTIFICATION STUDY GUIDE

Rigor Table

Easy
8, 9, 15, 18, 21, 23, 30, 31

Average
3, 4, 6, 7, 10, 12, 13, 14, 16, 19, 22, 24, 29, 34, 38, 39

Rigorous
1, 2, 5, 11, 17, 20, 25, 26, 27, 28, 32, 33, 35, 36, 37, 40

TEACHER CERTIFICATION STUDY GUIDE

ELEMENTS OF COMPOSITION SAMPLE TEST WITH RATIONALES

Directions: The passage below contains many errors. Read the passage. Then, answer each test item by choosing the option that corrects an error in the underlined portion(s). No more than one underlined error will appear in each item. If no error exists, choose "No change is necessary."

Climbing to the top of Mount Everest is an adventure. One which everyone--whether physically fit or not--seems eager to try. The trail stretches for miles, the cold temperatures are usually frigid and brutal.

Climbers must endure severel barriers on the way, including other hikers, steep jagged rocks, and lots of snow. Plus, climbers often find the most grueling part of the trip is their climb back down, just when they are feeling greatly exhausted. Climbers who take precautions are likely to find the ascent less arduous than the unprepared. By donning heavy flannel shirts, gloves, and hats, climbers prevented hypothermia, as well as simple frostbite. A pair of rugged boots is also one of the necesities. If climbers are to avoid becoming dehydrated, there is beverages available for them to transport as well.

Once climbers are completely ready to begin their lengthy journey, they can comfortable enjoy the wonderful scenery. Wide rock formations dazzle the observers eyes with shades of gray and white, while the peak forms a triangle that seems to touch the sky. Each of the climbers are reminded of the splendor and magnificence of God's great Earth.

1. If climbers are to avoid <u>becoming</u> dehydrated, there <u>is</u> beverages available for <u>them</u> to transport as well.
   (Rigorous)

   A. becommming
   B. are
   C. him
   D. No change is necessary.

Answer: B. are
The plural verb *are* must be used with the plural subject *beverages*. Option A is incorrect because *becoming* has only one *m*. Option C is incorrect because the plural pronoun *them* is needed to agree with the referent *climbers*.

TEACHER CERTIFICATION STUDY GUIDE

2. Each of the climbers <u>are</u> reminded of the splendor and <u>magnificence</u> of <u>God's</u> great Earth.
   (Rigorous)

   A. is
   B. magnifisence
   C. Gods
   D. No change is necessary.

Answer: A. is
The singular verb *is* agrees with the singular subject *each*. Option B is incorrect because *magnificence* is misspelled. Option C is incorrect because an apostrophe is needed to show possession.

3. Climbing to the top of Mount Everest is an <u>adventure. One</u> which everyone —<u>whether</u> physically fit or not—<u>seems</u> eager to try.
   (Average)

   A. adventure, one
   B. everyone, whether
   C. seem
   D. No change is necessary.

Answer: A. adventure, one
A comma is needed between *adventure* and *one* to avoid creating a fragment of the second part. In Option B, a comma after *everyone* would not be appropriate when the dash is used on the other side of *not*. In Option C, the singular verb *seems* is needed to agree with the singular subject *everyone*.

4. A pair of rugged boots <u>is</u> <u>also one</u> of the <u>necesities</u>.
   (Average)

   A. are
   B. also, one
   C. necessities
   D. No change is necessary.

Answer: C. necessities
The word *necessities* is misspelled in the text. Option A is incorrect because the singular verb *is* must agree with the singular noun *pair* (a collective singular). Option B is incorrect because *is also* is set off with commas (potential correction); it should be set off on both sides.

TEACHER CERTIFICATION STUDY GUIDE

5. **Plus, climbers often find the most grueling part of the trip is <u>their</u> climb back <u>down, just</u> when they <u>are</u> feeling greatly exhausted.**
   (Rigorous)

   A. his
   B. down; just
   C. were
   D. No change is necessary.

Answer: D. No change is necessary.
The present tense must be used consistently throughout; therefore, Option C is incorrect. Option A is incorrect because the singular pronoun *his* does not agree with the plural antecedent *climbers*. Option B is incorrect because a comma, not a semicolon, is needed to separate the dependent clause from the main clause.

6. **By donning heavy flannel shirts, boots, and <u>hats, climbers</u> <u>prevented</u> hypothermia, as well as simple frostbite.**
   (Average)

   A. hats climbers
   B. can prevent
   C. hypothermia;
   D. No change is necessary.

Answer: B. can prevent
The verb *prevented* is in the past tense and must be changed to the present *can prevent* to be consistent. Option A is incorrect because a comma is needed after a long introductory phrase. Option C is incorrect because the semicolon creates a fragment of the phrase *as well as simple frostbite*.

7. **Climbers must endure <u>severel</u> barriers <u>on the way, including</u> other <u>hikers</u>, steep jagged rocks, and lots of snow.**
   (Average)

   A. several
   B. on the way: including
   C. hikers'
   D. No change is necessary.

Answer: A. several
The word *several* is misspelled in the text. Option B is incorrect because a comma, not a colon, is needed to set off the modifying phrase. Option C is incorrect because no apostrophe is needed after *hikers* since possession is not involved.

TEACHER CERTIFICATION STUDY GUIDE

8. **Climbers who** take precautions are likely to find the ascent **less difficult than** the unprepared.
   (Easy)

   A. Climbers, who
   B. least difficult
   C. then
   D. No change is necessary.

Answer: D. No change is necessary.
No change is needed. Option A is incorrect because a comma would make the phrase *who take precautions* seem less restrictive or less essential to the sentence. Option B is incorrect because *less* is appropriate when two items—the prepared and the unprepared—are compared. Option C is incorrect because the comparative adverb *than*, not *then*, is needed.

9. Once climbers are completely prepared for **their** lengthy **journey, they** can **comfortable** enjoy the wonderful scenery.
   (Easy)

   A. they're
   B. journey; they
   C. comfortably
   D. No change is necessary.

Answer: C. comfortably
The adverb form *comfortably* is needed to modify the verb phrase *can enjoy*. Option A is incorrect because the possessive plural pronoun is spelled *their*. Option B is incorrect because a semicolon would make the first half of the item seem like an independent clause when the subordinating conjunction *once* makes that clause dependent.

10. **Wide rock formations dazzle the <u>observers eyes</u> with shades of gray and <u>white, while</u> the peak <u>forms</u> a triangle that seems to touch the sky.**
    (Average)

    A. observers' eyes
    B. white; while
    C. formed
    D. No change is necessary.

Answer: A. observers' eyes
An apostrophe is needed to show the plural possessive form *observers' eyes*. Option B is incorrect because the semicolon would make the second half of the item seem like an independent clause when the subordinating conjunction *while* makes that clause dependent. Option C is incorrect because *formed* is in the wrong tense.

11. **The <u>trail</u> stretches for <u>miles</u>, the cold temperatures are <u>usually</u> frigid and brutal.**
    (Rigorous)

    A. trails
    B. miles;
    C. usual
    D. No change is necessary.

Answer: B. miles;
A semicolon, not a comma, is needed to separate the first independent clause from the second independent clause. Option A is incorrect because the plural subject *trails* needs the singular verb *stretch*. Option C is incorrect because the adverb form *usually* is needed to modify the adjective *frigid*.

TEACHER CERTIFICATION STUDY GUIDE

Directions: The passage below contains several errors. Read the passage. Then, answer each test item by choosing the option that corrects an error in the underlined portion(s). No more than one underlined error will appear in each item. If no error exists, choose "No change is necessary."

Every job places different kinds of demands on their employees. For example, whereas such jobs as accounting and bookkeeping require mathematical ability; graphic design requires creative/artistic ability.

Doing good at one job does not usually guarantee success at another. However, one of the elements crucial to all jobs are especially notable: the chance to accomplish a goal.

The accomplishment of the employees varies according to the job. In many jobs, the employees become accustom to the accomplishment provided by the work they do every day.

In medicine, for example, every doctor tests him self by treating badly injured or critically ill people. In the operating room, a team of Surgeons, is responsible for operating on many of these patients. In addition to the feeling of accomplishment that the workers achieve, some jobs also give a sense of identity to the employees'. Profesions like law, education, and sales offer huge financial and emotional rewards. Politicians are public servants: who work for the federal and state governments. President obama is basically employed by the American people to make laws and run the country.

Finally; the contributions that employees make to their companies and to the world cannot be taken for granted. Through their work, employees are performing a service for their employers and are contributing something to the world.

12. Every job <u>places</u> different kinds of demands on <u>their</u> <u>employees</u>. *(Average)*

   A. place
   B. its
   C. employes
   D. No change is necessary.

Answer: B. its
The singular possessive pronoun *its* must agree with its antecedent *job*, which is singular also. Option A is incorrect because *place* is a plural form, and the subject, *job*, is singular. Option C is incorrect because the correct spelling of employees is given in the sentence.

TEACHER CERTIFICATION STUDY GUIDE

13. <u>However,</u> one of the elements crucial to all jobs <u>are</u> especially <u>notable:</u> the accomplishment of a goal.
    (Average)

    A. However
    B. is
    C. notable;
    D. No change is necessary.

Answer: B. is
The singular verb *is* is needed to agree with the singular subject *one*. Option A is incorrect because a comma is needed to set off the transitional word *however*. Option C is incorrect because a colon, not a semicolon, is needed to set off an item.

14. The <u>accomplishment</u> of the <u>employees</u> <u>varies</u> according to the job.
    (Average)

    A. accomplishment,
    B. employee's
    C. vary
    D. No change is necessary.

Answer: C. vary
The singular verb *vary* is needed to agree with the singular subject *accomplishment*. Option A is incorrect because a comma after *accomplishment* would suggest that the modifying phrase *of the employees* is additional instead of essential. Option B is incorrect because *employees* is not possessive.

15. <u>Profesions</u> like law, <u>education,</u> and sales <u>offer</u> huge financial and emotional rewards.
    (Easy)

    A. Professions
    B. education;
    C. offered
    D. No change is necessary.

Answer: A. Professions
Option A is correct because *professions* is misspelled in the sentence. Option B is incorrect because a comma, not a semi-colon, is needed after *education*. In Option C, *offered* is in the wrong tense.

TEACHER CERTIFICATION STUDY GUIDE

16. Doing <u>good</u> at one job does not <u>usually</u> guarantee <u>success</u> at another.
    (Average)

    A. well
    B. usualy
    C. succeeding
    D. No change is necessary.

Answer: A. well
The adverb *well* modifies the word *doing*. Option B is incorrect because *usually* is spelled correctly in the sentence. Option C is incorrect because *succeeding* is in the wrong tense.

17. In many jobs, the employees <u>become</u> <u>accustom</u> to the accomplishment <u>provided</u> by the work they do every day.
    (Rigorous)

    A. became
    B. accustomed
    C. provides
    D. No change is necessary.

Answer: B. accustomed
The past participle *accustomed* is needed with the verb *become*. Option A is incorrect because the verb tense does not need to change to the past *became*. Option C is incorrect because *provides* is the wrong tense.

18. In medicine, for example, every doctor <u>tests</u> <u>him self</u> by treating badly-injured and critically ill people.
    (Easy)

    A. test
    B. himself
    C. critical
    D. No change is necessary.

Answer: B. himself
The reflexive pronoun *himself* is needed. (Him self is nonstandard and never correct.) Option A is incorrect because the singular verb *test* is needed to agree with the singular subject *doctor*. Option C is incorrect because the adverb *critically* is needed to modify the verb *ill*.

TEACHER CERTIFICATION STUDY GUIDE

19. In addition to the feeling of accomplishment that the workers <u>achieve</u>, some jobs also <u>give</u> a sense of self-identity to the <u>employees'</u>.
    (Average)

    A. acheve
    B. gave
    C. employees
    D. No change is necessary.

Answer: C. employees
Option C is correct because *employees* is not possessive. Option A is incorrect because *achieve* is spelled correctly in the sentence. Option B is incorrect because *gave* is the wrong tense.

20. <u>For example, whereas</u> such jobs as accounting and bookkeeping require mathematical <u>ability;</u> graphic design requires creative/artistic ability.
    (Rigorous)

    A. For example
    B. whereas,
    C. ability,
    D. No change is necessary.

Answer: C. ability,
An introductory dependent clause is set off with a comma, not a semicolon. Option A is incorrect because the transitional phrase *for example* should be set off with a comma. Option B is incorrect because the adverb *whereas* functions like *while* and does not take a comma after it.

21. In the <u>operating room,</u> a team of <u>Surgeons, is</u> responsible for operating on many of <u>these</u> patients.
    (Easy)

    A. operating room:
    B. surgeons is
    C. those
    D. No change is necessary.

Answer: B. surgeons is
Surgeons is not a proper name, so it does not need to be capitalized. A comma is not needed to break up *a team of surgeons* from the rest of the sentence. Option A is incorrect because a comma, not a colon, is needed to set off an item. Option C is incorrect because *those* is an incorrect pronoun.

TEACHER CERTIFICATION STUDY GUIDE

22. Politicians <u>are</u> public <u>servants: who</u> <u>work</u> for the federal and state governments.
    (Average)

    A. were
    B. servants who
    C. worked
    D. No change is necessary.

Answer: B. servants who
A colon is not needed to set off the introduction of the sentence. In Option A, *were* is the incorrect tense of the verb. In Option C, *worked* is in the wrong tense.

23. President obama is basically employed <u>by</u> the American people to <u>make</u> laws and run the country.
    (Easy)

    A. Obama
    B. to
    C. made
    D. No change is necessary.

Answer: A. Obama
Obama is a proper name and should be capitalized. In Option B, *to* does not fit with the verb *employed*. Option C uses the wrong form of the verb *make*.

24. <u>Finally;</u> the contributions that employees make to <u>their</u> companies and to the world cannot be <u>taken</u> for granted.
    (Average)

    A. Finally,
    B. thier
    C. took
    D. No change is necessary.

Answer: A. Finally,
A comma is needed to separate *Finally* from the rest of the sentence. *Finally* is a preposition which usually heads a dependent sentence, hence a comma is needed. Option B is incorrect because *their* is misspelled. Option C is incorrect because *took* is the wrong form of the verb.

TEACHER CERTIFICATION STUDY GUIDE

Directions: For the underlined sentence(s), choose the option that expresses the meaning with the most fluency and the clearest logic within the context. If the underlined sentence should not be changed, choose Option A, which shows no change.

25. **Which of the following sentences logically and correctly expresses the comparison?**
    (Rigorous)

    A. The Empire State Building in New York is taller than buildings in the city.
    B. The Empire State Building in New York is taller than any other building in the city.
    C. The Empire State Building in New York is tallest than other buildings in the city.

Answer: B. The Empire State Building in New York is taller than any other building in the city.

Because the Empire State Building is a building in New York City, the phrase *any other* must be included. Option A is incorrect because the Empire State Building is implicitly compared to itself since it is one of the buildings. Option C is incorrect because *tallest* is the incorrect form of the adjective.

26. Treating patients for drug and/or alcohol abuse is a sometimes difficult process. <u>Even though there are a number of different methods for helping the patient overcome a dependency, there is no way of knowing which is best in the long run.</u>
    (Rigorous)

    A. Even though there are a number of different methods for helping the patient overcome a dependency, there is no way of knowing which is best in the long run.
    B. Even though different methods can help a patient overcome a dependency, there is no way to know which is best in the long run.
    C. Even though there is no way to know which way is best in the long run, patients can overcome their dependencies when they are helped.
    D. There is no way to know which method will help the patient overcome a dependency in the long run, even though there are many different ones.

Answer: B. Even though different methods can help a patient overcome a dependency, there is no way to know which is best in the long run.
Option B is concise and logical. Option A tends to ramble with the use of *there are* and the verbs *helping* and *knowing*. Option C is awkwardly worded and repetitive in the first part of the sentence, and vague in the second because it never indicates how the patients can be helped. Option D contains the unnecessary phrase *even though there are many different ones*.

TEACHER CERTIFICATION STUDY GUIDE

27. Selecting members of a President's cabinet can often be an aggravating process. <u>Either there are too many or too few qualified candidates for a certain position, and then they have to be confirmed by the Senate, where there is the possibility of rejection.</u>
    (Rigorous)

    A. Either there are too many or too few qualified candidates for a certain position, and then they have to be confirmed by the Senate, where there is the possibility of rejection.
    B. Qualified candidates for certain positions face the possibility of rejection, when they have to be confirmed by the Senate.
    C. The Senate has to confirm qualified candidates, who face the possibility of rejection.
    D. Because the Senate has to confirm qualified candidates; they face the possibility of rejection.

Answer: C. The Senate has to confirm qualified candidates, who face the possibility of rejection.
Option C is the most straightforward and concise sentence. Option A is too unwieldy with the wordy *Either...or* phrase at the beginning. Option B doesn't make clear the fact that candidates face rejection by the Senate. Option D illogically implies that candidates face rejection because they have to be confirmed by the Senate.

28. Many factors account for the decline in the quality of public education. <u>Overcrowding, budget cutbacks, and societal deterioration which have greatly affected student learning</u>.
    (Rigorous)

    A. Overcrowding, budget cutbacks, and societal deterioration which have greatly affected student learning.
    B. Student learning has been greatly affected by overcrowding, budget cutbacks, and societal deterioration.
    C. Due to overcrowding, budget cutbacks, and societal deterioration, student learning has been greatly affected.
    D. Overcrowding, budget cutbacks, and societal deterioration have affected students learning greatly.

Answer: B. Student learning has been greatly affected by overcrowding, budget cutbacks, and societal deterioration.
Option B is concise and best explains the causes of the decline in student education. The unnecessary use of *which* in Option A makes the sentence feel incomplete. Option C has weak coordination between the reasons for the decline in public education and the fact that student learning has been affected. Option D incorrectly places the adverb *greatly* after learning, instead of before *affected*.

TEACHER CERTIFICATION STUDY GUIDE

Directions: Choose the most effective word within the context of the sentence.

29. Many of the clubs in Boca Raton are noted for their _____ elegance.
(Average)

    A. vulgar
    B. tasteful
    C. ordinary

Answer: B. tasteful
Tasteful means beautiful or charming, which would correspond to an elegant club. The words *vulgar* and *ordinary* have negative connotations.

30. When a student is expelled from school, the parents are usually _____ in advance.
(Easy)

    A. rewarded
    B. congratulated
    C. notified

Answer: C. notified
Notified means informed or told, which fits into the logic of the sentence. The words *rewarded* and *congratulated* are positive actions, which don't make sense regarding someone being expelled from school.

31. Before appearing in court, the witness was _____ the papers requiring her to show up.
(Easy)

    A. condemned
    B. served
    C. criticized

Answer: B. served
Served means given, which makes sense in the context of the sentence. *Condemned* and *criticized* do not make sense within the context of the sentence.

TEACHER CERTIFICATION STUDY GUIDE

Directions: Choose the underlined word or phrase that is unnecessary within the context of the passage.

32. <u>Considered by many to be</u> one of the worst <u>terrorist</u> incidents <u>on American soil</u> was the bombing of the Oklahoma City Federal Building, which will be remembered <u>for years to come</u>.
    (Rigorous)

    A. considered by many to be
    B. terrorist
    C. on American soil
    D. for years to come

Answer: A. considered by many to be
Considered by many to be is a wordy phrase and unnecessary in the context of the sentence. All other words are necessary within the context of the sentence.

33. The <u>flu</u> epidemic struck <u>most of</u> the <u>respected</u> faculty and students of The Woolbright School, forcing the Boynton Beach School Superintendent to close it down <u>for two weeks</u>.
    (Rigorous)

    A. flu
    B. most of
    C. respected
    D. for two weeks

Answer: C. respected
The fact that the faculty might have been *respected* is not really necessary to mention in the sentence. The other words and phrases are all necessary to complete the meaning of the sentence. The correct answer is C.

34. The <u>expanding</u> number of television channels has <u>prompted</u> cable operators to raise their prices, <u>even though</u> many consumers do not want to pay a higher <u>increased</u> amount for their service.
(Average)

- A. expanding
- B. prompted
- C. even though
- D. increased

Answer: D. increased

The word *increased* is redundant with *higher* and should be removed. All the other words are necessary within the context of the sentence.

TEACHER CERTIFICATION STUDY GUIDE

Directions: The passage below contains several errors. Read the passage. Then, answer each test item by choosing the option that corrects an error in the underlined portion(s). No more than one underlined error will appear in each item. If no error exists, choose "No change is necessary."

The discovery of a body at Paris Point marina in Boca Raton shocked the residents of Palmetto Pines, a luxury condominium complex located next door to the marina.

The victim is a thirty-five year old woman who had been apparently bludgeoned to death and dumped in the ocean late last night. Many neighbors reported terrible screams, gunshots: as well as the sound of a car backfiring loudly to Boca Raton Police shortly after midnight. The woman had been spotted in the lobby of Palmetto Pines around ten thirty, along with an older man, estimated to be in his fifties, and a younger man, in his late twenties.

"Apparently, the victim had been driven to the complex by the older man and was seen arguing with him when the younger man intervened," said Sheriff Fred Adams, "all three of them left the building together and walked to the marina, where gunshots rang out an hour later." Deputies found five bullets on the sidewalk and some blood, along with a steel pipe that is assumed to be the murder weapon. Two men were seen fleeing the scene in a red Mercedes shortly after, rushing toward the Interstate. The Palm Beach County Coroner, Melvin Watts, said he concluded the victim's skull had been crushed by a blunt tool, which resulted in a brain hemorrhage. As of now, there is no clear motive for the murder.

35. **The victim is a thirty-five-year-old who had been apparently bludgeoned to death and dumped in the ocean late last night.**
    (Rigorous)

    A. was
    B. bludgoned
    C. ocean: late
    D. No change is necessary.

Answer: A. was
The past tense *was* is needed to maintain consistency. Option B creates a misspelling. Option C incorrectly uses a colon when none is needed.

PPR EC-12 BONUS EDITION

TEACHER CERTIFICATION STUDY GUIDE

36. The discovery of a body at Paris Point <u>marina</u> in Boca Raton shocked the <u>residents</u> of Palmetto Pines, a luxury <u>condominium</u> complex located next door to the marina.
    (Rigorous)

    A. Marina
    B. residence
    C. condominnium
    D. No change is necessary.

Answer: A. Marina
Marina is a name that needs to be capitalized. Options B and C create misspellings.

37. Deputies found five bullets on the sidewalk and some <u>blood,</u> along with a steel pipe that is <u>assumed</u> <u>to be</u> the murder weapon.
    (Rigorous)

    A. blood;
    B. assuming
    C. to have been
    D. No change is necessary.

Answer: C. to have been
The past tense *to have been* is needed to maintain consistency. Option A incorrectly uses a semicolon, instead of a comma. Option B uses the wrong form of the verb *assumed*.

38. Many <u>neighbors</u> reported terrible screams, <u>gunshots: as</u> well as the sound of a car, backfiring <u>loudly</u> to Boca Raton Police shortly after midnight.
    (Average)

    A. nieghbors
    B. gunshots, as
    C. loud
    D. No change is necessary.

Answer: B. gunshots, as
Option B correctly uses a comma, not a colon to separate the items. Option A creates a misspelling. Option C incorrectly changes the adverb into an adjective.

TEACHER CERTIFICATION STUDY GUIDE

39. The woman <u>had</u> been spotted in the lobby of Palmetto Pines around ten <u>thirty,</u> along with an older <u>man, estimated</u> to be in his fifties, and a younger man in his late twenties.
   (Average)

   A. has
   B. thirty;
   C. man estimated
   D. No change is necessary.

Answer: C. man estimated
A comma is not needed to separate the item because *an older man estimated to be in his fifties* is one complete fragment. Option A incorrectly uses the present tense *has* instead of the past tense *had*. Option B incorrectly uses a colon when a comma is needed.

40. "Apparently, the victim had been driven to the complex by the older man and was seen arguing with him when the younger man intervened," said <u>Sheriff Fred Adams, "all</u> three of them left the building together and walked to the marina, where gunshots rang out an hour later."
    (Rigorous)

    A. sheriff Fred Adams, "all
    B. sheriff Fred Adams, "All
    C. Sheriff Fred Adams. "All
    D. No change is necessary.

Answer: C. Sheriff Fred Adams. "All
The quote's source comes in the middle of two independent clauses, so a period should follow *Adams*. Option A is incorrect because titles, when they come before a name, must be capitalized. Punctuation is also faulty. Option B is incorrect because the word *Adams* ends a sentence; a comma is not strong enough to support two sentences.

TEACHER CERTIFICATION STUDY GUIDE

TExES GENERALIST 4-8 111

TEACHER CERTIFICATION STUDY GUIDE

LANGUAGE ARTS SAMPLE TEST

1. **If a student has a poor vocabulary the teacher should recommend that:**
   (Rigorous)

   A. The student read newspapers, magazines, and books on a regular basis
   B. The student enroll in a Latin class
   C. The student write the words repeatedly after looking them up in the dictionary
   D. The student use a thesaurus to locate synonyms and incorporate them into his/her vocabulary

2. **The arrangement and relationship of words in sentences or sentence structure best describes**
   (Rigorous)

   A. Style
   B. Discourse
   C. Thesis
   D. Syntax

3. **Which of the following is a formal reading assessment?**
   (Rigorous)

   A. A standardized reading test
   B. A teacher-made reading test
   C. An interview
   D. A reading diary

4. **The literary device of personification is used in which example below?**
   (Average)

   A. "Beg me no beggary by soul or parents, whining dog!"
   B. "Happiness sped through the halls cajoling as it went."
   C. "O wind thy horn, thou proud fellow."
   D. "And that one talent which is death to hide."

5. **Which teaching method would be the most effective for interesting underachievers in the required senior English class?**
   (Rigorous)

   A. Assign use of glossary work and extensively footnoted excerpts of great works
   B. Have students take turns reading aloud the anthology selection
   C. Let students choose which readings they'll study and write about
   D. Use a chronologically arranged, traditional text, but assigning group work, panel presentations, and portfolio management

6. Which definition is the best for defining diction?
   (Rigorous)

   A. The specific word choices of an author to create a particular mood or feeling in the reader
   B. Writing which explains something thoroughly
   C. The background, or exposition, for a short story or drama
   D. Word choices which help teach a truth or moral

7. Which is **not** a true statement concerning an author's literary tone?
   (Rigorous)

   A. Tone is partly revealed through the selection of details
   B. Tone is the expression of the author's attitude towards his/her subject
   C. Tone in literature is usually satiric or angry
   D. Tone in literature corresponds to the tone of voice a speaker uses

8. What were two major characteristics of the first American literature?
   (Rigorous)

   A. Vengefulness and arrogance
   B. Bellicosity and derision
   C. Oral delivery and reverence for the land
   D. Maudlin and self-pitying egocentricism

9. An example of the subject of a tall tale is
   (Rigorous)

   A. John Henry
   B. Paul Bunyan
   C. George Washington
   D. Rip Van Winkle

10. Which term best describes the form of the following poetic excerpt?
    (Rigorous)

    And more to lulle him in his slumber soft,
    A trickling streake from high rock tumbling downe,
    And ever-drizzling raine upon the loft.
    Mixt with a murmuring winde, much like a swowne
    No other noyse, nor peoples troubles cryes.
    As still we wont t'annoy the walle'd towne,
    Might there be heard: but careless Quiet lyes,
    Wrapt in eternall silence farre from enemyes.

    A. Ballad
    B. Elegy
    C. Spenserian stanza
    D. Octava rima

11. Which sonnet form describes the following?
(Rigorous)

My galley charg'd with forgetfulness,
Through sharp seas, in winter night doth pass
'Tween rock and rock; and eke mine enemy, alas,
That is my lord steereth with cruelness.
And every oar a thought with readiness,
As though that death were light in such a case.
An endless wind doth tear the sail apace
Or forc'ed sighs and trusty fearfulness.
A rain of tears, a cloud of dark disdain,
Hath done the wearied cords great hinderance,
Wreathed with error and eke with ignorance.
The stars be hid that led me to this pain
Drowned is reason that should me consort,
And I remain despairing of the poet

A. Petrarchan or Italian sonnet
B. Shakespearian or Elizabethan sonnet
C. Romantic sonnet
D. Spenserian sonnet

12. A figure of speech in which someone absent or something inhuman is addressed as though present and able to respond describes
(Average)

A. Personification
B. Synechdoche
C. Metonymy
D. Apostrophe

13. The quality in a work of literature which evokes feelings of pity or compassion is called
(Easy)

A. Colloquy
B. Irony
C. Pathos
D. Paradox

14. An extended metaphor which compares two very dissimilar things—one lofty, one lowly, is a definition of a/an
(Average)

A. Antithesis
B. Aphorism
C. Apostrophe
D. Conceit

15. Which of the following is a complex sentence?
    (Easy)

    A. Anna and Margaret read a total of fifty-four books during summer vacation.
    B. The youngest boy on the team had the best earned run average which mystifies the coaching staff.
    C. Earl decided to attend Princeton; his twin brother Roy, who aced the ASVAB test, will be going to Annapolis.
    D. "Easy come, easy go," Marcia moaned.

16. Middle and high school students are more receptive to studying grammar and syntax
    (Rigorous)

    A. Through worksheets and end of lessons practices in textbooks
    B. Through independent, homework assignment
    C. Through analytical examination of the writings of famous authors
    D. Through application to their own writing

17. A punctuation mark indicating omission, interrupted thought, or an incomplete statement is a/an
    (Easy)

    A. Ellipsis
    B. Anachronism
    C. Colloquy
    D. Idiom

18. Which of the following contains an error in possessive inflection?
    (Easy)

    A. Doris's shawl
    B. Mother's-in-law frown
    C. Children's lunches
    D. Ambassador's briefcase

19. Wally <u>groaned, "Why</u> do I have to do an oral interpretation of "The Raven."
    (Average)

    A. Groaned "Why… of 'The Raven'?"
    B. Groaned "Why… of "The Raven"?
    C. Groaned ", Why… of "The Raven?"
    D. Groaned, "Why… of "The Raven."

20. Mr. Smith <u>respectfully submitted his resignation and had</u> a new job.
    (Average)

    A. Respectfully submitted his resignation and has
    B. Respectfully submitted his resignation before accepting
    C. Respectfully submitted his resignation because of
    D. Respectfully submitted his resignation and had

21. There were fewer pieces of evidence presented during the second trial
    (Average)

    A. fewer peaces
    B. less peaces
    C. less pieces
    D. fewer pieces

22. The teacher implied from our angry words that there was conflict between you and me.
    (Easy)

    A. Implied... between you and I.
    B. Inferred... between you and I.
    C. Inferred... between you and me.
    D. Implied... between you and me.

23. Which of the following is not one of the four forms of discourse?
    (Average)

    A. Exposition
    B. Description
    C. Rhetoric
    D. Persuasion

24. "Clean as a whistle or "Easy as falling off a log" are examples of
    (Average)

    A. Semantics
    B. Parody
    C. Irony
    D. Clichés

25. What is the figure of speech present in line one below in which the dead body of Caesar is addressed as though he were still a living being?
    (Average)

    O, pardon me, though Bleeding piece of earth
    That I am meek and gentle with These butchers.

    Marc Antony from *Julius Caesar*

    A. Apostrophe
    B. Allusion
    C. Antithesis
    D. Anachronism

26. A sixth-grade science teacher has given her class a paper to read on the relationship between food and weight gain. The writing contains signal words such as "because," "consequently," "this is how," and "due to." This paper has which text structure?
    (Rigorous)

    A. Cause & effect
    B. Compare & contrast
    C. Description
    D. Sequencing

27. A form or discourse which explains or informs is
    (Average)

    A. Exposition
    B. Narration
    C. Persuasion
    D. Description

28. **The following passage is written from which point of view?**
(Rigorous)

As she mused the pitiful vision of her mother's life laid its spell on the very quick of her being –that life of commonplace sacrifices closing in final craziness. She trembled as she heard again her mother's voice saying constantly with foolish insistence: Dearevaun Seraun! Dearevaun Seraun!* * "The end of pleasure is pain!" (Gaelic)

A. First person, narrator
B. Second person, direct address
C. Third person, omniscient
D. First person, omniscient

29. **Which of the following should not be included in the opening paragraph of an informative essay?**
(Average)

A. Thesis sentence
B. Details and examples supporting the main idea
C. A broad general introduction to the topic
D. A style and tone that grabs the reader's attention

30. **Which of the following is not a technique of prewriting?**
(Average)

A. Clustering
B. Listing
C. Brainstorming
D. Proofreading

31. **Which of the following is not an approach to keep students ever conscious of the need to write for audience appeal?**
(Rigorous)

A. Pairing students during the writing process
B. Reading all rough drafts before the students write the final copies
C. Having students compose stories or articles for publication in school literary magazines or newspaper
D. Writing letters to friends or relatives

Answer Key

1.	A		17.	A
2.	D		18.	B
3.	A		19.	A
4.	C		20.	C
5.	C		21.	D
6.	A		22.	C
7.	C		23.	C
8.	D		24.	D
9.	B		25.	B
10.	D		26.	A
11.	A		27.	A
12.	D		28.	C
13.	C		29.	B
14.	D		30.	D
15.	B		31.	B
16.	D			

Rigor Table

Easy
13, 15, 17, 18, 22

Average
4, 12, 14, 19, 20, 21, 23, 24, 25, 27, 29, 30

Rigorous
1, 2, 3, 5, 6, 7, 8, 9, 10, 11, 16, 26, 28, 31

TEACHER CERTIFICATION STUDY GUIDE

LANGUAGE ARTS SAMPLE TEST WITH RATIONALES

1. **If a student has a poor vocabulary the teacher should recommend that:**
   (Rigorous)

   A. The student read newspapers, magazines, and books on a regular basis
   B. The student enroll in a Latin class
   C. The student write the words repeatedly after looking them up in the dictionary
   D. The student use a thesaurus to locate synonyms and incorporate them into his/her vocabulary

   Answer: A. The student read newspapers, magazines, and books on a regular basis
   It is up to the teacher to help the student choose reading material, but the student must be able to choose where s/he will search for the reading pleasure indispensable for enriching vocabulary.

2. **The arrangement and relationship of words in sentences or sentence structure best describes**
   (Rigorous)

   A. Style
   B. Discourse
   C. Thesis
   D. Syntax

   Answer: D. Syntax
   Syntax is the grammatical structure of sentences.

3. **Which of the following is a formal reading assessment?**
   (Rigorous)

   A. A standardized reading test
   B. A teacher-made reading test
   C. An interview
   D. A reading diary

   Answer: A. A standardized reading text
   If assessment is standardized, it has to be objective, whereas B, C and D are all subjective assessments.

TEACHER CERTIFICATION STUDY GUIDE

4. **The literary device of personification is used in which example below?**
   (Average)

   A. "Beg me no beggary by soul or parents, whining dog!"
   B. "Happiness sped through the halls cajoling as it went."
   C. "O wind thy horn, thou proud fellow."
   D. "And that one talent which is death to hide."

Answer: C. "O wind thy horn, thou proud fellow."
Personification gives human characteristics to an inanimate object, such as wind in the sentence above.

5. **Which teaching method would be the most effective for interesting underachievers in the required senior English class?**
   (Rigorous)

   A. Assign use of glossary work and extensively footnoted excerpts of great works
   B. Have students take turns reading aloud the anthology selection
   C. Let students choose which readings they'll study and write about
   D. Use a chronologically arranged, traditional text, but assigning group work, panel presentations, and portfolio management

Answer: C. Let students choose which readings they'll study and write about
It will encourage students to react honestly to literature. Students should take notes on what they're reading so they will be able to discuss the material. They should not only react to literature, but also experience it. Small-group work is a good way to encourage them. The other answers are not fit for junior-high or high school students. They should be encouraged, however, to read critics of works in order to understand criteria work.

6. **Which definition is the best for defining diction?**
   (Rigorous)

   A. The specific word choices of an author to create a particular mood or feeling in the reader
   B. Writing which explains something thoroughly
   C. The background, or exposition, for a short story or drama
   D. Word choices which help teach a truth or moral

Answer: A. The specific word choices of an author to create a particular mood or feeling in the reader
Diction refers to an author's choice of words, expressions, and style to convey his/her meaning.

7. Which is not a true statement concerning an author's literary tone? *(Rigorous)*

   A. Tone is partly revealed through the selection of details
   B. Tone is the expression of the author's attitude towards his/her subject
   C. Tone in literature is usually satiric or angry
   D. Tone in literature corresponds to the tone of voice a speaker uses

Answer: C. Tone in literature is usually satiric or angry
Tone in literature conveys a mood and can be as varied as the tone of voice of a speaker (see D), e.g., sad, nostalgic, whimsical, angry, formal, intimate, satirical, sentimental, etc.

8. What were two major characteristics of the first American literature? *(Rigorous)*

   A. Vengefulness and arrogance
   B. Bellicosity and derision
   C. Oral delivery and reverence for the land
   D. Maudlin and self-pitying egocentricism

Answer: D. Maudlin and self-pitying egocentricism
This characteristic can be seen in Captain John Smith's work as well as William Bradford's, and Michael Wigglesworth's works.

9. An example of the subject of a tall tale is *(Rigorous)*

   A. John Henry
   B. Paul Bunyan
   C. George Washington
   D. Rip Van Winkle

Answer: B. Paul Bunyan
A tall tale is a Folklore genre, originating on the American frontier, in which the physical attributes, capabilities, and exploits of characters are wildly exaggerated. This is the case of giant logger Paul Bunyan of the American Northwestern forests. James Stevens traced Paul Bunyan to a French Canadian logger named Paul Bunyon. He won a reputation as a great fighter in the Papineau Rebellion against England in 1837 and later became famous as the boss of a logging camp. Paul Bunyan's first appearance in print seems to be in an advertising pamphlet, *Paul Bunyan and His Big Blue Ox*, published by the Red River Company. It immediately became very popular and was reissued many times.

TEACHER CERTIFICATION STUDY GUIDE

10. Which term best describes the form of the following poetic excerpt? *(Rigorous)*

   And more to lulle him in his slumber soft,
   A trickling streake from high rock tumbling downe,
   And ever-drizzling raine upon the loft.
   Mixt with a murmuring winde, much like a swowne
   No other noyse, nor peoples troubles cryes.
   As still we wont t'annoy the walle'd towne,
   Might there be heard: but careless Quiet lyes,
   Wrapt in eternall silence farre from enemyes.

   A. Ballad
   B. Elegy
   C. Spenserian stanza
   D. Octava rima

Answer: D. Octava rima
The Octava Rima is a specific eight-line stanza whose rhyme scheme is abababcc.

11. Which sonnet form describes the following?
(Rigorous)

My galley charg'd with forgetfulness,
Through sharp seas, in winter night doth pass
'Tween rock and rock; and eke mine enemy, alas,
That is my lord steereth with cruelness.
And every oar a thought with readiness,
As though that death were light in such a case.
An endless wind doth tear the sail apace
Or forc'ed sighs and trusty fearfulness.
A rain of tears, a cloud of dark disdain,
Hath done the wearied cords great hinderance,
Wreathed with error and eke with ignorance.
The stars be hid that led me to this pain
Drowned is reason that should me consort,
And I remain despairing of the poet

- A. Petrarchan or Italian sonnet
- B. Shakespearian or Elizabethan sonnet
- C. Romantic sonnet
- D. Spenserian sonnet

Answer: A. Petrarchan or Italian sonnet

The Petrarchan sonnet, also known as the Italian sonnet, is named after the Italian poet Petrarch (1304-74). It is divided into an octave rhyming *abbaabba* and a sestet normally rhyming *cdecde*.

TEACHER CERTIFICATION STUDY GUIDE

12. **A figure of speech in which someone absent or something inhuman is addressed as though present and able to respond describes**
    (Average)

    A. Personification
    B. Synechdoche
    C. Metonymy
    D. Apostrophe

Answer: D. Apostrophe
Apostrophe gives human reactions and thoughts to animals, things, and abstract ideas alike. This figure of speech is often present in allegory: for instance, the Giant Despair in John Bunyon's *Pilgrim's Progress.* Also, fables use personification to make animals able to speak.

13. **The quality in a work of literature which evokes feelings of pity or compassion is called**
    (Easy)

    A. Colloquy
    B. Irony
    C. Pathos
    D. Paradox

Answer: C. Pathos
A very well known example of pathos is Desdemona's death in Othello, but there are many other examples of pathos.

14. **An extended metaphor which compares two very dissimilar things—one lofty, one lowly, is a definition of a/an**
    (Average)

    A. Antithesis
    B. Aphorism
    C. Apostrophe
    D. Conceit

Answer: D. Conceit
A conceit is an unusually far-fetched metaphor in which an object, person, or situation is presented in a parallel and simpler analogue between two apparently very different things or feelings, one very sophisticated and one very ordinary, usually taken either from nature or a well known every day concept familiar to both reader and author alike. The conceit was first developed by Petrarch and spread to England in the sixteenth century.

TEACHER CERTIFICATION STUDY GUIDE

15. **Which of the following is a complex sentence?**
    (Easy)

    A. Anna and Margaret read a total of fifty-four books during summer vacation.
    B. The youngest boy on the team had the best earned run average which mystifies the coaching staff.
    C. Earl decided to attend Princeton; his twin brother Roy, who aced the ASVAB test, will be going to Annapolis.
    D. "Easy come, easy go," Marcia moaned.

Answer: B. The youngest boy on the team had the best earned run average which mystifies the coaching staff.
Here, the use of the relative pronoun "which", whose antecedent is "the best run average", introduces a clause that is dependent on the independent clause "The youngest boy on the team had the best run average". The idea expressed in the subordinate clause is subordinate to the one expressed in the independent clause.

16. **Middle and high school students are more receptive to studying grammar and syntax**
    (Rigorous)

    A. Through worksheets and end of lessons practices in textbooks
    B. Through independent, homework assignment
    C. Through analytical examination of the writings of famous authors
    D. Through application to their own writing

Answer: D. Through application to their own writing
At this age, students learn grammatical concepts best through practical application in their own writing.

17. **A punctuation mark indicating omission, interrupted thought, or an incomplete statement is a/an**
    (Easy)

    A. Ellipsis
    B. Anachronism
    C. Colloquy
    D. Idiom

Answer: A. Ellipsis
In an ellipsis, a word or words that would clarify the sentence's message are missing, yet it is still possible to understand them from the context.

TEACHER CERTIFICATION STUDY GUIDE

18. Which of the following contains an error in possessive inflection? *(Easy)*

    A. Doris's shawl
    B. Mother's-in-law frown
    C. Children's lunches
    D. Ambassador's briefcase

Answer: B. Mother's-in-law frown
Mother-in-Law is a compound common noun and the inflection should be at the end of the word, according to the rule.

19. Wally <u>groaned, "Why</u> do I have to do an oral interpretation of "The Raven." *(Average)*

    A. Groaned "Why… of 'The Raven'?"
    B. Groaned "Why… of "The Raven"?
    C. Groaned ", Why… of "The Raven?"
    D. Groaned, "Why… of "The Raven."

Answer: A. Groaned "Why… of 'The Raven'?"
The question mark in a quotation that is an interrogation should be within the quotation marks. Also, when quoting a work of literature within another quotation, one should use single quotation marks ('…') for the title of this work, and they should close before the final quotation mark.

20. Mr. Smith <u>respectfully submitted his resignation and had</u> a new job. *(Average)*

    A. Respectfully submitted his resignation and has
    B. Respectfully submitted his resignation before accepting
    C. Respectfully submitted his resignation because of
    D. Respectfully submitted his resignation and had

Answer: C. Respectfully submitted his resignation because of
Choice A eliminates any relationship of causality between submitting the resignation and having the new job. Choice B just changes the sentence and does not indicate the fact that Mr. Smith had a new job before submitting his resignation. Choice D means that Mr. Smith first submitted his resignation then got a new job.

TEACHER CERTIFICATION STUDY GUIDE

21. There were <u>fewer pieces</u> of evidence presented during the second trial
    (Average)

    A. fewer peaces
    B. less peaces
    C. less pieces
    D. fewer pieces

Answer: D. fewer pieces
"Less" is impossible in the plural, and "peace" is the opposite of war, not a "piece" of evidence.

22. The teacher <u>implied</u> from our angry words that there was conflict <u>between you and me.</u>
    (Easy)

    A. Implied... between you and I.
    B. Inferred... between you and I.
    C. Inferred... between you and me.
    D. Implied... between you and me.

Answer: C. Inferred....between you and me.
The difference between the verb "to imply" and the verb "to infer" is that implying is directing an interpretation toward other people; to infer is to deduce an interpretation from someone else's discourse. Moreover, "between you and I" is grammatically incorrect: after a preposition here "and", a disjunctive pronoun (me, you, him, her, us, you, them) is needed.

23. Which of the following is not one of the four forms of discourse?
    (Average)

    A. Exposition
    B. Description
    C. Rhetoric
    D. Persuasion

Answer: C. Rhetoric
Exposition, description, and persuasion are styles of writing and ways of influencing a reader or a listener. Rhetoric, on the other hand, is theoretical. It is the theory of expressive and effective speech. Rhetorical figures are ornaments of speech such as anaphora, antithesis, metaphor, etc.

TEACHER CERTIFICATION STUDY GUIDE

24. "Clean as a whistle or "Easy as falling off a log" are examples of
    (Average)

    A. Semantics
    B. Parody
    C. Irony
    D. Clichés

Answer: D. Clichés
A cliché is a phrase or expression that has become dull due to overuse.

25. What is the figure of speech present in line one below in which the dead body of Caesar is addressed as though he were still a living being?
    (Average)

    O, pardon me, though Bleeding piece of earth
    That I am meek and gentle with
    These butchers.

    Marc Antony from *Julius Caesar*

    A. Apostrophe
    B. Allusion
    C. Antithesis
    D. Anachronism

Answer: B. Allusion
This rhetorical figure addresses personified things, absent people or gods. An antithesis is a contrast between two opposing viewpoints, ideas, or presentation of characters. An anachronism is the placing of an object or person out of its time with the time of the text. The best known example is the clock in Shakespeare's *Julius Caesar*.

26. A sixth-grade science teacher has given her class a paper to read on the relationship between food and weight gain. The writing contains signal words such as "because," "consequently," "this is how," and "due to." This paper has which text structure?
(Rigorous)

   A. Cause & effect
   B. Compare & contrast
   C. Description
   D. Sequencing

Answer: A. Cause & effect
Cause and effect is the relationship between two things when one thing makes something else happen. Writers use this text structure to show order, inform, speculate, and change behavior. This text structure uses the process of identifying potential causes of a problem or issue in an orderly way. It is often used to teach social studies and science concepts. It is characterized by signal words such as because, so, so that, if… then, consequently, thus, since, for, for this reason, as a result of, therefore, due to, this is how, nevertheless, and accordingly.

27. A form or discourse which explains or informs is
(Average)

   A. Exposition
   B. Narration
   C. Persuasion
   D. Description

Answer: A. Exposition
Exposition sets forth a systematic explanation of any subject. It can also introduce the characters of a literary work and their situations in the story.

TEACHER CERTIFICATION STUDY GUIDE

28. **The following passage is written from which point of view?**
    (Rigorous)

    As she mused the pitiful vision of her mother's life laid its spell on the very quick of her being –that life of commonplace sacrifices closing in final craziness. She trembled as she heard again her mother's voice saying constantly with foolish insistence: Dearevaun Seraun! Dearevaun Seraun!* * "The end of pleasure is pain!" (Gaelic)

    A. First person, narrator
    B. Second person, direct address
    C. Third person, omniscient
    D. First person, omniscient

Answer: C. Third person, omniscient
The passage is clearly in the third person (the subject is "she"), and it is omniscient since it gives the characters' inner thoughts.

29. **Which of the following should not be included in the opening paragraph of an informative essay?**
    (Average)

    A. Thesis sentence
    B. Details and examples supporting the main idea
    C. A broad general introduction to the topic
    D. A style and tone that grabs the reader's attention

Answer: B. Details and examples supporting the main idea
The introductory paragraph should introduce the topic, capture the reader's interest, state the thesis and prepare the reader for the main points in the essay. Details and examples, however, should be given in the second part of the essay, so as to help develop the thesis presented at the end of the introductory paragraph, following the inverted triangle method consisting of a broad general statement followed by some information, and then the thesis at the end of the paragraph.

30. **Which of the following is not a technique of prewriting?**
    (Average)

    A. Clustering
    B. Listing
    C. Brainstorming
    D. Proofreading

Answer: D. Proofreading
Proofreading should be reserved for the final draft.

31. **Which of the following is not an approach to keep students ever conscious of the need to write for audience appeal?**
    (Rigorous)

    A. Pairing students during the writing process
    B. Reading all rough drafts before the students write the final copies
    C. Having students compose stories or articles for publication in school literary magazines or newspaper
    D. Writing letters to friends or relatives

Answer: B. Reading all rough drafts before the students write the final copies
Reading all rough drafts will not encourage the students to take control of their text and might even inhibit their creativity. On the contrary, pairing students will foster their sense of responsibility, and having them compose stories for literary magazines will boost their self esteem as well as their organization skills. As far as writing letters is concerned, the work of authors such as Madame de Sevigne in the seventeenth century is a good example of epistolary literary work.

MATHEMATICS SAMPLE TEST

1. $\dfrac{2^{10}}{2^5} =$
   (Average)

   A. 2^2
   B. 2^5
   C. 2^{50}
   D. $2^{\frac{1}{2}}$

2. $\left(\dfrac{-4}{9}\right) + \left(\dfrac{-7}{10}\right) =$
   (Average)

   A. $\dfrac{23}{90}$
   B. $\dfrac{-23}{90}$
   C. $\dfrac{103}{90}$
   D. $\dfrac{-103}{90}$

3. $0.74 =$
   (Easy)

   A. $\dfrac{74}{100}$
   B. 7.4%
   C. $\dfrac{33}{50}$
   D. $\dfrac{74}{10}$

4. $(5.6) \times (^-0.11) =$
   (Average)

   A. $^-0.616$
   B. 0.616
   C. $^-6.110$
   D. 6.110

5. **An item that sells for $375 is put on sale at $120. What is the percent of decrease?**
   (Easy)

   A. 25%
   B. 28%
   C. 68%
   D. 34%

TEACHER CERTIFICATION STUDY GUIDE

6. Which denotes an irrational number?
   (Easy)

   A. 4.2500000
   B. $\sqrt{16}$
   C. 0.25252525
   D. π=3.141592

7. What is the greatest common factor of 16, 28, and 36?
   (Average)

   A. 2
   B. 4
   C. 8
   D. 16

8. Compute the surface area of the prism below.
   (Average)

   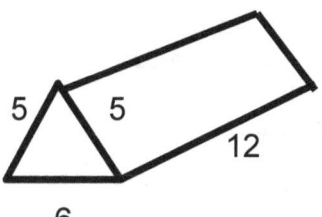

   A. 204
   B. 216
   C. 360
   D. 180

9. What is the area of a square whose side is 13 feet?
   (Easy)

   A. 169 feet
   B. 169 square feet
   C. 52 feet
   D. 52 square feet

10. The owner of a rectangular piece of land 40 yards in length and 30 yards in width wants to divide it into two parts. She plans to join two opposite corners with a fence as shown in the diagram below. The cost of the fence will be approximately $25 per linear foot. What is the estimated cost for the fence needed by the owner?
    (Rigorous)

    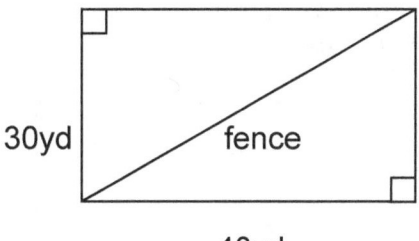

    A. $1,250
    B. $62,500
    C. $5,250
    D. $3,750

11. Find the surface area of a box which is 3 feet wide, 5 feet tall, and 4 feet deep.
    (Average)

    A. 47 sq. ft.
    B. 60 sq. ft.
    C. 94 sq. ft
    D. 188 sq. ft.

12. The trunk of a tree has a 2.1 meter radius. What is its circumference?
(Average)

    A. 2.1π square meters
    B. 4.2π meters
    C. 2.1π meters
    D. 4.2π square meters

13. Set A, B, C, and U are related as shown in the diagram. Which of the following is true, assuming not one of the six regions is empty?
(Average)

    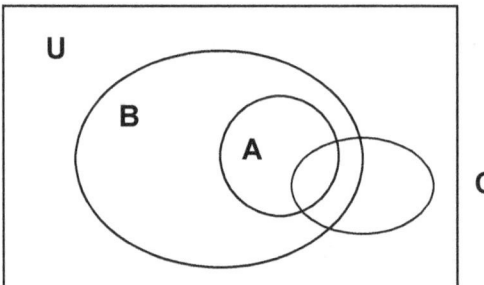

    A. Any element that is a member of set B is also a member of set A.
    B. No element is a member of all three sets A, B, and C.
    C. Any element that is a member of set U is also a member of set B.
    D. None of the above statements is true.

14. If $4x - (3 - x) = 7(x - 3) + 10$, then
(Rigorous)

    A. $x = 8$
    B. $x = -8$
    C. $x = 4$
    D. $x = -4$

15. It takes 5 equally skilled people 9 hours to shingle Mr. Joe's roof. Let t be the time required for only 3 of these men to do the same job. Select the correct statement of the given condition
(Rigorous)

    A. $\dfrac{3}{5} = \dfrac{9}{t}$

    B. $\dfrac{9}{5} = \dfrac{3}{t}$

    C. $\dfrac{5}{9} = \dfrac{3}{t}$

    D. $\dfrac{14}{9} = \dfrac{t}{5}$

16. Find the equation of a line through (5,6) and (-1,-2) in standard form.
(Rigorous)

    A. $3y = 4x - 2$

    B. $-2y = \dfrac{4}{3}x - 1$

    C. $6y + 5x - 1$

    D. $y = 4x - 6$

17. Find the real roots of the equation $3x^2 - 45 + 22x$.
    (Rigorous)

    A. $\dfrac{-5}{3}$ and 9

    B. $\dfrac{5}{3}$ and -9

    C. 5 and 9

    D. -5 and -9

18. {1,4,7,10, . . .} What is the 40th term in this sequence?
    (Rigorous)

    A. 43
    B. 121
    C. 118
    D. 120

19. Which term most accurately describes two coplanar lines without any common points?
    (Average)

    A. Perpendicular
    B. Parallel
    C. Intersecting
    D. Skew

20. Given similar polygons with corresponding sides 6 and 8, what is the area of the smaller polygon if the area of the larger polygon is 64?
    (Rigorous)

    A. 48
    B. 36
    C. 144
    D. 78

21. Study figures A, B, C, and D. Select the letter in which all triangles are similar.
    (Easy)

    A.

    B.

    C.

    D.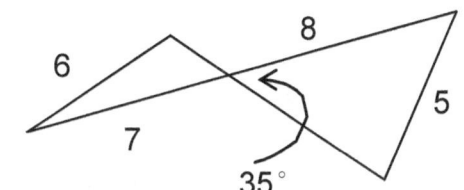

22. Find the midpoint of (2,5) and (7,-4).
    (Rigorous)

    A. (9,-1)
    B. (5, 9)
    C. (9/2, -1/2)
    D. (9/2, 1/2)

23. The following chart shows the yearly average number of international tourists visiting Palm Beach for 1990-1994. How many more international tourists visited Palm Beach in 1994 than in 1991?
(Average)

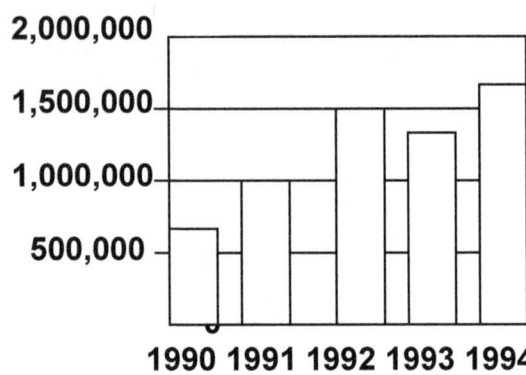

A. 100,000
B. 600,000
C. 1,600,000
D. 8,000,000

24. What conclusion can be drawn from the graph below?
(Rigorous)

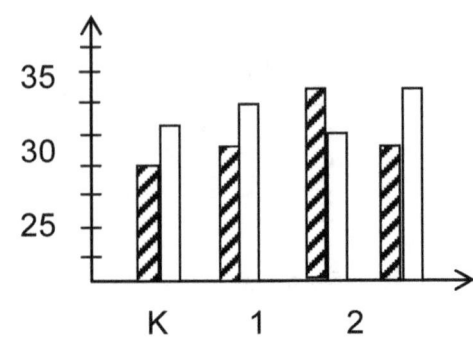

MLK Elementary Student Enrollment   Girls   Boys

A. The number of students in first grade exceeds the number in second grade
B. There are more boys than girls in the entire school
C. There are more girls than boys in the first grade
D. Third grade has the largest number of students

25. Mary did comparison shopping on her favorite brand of coffee. Over half of the stores priced the coffee at $1.70. Most of the remaining stores priced the coffee at $1.80, except for a few who charged $1.90. Which of the following statements is true about the distribution of prices?
    (Rigorous)

    A. The mean and the mode are the same
    B. The mean is greater than the mode
    C. The mean is less than the mode
    D. The mean is less than the median

26. What is the mode of the data in the following sample?
    (Easy)

    9, 10, 11, 9, 10, 11, 9, 13

    A. 9
    B. 9.5
    C. 10
    D. 11

27. A coin is tossed and a die is rolled. What is the probability of landing on the head side of the coin and rolling a 3 on the dice?
    (Rigorous)

    A. $\dfrac{1}{2}$

    B. $\dfrac{1}{6}$

    C. $\dfrac{1}{12}$

    D. $\dfrac{1}{15}$

28. What is the probability of drawing 2 consecutive aces from a standard deck of cards?
    (Rigorous)

    A. $\dfrac{3}{51}$

    B. $\dfrac{1}{221}$

    C. $\dfrac{2}{104}$

    D. $\dfrac{2}{52}$

Answer Key

1. B
2. D
3. A
4. A
5. C
6. D
7. B
8. B
9. B
10. D
11. C
12. B
13. D
14. C
15. A
16. A
17. B
18. C
19. B
20. B
21. B
22. D
23. B
24. B
25. B
26. A
27. C
28. B

Rigor Table

Easy
3, 5, 6, 9, 21, 26

Average
1, 2, 4, 7, 8, 11, 12, 13, 19, 23

Rigorous
10, 14, 15, 16, 17, 18, 20, 22, 24, 25, 27, 28

TEACHER CERTIFICATION STUDY GUIDE

MATHEMATICS SAMPLE TEST WITH RATIONALES

1. $\dfrac{2^{10}}{2^5} =$

   (Average)

   A. 2^2
   B. 2^5
   C. 2^{50}
   D. $2^{\frac{1}{2}}$

Answer: B. 2^5

The quotient rule of exponents says $\dfrac{a^m}{a^n} = a^{(m-n)}$ so $\dfrac{2^{10}}{2^5} = 2^{(10-5)} = 2^5$

2. $\left(\dfrac{-4}{9}\right) + \left(\dfrac{-7}{10}\right) =$

   (Average)

   A. $\dfrac{23}{90}$

   B. $\dfrac{-23}{90}$

   C. $\dfrac{103}{90}$

   D. $\dfrac{-103}{90}$

Answer: D. $\dfrac{-103}{90}$

Find the LCD of $\dfrac{-4}{9}$ and $\dfrac{-7}{10}$. The LCD is 90, so you get $\dfrac{-40}{90} + \dfrac{-63}{90} = \dfrac{-103}{90}$

3. **0.74 =**
    (Easy)

    A. $\dfrac{74}{100}$

    B. 7.4%

    C. $\dfrac{33}{50}$

    D. $\dfrac{74}{10}$

Answer: A. $\dfrac{74}{100}$

0.74 ⑧ the 4 is in the hundredths place, so the answer is $\dfrac{74}{100}$

4. $(5.6) \times (^-0.11) =$
    (Average)

    A. $^-0.616$
    B. 0.616
    C. $^-6.110$
    D. 6.110

Answer: A. $^-0.616$
Simply multiply 5.6 by -0.11. The answer will be negative because a positive times a negative is a negative number.

TEACHER CERTIFICATION STUDY GUIDE

5. An item that sells for $375 is put on sale at $120. What is the percent of decrease?
   (Easy)

   A. 25%
   B. 28%
   C. 68%
   D. 34%

Answer: C. 68%
Use $(1 - x)$ as the discount. $375x = 120$.
$375(1 - x) = 120 \rightarrow 375 - 375x = 120 \rightarrow 375x = 255 \rightarrow x = 0.68 = 68\%$

6. Which denotes an irrational number?
   (Easy)

   A. 4.2500000
   B. $\sqrt{16}$
   C. 0.25252525
   D. π=3.141592

Answer: D. π=3.141592
An irrational number is neither terminal nor repeating. Rational numbers are either terminal or repeating. Of the choices given, only the value of pi (π) is an irrational number.

7. What is the greatest common factor of 16, 28, and 36?
   (Average)

   A. 2
   B. 4
   C. 8
   D. 16

Answer: B. 4
The smallest number in this set is 16; its factors are 1, 2, 4, 8 and 16. 16 is the largest factor, but it does not divide into 28 or 36. Neither does 8. 4 does factor into both 28 and 36.

TEACHER CERTIFICATION STUDY GUIDE

8. Compute the surface area of the prism below.
   (Average)

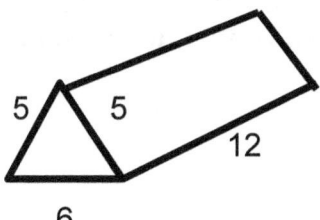

- A. 204
- B. 216
- C. 360
- D. 180

Answer: B. 216
There are five surfaces which make up the prism. The bottom rectangle has area 6 x 12 = 72. The sloping sides are two rectangles each with an area of 5 x 12 = 60. The height of the triangles is determined to be 4 using the Pythagorean Theorem. Therefore each triangle has area 1/2bh = 1/2(6)(4) =12. Thus, the surface area is 72 + 60 + 60 + 12 + 12 = 216.

9. What is the area of a square whose side is 13 feet?
   (Easy)

- A. 169 feet
- B. 169 square feet
- C. 52 feet
- D. 52 square feet

Answer: B. 169 square feet
Area = length times width (*lw*).
Length = 13 feet
Width = 13 feet (square, so length and width are the same).
Area = $13 \times 13 = 169$ square feet.
Area is measured in square feet.

10. The owner of a rectangular piece of land 40 yards in length and 30 yards in width wants to divide it into two parts. She plans to join two opposite corners with a fence as shown in the diagram below. The cost of the fence will be approximately $25 per linear foot. What is the estimated cost for the fence needed by the owner?
(Rigorous)

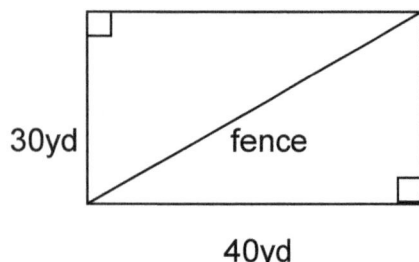

A. $1,250
B. $62,500
C. $5,250
D. $3,750

Answer: D. $3,750
Find the length of the diagonal by using the Pythagorean theorem. Let *x* be the length of the diagonal.

$$30^2 + 40^2 = x^2 \rightarrow 900 + 1600 = x^2$$
$$2500 = x^2 \rightarrow \sqrt{2500} = \sqrt{x^2}$$
$$x = 50 \text{ yards}$$

Convert to feet. $\dfrac{50 \text{ yards}}{x \text{ feet}} = \dfrac{1 \text{ yard}}{3 \text{ feet}} \rightarrow 150 \text{ feet}$

It cost $25.00 per linear foot, so the cost is (150 ft)($25) = $3750

TEACHER CERTIFICATION STUDY GUIDE

11. Find the surface area of a box which is 3 feet wide, 5 feet tall, and 4 feet deep.
    (Average)

    A. 47 sq. ft.
    B. 60 sq. ft.
    C. 94 sq. ft
    D. 188 sq. ft.

Answer: C. 94 sq. ft.
Let's assume the base of the rectangular solid (box) is 3 by 4, and the height is 5. Then the surface area of the top and bottom together is 2(12) = 24. The sum of the areas of the front and back are 2(15) = 30, while the sum of the areas of the sides are 2(20)=40. The total surface area is therefore 94 square feet.

12. The trunk of a tree has a 2.1 meter radius. What is its circumference?
    (Average)

    A. 2.1π square meters
    B. 4.2π meters
    C. 2.1π meters
    D. 4.2π square meters

Answer: B. 4.2π meters
Circumference is $2\pi r$, where r is the radius. The circumference is $2\pi 2.1 = 4.2\pi$ meters (not square meters because not measuring area).

13. Set A, B, C, and U are related as shown in the diagram. Which of the following is true, assuming not one of the six regions is empty?
    (Average)

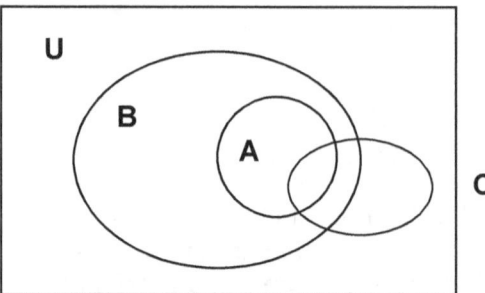

   A. Any element that is a member of set B is also a member of set A.
   B. No element is a member of all three sets A, B, and C.
   C. Any element that is a member of set U is also a member of set B.
   D. None of the above statements is true.

Answer: D. None of the above statements is true.
Answer A is incorrect because not all members of set B are also in set A. Answer B is incorrect because there are elements that are members of all three sets A, B, and C. Answer C is incorrect because not all members of set U is a member of set B. This leaves answer D, which states that none of the above choices are true.

14. If $4x - (3 - x) = 7(x - 3) + 10$, then
    (Rigorous)

   A. $x = 8$
   B. $x = -8$
   C. $x = 4$
   D. $x = -4$

Answer: C. $x = 4$
The answer is **C**. Solve for x.

$4x - (3 - x) = 7(x - 3) + 10$

$4x - 3 + x = 7x - 21 + 10$

$5x - 3 = 7x - 11$

$5x = 7x - 11 + 3$

$5x - 7x = {}^-8$

${}^-2x = {}^-8$

$x = 4$

15. It takes 5 equally skilled people 9 hours to shingle Mr. Joe's roof. Let t be the time required for only 3 of these men to do the same job. Select the correct statement of the given condition
 (Rigorous)

 A. $\dfrac{3}{5} = \dfrac{9}{t}$

 B. $\dfrac{9}{5} = \dfrac{3}{t}$

 C. $\dfrac{5}{9} = \dfrac{3}{t}$

 D. $\dfrac{14}{9} = \dfrac{t}{5}$

Answer: A. $\dfrac{3}{5} = \dfrac{9}{t}$

$$\dfrac{3 \text{ people}}{5 \text{ people}} = \dfrac{9 \text{ hours}}{t \text{ hours}}$$

16. Find the equation of a line through (5,6) and (-1,-2) in standard form. *(Rigorous)*

   A. $3y=4x-2$

   B. $-2y = \dfrac{4}{3}x - 1$

   C. $6y + 5x - 1$

   D. $y = 4x - 6$

Answer: A. 3y=4x-2

$$\text{slope} = \frac{y_2 - y_1}{x_2 - x_1} = \frac{-2-6}{-1-5} = \frac{-8}{-6} = \frac{4}{3}$$

$$Y - y_a = m(X - x_a) \rightarrow Y + 2 = \frac{4}{3}(X + 1) \rightarrow$$

$$Y + 2 = \frac{4}{3}x + \frac{4}{3}$$

$$Y = \frac{4}{3}x - \frac{2}{3} \qquad \text{This is the slope-intercept form.}$$

Multiply by 3 to eliminate fractions

$$3y = 4x - 2 \qquad \text{This is the standard form.}$$

TEACHER CERTIFICATION STUDY GUIDE

17. Find the real roots of the equation $3x^2 - 45 + 22x$.
    (Rigorous)

    A. $\dfrac{-5}{3}$ and 9

    B. $\dfrac{5}{3}$ and $^-9$

    C. 5 and 9

    D. -5 and -9

Answer: B. $\dfrac{5}{3}$ and $^-9$

Factor the equation $3x^2 - 45 + 22x$
(−)(+)
$(3x - 5)(x + 9)$ Set each part equal to 0 and solve for x.
$3x - 5 = 0$
$3x = 5$ $x + 9 = 0$
$x = \dfrac{5}{3}$ $x = ^-9$

18. $\{1, 4, 7, 10, \ldots\}$ What is the 40th term in this sequence?
    (Rigorous)

    A. 43
    B. 121
    C. 118
    D. 120

Answer: C. 118
To find a term in an arithmetic series in which each term is separated from the next by a fixed number, use the following formula: $a_n = a_1 + (n - 1)d$, where a_1 = the first term in the series, a_n = the nth term in the series, and d = the common difference between the terms.

$a_n = 1 + (40 - 1)3$
$a_n = 1 + (39)3$
$a_n = 118$

19. Which term most accurately describes two coplanar lines without any common points?
    (Average)

    A. Perpendicular
    B. Parallel
    C. Intersecting
    D. Skew

Answer: B. Parallel
By definition, parallel lines are coplanar lines without any common points.

20. Given similar polygons with corresponding sides 6 and 8, what is the area of the smaller polygon if the area of the larger polygon is 64?
    (Rigorous)

    A. 48
    B. 36
    C. 144
    D. 78

Answer: B. 36
In similar polygons, the areas are proportional to the squares of the sides. 36/64 = x/64.

21. Study figures A, B, C, and D. Select the letter in which all triangles are similar.
    (Easy)

A.

B.

C.

D.

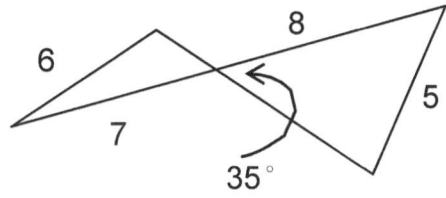

Answer: B.
Choice A is not correct because one triangle is equilateral and the other is isosceles. Choice C is not correct because the two smaller triangles are similar, but the large triangle is not. Choice D is not correct because the lengths and angles are not proportional to each other. Therefore, the correct answer is B because all the triangles have the same angles.

TEACHER CERTIFICATION STUDY GUIDE

22. Find the midpoint of (2,5) and (7,-4).
    (Rigorous)

    A. (9,-1)
    B. (5, 9)
    C. (9/2, -1/2)
    D. (9/2, 1/2)

Answer: D. (9/2, 1/2)
Using the midpoint formula x = (2 + 7)/2   y = (5 + -4)/2

23. The following chart shows the yearly average number of international tourists visiting Palm Beach for 1990-1994. How many more international tourists visited Palm Beach in 1994 than in 1991?
    (Average)

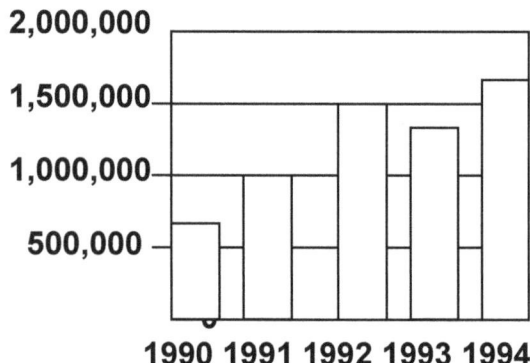

    A. 100,000
    B. 600,000
    C. 1,600,000
    D. 8,000,000

Answer: B. 600,000
The number of tourists in 1991 was 1,000,000 and the number in 1994 was 1,600,000. Subtract to get a difference of 600,000.

TEACHER CERTIFICATION STUDY GUIDE

24. What conclusion can be drawn from the graph below?
    (Rigorous)

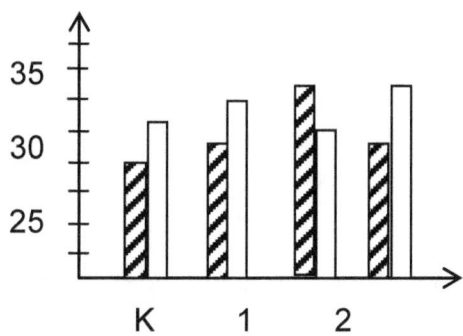

MLK Elementary Student Enrollment   Girls   Boys

   A. The number of students in first grade exceeds the number in second grade
   B. There are more boys than girls in the entire school
   C. There are more girls than boys in the first grade
   D. Third grade has the largest number of students

Answer: B. There are more boys than girls in the entire school
In Kindergarten, first grade, and third grade, there are more boys than girls. The number of extra girls in grade two is more than made up for by the extra boys in all the other grades put together.

25. Mary did comparison shopping on her favorite brand of coffee. Over half of the stores priced the coffee at $1.70. Most of the remaining stores priced the coffee at $1.80, except for a few who charged $1.90. Which of the following statements is true about the distribution of prices?
    (Rigorous)

   A. The mean and the mode are the same
   B. The mean is greater   than the mode
   C. The mean is less than the mode
   D. The mean is less than the median

Answer: B. The mean is greater than the mode
Over half the stores priced the coffee at $1.70, so this means that this is the mode. The mean would be slightly over $1.70 because other stores priced the coffee at over $1.70.

TEACHER CERTIFICATION STUDY GUIDE

26. What is the mode of the data in the following sample?
    (Easy)

    9, 10, 11, 9, 10, 11, 9, 13

    A. 9
    B. 9.5
    C. 10
    D. 11

Answer: A. 9
The mode is the number that appears most frequently. Nine appears 3 times, which is more than the other numbers.

27. A coin is tossed and a die is rolled. What is the probability of landing on the head side of the coin and rolling a 3 on the dice?
    (Rigorous)

    A. $\dfrac{1}{2}$

    B. $\dfrac{1}{6}$

    C. $\dfrac{1}{12}$

    D. $\dfrac{1}{15}$

Answer: C. $\dfrac{1}{12}$

$P(\text{head}) = \dfrac{1}{2}$. $P(3) = \dfrac{1}{6}$

$P(\text{head and 3}) = P(\text{head}) \times P(3)$
$$= \dfrac{1}{2} \times \dfrac{1}{6} = \dfrac{1}{12}$$

TEACHER CERTIFICATION STUDY GUIDE

28. What is the probability of drawing 2 consecutive aces from a standard deck of cards?
    (Rigorous)

    A. $\dfrac{3}{51}$

    B. $\dfrac{1}{221}$

    C. $\dfrac{2}{104}$

    D. $\dfrac{2}{52}$

Answer: B. $\dfrac{1}{221}$

There are 4 aces in the 52 card deck. P(first ace) = $\dfrac{4}{52}$. P(second ace) = $\dfrac{3}{51}$. P(first ace and second ace) = P(one ace)xP(second ace/first ace) = $\dfrac{4}{52} \times \dfrac{3}{51} = \dfrac{1}{221}$.

TEACHER CERTIFICATION STUDY GUIDE

SOCIAL SCIENCE SAMPLE TEST

1. The belief that the United States should control all of North America was called:
   (Easy)

   A. Westward expansion
   B. Pan Americanism
   C. Manifest Destiny
   D. Nationalism

2. The area of the United States was effectively doubled through purchase of the Louisiana Territory under which President?
   (Average)

   A. John Adams
   B. Thomas Jefferson
   C. James Madison
   D. James Monroe

3. A major quarrel between colonial Americans and the British concerned a series of British Acts of Parliament dealing with:
   (Easy)

   A. Taxes
   B. Slavery
   C. Native Americans
   D. Shipbuilding

4. The international organization established to work for world peace at the end of the Second World War is the:
   (Average)

   A. League of Nations
   B. United Federation of Nations
   C. United Nations
   D. United World League

5. Which famous battle fought on Texas soil resulted in Texas independence from Mexico?
   (Rigorous)

   A. The Battle of the Alamo
   B. The Battle of San Jacinto
   C. The Battle of the Rio Grande
   D. The Battle of Shiloh

6. Why is the system of government in the United States referred to as a federal system?
   (Rigorous)

   A. There are different levels of government
   B. There is one central authority in which all governmental power is vested
   C. The national government cannot operate except with the consent of the governed
   D. Elections are held at stated periodic times, rather than as called by the head of the government

7. **The U.S. Constitution, adopted in 1789, provided for:**
   (Rigorous)

   A. Direct election of the President by all citizens
   B. Direct election of the President by citizens meeting a standard of wealth
   C. Indirect election of the President by electors
   D. Indirect election of the President by the U.S. Senate

8. **From about 1870 to 1900 the settlement of America's "last frontier," the West, was completed. One attraction for settlers was free land, but it would have been to no avail without:**
   (Rigorous)

   A. Better farming methods and technology
   B. Surveying to set boundaries
   C. Immigrants and others to seek new land
   D. The railroad to get them there

9. **Slavery arose in the Southern Colonies partly as a perceived economical way to:**
   (Average)

   A. Increase the owner's wealth through human beings used as a source of exchange
   B. Cultivate large plantations of cotton, tobacco, rice, indigo, and other crops
   C. Provide Africans with humanitarian aid, such as health care, Christianity, and literacy
   D. Keep ships' holds full of cargo on two out of three legs of the "triangular trade" voyage.

10. **The post-Civil War years were a time of low public morality, a time of greed, graft, and dishonesty. Which one of the reasons listed below would not be accurate reasons for this?**
    (Rigorous)

    A. The war itself, because of the money and materials needed to conduct the War
    B. The very rapid growth of industry and big business after the War
    C. The personal example set by President Grant
    D. Unscrupulous heads of large impersonal corporations

11. A number of women worked hard in the first half of the 19th century for women's rights, but decisive gains did not come until after 1850. The earliest accomplishments were in:
    (Average)

    A. Medicine
    B. Education
    C. Writing
    D. Temperance

12. Of all the major causes of both World Wars I and II, the most significant one is considered to be:
    (Average)

    A. Extreme nationalism
    B. Military buildup and aggression
    C. Political unrest
    D. Agreements and alliances

13. Meridians, or lines of longitude, not only help in pinpointing locations but are also used for:
    (Rigorous)

    A. Measuring distance from the Poles
    B. Determining direction of ocean currents
    C. Determining the time around the world
    D. Measuring distance on the equator

14. The study of the ways in which different societies around the world deal with the problems of limited resources and unlimited needs and wants is in the area of:
    (Average)

    A. Economics
    B. Sociology
    C. Anthropology
    D. Political science

15. Capitalism and communism are alike in that they are both:
    (Easy)

    A. Organic systems
    B. Political systems
    C. Centrally planned systems
    D. Economic systems

16. The purchase of goods or services on one market for immediate resale on another market is:
    (Average)

    A. Output
    B. Enterprise
    C. Arbitrage
    D. Mercantile

17. The economic system promoting individual ownership of land, capital, and businesses with minimal governmental regulations is called:
    (Easy)

    A. Macro-economy
    B. Micro-economy
    C. Laissez-faire
    D. Free enterprise

18. **The American labor union movement started gaining new momentum:**
    (Rigorous)

    A. During the building of the railroads
    B. After 1865 with the growth of cities
    C. With the rise of industrial giants such as Carnegie and Vanderbilt
    D. During the war years of 1861-1865

19. **It can be reasonably stated that the change in the United States from primarily an agricultural country into an industrial power was due to all of the following except:**
    (Average)

    A. Tariffs on foreign imports
    B. Millions of hardworking immigrants
    C. An increase in technological developments
    D. The change from steam to electricity for powering industrial machinery

20. **There is no doubt of the vast improvement of the U.S. Constitution over the weak Articles of Confederation. Which one of the four accurate statements below is a unique yet eloquent description of the document?**
    (Rigorous)

    A. The establishment of a strong central government in no way lessened or weakened the individual states
    B. Individual rights were protected and secured
    C. The Constitution is the best representation of the results of the American genius for compromise
    D. Its flexibility and adaptation to change gives it a sense of timelessness

21. **Marbury vs Madison (1803) was an important Supreme Court case which set the precedent for:**
    (Rigorous)

    A. The elastic clause
    B. Judicial review
    C. The supreme law of the land
    D. Popular sovereignty in the Territories

22. Which one of the following is not a function or responsibility of U.S. political parties?
    (Rigorous)

    A. Conducting elections or the voting process
    B. Obtaining funds needed for election campaigns
    C. Choosing candidates to run for public office
    D. Making voters aware of issues and other public affairs information

23. Which of the following choices lists elements usually considered to be responsibilities of citizenship under the American system of government?
    (Easy)

    A. Serving in public office, voluntary government service, military duty
    B. Paying taxes, jury duty, upholding the Constitution
    C. Maintaining a job, giving to charity, turning in fugitives
    D. Quartering of soldiers, bearing arms, government service

24. In which of the following disciplines would the study of physical mapping, modern or ancient, and the plotting of points and boundaries be least useful?
    (Average)

    A. Sociology
    B. Geography
    C. Archaeology
    D. History

25. The study of the exercise of power and political behavior in human society today would be conducted by experts in:
    (Average)

    A. History
    B. Sociology
    C. Political science
    D. Anthropology

Answer Key

1. C
2. B
3. A
4. C
5. B
6. A
7. C
8. D
9. B
10. C
11. B
12. A
13. C
14. A
15. D
16. C
17. D
18. B
19. A
20. C
21. B
22. A
23. B
24. A
25. C

Rigor Table

Easy
1, 3, 15, 17, 23

Average
2, 4, 9, 11, 12, 14, 16, 19, 24, 25

Rigorous
5, 6, 7, 8, 10, 13, 18, 20, 21, 22

TEACHER CERTIFICATION STUDY GUIDE

SOCIAL SCIENCE SAMPLE TEST WITH RATIONALES

1. **The belief that the United States should control all of North America was called:**
   (Easy)

   A. Westward expansion
   B. Pan Americanism
   C. Manifest Destiny
   D. Nationalism

Answer: C. Manifest Destiny
The belief that the United States should control all of North America was called Manifest Destiny. This idea fueled much of the violence and aggression towards those already occupying the lands such as the Native Americans. Manifest Destiny was certainly driven by sentiments of nationalism, and gave rise to westward expansion.

2. **The area of the United States was effectively doubled through purchase of the Louisiana Territory under which President?**
   (Average)

   A. John Adams
   B. Thomas Jefferson
   C. James Madison
   D. James Monroe

Answer: B. Thomas Jefferson
The Louisiana Purchase, an acquisition of territory from France in 1803, occurred during the presidency of Thomas Jefferson. John Adams (1735-1826) was president from 1797–1801, before the purchase. James Madison (1751-1836) was president after the purchase (1809-1817). James Monroe (1758-1831) was actually a signatory on the Purchase, but did not become President until 1817.

3. A major quarrel between colonial Americans and the British concerned a series of British Acts of Parliament dealing with:
(Easy)

   A. Taxes
   B. Slavery
   C. Native Americans
   D. Shipbuilding

Answer: A. Taxes
Acts of Parliament imposing taxes on the colonists always provoked resentment. Because the colonies had no direct representation in Parliament, they felt it unjust that that body should impose taxes on them, with so little knowledge of their very different situation in America and no real concern for the consequences of such taxes. While slavery (B) continued to exist in the colonies long after it had been completely abolished in Britain, it never was a source of serious debate between Britain and the colonies. By the time Britain outlawed slavery in its colonies in 1833, the American Revolution had already occurred and the United States was free of British control. There was no series of British Acts of Parliament passed concerning Native Americans (C). Colonial shipbuilding (D) was an industry which received little interference from the British.

4. The international organization established to work for world peace at the end of the Second World War is the:
(Average)

   A. League of Nations
   B. United Federation of Nations
   C. United Nations
   D. United World League

Answer: C. United Nations
The international organization established to work for world peace at the end of the Second World War was the United Nations. From the ashes of the failed League of Nations, established following World War I, the United Nations continues to be a major player in world affairs today.

TEACHER CERTIFICATION STUDY GUIDE

5. **Which famous battle fought on Texas soil resulted in Texas independence from Mexico?**
   (Rigorous)

   A. The Battle of the Alamo
   B. The Battle of San Jacinto
   C. The Battle of the Rio Grande
   D. The Battle of Shiloh

Answer: B. The Battle of San Jacinto
It was the Battle of San Jacinto in which Sam Houston and the Texicans roundly defeated the Mexican army and captured Mexican General and Commander Santa Anna. The result was the independence of the Republic of Texas from Mexican control. The Battle of the Alamo (A), despite the defeat of the Texans by Santa Anna's troops, was a critical event which enabled Houston to gather troops and prepare for the Battle of San Jacinto. The Battle of Shiloh (D) occurred during the Civil War, and it was not in Texas. There was no major battle called the Battle of the Rio Grande (C).

6. **Why is the system of government in the United States referred to as a federal system?**
   (Rigorous)

   A. There are different levels of government
   B. There is one central authority in which all governmental power is vested
   C. The national government cannot operate except with the consent of the governed
   D. Elections are held at stated periodic times, rather than as called by the head of the government

Answer: A. There are different levels of government
The United States is composed of fifty states, each responsible for its own affairs, but united under a federal government. A centralized system (B) is the opposite of a federal system. That national government cannot operate except with the consent of the governed (C) is a founding principle of American politics but is not a political system like federalism. A centralized democracy could still be consensual, but would not be federal. (D) is a description of electoral procedure, not a political system like federalism.

TEACHER CERTIFICATION STUDY GUIDE

7. **The U.S. Constitution, adopted in 1789, provided for:**
   (Rigorous)

   A. Direct election of the President by all citizens
   B. Direct election of the President by citizens meeting a standard of wealth
   C. Indirect election of the President by electors
   D. Indirect election of the President by the U.S. Senate

Answer: C. Indirect election of the President by electors
The United States Constitution has always arranged for the indirect election of the President by electors. The question, by mentioning the original date of adoption, might mislead someone to choose B, but while standards of citizenship have been changed by amendment, the President has never been directly elected. Nor does the Senate have anything to do with presidential elections. The House of Representatives, not the Senate, settles cases where neither candidate wins in the Electoral College.

8. **From about 1870 to 1900 the settlement of America's "last frontier," the West, was completed. One attraction for settlers was free land, but it would have been to no avail without:**
   (Rigorous)

   A. Better farming methods and technology
   B. Surveying to set boundaries
   C. Immigrants and others to seek new land
   D. The railroad to get them there

Answer: D. The railroad to get them there
From about 1870 to 1900, the settlement of America's "last frontier" in the West was made possible by the building of the railroad. Without the railroad, the settlers never could have traveled such distances in an efficient manner.

TEACHER CERTIFICATION STUDY GUIDE

9. **Slavery arose in the Southern Colonies partly as a perceived economical way to:**
   (Average)

   A. Increase the owner's wealth through human beings used as a source of exchange
   B. Cultivate large plantations of cotton, tobacco, rice, indigo, and other crops
   C. Provide Africans with humanitarian aid, such as health care, Christianity, and literacy
   D. Keep ships' holds full of cargo on two out of three legs of the "triangular trade" voyage.

Answer: B. Cultivate large plantations of cotton, tobacco, rice, indigo, and other crops

The Southern states, with their smaller populations, were heavily dependent on slave labor as a means of being able to fulfill their role and remain competitive in the greater U.S. economy. When slaves arrived in the South, the vast majority would become permanent fixtures on plantations, intended for work, not as a source of exchange. While some slave owners instructed their slaves in Christianity, provided health care or some level of education, such attention were not their primary reasons for owning slaves – a cheap and ready labor force was their reason. Whether or not ships' holds were full on two or three legs of the triangular journey was not the concern of Southerners as the final purchasers of slaves. Such details would have concerned the slave traders.

TEACHER CERTIFICATION STUDY GUIDE

10. The post-Civil War years were a time of low public morality, a time of greed, graft, and dishonesty. Which one of the reasons listed below would not be accurate reasons for this?
    (Rigorous)

    A. The war itself, because of the money and materials needed to conduct the War
    B. The very rapid growth of industry and big business after the War
    C. The personal example set by President Grant
    D. Unscrupulous heads of large impersonal corporations

Answer: C. The personal example set by President Grant
The post-Civil War years were a particularly difficult time for the nation, and public morale was especially low. The war had plunged the country into debt, and ultimately into a recession by the 1890s. Racism was rampant throughout the South and the North, where freed Blacks were taking jobs for low wages. The rapid growth of industry and big business caused a polarization of rich and poor, workers and owners. Many people moved into the urban centers to find work in the new industrial sector. These jobs typically paid low wages, required long hours, and offered poor working conditions. The heads of large impersonal corporations treated their workers inhumanely, letting morale drop to a record low. The heads of corporations tried to prevent and disband labor unions.

11. A number of women worked hard in the first half of the 19th century for women's rights, but decisive gains did not come until after 1850. The earliest accomplishments were in:
    (Average)

    A. Medicine
    B. Education
    C. Writing
    D. Temperance

Answer: B. Education
Although women worked hard in the early nineteenth century to make gains in medicine, writing, and temperance movements, the most prestigious accomplishments of the early women's movement were in the field of education. Women such as May Wollstonecraft (1759-1797), Alice Palmer (1855-1902), and, of course, Elizabeth Blackwell (1821-1910) led the way for women, particularly in the area of higher education.

TEACHER CERTIFICATION STUDY GUIDE

12. Of all the major causes of both World Wars I and II, the most significant one is considered to be:
    (Average)

    A. Extreme nationalism
    B. Military buildup and aggression
    C. Political unrest
    D. Agreements and alliances

Answer: A. Extreme nationalism
Although military buildup and aggression, political unrest, and agreements and alliances were all characteristic of the world climate before and during World War I and World War II, the most significant cause of both wars was extreme nationalism. Nationalism is the idea that the interests and needs of a particular nation are of the utmost and primary importance above all else. Some nationalist movements could be liberation movements while others were oppressive regimes, much depends on their degree of nationalism.

The nationalism that sparked WWI included a rejection of German, Austro-Hungarian, and Ottoman imperialism by Serbs, Slavs and others culminating in the assassination of Archduke Ferdinand by a Serb nationalist in 1914. Following WWI and the Treaty of Versailles, many Germans and others in the Central Alliance Nations, malcontent at the concessions and reparations of the treaty, started a new form of nationalism. Adolf Hitler and the Nazi regime led this extreme nationalism. Hitler's ideas were examples of extreme, oppressive nationalism combined with political, social, and economic scapegoating and were the primary cause of WWII.

13. Meridians, or lines of longitude, not only help in pinpointing locations but are also used for:
    (Rigorous)

    A. Measuring distance from the Poles
    B. Determining direction of ocean currents
    C. Determining the time around the world
    D. Measuring distance on the equator

Answer: C. Determining the time around the world
Meridians, or lines of longitude, are the determining factor in separating time zones and determining time around the world.

TEACHER CERTIFICATION STUDY GUIDE

14. The study of the ways in which different societies around the world deal with the problems of limited resources and unlimited needs and wants is in the area of:
    (Average)

    A. Economics
    B. Sociology
    C. Anthropology
    D. Political science

Answer: A. Economics
The study of the ways in which different societies around the world deal with the problems of limited resources and unlimited needs and wants is a study of economics. Economists consider the law of supply and demand as fundamental to the study of the economy. However, sociology and political science also consider the study of economics and its importance in understanding social and political systems.

15. Capitalism and communism are alike in that they are both:
    (Easy)

    A. Organic systems
    B. Political systems
    C. Centrally planned systems
    D. Economic systems

Answer: D. Economic systems
While economic and political systems are often closely connected, capitalism and communism are primarily economic systems. Capitalism is a system of economics that allows the open market to determine the relative value of goods and services. Communism is an economic system where the market is planned by a central state. While communism is a centrally planned system, this is not true of capitalism. Organic systems (A) are studied in biology, a natural science.

TEACHER CERTIFICATION STUDY GUIDE

16. **The purchase of goods or services on one market for immediate resale on another market is:**
    (Average)

    A. Output
    B. Enterprise
    C. Arbitrage
    D. Mercantile

Answer: C. Arbitrage
Output is an amount produced or manufactured by an industry. Enterprise is simply any business organization. Mercantile is one of the first systems of economics in which goods were exchanged. Arbitrage is an item or service that an industry produces. The dictionary definition of arbitrage is the purchase of securities on one market for immediate resale on another market in order to profit from a price discrepancy.

17. **The economic system promoting individual ownership of land, capital, and businesses with minimal governmental regulations is called:**
    (Easy)

    A. Macro-economy
    B. Micro-economy
    C. Laissez-faire
    D. Free enterprise

Answer: D. Free enterprise
Free enterprise or capitalism is the economic system that promotes private ownership of land, capital, and business with minimal government interference. Laissez-faire is the idea that an "invisible hand" will guide the free enterprise system to the maximum potential efficiency.

TEACHER CERTIFICATION STUDY GUIDE

18. **The American labor union movement started gaining new momentum:**
    (Rigorous)

    A. During the building of the railroads
    B. After 1865 with the growth of cities
    C. With the rise of industrial giants such as Carnegie and Vanderbilt
    D. During the war years of 1861-1865

Answer: B. After 1865 with the growth of cities
The American Labor Union movement had been around since the late 18th and early 19th centuries. The Labor movement began to first experience persecution by employers in the early 1800s. The American Labor Movement remained relatively ineffective until after the Civil War. In 1866, the National Labor Union was formed, pushing such issues as the eight-hour workday and new policies of immigration. This gave rise to the Knights of Labor and eventually the American Federation of Labor (AFL) in the 1890s and the Industrial Workers of the World (1905). Therefore, it was the period following the Civil War that empowered the labor movement in terms of numbers, militancy, and effectiveness.

19. **It can be reasonably stated that the change in the United States from primarily an agricultural country into an industrial power was due to all of the following except:**
    (Average)

    A. Tariffs on foreign imports
    B. Millions of hardworking immigrants
    C. An increase in technological developments
    D. The change from steam to electricity for powering industrial machinery

Answer: A. Tariffs on foreign imports
It can be reasonably stated that the change in the United States from primarily an agricultural country into an industrial power was due to a great degree to three of the reasons listed above. It was a combination of millions of hard-working immigrants, an increase in technological developments, and the change from steam to electricity for powering industrial machinery. The only reason given that really had little effect was the tariffs on foreign imports.

TEACHER CERTIFICATION STUDY GUIDE

20. There is no doubt of the vast improvement of the U.S. Constitution over the weak Articles of Confederation. Which one of the four accurate statements below is a unique yet eloquent description of the document?
    (Rigorous)

    A. The establishment of a strong central government in no way lessened or weakened the individual states
    B. Individual rights were protected and secured
    C. The Constitution is the best representation of the results of the American genius for compromise
    D. Its flexibility and adaptation to change gives it a sense of timelessness

Answer: C. The Constitution is the best representation of the results of the American genius for compromise
The U.S. Constitution was indeed a vast improvement over the Articles of Confederation and the authors of the document took great care to assure longevity. It clearly stated that the establishment of a strong central government in no way lessened or weakened the individual states. In the Bill of Rights, citizens were assured that individual rights were protected and secured. Possibly the most important feature of the new Constitution was its flexibility and adaptation to change which assured longevity.

21. Marbury vs Madison (1803) was an important Supreme Court case which set the precedent for:
    (Rigorous)

    A. The elastic clause
    B. Judicial review
    C. The supreme law of the land
    D. Popular sovereignty in the Territories

Answer: B. Judicial review
Marbury vs. Madison (1803) was an important case for the Supreme Court as it established judicial review. In that case, the Supreme Court set precedence to declare laws passed by Congress as unconstitutional.

22. Which one of the following is not a function or responsibility of U.S. political parties?
    (Rigorous)

    A. Conducting elections or the voting process
    B. Obtaining funds needed for election campaigns
    C. Choosing candidates to run for public office
    D. Making voters aware of issues and other public affairs information

Answer: A. Conducting elections or the voting process
U.S. political parties have numerous functions and responsibilities. Among them are obtaining funds needed for election campaigns, choosing the candidates to run for office, and making voters aware of the issues. The political parties, however, do not conduct elections or the voting process, as that would be an obvious conflict of interest.

23. Which of the following choices lists elements usually considered to be responsibilities of citizenship under the American system of government?
    (Easy)

    A. Serving in public office, voluntary government service, military duty
    B. Paying taxes, jury duty, upholding the Constitution
    C. Maintaining a job, giving to charity, turning in fugitives
    D. Quartering of soldiers, bearing arms, government service

Answer: B. Paying taxes, jury duty, upholding the Constitution
Only paying taxes, jury duty and upholding the Constitution are responsibilities of citizens as a result of rights and commitments outlined in the Constitution. For example, the right of citizens to a jury trial in the Sixth and Seventh Amendments and the right of the federal government to collect taxes in Article 1, Section 8. Serving in public office, voluntary government service and military duty, maintaining a job, giving to charity and turning in fugitives are all considered purely voluntary actions, even when officially recognized and compensated. The United States has none of the compulsory military or civil service requirements of many other countries. The quartering of soldiers is an act which, according to Amendment III of the Bill of Rights, requires a citizen's consent. Bearing arms is a right guaranteed under Amendment II of the Bill of Rights.

TEACHER CERTIFICATION STUDY GUIDE

24. In which of the following disciplines would the study of physical mapping, modern or ancient, and the plotting of points and boundaries be least useful?
    (Average)

    A. Sociology
    B. Geography
    C. Archaeology
    D. History

Answer: A. Sociology
In geography, archaeology, and history, the study of maps and plotting of points and boundaries is very important as all three of these disciplines hold value in understanding the spatial relations and regional characteristics of people and places. Sociology, however, mostly focuses on the social interactions of people and while location is important, the physical location is not as important as the social location such as the differences between studying people in groups or as individuals.

25. The study of the exercise of power and political behavior in human society today would be conducted by experts in:
    (Average)

    A. History
    B. Sociology
    C. Political science
    D. Anthropology

Answer: C. Political science
Experts in the field of political science today would likely conduct the study of exercise of power and political behavior in human society. However, it is also reasonable to suggest that such studies would be important to historians (study of the past, often in an effort to understand the present), sociologists (often concerned with power structure in the social and political worlds), and even some anthropologists (study of culture and their behaviors).

TEACHER CERTIFICATION STUDY GUIDE

SCIENCE SAMPLE TEST

1. **Chemicals should be stored**
   (Easy)

   A. In the principal's office
   B. In a dark room
   C. In an off-site research facility
   D. According to their reactivity with other substances

2. **When measuring the volume of water in a graduated cylinder, where does one read the measurement?**
   (Average)

   A. At the highest point of the liquid
   B. At the bottom of the meniscus curve
   C. At the closest mark to the top of the liquid
   D. At the top of the plastic safety ring

3. **When is a hypothesis formed?**
   (Easy)

   A. Before the data is taken
   B. After the data is taken
   C. After the data is analyzed
   D. Concurrent with graphing the data

4. **Which of the following is the most accurate definition of a non-renewable resource?**
   (Average)

   A. A nonrenewable resource is never replaced once used
   B. A nonrenewable resource is replaced on a timescale that is very long relative to human life-spans
   C. A nonrenewable resource is a resource that can only be manufactured by humans
   D. A nonrenewable resource is a species that has already become extinct

5. A scientist exposes mice to cigarette smoke, and notes that their lungs develop tumors. Mice that were not exposed to the smoke do not develop as many tumors. Which of the following conclusions may be drawn from these results?
(Rigorous)

   I. Cigarette smoke causes lung tumors
   II. Cigarette smoke exposure has a positive correlation with lung tumors in mice
   III. Some mice are predisposed to develop lung tumors
   IV. Cigarette smoke exposure has a positive correlation with lung tumors in humans

   A. I and II only
   B. II only
   C. I, II, III and IV
   D. II and IV only

6. Which of the following is a correct explanation for an astronaut's 'weightlessness'?
(Average)

   A. Astronauts continue to feel the pull of gravity in space, but they are so far from planets that the force is small
   B. Astronauts continue to feel the pull of gravity in space, but spacecraft have such powerful engines that those forces dominate, reducing effective weight
   C. Astronauts do not feel the pull of gravity in space, because space is a vacuum
   D. The cumulative gravitational forces, that the astronaut is experiencing, from all sources in the solar system equal out to a net gravitational force of zero

7. Physical properties are observable characteristics of a substance in its natural state. Which of the following are considered physical properties?
(Rigorous)

   I. Color
   II. Density
   III. Specific gravity
   IV. Melting point

   A. I only
   B. I and II only
   C. I, II, and III only
   D. III and IV only

8. The change in phase from liquid to gas is called:
   (Rigorous)

   A. Evaporation
   B. Condensation
   C. Vaporization
   D. Boiling

9. Which of the following statements is true of all transition elements?
   (Rigorous)

   A. They are all hard solids at room temperature
   B. They tend to form salts when reacted with Halogens
   C. They all have a silvery appearance in their pure state
   D. All of the above

10. A boulder sitting on the edge of a cliff has which type of energy?
    (Easy)

    A. Kinetic energy
    B. Latent energy
    C. No energy
    D. Potential energy

11. A converging lens produces a real image _____.
    (Rigorous)

    A. always
    B. never
    C. when the object is within one focal length of the lens
    D. when the object is further than one focal length from the lens

12. Which of the following is not a factor in how different materials will conduct seismic waves?
    (Average)

    A. Density
    B. Incompressiblity
    C. Rigidty
    D. Tensile strength

13. The Law of Conservation of Energy states that:
    (Average)

    A. There must be the same number of products and reactants in any chemical equation
    B. Mass and energy can be interchanged
    C. Energy is neither created nor destroyed, but may change form
    D. One form energy must remain intact (or conserved) in all reactions

14. When you step out of the shower, the floor feels colder on your feet than the bathmat. Which of the following is the correct explanation for this phenomenon?
(Rigorous)

   A. The floor is colder than the bathmat
   B. The bathmat, being smaller than the floor, quickly reaches equilibrium with your body temperature
   C. Heat is conducted more easily into the floor
   D. Water is absorbed from your feet into the bathmat so it doesn't evaporate as quickly as it does off the floor, thus not cooling the bathmat as quickly

15. Identify the correct sequence of organization of living things from lower to higher order:
(Average)

   A. Cell, organelle, organ, tissue, system, organism
   B. Cell, tissue, organ, organelle, system, organism
   C. Organelle, cell, tissue, organ, system, organism
   D. Organelle, tissue, cell, organ, system, organism

16. Catalysts assist reactions by _____ .
(Easy)

   A. lowering required activation energy
   B. maintaining precise pH levels
   C. keeping systems at equilibrium
   D. changing the starting amounts of reactants

17. Which process results in a haploid chromosome number?
(Rigorous)

   A. Mitosis
   B. Meiosis I
   C. Meiosis II
   D. Neither mitosis nor meiosis

18. A carrier of a genetic disorder is heterozygous for a disorder that is recessive in nature. Hemophilia is a sex-linked disorder. This means that:
(Easy)

   A. Only females can be carriers
   B. Only males can be carriers
   C. Both males and females can be carriers
   D. Neither females nor males can be carriers

19. Which of the following is a correct explanation for scientific biological adaptation?
    (Average)

    A. Giraffes need to reach higher for leaves to eat, so their necks stretch. The giraffe babies are then born with longer necks. Eventually, there are more long-necked giraffes in the population.
    B. Giraffes with longer necks are able to reach more leaves, so they eat more and have more babies than other giraffes. Eventually, there are more long-necked giraffes in the population.
    C. Giraffes want to reach higher for leaves to eat, so they release enzymes into their bloodstream, which in turn causes fetal development of longer-necked giraffes. Eventually, there are more long-necked giraffes in the population.
    D. Giraffes with long necks are more attractive to other giraffes, so they get the best mating partners and have more babies. Eventually, there are more long-necked giraffes in the population.

20. An animal choosing its mate because of attractive plumage or a strong mating call is an example of:
    (Average)

    A. Sexual selection
    B. Natural selection
    C. Mechanical isolation
    D. Linkage

21. Many male birds sing long, complicated songs that describe thier identity and the area of land that they claim. Which of the answers below is the best decription of this behavior?
    (Rigorous)

    A. Innate territorial behavior
    B. Learned competitve behavior
    C. Innate mating behavior
    D. Learned territorial behavior

22. A wrasse (fish) cleans the teeth of other fish by eating away plaque. This is an example of _____ between the fish.
    (Average)

    A. parasitism
    B. symbiosis (mutualism)
    C. competition
    D. predation

23. **Which of the following causes the aurora borealis?**
    (Rigorous)

    A. Gases escaping from earth
    B. Particles from the sun
    C. Particles from the moon
    D. Electromagnetic discharges from the North pole

24. **The transfer of heat from the earth's surface to the atmosphere is called:**
    (Average)

    A. Convection
    B. Radiation
    C. Conduction
    D. Advection

25. **What is the most accurate description of the Water Cycle?**
    (Rigorous)

    A. Rain comes from clouds, filling the ocean. The water then evaporates and becomes clouds again.
    B. Water circulates from rivers into groundwater and back, while water vapor circulates in the atmosphere.
    C. Water is conserved except for chemical or nuclear reactions, and any drop of water could circulate through clouds, rain, ground-water, and surface-water.
    D. Water flows toward the oceans, where it evaporates and forms clouds, which causes rain, which in turn flow back to the oceans after it falls.

26. **What makes up the largest abiotic portion of the Nitrogen Cycle?**
    (Average)

    A. Nitrogen fixing bacteria
    B. Nitrates
    C. Decomposers
    D. Atomsphere

27. **What are the most significant and prevalent elements in the biosphere?**
    (Easy)

    A. Carbon, Hydrogen, Oxygen, Nitrogen, Phosphorus
    B. Carbon, Hydrogen, Sodium, Iron, Calcium
    C. Carbon, Oxygen, Sulfur, Manganese, Iron
    D. Carbon, Hydrogen, Oxygen, Nickel, Sodium, Nitrogen

28. **Neap Tides are especially weak tides that occur when the Sun and Moon are in a perpendicular arrangment to the Earth, and Spring Tides are especially strong tides that occur when the Sun and Moon are in line. At which combination of lunar phases do these tides occur (respectively)?**
    (Rigorous)

    A. Half Moon and Full Moon
    B. Quarter Moon and New Moon
    C. Gibbous Moon and Quarter Moon
    D. Full Moon and New Moon

29. The planet with true retrograde rotation is:
    (Rigorous)

    A. Pluto
    B. Neptune
    C. Venus
    D. Saturn

30. The phases of the Moon are the result of its _____ in relation to the Sun.
    (Average)

    A. revolution
    B. rotation
    C. position
    D. inclination

31. The end of a geologic era is most often characterized by:
    (Average)

    A. A general uplifting of the crust
    B. The extinction of the dominant plants and animals
    C. The appearance of new life forms
    D. All of the above

32. The best preserved animal remains have been discovered in:
    (Rigorous)

    A. Resin
    B. Fossil mold
    C. Tar pits
    D. Glacial ice

33. Which type of student activity is most likely to expose a student's misconceptions about science?
    (Average)

    A. Multiple-choice and fill-in-the-blank worksheets
    B. Laboratory activities, where the lab is laid out step-by-step with no active thought on the part of the student
    C. Teacher-lead demonstrations
    D. Laboratories in which the students are forced to critically consider the steps taken and the results obtained

34. In an experiment measuring the inhibition effect of different antibiotic discs of bacteria grown in Petri dishes, what are the independent and dependent variables respectively?
    (Rigorous)

    A. Number of bacterial colonies and the antibiotic type
    B. Antibiotic type and the distance between antibiotic and the closest colony
    C. Antibiotic type and the number of bacterial colonies
    D. Presence of bacterial colonies and the antibiotic type

TEACHER CERTIFICATION STUDY GUIDE

Answer Key

1.	D	18.	A
2.	B	19.	B
3.	A	20.	A
4.	B	21.	D
5.	B	22.	B
6.	A	23.	B
7.	C	24.	C
8.	A	25.	C
9.	B	26.	D
10.	D	27.	A
11.	D	28.	B
12.	D	29.	C
13.	C	30.	C
14.	C	31.	D
15.	C	32.	C
16.	A	33.	D
17.	C	34.	B

Rigor Table

Easy
1, 3, 10, 16, 18, 27

Average
2, 4, 6, 12, 13, 15, 19, 20, 22, 24, 26, 30, 31, 33

Rigorous
5, 7, 8, 9, 11, 14, 17, 21, 23, 25, 28, 29, 32, 34

TEACHER CERTIFICATION STUDY GUIDE

SCIENCE SAMPLE TEST WITH RATIONALES

1. **Chemicals should be stored**
   (Easy)

   A. In the principal's office
   B. In a dark room
   C. In an off-site research facility
   D. According to their reactivity with other substances

Answer: D. According to their reactivity with other substances
Chemicals should be stored with other chemicals of similar properties (e.g., acids with other acids), to reduce the potential for either hazardous reactions in the store-room, or mistakes in reagent use. Certainly, chemicals should not be stored in anyone's office, and the light intensity of the room is not very important because light-sensitive chemicals are usually stored in dark containers. In fact, good lighting is desirable in a store-room, so that labels can be read easily. Chemicals may be stored off-site, but that makes their use inconvenient.

2. **When measuring the volume of water in a graduated cylinder, where does one read the measurement?**
   (Average)

   A. At the highest point of the liquid
   B. At the bottom of the meniscus curve
   C. At the closest mark to the top of the liquid
   D. At the top of the plastic safety ring

Answer: B. At the bottom of the meniscus curve
To measure water in glass, you must look at the top surface at eye-level, and ascertain the location of the bottom of the meniscus (the curved surface at the top of the water). The meniscus forms because water molecules adhere to the sides of the glass, which is a slightly stronger force than their cohesion to each other. This leads to a U-shaped top of the liquid column, the bottom of which gives the most accurate volume measurement. (Other liquids have different forces, e.g., mercury in glass, which has a convex meniscus.)

3. **When is a hypothesis formed?**
   (Easy)

   A. Before the data is taken
   B. After the data is taken
   C. After the data is analyzed
   D. Concurrent with graphing the data

Answer: A. Before the data is taken
A hypothesis is an educated guess, made before undertaking an experiment. The hypothesis is then evaluated based on the observed data. Therefore, the hypothesis must be formed before the data is taken, not during or after the experiment.

4. **Which of the following is the most accurate definition of a non-renewable resource?**
   (Average)

   A. A nonrenewable resource is never replaced once used
   B. A nonrenewable resource is replaced on a timescale that is very long relative to human life-spans
   C. A nonrenewable resource is a resource that can only be manufactured by humans
   D. A nonrenewable resource is a species that has already become extinct

Answer: B. A nonrenewable resource is replaced on a timescale that is very long relative to human life-spans
Renewable resources are those that are renewed, or replaced, in time for humans to use more of them. Examples include fast-growing plants, animals, or oxygen gas. (Note that while sunlight is often considered a renewable resource, it is actually a nonrenewable but extremely abundant resource.) Nonrenewable resources are those that renew themselves only on very long timescales, usually geologic timescales. Examples include minerals, metals, or fossil fuels.

TEACHER CERTIFICATION STUDY GUIDE

5. A scientist exposes mice to cigarette smoke, and notes that their lungs develop tumors. Mice that were not exposed to the smoke do not develop as many tumors. Which of the following conclusions may be drawn from these results?
   (Rigorous)

   I. Cigarette smoke causes lung tumors
   II. Cigarette smoke exposure has a positive correlation with lung tumors in mice
   III. Some mice are predisposed to develop lung tumors
   IV. Cigarette smoke exposure has a positive correlation with lung tumors in humans

   A. I and II only
   B. II only
   C. I, II, III and IV
   D. II and IV only

Answer: B. II only
Although cigarette smoke has been found to cause lung tumors (and many other problems), this particular experiment shows only that there is a positive correlation between smoke exposure and tumor development in these mice. It may be true that some mice are more likely to develop tumors than others, which is why a control group of identical mice should have been used for comparison. Mice are often used to model human reactions, but this is as much due to their low financial and emotional cost as it is due to their being a "good model" for humans, and thus this scientist cannot make the conclusion that cigarette smoke exposure has a positive correlation with lung tumors in humans based on this data alone.

TEACHER CERTIFICATION STUDY GUIDE

6. **Which of the following is a correct explanation for an astronaut's 'weightlessness'?**
   (Average)

   A. Astronauts continue to feel the pull of gravity in space, but they are so far from planets that the force is small
   B. Astronauts continue to feel the pull of gravity in space, but spacecraft have such powerful engines that those forces dominate, reducing effective weight
   C. Astronauts do not feel the pull of gravity in space, because space is a vacuum
   D. The cumulative gravitational forces, that the astronaut is experiencing, from all sources in the solar system equal out to a net gravitational force of zero

Answer: A. Astronauts continue to feel the pull of gravity in space, but they are so far from planets that the force is small
Gravity acts over tremendous distances in space (theoretically, infinite distance, though certainly at least as far as any astronaut has traveled). However, gravitational force is inversely proportional to distance squared from a massive body. This means that when an astronaut is in space, s/he is far enough from the center of mass of any planet that the gravitational force is very small, and s/he feels 'weightless'. Space is mostly empty (i.e., a vacuum), and spacecraft do have powerful engines. However, none of these has the effect attributed to it in the incorrect answer choices (B) or (C). Although, theoretically there is a point in space where the cumulative gravitational forces of sources within the solar system would equal a net force of zero, that point would be in constant motion and difficult to find, making answer D unlikely at best.

TEACHER CERTIFICATION STUDY GUIDE

7. Physical properties are observable characteristics of a substance in its natural state. Which of the following are considered physical properties? *(Rigorous)*

   I. Color
   II. Density
   III. Specific gravity
   IV. Melting point

   A. I only
   B. I and II only
   C. I, II, and III only
   D. III and IV only

Answer: C. I, II, and III only
Of the possibilities only the melting point of a substance cannot be found without altering the substance itself. Color is readily observable. Density can be measured without changing a substances form or structure, and specific gravity is a ratio based on density, so once one is known the other can be calculated. Thus answer (C) is the only possible answer.

8. The change in phase from liquid to gas is called: *(Rigorous)*

   A. Evaporation
   B. Condensation
   C. Vaporization
   D. Boiling

Answer: A. Evaporation
Condensation is the change in phase from a gas to a liquid. Vaporization is the conversion of matter to vapor - not all gases are vapors. Boiling is one method of inducing the change from a liquid to a gas; the process is called evaporation.

TEACHER CERTIFICATION STUDY GUIDE

9. **Which of the following statements is true of all transition elements?**
   (Rigorous)

   A. They are all hard solids at room temperature
   B. They tend to form salts when reacted with Halogens
   C. They all have a silvery appearance in their pure state
   D. All of the above

Answer: B. They tend to form salts when reacted with Halogens
Answer (A) is incorrect because of Mercury, which has a low melting point and is thus a liquid at room temperature. Answer (C) is incorrect because Copper and Gold do not have a silvery appearance in their natural states. Since answers (A) and (C) are not correct then answer (D) cannot be correct either. This leaves only answer (B).

10. **A boulder sitting on the edge of a cliff has which type of energy?**
    (Easy)

    A. Kinetic energy
    B. Latent energy
    C. No energy
    D. Potential energy

Answer: D. Potential energy
Answer (A) would be true if the boulder fell off the cliff and started falling. Answer (C) would be a difficult condition to find since it would mean that no outside forces where operating on an object, and gravity is difficult to avoid. Answer (B) might be a good description of answer (D) which is the correct energy. The boulder has potential energy is imparted from the force of gravity.

11. **A converging lens produces a real image _____.**
    (Rigorous)

    A. always
    B. never
    C. when the object is within one focal length of the lens
    D. when the object is further than one focal length from the lens

Answer: D. when the object is further than one focal length from the lens
A converging lens produces a real image whenever the object is far enough from the lens (outside one focal length) so that the rays of light from the object can hit the lens and be focused into a real image on the other side of the lens. When the object is closer than one focal length from the lens, rays of light do not converge on the other side; they diverge. This means that only a virtual image can be formed, i.e., the theoretical place where those diverging rays would have converged if they had originated behind the object.

TEACHER CERTIFICATION STUDY GUIDE

12. **Which of the following is not a factor in how different materials will conduct seismic waves?**
    (Average)

    A. Density
    B. Incompressiblity
    C. Rigidty
    D. Tensile strength

Answer: D. Tensile strength
Density affects the speed at which seismic waves travel through the material. Incompressibilty has to do with how quickly a material compresses and rebounds as the waves hit it. The more compressable a material (and thus the slower the rebound) the slower the wave travels trhough the material. Seismic waves create a shearing force as they travel through a material, rigidity is the measure of the material's resistance to that shearing force. Tensile strength measures how far something can be stretched before breaking. Since seismic waves compress materials and are not stretching them that makes answer (D) the correct answer.

13. **The Law of Conservation of Energy states that:**
    (Average)

    A. There must be the same number of products and reactants in any chemical equation
    B. Mass and energy can be interchanged
    C. Energy is neither created nor destroyed, but may change form
    D. One form energy must remain intact (or conserved) in all reactions

Answer: C. Energy is neither created nor destroyed, but may change form
Answer (C) is a summary of the Law of Conservation of Energy (for non-nuclear reactions). In other words, energy can be transformed into various forms such as kinetic, potential, electric, or heat energy, but the total amount of energy remains constant. Answer (A) is untrue, as demonstrated by many synthesis and decomposition reactions. Answers (B) and (D) may be sensible, but they are not relevant in this case.

TEACHER CERTIFICATION STUDY GUIDE

14. **When you step out of the shower, the floor feels colder on your feet than the bathmat. Which of the following is the correct explanation for this phenomenon?**
    (Rigorous)

    A. The floor is colder than the bathmat
    B. The bathmat, being smaller than the floor, quickly reaches equilibrium with your body temperature
    C. Heat is conducted more easily into the floor
    D. Water is absorbed from your feet into the bathmat so it doesn't evaporate as quickly as it does off the floor, thus not cooling the bathmat as quickly

Answer: C. Heat is conducted more easily into the floor
When you step out of the shower and onto a surface, the surface is most likely at room temperature, regardless of its composition (eliminating answer (A)). The bathmat is likely a good insulator and is unlikely to reach equilibrium with your body temperature after a short exposure so answer (B) is incorrect. Although evaporation does have a cooling effect, in the short time it takes you to step from the bathmat to the floor, it is unlikely to have a significant effect on the floor temperature (eliminating answer (D)).

Your feet feel cold when heat is transferred from them to the surface, which happens more easily on a hard floor than a soft bathmat. This is because of differences in specific heat (the energy required to change temperature, which varies by material). Therefore, the answer must be (C), i.e., heat is conducted more easily into the floor from your feet.

15. **Identify the correct sequence of organization of living things from lower to higher order:**
    (Average)

    A. Cell, organelle, organ, tissue, system, organism
    B. Cell, tissue, organ, organelle, system, organism
    C. Organelle, cell, tissue, organ, system, organism
    D. Organelle, tissue, cell, organ, system, organism

Answer: C. Organelle, cell, tissue, organ, system, organism
Organelles are parts of the cell; cells make up tissue, which makes up organs. Organs work together in systems (e.g., the respiratory system), and the organism is the living thing as a whole.

TEACHER CERTIFICATION STUDY GUIDE

16. Catalysts assist reactions by _____ .
    (Easy)

    A. lowering required activation energy
    B. maintaining precise pH levels
    C. keeping systems at equilibrium
    D. changing the starting amounts of reactants

Answer: A. Lowering required activation energy
Chemical reactions can be enhanced or accelerated by catalysts, which are present both with reactants and with products. They induce the formation of activated complexes, thereby lowering the required activation energy—so that less energy is necessary for the reaction to begin. Catalysts may require a well maintained pH to operate effectively, however they do not do this themselves. A catalyst, by lowering activation energy, may change a reaction's equilibrium point however, it does not maintain a system at equilibrium. The starting level of reactants is controlled separately from the addition of the catalyst, and has no direct correlation. Thus the correct answer is (A).

17. Which process results in a haploid chromosome number?
    (Rigorous)

    A. Mitosis
    B. Meiosis I
    C. Meiosis II
    D. Neither mitosis nor meiosis

Answer: C. Meiosis II
Meiosis is the division of sex cells. The resulting chromosome number is half the number of parent cells, i.e., a haploid chromosome number. Meiosis I mirrors Mitosis, resulting in diploid cells. It is only during Meiosis II that the number of chromosomes is halved. Mitosis, however, is the division of other cells, in which the chromosome number is the same as the parent cell chromosome number. Therefore, the answer is (B).

18. A carrier of a genetic disorder is heterozygous for a disorder that is recessive in nature. Hemophilia is a sex-linked disorder. This means that: *(Easy)*

    A. Only females can be carriers
    B. Only males can be carriers
    C. Both males and females can be carriers
    D. Neither females nor males can be carriers

Answer: A. Only females can be carriers
Sice Hemophilia is a sex-linked disorder, the gene only appears on the X chromosome, with no counterpart on the Y chromosome. Since males are XY, they cannot be heterozygous for the trait; whatever is on the single X chromosome will be expressed. Females being XX can be heterozygous.

Answer (C) would describe a genetic disorder that is recessive and expressed on one of the somatic chromosomes (not sex-linked). Answer (D) would describe a genetic disorder that is dominant and expressed on any of the chromosomes. An example of answer (C) is sickle cell anemia. An example of answer (D) is Achondroplasia (the most common type of short-limbed dwarfism), in fact for this condition people that are Homozygous dominant for the gene that creates the disorder usually have severe health problems if they live past infancy, so almost all individuals with this disorder are carriers.

TEACHER CERTIFICATION STUDY GUIDE

19. **Which of the following is a correct explanation for scientific biological adaptation?**
    (Average)

    A. Giraffes need to reach higher for leaves to eat, so their necks stretch. The giraffe babies are then born with longer necks. Eventually, there are more long-necked giraffes in the population.
    B. Giraffes with longer necks are able to reach more leaves, so they eat more and have more babies than other giraffes. Eventually, there are more long-necked giraffes in the population.
    C. Giraffes want to reach higher for leaves to eat, so they release enzymes into their bloodstream, which in turn causes fetal development of longer-necked giraffes. Eventually, there are more long-necked giraffes in the population.
    D. Giraffes with long necks are more attractive to other giraffes, so they get the best mating partners and have more babies. Eventually, there are more long-necked giraffes in the population.

Answer: B. Giraffes with longer necks are able to reach more leaves, so they eat more and have more babies than other giraffes. Eventually, there are more long-necked giraffes in the population.
Although evolution is often misunderstood, it occurs via natural selection. Organisms with a life/reproductive advantage will produce more offspring. Over many generations, this changes the proportions of the population. In any case, it is impossible for a stretched neck (A) or a fervent desire (C) to result in a biologically mutated baby. Although there are traits that are naturally selected because of mate attractiveness and fitness (D), this is not the primary situation here, so answer (B) is the best choice.

20. **An animal choosing its mate because of attractive plumage or a strong mating call is an example of:**
    (Average)

    A. Sexual selection
    B. Natural selection
    C. Mechanical isolation
    D. Linkage

Answer: A. Sexual Selection
The coming together of genes determines the makeup of the gene pool. Sexual selection, the act of choosing a mate, allows animals to have some choice in the breeding of its offspring.

21. Many male birds sing long, complicated songs that describe thier identity and the area of land that they claim. Which of the answers below is the best decription of this behavior?
(Rigorous)

   A. Innate territorial behavior
   B. Learned competitve behavior
   C. Innate mating behavior
   D. Learned territorial behavior

Answer: D. Learned territorial behavior
Birds often learn their songs, through a combination of trial and error, and listening to the songs of other members of their species (in some cases other species; this is called mimicry). Thus answers (A) and (C) are not correct. Typically a male bird will use a short song to impress a mate, the longer song is territorial because it is trying to convey to other males both identity and the territory that it claims.

22. A wrasse (fish) cleans the teeth of other fish by eating away plaque. This is an example of _____ between the fish.
(Average)

   A. parasitism
   B. symbiosis (mutualism)
   C. competition
   D. predation

Answer: B. symbiosis (mutualism)
When both species benefit from their interaction in their habitat, this is called symbiosis, or mutualism. In this example, the wrasse benefits from having a source of food, and the other fish benefit by having healthier teeth. Note that parasitism is when one species benefits at the expense of the other; competition is when two species compete with one another for the same habitat or food, and predation is when one species feeds on another.

TEACHER CERTIFICATION STUDY GUIDE

23. **Which of the following causes the aurora borealis?**
    (Rigorous)

    A. Gases escaping from earth
    B. Particles from the sun
    C. Particles from the moon
    D. Electromagnetic discharges from the North pole

Answer: B. Particles from the sun
Aurora Borealis is a phenomenon caused by particles escaping from the sun. The particles escaping from the sun include a mixture of gases, electrons and protons, and are sent out at as force that scientists call solar wind. Together, we have the Earth's magnetosphere and the solar wind squeezing the magnetosphere and charged particles everywhere in the field. When conditions are right, the build-up of pressure from the solar wind creates an electric voltage that pushes electrons into the ionosphere. Here they collide with gas atoms, causing them to release both light and more electrons.

24. **The transfer of heat from the earth's surface to the atmosphere is called:**
    (Average)

    A. Convection
    B. Radiation
    C. Conduction
    D. Advection

Answer: C. Conduction
Radiation is the process of warming through rays or waves of energy, such as the Sun's rays warming the earth. The Earth returns heat to the atmosphere through conduction. Conduction is the transfer of heat through matter, such that areas of greater heat move to areas of lesser heat in an attempt to balance temperature.

TEACHER CERTIFICATION STUDY GUIDE

25. **What is the most accurate description of the Water Cycle?**
    (Rigorous)

    A. Rain comes from clouds, filling the ocean. The water then evaporates and becomes clouds again.
    B. Water circulates from rivers into groundwater and back, while water vapor circulates in the atmosphere.
    C. Water is conserved except for chemical or nuclear reactions, and any drop of water could circulate through clouds, rain, ground-water, and surface-water.
    D. Water flows toward the oceans, where it evaporates and forms clouds, which causes rain, which in turn flow back to the oceans after it falls.

Answer: C. Water is conserved except for chemical or nuclear reactions, and any drop of water could circulate through clouds, rain, ground-water, and surface-water.
All natural chemical cycles, including the Water Cycle, depend on the principle of Conservation of Mass. Any drop of water may circulate through the hydrologic system, ending up in a cloud, as rain, or as surface or ground-water. Although answers (A), (B) and (D) describe parts of the water cycle, the most comprehensive and correct answer is (C).

26. **What makes up the largest abiotic portion of the Nitrogen Cycle?**
    (Average)

    A. Nitrogen fixing bacteria
    B. Nitrates
    C. Decomposers
    D. Atomsphere

Answer: D. Atomsphere
Since answers (A) and (C) are both examples of living organisms, they are biotic components of the nitrogen cycle. Nitrates are one type of nitrogen compound, (making it abiotic) that can be found in soil and in living organisms, however it makes up a small portion of the avaible nitrogen. The atmosphere being 78% Nitrogen gas (an abiotic component) makes up the largest source available to the Nitrogen Cycle.

TEACHER CERTIFICATION STUDY GUIDE

27. **What are the most significant and prevalent elements in the biosphere?**
    (Easy)

    A. Carbon, Hydrogen, Oxygen, Nitrogen, Phosphorus
    B. Carbon, Hydrogen, Sodium, Iron, Calcium
    C. Carbon, Oxygen, Sulfur, Manganese, Iron
    D. Carbon, Hydrogen, Oxygen, Nickel, Sodium, Nitrogen

Answer: A. Carbon, Hydrogen, Oxygen, Nitrogen, Phosphorus
Organic matter (and life as we know it) is based on Carbon atoms, bonded to Hydrogen and Oxygen. Nitrogen and Phosphorus are the next most significant elements, followed by Sulfur and then trace nutrients such as Iron, Sodium, Calcium, and others. If you know that the formula for any carbohydrate contains Carbon, Hydrogen, and Oxygen, that will help you narrow the choices to (A) and (D) in any case.

28. **Neap Tides are especially weak tides that occur when the Sun and Moon are in a perpendicular arrangment to the Earth, and Spring Tides are especially strong tides that occur when the Sun and Moon are in line. At which combination of lunar phases do these tides occur (respectively)?**
    (Rigorous)

    A. Half Moon and Full Moon
    B. Quarter Moon and New Moon
    C. Gibbous Moon and Quarter Moon
    D. Full Moon and New Moon

Answer: B. Quarter Moon and New Moon
Spring tides are especially strong tides that occur when the Earth, Sun and Moon are in line, allowing both the Sun and the Moon to exert gravitational force on the Earth and increase tidal bulge height. These tides occur during the full moon and the new moon.

Neap tides occur during quarter moons, when the sun is illuminating half of the Moon's surface (the term quarter is used to refer to the fact that the Moon has traveled 1/2 of it's way through its cycle, not the amount of the surface illuminated by the Sun).

TEACHER CERTIFICATION STUDY GUIDE

29. The planet with true retrograde rotation is:
    (Rigorous)

    A. Pluto
    B. Neptune
    C. Venus
    D. Saturn

Answer: C. Venus
Venus has an axial tilt of only 3 degrees and a very slow rotation. It spins in the direction opposite of its counterparts (who spin in the same direction as the Sun). Uranus is also tilted and orbits on its side. However, this is thought to be the consequence of an impact that left the previously prograde rotating planet tilted in such a manner.

30. The phases of the Moon are the result of its _____ in relation to the Sun.
    (Average)

    A. revolution
    B. rotation
    C. position
    D. inclination

Answer: C. position
The Moon is visible in varying amounts during its orbit around the earth. One half of the Moon's surface is always illuminated by the Sun (appears bright), but the amount observed can vary from full Moon to none.

31. The end of a geologic era is most often characterized by:
    (Average)

    A. A general uplifting of the crust
    B. The extinction of the dominant plants and animals
    C. The appearance of new life forms
    D. All of the above

Answer: D. All of the above
Any of these things can be used to characterize the end of a geologic era, and often a combination of factors are applied to determining the end of an era.

TEACHER CERTIFICATION STUDY GUIDE

32. **The best preserved animal remains have been discovered in:**
    (Rigorous)

    A. Resin
    B. Fossil mold
    C. Tar pits
    D. Glacial ice

Answer: C. Tar pits
Tar pits provide a wealth of information when it comes to fossils. Tar pits are oozing areas of asphalt, which were so sticky as to trap animals. These animals, without a way out, would die of starvation or be preyed upon. Their bones would remain in the tar pits, and be covered by the continued oozing of asphalt. Because the asphalt deposits were continuously added to, the bones were not exposed to much weathering, and we have found some of the most complete and unchanged fossils from these areas, including mammoths and saber toothed cats.

33. **Which type of student activity is most likely to expose a student's misconceptions about science?**
    (Average)

    A. Multiple-choice and fill-in-the-blank worksheets
    B. Laboratory activities, where the lab is laid out step-by-step with no active thought on the part of the student
    C. Teacher- lead demonstrations
    D. Laboratories in which the students are forced to critically consider the steps taken and the results obtained

Answer: D. Laboratories in which the students are forced to critically consider the steps taken and the results obtained
Answer (A) is a typical retain and repeat exercise, where a student just needs to remember the answer and doesn't need to understand it. Answer (B) is often called a cookie cutter lab because everything fits into a specific plan. Students are often able to guess the right answer without understanding the process. Teacher-lead demonstrations can be interesting for the students, and may challenge a student's misconceptions but misconceptions are often firmly routed and will require critical thought and reflection to change. Answer (D) requires active mental participation on the part of the student and thus is most likely to alter their understanding. These types of labs are often refered to as guided discovery laboratories.

TEACHER CERTIFICATION STUDY GUIDE

34. In an experiment measuring the inhibition effect of different antibiotic discs of bacteria grown in Petri dishes, what are the independent and dependent variables respectively?
    (Rigorous)

    A. Number of bacterial colonies and the antibiotic type
    B. Antibiotic type and the distance between antibiotic and the closest colony
    C. Antibiotic type and the number of bacterial colonies
    D. Presence of bacterial colonies and the antibiotic type

Answer: B. Antibiotic type and the distance between antibiotic and the closest colony

To answer this question, recall that the independent variable in an experiment is the entity that is changed by the scientist, in order to observe the effects of the change on the dependent variable. In this experiment, the antibiotic used is purposely changed so it is the independent variable.

Answers (A) and (D) list antibiotic type as the dependent variable and thus cannot be the correct answer, leaving answers (B) and (C) as the only two viable choices. The best answer is (B), because it measures at what concentration of the antibiotic the bacteria are able to grow, (as you move from the source of the antibiotic, the concentration decreases).

SAMPLE ESSAYS: SCIENCE

1. Use your accumulated knowledge to discuss the components of biogeochemical cycles.

BEST

Essential elements are recycled through an ecosystem. At times, the element needs to be made available in a useable form. Cycles are dependent on plants, algae and bacteria to fix nutrients for use by animals. The four main cycles are: water, carbon, nitrogen, and phosphorous.

Two percent of all the water is fixed in ice or the bodies of organisms, rendering it unavailable. Available water includes surface water (lakes, ocean, and rivers) and ground water (aquifers, wells). The majority (96%) of all available water is from ground water. Water is recycled through the processes of evaporation and precipitation. The water present now is the water that has been here since our atmosphere was formed.

Ten percent of all available carbon in the air (in the form of carbon dioxide gas) is fixed by photosynthesis. Plants fix carbon in the form of glucose; animals eat the plants and are able to obtain the carbon necessary to sustain themselves. When animals release carbon dioxide through respiration, the cycle begins again as plants recycle the carbon through photosynthesis.

Eighty percent of the atmosphere is in the form of nitrogen gas. Nitrogen must be fixed and taken out of gaseous form to be incorporated into an organism. Only a few genera of bacteria have the correct enzymes to break the strong triple bond between nitrogen atoms. These special bacteria live within the roots of legumes (peas, beans, alfalfa) and add bacteria to the soil so it may be taken-up by the plant. Nitrogen is necessary in the building of amino acids and the nitrogenous bases of DNA.

Phosphorus exists as a mineral and is not found in the atmosphere. Fungi and plant roots have structures called mycorrhizae that are able to fix insoluble phosphates into useable phosphorus. Urine and decayed matter returns phosphorus to the earth where it can be fixed in the plant. Phosphorus is needed for the backbone of DNA and for the manufacture of ATP.

The four biogeochemical cycles are present concurrently. Water is continually recycled, and is utilized by organisms to sustain life. Carbon is also a necessary component for life. Both water and carbon can be found in the air and on the ground. Nitrogen and phosphorous are commonly found in the ground. Special organisms, called decomposers, help to make these elements available in the environment. Plants use the recycled materials for energy and when they are consumed, the cycle begins again.

BETTER
Essential elements are recycled through an ecosystem. Cycles are dependent on plants, algae and bacteria to make nutrients available for use by animals. The four main cycles are: water, carbon, nitrogen, and phosphorous. Water is typically available as surface water (large bodies of water) or ground water. Water is recycled through the states of gas, liquid (rain), and solid (ice or snow). Carbon is necessary for life as it is the basis for organic matter. It is a byproduct of photosynthesis and is found in the air as carbon dioxide gas. Nitrogen is the largest component of the atmosphere. It is also necessary for the creation of amino acids and the nitrogenous bases of DNA. Phosphorous is another elemental cycle. Phosphorous is found in the soil and is made available by decomposition. It is then converted for use in the manufacture of DNA and ATP.

BASIC
Elements are recycled through an ecosystem. This occurs through cycles. These important cycles are called biogeochemical cycles. The water cycle consists of water moving from bodies of water into the air and back again as precipitation. The carbon cycle includes all organisms, as mammals breathe out carbon dioxide and are made of carbon molecules. Nitrogen is an amino building block and is found in soil. As things are broken down phosphorous is added to the earth, enriching the soil.

TEACHER CERTIFICATION STUDY GUIDE

2. Examine the components of a eukaryotic cell.

BEST

The cell is the basic unit of all living things. Eukaryotic cells are found in protists, fungi, plants, and animals. Eukaryotic cells are organized. They contain many organelles, which are membrane bound areas for specific functions. Their cytoplasm contains a cytoskeleton that provides a protein framework for the cell. The cytoplasm also supports the organelles and contains the ions and molecules necessary for cell function. The cytoplasm is contained by the plasma membrane. The plasma membrane allows molecules to pass in and out of the cell. The membrane can bud inward to engulf outside material in a process called endocytosis. Exocytosis is a secretory mechanism, the reverse of endocytosis.

Eukaryotes have a nucleus. The nucleus is the brain of the cell that contains all of the cell's genetic information. The genetic information is contained on chromosomes that consist of chromatin, which is a complex of DNA and proteins. The chromosomes are tightly coiled to conserve space while providing a large surface area. The nucleus is the site of transcription of the DNA into RNA. The nucleolus is where ribosomes are made. There is at least one of these dark-staining bodies inside the nucleus of most eukaryotes. The nuclear envelope is two membranes separated by a narrow space. The envelope contains many pores that let RNA out of the nucleus.

Ribosomes are the site for protein synthesis. They may be free floating in the cytoplasm or attached to the endoplasmic reticulum. There may be up to a half a million ribosomes in a cell, depending on how much protein is made by the cell.

The endoplasmic reticulum (ER) is folded and provides a large surface area. It is the "roadway" of the cell and allows for transport of materials through and out of the cell. There are two types of ER. Smooth endoplasmic reticulum contains no ribosomes on their surface. This is the site of lipid synthesis. Rough endoplasmic reticulum has ribosomes on its surfaces. They aid in the synthesis of proteins that are membrane bound or destined for secretion.

Many of the products made in the ER proceed on to the Golgi apparatus. The Golgi apparatus functions to sort, modify, and package molecules that are made in the other parts of the cell. These molecules are either sent out of the cell or to other organelles within the cell. The Golgi apparatus is a stacked structure to increase the surface area.

Lysosomes are found mainly in animal cells. These contain digestive enzymes that break down food, substances not needed, viruses, damaged cell components and eventually the cell itself. It is believed that lysomomes are responsible for the aging process.

Mitochondria are large organelles that are the site of cellular respiration, where ATP is made to supply energy to the cell. Muscle cells have many mitochondria because they use a great deal of energy. Mitochondria have their own DNA, RNA, and ribosomes and are capable of reproducing by binary fission if there is a greater demand for additional energy. Mitochondria have two membranes: a smooth outer membrane and a folded inner membrane. The folds inside the mitochondria are called cristae. They provide a large surface area for cellular respiration to occur.

Plastids are found only in photosynthetic organisms. They are similar to the mitochondria due to the double membrane structure. They also have their own DNA, RNA, and ribosomes and can reproduce if the need for the increased capture of sunlight becomes necessary. There are several types of plastids. Chloroplasts are the sight of photosynthesis. The stroma is the chloroplast's inner membrane space. The stoma encloses sacs called thylakoids that contain the photosynthetic pigment chlorophyll. The chlorophyll traps sunlight inside the thylakoid to generate ATP which is used in the stroma to produce carbohydrates and other products. The chromoplasts make and store yellow and orange pigments. They provide color to leaves, flowers, and fruits. The amyloplasts store starch and are used as a food reserve. They are abundant in roots like potatoes.

The Endosymbiotic Theory states that mitochondria and chloroplasts were once free living and possibly evolved from prokaryotic cells. At some point in our evolutionary history, they entered the eukaryotic cell and maintained a symbiotic relationship with the cell, with both the cell and organelle benefiting from the relationship. The fact that they both have their own DNA, RNA, ribosomes, and are capable of reproduction helps to confirm this theory.

Found in plant cells only, the cell wall is composed of cellulose and fibers. It is thick enough for support and protection, yet porous enough to allow water and dissolved substances to enter. Vacuoles are found mostly in plant cells. They hold stored food and pigments. Their large size allows them to fill with water in order to provide turgor pressure. Lack of turgor pressure causes a plant to wilt.

The cytoskeleton, found in both animal and plant cells, is composed of protein filaments attached to the plasma membrane and organelles. They provide a framework for the cell and aid in cell movement. They constantly change shape and move about. Three types of fibers make up the cytoskeleton:

> 1. Microtubules – the largest of the three, they make up cilia and flagella for locomotion. Some examples are sperm cells, cilia that line the fallopian tubes, and tracheal cilia. Centrioles are also composed of microtubules. They aid in cell division to form the spindle fibers that pull the cell apart into two new cells. Centrioles are not found in the cells of higher plants.

2. Intermediate filaments – intermediate in size, they are smaller than microtubules but larger than microfilaments. They help the cell to keep its shape.

3. Microfilaments – smallest of the three, they are made of actin and small amounts of myosin (like in muscle tissue). They function in cell movement like cytoplasmic streaming, endocytosis, and ameboid movement. This structure pinches the two cells apart after cell division, forming two new cells.

BETTER
The cell is the basic unit of all living things. Eukaryotic cells are found in protists, fungi, plants, and animals. Eukaryotic cells are organized. Their cytoplasm contains a cytoskeleton that provides a protein framework for the cell. The cytoplasm is contained by the plasma membrane. The plasma membrane allows molecules to pass in and out of the cell.

Eukaryotes have a nucleus. The nucleus is the brain of the cell that contains all of the cell's genetic information. The chromosomes house genetic information and are tightly coiled to conserve space while providing a large surface area. The nucleus is the site of transcription of the DNA into RNA. The nucleolus is where ribosomes are made.

Ribosomes are the site for protein synthesis. There may be up to a half a million ribosomes in a cell, depending on how much protein is made by the cell.

The endoplasmic reticulum (ER) is folded and provides a large surface area. It is the "roadway" of the cell and allows for transport of materials through and out of the cell. It may be smooth or rough.

Many of the products made in the ER proceed on to the Golgi apparatus. The Golgi apparatus functions to sort, modify, and package molecules that are made in the other parts of the cell.

Mitochondria are large organelles that are the site of cellular respiration, where ATP is made to supply energy to the cell. Mitochondria have their own DNA, RNA, and ribosomes and are capable of reproducing by binary fission if there is a greater demand for additional energy.

Plastids are found only in photosynthetic organisms. They are similar to the mitochondria. They also have their own DNA, RNA, and ribosomes and can reproduce if the need for the increased capture of sunlight becomes necessary.

Found in plant cells only, the cell wall is composed of cellulose and fibers. It is thick enough for support and protection, yet porous enough to allow water and dissolved substances to enter.

The cytoskeleton, found in both animal and plant cells, is composed of protein filaments attached to the plasma membrane and organelles. They provide a framework for the cell and aid in cell movement. They constantly change shape and move about. Three types of fibers make up the cytoskeleton (in order of size: largest-smallest): microtubules, intermediate filaments, microfilaments.

BASIC

The cell is the basic unit of all living things. Eukaryotic cells contain many organelles. Eukaryotes have a nucleus. The nucleus is the brain of the cell that contains all of the cell's genetic information. The nucleus is the site of DNA transcription. There is at least one nucleolus inside the nucleus of most eukaryotes. Ribosomes are the site for protein synthesis and can be found on the endoplasmic reticulum (ER). The Golgi apparatus functions to sort, modify, and package molecules that are made in the other parts of the cell. Mitochondria are large organelles that are the site of cellular respiration, where ATP is made to supply energy to the cell.

In plant cells, the cell wall is composed of cellulose and fibers. The cytoskeleton, found in both animal and plant cells, is composed of protein filaments. The three types of fibers differ in size and help the cell to keep its shape and aid in movement.

TEACHER CERTIFICATION STUDY GUIDE

3. Discuss the scientific process.

BEST
Science may be defined as a body of knowledge that is systematically derived from study, observations, and experimentation. Its goal is to identify and establish principles and theories that may be applied to solve problems. Pseudoscience, on the other hand, is a belief that is not warranted. There is no scientific methodology or application. Some of the more classic examples of pseudoscience include witchcraft, alien encounters or any topic that is explained by hearsay.

Scientific theory and experimentation must be repeatable. It is also possible to be disproved and is capable of change. Science depends on communication, agreement, and disagreement among scientists. It is composed of theories, laws, and hypotheses.

Theory - the formation of principles or relationships which have been verified and accepted.

Law - an explanation of events that occur with uniformity under the same conditions (laws of nature, law of gravitation).

Hypothesis - an unproved theory or educated guess followed by research to best explain a phenomena. A theory is a proven hypothesis.

Science is limited by the available technology. An example of this would be the relationship of the discovery of the cell and the invention of the microscope. As our technology improves, more hypotheses will become theories and possibly laws. Science is also limited by the data that is able to be collected. Data may be interpreted differently on different occasions. Science limitations cause explanations to be changeable as new technologies emerge.

The first step in scientific inquiry is posing a question to be answered. Next, a hypothesis is formed to provide a plausible explanation. An experiment is then proposed and performed to test this hypothesis. A comparison between the predicted and observed results is the next step. Conclusions are then formed and it is determined whether the hypothesis is correct or incorrect. If incorrect, the next step is to form a new hypothesis and the process is repeated.

BETTER
Science is derived from study, observations, and experimentation. Its goal is to identify and establish principles and theories that may be applied to solve problems. Scientific theory and experimentation must be repeatable. It is also possible to disprove or change a theory. Science depends on communication, agreement, and disagreement among scientists. It is composed of theories, laws, and hypotheses. A theory is a principle or relationship that has been verified and accepted through experiments. A law is an explanation of events that occur with uniformity under the same conditions. A hypothesis is an educated guess followed by research. A theory is a proven hypothesis.

Science is limited by the available technology. An example of this would be the relationship of the discovery of the cell and the invention of the microscope. The first step in scientific inquiry is posing a question to be answered. Next, a hypothesis is formed to provide a plausible explanation. An experiment is then proposed and performed to test this hypothesis. A comparison between the predicted and observed results is the next step. Conclusions are then formed and it is determined whether the hypothesis is correct or incorrect. If incorrect, the next step is to form a new hypothesis and the process is repeated.

BASIC
Science is composed of theories, laws, and hypotheses. The first step in scientific inquiry is posing a question to be answered. Next, a hypothesis is formed to provide a plausible explanation. An experiment is then proposed and performed to test this hypothesis. A comparison between the predicted and observed results is the next step. Conclusions are then formed and it is determined whether the hypothesis is correct or incorrect. If incorrect, the next step is to form a new hypothesis and the process is repeated. Science is always limited by the available technology.

www.ingramcontent.com/pod-product-compliance
Lightning Source LLC
Chambersburg PA
CBHW080933300426
44115CB00017B/2802